Colleen Moore

Colleen Moore
A Biography of the Silent Film Star

Jeff Codori

Forewords by Joseph Yranski *and*
Judith Hargrave Coleman

McFarland & Company, Inc., Publishers
Jefferson, North Carolina, and London

Uncredited photographs are from the author's collecton.

LIBRARY OF CONGRESS CATALOGUING-IN-PUBLICATION DATA

Codori, Jeff, 1966–
Colleen Moore : a biography of the silent film star / Jeff Codori ;
forewords by Joseph Yranski and Judith Hargrave Coleman.
p.   cm.
Includes bibliographical references and index.

ISBN 978-0-7864-4969-9
softcover : acid free paper ∞

1. Moore, Colleen, 1900–1988.   2. Motion picture actors and
actresses — United States — Biography. I. Title.
PN2287.M695C84 2012   791.4302'8092 — dc23   [B]   2012001140

BRITISH LIBRARY CATALOGUING DATA ARE AVAILABLE

©2012 Jeff Codori. All rights reserved

*No part of this book may be reproduced or transmitted in any form
or by any means, electronic or mechanical, including photocopying
or recording, or by any information storage and retrieval system,
without permission in writing from the publisher.*

On the cover Colleen Moore's engagement portrait, 1922

Manufactured in the United States of America

*McFarland & Company, Inc., Publishers
Box 611, Jefferson, North Carolina 28640
www.mcfarlandpub.com*

Table of Contents

Forewords by Joseph Yranski and Judith Hargrave Coleman	1
Preface	3
1. September 1895	5
2. Port Huron, 1890–1902	7
3. Port Huron and Hillsdale, Michigan, 1905–1908	12
4. Atlanta, Georgia, 1908–1911	17
5. Chicago and Tampa, 1911–1916	23
6. November, 1916	27
7. *The Bad Boy,* December 1916–January 1917	30
8. April–December, 1917	37
9. Selig Polyscope, 1918	41
10. 1919	46
11. Discovering Comedy	53
12. "Dry Land; That's All."	60
13. August 1920	66
14. November 1920–March 1921	72
15. April–June 1921	78
16. Censorship	85
17. August 1921–December 1921	92
18. *The Bitterness of Sweets* (*Look Your Best*), March–May 1922	98
19. *Forsaking All Others,* September–October 1922	106
20. *The Nth Commandment,* November–December 1922	111
21. *The Huntress,* May–July 1923	120
22. *The Swamp Angel* (*Painted People*), October–November 1923	128
23. *The Perfect Flapper,* January–April 1924	133
24. *Sally*	140

25. *The Desert Flower,* February–April 1925	143
26. European Tour, April–July 1925	149
27. First National, *Irene*	157
28. *Ella Cinders,* February 19–April 6, 1926	162
29. *Twinkletoes,* July 26–September 15, 1926	168
30. October 1926–April 1927	179
31. Break with First National, May–June 1927	188
32. New York and Arbitration, June–August 1927	197
33. October–November 1927	204
34. *Oh, Kay!,* April–July 1928	212
35. Colleen and Sound, August–October 1928	222
36. *Why Be Good?,* November 1928–January 1929	232
37. The Bel Air House and a Fairy Castle	243
Filmography	251
Chapter Notes	257
Bibliography	287
Index	291

Forewords by Joseph Yranski and Judith Hargrave Coleman

Joseph Yranski Upon first discovering Colleen Moore when Public Television broadcast her film *Ella Cinders*, I found her to be a revelation: funny, quirky, and winsome, while displaying a remarkable sense of individuality. A decade later I met this amazing lady at the gala opening of director King Vidor's retrospective at the Museum of Modern Art. I skipped all of my university classes that day in order to secure tickets. There I spoke with her and discovered her to be remarkably gracious, yet humble, stating that "it was King's evening and not mine." Later when Mr. Vidor left for a radio station interview, I was invited to keep Colleen company. I discovered her to be an intelligent woman who blazed many and varied paths in life: silent film actress, philanthropist, astute businesswoman, mother and grandmother. We discussed topics that ranged from politics, art, and history to Hollywood, ecology and business. Thus began a blessed 18 year friendship with the lady, a friendship that continued until her death.

Over the years there have been many film star biographies. Some center on the private lives of the stars, while others focus on their careers. With Jeff Codori's, there is now a work that traces the entire improbable course with first-hand documentation of an amazing girl with one brown and one blue eye. She miraculously managed to parlay a six-month "payoff" contract into a career as the number-one international female star of the 1920s. More importantly, once she had achieved her dream, Miss Moore knew when to end that aspect of her life and go on to successfully blaze many other paths.

For nearly 30 years, Joe Yranski has been the senior film and video historian for the New York Public Library. He has contributed to a dozen books about various aspects of film history and nine documentary films.

Judith Hargrave Coleman I first met Colleen Moore, film star, as she greeted me at the great hall of her Fairy Castle. I was five years old.

She married my father, a widower with two children, my brother and I, and we all lived happily together in that Fairy Castle.

One of the many things I learned from Colleen Moore, film star, was her gift of taking on any challenge.

One challenge was becoming a film star ... and she did. But then she accepted another challenge ... knowing when to leave the cameras behind and move on.

And move on she did, by creating the Fairy Castle with the help of her artist friends in Hollywood.

She went on tour with the Castle all over America, once again touching the lives of so many, but in a different way. She touched their lives by giving them, for a brief time, a glimpse of a make-believe world, untouched by a troubled country dealing with the Great Depression. An imaginary world of fairy tales, princesses, floating stairways, with Christmas every day.

Another challenge was Colleen Moore, mother and housewife, community service leader and fund raiser.

After becoming a widow, she once again moved on; she wrote three books, traveled the world with old friends, gathering new friends as she went along. She then built a house, entertained the famous and not so famous. Not to tell her stories but to sit back and listen to theirs.

She said to me, shortly before she died, "Life's been good to me ... I've had it all."

I will always remember her as that magical lady coming to meet me in the grand hall of her Fairy Castle, not as Colleen Moore, film star, but as Colleen Moore, mother. My mother!

Judy Coleman, Moore's daughter, lives in California.

Preface

Colleen Moore is an actress who should be better remembered than she is. Today, if she is recalled at all, it is usually as the quintessential film flapper. Her vibrant, beaming smile, geometric bobbed hairstyle and slim figure are iconic. When the economy went south in the early 1930s, the flapper as a social figure was considered irrelevant. Colleen's place in the pantheon of film actresses was supplanted because she was so strongly associated with flappers; forgotten is the fact that flapper roles were a small portion of the characters she played throughout her career. Even if the characterization of Colleen as a flapper was accurate, she would still be worthy of note for having opened the door for the likes of Clara Bow, Joan Crawford and Louise Brooks.

In fact, Colleen had been working her way up the ladder of motion pictures before her sudden, explosive fame, playing the part of Patricia Frentiss in *Flaming Youth*. Her earlier film roles covered the full spectrum from drama to comedy, from innocent girl to sophisticated city girls. Colleen had grown up as one of the first generation of a world in which motion pictures were ubiquitous, and when the art form was still in its infancy she had already decided to become a star. She had not been drafted into films from the stage or discovered at a druggist's soda fountain. As a favor to a relative, she was given a six-month contract, and she spun that into a successful career.

This biography is an examination of Colleen's silent film career, from her arrival in Hollywood to the end of her affiliation with First National Pictures, the studio that made some of her most important and influential films, with a brief look at her foray into talking films before she retired. In addition to a survey of her career, this book covers her childhood, her upbringing and her life. One cannot understand the choices she made in her career without understanding her life and the times in which she lived. Colleen is one of the few actresses who found sudden fame and did not let it go to her head. With the support of her family, she managed to keep the screen persona "Colleen Moore" seperate from the woman she was born, Kathleen Morrison. In this biography, she is referred throughout her childhood as "Kathleen" until her arrival in Hollywood, when she became "Colleen." I hope it does not cause confusion.

In the late 1960s Colleen wrote her autobiography, *Silent Star* (Doubleday, 1968), which has been the most used resource for people writing about her and is often combined with newspaper clippings from her scrapbooks (36 scrapbooks, Colleen Moore Collection, Academy of Motion Picture Arts and Sciences, Margaret Herrick Library). A third resource is a short authorized *The Story of My Life*, written by Colleen shortly after the completion of *Irene* for release to the press in 1926. Of these, *Silent Star* is perhaps the most valuable resource, being the closest thing to a diary she left. The autobiography has the virtue of being an honest account of her feelings during important events in her life, though it suffers from many minor inaccuracies. It was written, after all, 40 years after the events described. While Colleen had excellent recall, the book was written with the aid of her friend Adela Rogers St. Johns, a former Hollywood columnist with a tendency to embellish stories.

To gain a better look into her career, this book uses her autobiography and scrapbooks as guides, but relies on a variety of resources. While motion picture journals often printed publicity materials issued by the studios verbatim, they also recorded the comings and goings of individuals and productions, helping to establish a timeline of when Colleen was in or out of town, and where she was. The same is true of newspapers, especially local papers in towns where location work was done. Local papers often followed film productions with great interest. Where studio materials exist, they are relied upon. First National, especially after 1925, kept extensive records on Colleen and her production unit. They give a unique insight into Colleen's decision-making process and the way the dream-manufacturing machine of First National Pictures produced her films.

This biography would not have been possible without the help of many people with an interest in Colleen or an interest in the project. What started as a general curiosity about an actress who was obviously famous at one time but unknown today, grew first into a website, and then into this book. There are several hundred people who deserve thanks, but thanking them all would double the size of this book. So here are the top half-dozen or so: Kevin Brownlow who, when I first wrote asking about Colleen, copied his complete notes and correspondence and sent them to me; Joseph Yranski, a friend of Colleen's, a virtual human encyclopedia of all things film-related (he is saying "pish-posh" as he reads this), and a scholar who is always happy to assist researchers; and most of all to Judy Coleman, Colleen's step-daughter, who has had me as her guest in her home, allowed me to rifle through family albums, and has answered many questions about a woman who was, first and foremost her mother.

I also need to thank Rick Levinson, who first put me in contact with Joe Yranski ... some day he and the rest of the world will get his Colleen Moore DVD box set; Steve Moore, related to Colleen through her aunt Elizabeth Moore, who provided information on Colleen's Port Huron years whenever he found it; Lisa Bradberry in Tampa, Florida, whose research there has helped fill in details on Colleen's childhood; and Liesl Ehardt for providing me with the research of her aunt, Jane Moore, into the life of John McCormick. John was married to actress Zita Johann; Liesl is Zita's second cousin twice removed. And a special thanks to all the various relatives of Colleen's who contacted me through my website and shared their unique stories of Colleen and her brother, Cleeve. I must also thank my small army of proofreaders, without whom this biography would be an overlong and incomprehensible mess: Don Ciccone, Betsy Shelton, Lisa Taner, Dana Riggs, and Jeff Nelson.

Finally, Colleen is now remembered fondly by a whole other generation aware of her through her Fairy Castle, still on display in the Chicago Museum of Science and Industry. She was easily as proud of her castle as she was of anything she accomplished in motion pictures, and it continues to be enjoyed by children to this day.

1

September 1895

Before modern telecommunications, county fairs and their bigger cousins, international expositions, were the best way for the average citizen to encounter the latest inventions and innovations. One such exposition, the 1895 Cotton States and International Exposition in Atlanta, was a humdinger, displaying the latest products of American industry and technology. One of the midway attractions seemed at first a simple curiosity. It would grow with time to threaten the expositions as a showcase for the new and dramatic. It was set up by Charles Francis Jenkins and Thomas Armat. With a tent as a theater they demonstrated a device they that projected moving images on a screen before a seated audience. Their invention utilized film strips from Edison Kinetoscopes that previously could only viewed by an individual hunched over a hooded viewer. Now Jenkins and Armat had devised a way for groups to watch as an audience. They called their invention the "Phantoscope" and their demonstrations were the first commercial venture in America featuring projected moving pictures.

Compared to the other wonders on display, however, the Phantoscope receded into the background. The spectacle of the varied achievements of the South was the point of the exposition, and it reflected pride in Atlanta's recovery from the Civil War. It was also an international exhibition, the flavor of which was confirmed by the attention paid to a delegation of over 200 Chinese nationals intended as employees of the exposition. As their ship, the *Empress of China*, steamed towards the continent, the *New York Times* reported each step of their itinerary with fascination. "Telegraphic and written instructions were today sent to the Collector of Customs at Ogdensburg, N.Y. He is directed to see that the Chinamen presenting themselves at the port for admission are, beyond all question of a doubt, what they represent themselves to be, viz.: employees of the exhibitors at the Atlanta Exposition."[1] They were admitted, and they continued from New York to Atlanta where they were greeted by a crowd of over two thousand gawkers. From the station they walked to the grounds of the exhibition where they were met by an inspector and the sheriff for an inspection. "The entire lot was taken to the Chinese village and there locked in."[2]

The Chinese village was just one of several foreign villages recreated for the exposition; others were Mexican, Japanese, and German. In addition to villages, the midway featured mirror mazes, beauty shows, and even a recreated antebellum plantation. There was something for everyone along "Midway Heights." Souvenir spoons, souvenir cotton bales, key rings, aluminum novelties ... an almost endless array of goods and entertainment from the corners of the globe competed for the attention of visitors.[3]

For 50 cents — two bits for children under the age of 12 — one could view the spectaculars. The buildings were impressive, most over 100 feet to the tops of their domes. There were new mechanical wonders to behold: "The cotton picker at the exposition has become the topic of conversation.... It is safe to say that almost all, if not all that body of staid, conservative business men, have prophesied the impossibility of making such a machine, and now that it is upon them they can scarcely credit their own senses."[4] Every day — excepting Sundays when it was closed — the exposition was packed, as was the city.

Given the press of people and array of sights, it was no wonder the Phantoscope escaped the attention of most people. Even so, the idea of the projected image, and that one might make a profit from exhibiting projected moving pictures, formed the basis of a whole new industry.

Moving pictures were not a new idea in 1895. There had been optical tricks around for centuries, and a few years earlier Edison had introduced his Kinetoscope,[5] a projector in a cabinet that allowed a single viewer to see a film through a peephole. The Kinetoscope was represented at the Atlanta exposition, with displays in several buildings around the grounds.[6] To supply his device with filmed subjects, Edison's Kinetographic Theater — a small, stuffy, tar-papered studio with a roof that opened to the sky for light — had been built in East Orange, New Jersey, in 1893, one of the earliest motion picture studios.

Edison's Kinetoscope had begun to pop up in arcades immediately after its introduction. Already people were dropping their nickels into the coin slots to watch a variety of short shows. There were personalities such as the well-known strongman Eugen Sandow, who posed and flexed his muscles for the camera; Annabelle Whitford, who performed her Butterfly Dance; and even Edison employee Fred Ott sneezing for the camera after pinching snuff.[7] Only one person at a time could watch these films, which went against the long tradition of watching shows as an audience. Theatergoing was a social affair. People liked to sit and be comfortable, to share a guffaw with their neighbor, to light up a cigar, lean back in the seat and enjoy the show. An individual could stand hunched over a brass hood staring at small images only so long before exhaustion set in.

The crowds Jenkins and had hoped for failed to materialize. Among their small audiences it is possible that one attendee was Charles Runnles Morrison. He was a young man who had come to the exposition by way of the city of Port Huron, Michigan.[8] His father, Robert, was a patternmaker, work that was not strenuous but required a precise mind, knowledge of mechanical drawing, and the skilled use of edged tools.[9] Charles had inherited his father's precise mind and applied it towards the world of business. Any young man with dreams of securing a place in the vibrant and growing economy of the country would have been drawn to the exhibition.

Charles arrived in Atlanta on or about September 12.[10] By the next day he was no doubt scouting out the attractions of the exposition. Charles never recorded his experiences at the exposition, so it is impossible to know if he was drawn to Jenkins and Armat's display. The presence of Charles Morrison at the same exhibition that hosted the first commercially projected motion pictures in America seems to be prescient. The medium was, after all, in its infancy; the fact that his future offspring would one day be the top box-office draw for the motion picture business might seem to be the hand of fate at work.

Tempting as the thought might be, his presence there serves to better illustrate the explosive manner in which motion pictures had spread into society. It was only a few years after the invention of motion pictures, and already thousands were watching them. In a generation, moving pictures would change the way everyone saw the world.

2

Port Huron, 1890s–1902

Port Huron, Michigan, was a vibrant, bustling town. The city had a diversified industrial base, having "extensive shipbuilding interests, there being several dry docks and ship yards."[1] The railroads had come to the city in 1882. The Grand Trunk railroad had opened its Block I shops in Port Huron and by 1900 they would employ nearly 500 people. One employee was Robert Morrison, father of Charles Morrison.[2] It was not long before Port Huron became known as a railroad and industrial town. Port Huron was even one of Thomas Edison's childhood homes.[3] It was an industrious town filled with industrious families.

One family was the Kelly family, headed by John Patrick Kelly and Mary Moylan. Their house was crowded with seven daughters.[4] The Kelly house was a few blocks south of Pine Grove Park,[5] a picturesque spot bounded to the east by the St. Clair River and to the west by Pine Grove Avenue, which cut diagonally through the city parallel to the river.[6] From the river one could view the panorama of the river and the ships and ferries plying its waters.

Disaster struck in 1894 when the house burned down. Patrick Kelly was on the crew that fought the fire.[7] A new house went up on the property. As the Kelly daughters grew into adulthood each became a great beauty. They were photographed in the Gibson Girl fashion of the day with cascades of curls or hair upswept.[8] They were also spirited, especially Elizabeth, who had informally changed her name to "Liberty." She wanted men to say "give me Liberty or give me death."[9] Liberty Kelly's strategy worked; she was married to J.L. "Lew" Board, a round man in a silk top hat with a drooping moustache.[10] They lived on Pine Grove Avenue, and when her sister Kathleen (who had been a stenographer) was married, they hosted the wedding reception.

The Kelly house was a household constantly in flux and the center of a wide web of connections.[11] One of those connections was a frequent visitor named Charles Morrison, recently of Saginaw. Charles was one of five children in his family[12] and the youngest, born seven years after his brother William. Charles's older sister Lizzie — Elizabeth, younger of the two Morrison daughters — had married a prominent grocer. In marrying the grocer,[13] Lizzie had gained the prophetic surname of "Moore."

Charles Morrison courted Agnes Kelly, who was a schoolteacher. A photograph exists of her posed before an American flag wearing a white blouse with short poofy sleeves, the very image of a patriotic schoolmarm. As was the fashion of the day, everyone around the Kelly house had a camera and took snapshots. In many snapshots Charles can be seen with the people who would become his future in-laws when Agnes married him on October 23, 1897.[14]

The American Mutoscope and Biograph Company was founded in 1896, the same year as Edison debuted his refinement of the Phantoscope, rechristened the Vitascope. The company was built in part around the "Biograph" camera, the creation of William Kennedy-

Lavrie Dickson. To get around the patents Edison had taken on his own camera's workings, the Biograph employed a mechanism different enough to be considered original. Edison's film stock had sprocket holes. Inside his camera the mechanism grabbed the film and moved each frame into position for exposure. The Biograph's film stock was bigger and lacked sprocket holes. The film was moved into position by friction and sprocket holes were punched into the stock while inside the camera. Different principle; different mechanism.

In late 1899 a Biograph Company crew arrived in Port Huron to produce a film about the St. Clair River railroad tunnel, one of the marvels of engineering that American towns were turning out on a regular basis: "The St. Clair Tunnel is one of the most remarkable in all the world. The tunnel is six thousand feet long, about a mile and one-seventh."[15] The tunnel was the feat of engineering, and it was the genius that it represented that had attracted the film crew. When they made their debut, motion picture images of everyday happenings like fires and fights and sneezes possessed magic, but the magic had begun to fade. Times were changing. America was coming into its own, and audiences changed with them. They were hungry to see the world beyond their reach, to witness the miracles that America seemed to churn out daily. The film companies were happy to accommodate. The Bioscope camera had already captured the *Finish of the Brooklyn Handicap, 1899.* Sigmund Lubin had created the film *President McKinley and Cabinet at Camp Alger, May 28, 1898.* Edison had started shooting scenes with greater drama. *Astor Battery on Parade* had been filmed in New York. *Raising Old Glory Over Morro Castle* had shown the symbolic triumph of the New World over the Old. *Love and War* dramatized the story of a young man who leaves his parent's home a private in the army, marching off to war, and returning to them an officer with a wife.

The themes of war and honorable

Charles Morrison, ca. 1890 (courtesy Judy Coleman).

Agnes Kelly Morrison, ca. 1890 (courtesy Judy Coleman).

military service were no accidents: America was fresh from the Spanish–American War, swelling with ambition. The conflict had given the new medium of moving pictures an opportunity to prove its utility. The eye of the camera could allow the viewer to witness world events with a ringside seat for a pocketful of change. If a picture is worth a thousand words, then 30 seconds of moving pictures is worth volumes. The moving pictures gravitated towards the dramatic spectaculars of a country on the move, but until there was a motion picture camera in the hands of every proud father or new mother, there would always be little everyday miracles, like the miracle of birth that would escape the notice of the camera lens. The Biograph Company camera crew had been in Port Huron to film the miracle of the tunnel. It was left to the *Port Huron Daily Times* of August 24, 1899, to record the miracle of a birth under the "Personal Notes and Social Happenings" banner:

"A daughter was born to Mr. and Mrs. Charles Morrison on Tuesday."

Colleen Moore always insisted she was born on August 19, 1902. When Colleen wrote her autobiography *Silent Star*, she stated it clearly. When asked about the year of her birth, she was adamant on that point. In *Silent Star* she had gone out of her way to deconstruct many of the myths and stories that had been erected around her life. If she had known her birth to have fallen on some other year, she would have published it. That fact and family artifacts[16] would seem to support the year 1902 as the date of her birth. However, the bulk of official records tend to point towards an earlier date ... August 19, 1899.

What is known for sure is that the young woman who took on the persona of "Colleen Moore" was born Kathleen Morrison in Port Huron, Michigan. After that, the facts are less clear. In July of 1900 a birth was duly recorded in the county records. Record number 4010 indicates the birth of a child named "Kathlene Morrison," born to Chas. and Agnes Morrison on August 19, 1899, with a box checked indicating the child was a white male child. An announcement in the *Port Huron Daily Times* in 1899 states that the Morrison family was blessed with a daughter, though by the paper's reckoning the birthday would have fallen on Tuesday, August 22. It is entirely possible that there was a child born to the Morrison family in 1899, who lived long enough to be recorded in the 1900 census, and then, in 1902 the Kathleen Morrison who would become "Colleen Moore" was born.

It is impossible to say with 100 percent certainty which year was the year of her birth. Either way, it would not have affected the outcome of her life; its course had been set at an early age.[17] Nothing else that followed would have been different if she had been born on one date or the other.

In 1899, the Morrison and Kelly families played musical chairs with their residences. Charles and Agnes moved from the Morrison homestead into the Kelly home.[18] Charles's father, Robert Morrison, Sr., was in waning health at the time.[19] Fortunately for Charles and Agnes, the Kelly house was nearly empty. Patrick had died recently, and the only daughter left in the house was Kathleen Kelly, after whom Charles and Agnes named their child.[20]

In *Silent Star*, a photograph of Kathleen Morrison while an infant, enthroned upon a wicker perambulator, describes her as "bald, [with] one blue eye and one brown eye and a weight problem."[21] The infant was, nevertheless, adorable, and her family thought so as well. With the rest of the Kelly daughters moved out, she was a focus of affection for her grandmother, (whom she grew to hold in high esteem) and her many aunts, who frequently visited. "Of my mother's six sisters, three of them ... had no children of their own," she wrote, and so they showered her with gifts and toys. Kathleen had cousins as well. Her aunt Beatrice had two children. Her Aunt May had three boys.[22] Her namesake, Aunt Kathleen, had a daughter.[23] There were several aunts and uncles in the area, including those from Charles's side of the family. Her aunt Mary — Charles's sister — had four boys.[24] As she grew older, she would frequently visit Aunt Mary, who would "chalk up a mark on the wall each time to see how much taller she had grown."[25] Her uncle Robert, Jr., had four boys, too.[26]

With so many aunts showering Kathleen with toys, she had begun to amass a collection of dolls, and miniature furniture with which to furnish imaginary homes. Dolls would be a constant in her life, a source of joy, and provided endless hours of play.

By 1902, both of Charles's parents had died. Before the end of the year, he moved his young family out of the Kelly home at 817 Ontario Street and relocated two blocks north. Charles also moved from the Commercial Bank, where he had been a collector,[27] to the position of secretary and manager of the Crosby Company,[28] which manufactured plumbing supplies and furniture. He was an engineer, according to Colleen, but the bulk of his early jobs would be in the business field. His jobs would change often and would sometimes require relocating.

Charles was not strictly a businessman. He possessed a sense of improvisation that Kathleen would inherit. In 1904, he and his brother-in-law Morris Krakow traveled to

The Kelly house at 817 Ontario Street, Port Huron, Michigan, ca. 1900 (courtesy Judy Coleman).

Chicago to watch the hanging of the notorious "Car Barn Bandits." They were not able to gain admittance the first time, so they tried again using another tactic that was reported in the *Port Huron Times-Herald*, reprinted from the *Chicago American*. "Monsieur Krakow and Monsieur Morrison, special correspondents of the *Paris Figaro* have arrived in Chicago from Canada to attend the hanging.... The French journalists have been touring North America studying methods and purposes to give Paris a vivid description of the American idea of capital punishment." Afterwards, "Monsieur" Charles Morrison returned home to Port Huron.[29] It is an interesting display of acting ability, given how famous an actress his daughter would become.

The new house was larger[30] to better accommodate the growing family. Kathleen's grandmother moved in, and she gained a brother named Cleeve.[31] Before long, however, the family left Port Huron.

3

Port Huron and Hillsdale, Michigan, 1905–1908

Kathleen grew into a child with dark reddish brown hair and mismatched eyes: one eye was brown and the other was blue.[1] She and her brother got along well. They shared a sense of humor and were often co-conspirators in their antics. The both loved the outdoors and water, and Kathleen began to grow into a bit of a tomboy, stomping about in the underbrush with the boys as well as playing with her dolls at home.

Kathleen's collection of dolls and dollhouse furniture became impressive enough that her father built a wall-hung cabinet to house them, dubbing it "Kathleen's Collection." The household population of dolls grew and provided Kathleen with endless hours of fun. At night, the family gathered around her father, who read stories to them. Her grandmother told her about old Irish lore. Stories and fairy tales informed her play, and combined with a ready cast of characters in her dolls, stoked her imagination. As a young girl she spent hours with her dolls, making them actors in the stories she invented. As she learned to play the piano, she told stories to her friends, playing riffs on the keyboard to dramatize her narratives. She noted how her tiny audiences followed her stories with rapt attention and found the experience to be satisfying. Her storyteller's nature was beginning to emerge.

By 1905, the life of her household, rooted among the web of family connections in Port Huron, changed. Charles had a new job that took him on the road, and the family was forced to move.

"We were something of a nomadic family," Colleen would write, "for father's work called him to different cities and I soon became accustomed to packing trunks and getting used to hotels and new homes."[2] For seven years — until 1911 — they would relocate periodically, sometimes after years, sometimes after a few months. Sometimes their moves would leave behind no trace in the official records.

From Port Huron, the family is supposed to have relocated to Hillsdale, Michigan,[3] but there is no mention of the family in the local papers. The local paper, the *Hillsdale Democrat*, mainly covered local and state matters. A new family moving into town would have warranted a mention in the paper. A great number of items of daily life were printed on the pages in run-on sentences that were nevertheless witty and insightful. One item embodied a no-nonsense approach to the news: "A lighted match dropping into a show window full of fireworks caused a premature celebration in a grocery store at Hudson Tuesday night. The effect was dazzling, the damage considerable."[4] But, there was no

Kathleen Morrison with four of her dolls, around her first birthday (courtesy Judy Coleman).

mention of the Morrison family. Nor was there any mention of them in the city directory for Hillsdale or any of the surrounding towns.

The family did not always travel together. The logistics involved in moving a household were complicated enough for a long stay. For a short stay, it would make more sense for Agnes and Grandma Kelly and the kids to stay with family while Charles went off to work,[5] especially if the job was just one of a series of moves. A man staying in a residential hotel, doing a short job for a bank or business or using his room as a base as he traveled from town to town might escape notice and mention. There was mention in *Polk's Hillsdale City and County Directory* (1905–1906) of Charles Morrison, traveling agent for Alamo Manufacturing Company, boarding at 89 S. Howell.[6]

The town was known for the Baw Beese Lake which was becoming a popular tourist attraction, though its potential for attracting visitors was seen decades earlier: "It is nearly two miles long and three-quarters of a mile wide, and it has been made attractive to summer resorters and picnickers by improvements in the way of hotel, pavilion, toboggan slide and bath houses."[7] There were a picnic grounds and dance pavilions and rowboats for rent, a scenic lake. The building where Charles was boarding was in a residential area less than two miles from Baw Beese Lake.[8] Had Kathleen and Cleeve visited their father, they would have loved the lake. In winter or summer there would have been plenty to keep them busy.

Between the time when the family disappears from the directories of Port Huron and reappears in Atlanta, more than two years passed, too long for the family to have been lodged in a hotel. With many of Agnes's sisters married and living around the country, it's possible the family moved in with one of them. Her sister Elizabeth — Liberty — had remarried, to a newspaperman named Walter Howey. They lived in Chicago. Liberty was Kathleen's favorite aunt, and in later years she would write that the time she spent with them provided some of the best entertainment of her young life. They were both energetic, exciting people whose epic arguments were the stuff of legend, at least to Kathleen's mind.

Elizabeth "Liberty" Kelly Board Howey, Aunt Liberty, who prodded her husband, Walter Howey, into securing a contract from D.W. Griffith for Kathleen. According to an unidentified newspaper clipping courtesy Judy Coleman. "Mrs. Board [Liberty's first husband was Lew Board] is an 'enviable example' of American and European women and a hospitable and charming entertainer with a summer home in Port Huron."

About the same time the Morrison family began their zigzag course around the Northeast in November 1905, the country was seized by delight at a new stage play. In New York, "A line of messenger boys had formed in the lobby [of the Empire Theatre] to be the first to get seats for Maude Adams engagement in *Peter Pan*."[9] The show would prove a stellar hit, one of Charles Frohman's greatest triumphs. Filled with fantasy, the show gained fanciful reviews: "*Peter Pan* isn't a play. It is just a gentle jogging of the memory and a reminiscence of your childhood."[10] In a nervous time full of changes, a regression into the simplicity of childhood is just what the country was looking for. Adults as well as children flocked to the play. Soon people from around the country were making the trip to the Empire to see the show. Maude Adams was declared perfectly suited for the part: "*Peter Pan* is an epoch in our stage history. Out of the mass of problem plays and musical comedies, it shines like a star. It is a play for the children. If I were wealthy, I could think of no sweeter philanthropy than giving the old people back an hour of their youth."[11] In 1907, Charles Frohman took *Peter Pan* on the road for a tour of more than 20 cities, starting off nearby in Brooklyn, and then going farther afield to cities like Pittsburgh, Philadelphia, Cleveland, and Columbus before a southern and westward sprint that included St. Louis, Louisville, Denver, San Francisco, Los Angeles and Salt Lake City.

The production spent several successful weeks in Chicago. If Kathleen and her family were staying with the Howeys in March of 1907, when *Peter Pan* was showing at the Illinois Theater, Kathleen might have been in the audience. When Kathleen saw the play, it changed her life.[12]

She went to the play one afternoon, taken by her mother, Agnes. It was a matinee performance filled with children. Kathleen was taken in by the production. The children followed the play attentively, quiet at the tense moments, bursting with laughter at the light moments, Kathleen as engaged with the play as her neighbors. "Tears were running down my face," she wrote in *Silent Star*, "as Peter Pan came down to the footlights and spoke to the audience. 'All the children who believe in fairies raise their hands. If you believe, you can save Tinker Bell.'"

In an instant, Kathleen was on her chair, waving her arms frantically and screaming "I believe in fairies, I really do!"[13] Her outburst in that moment caused a swell of laughter as every set of eyes in the darkness of the audience turned her direction. An episode very much like it was described by the Chicago *Tribune*, near the end of the play's Chicago run: "(Peter) took out his pipe of Pan preparatory to skipping away to his home in the treetops. Just after the door had closed and he stood irresolute, a tiny voice came from the parquet and with all the earnest pleading of childhood in the tone cried: 'Don't doh (go) Peter, don't doh!'"[14] Colleen never noted if she saw the play near the end of its run, or if she and her mother were seated in the *parterre*, but the author of the article noted it as a pretty incident that added charm to the play. The pleading left Maude flustered a moment before she skipped off.

Kathleen was momentarily flustered as well, but she took note of the reaction of the audience right, the way her words had had a dramatic effect on everyone present. The laughter and applause her words had elicited excited her. It might be fun to perform with her dolls in private or on occasion for an audience of her family, but the reaction of a large audience was more gratifying. That was when her dream of becoming an actress began.

This period of flux for the Morrison family coincides roughly with the "nickelodeon" phase of the motion picture industry, wherein the nickel electric theaters began an uneven spread across the country.

Charles Edwards reported in the Chicago *Tribune* about businessman Aaron Jones, "King Jones," who had made his fortune "nickel by nickel" with a string of the small picture palaces offering, "high class, instructional and economical entertainments for ladies, gentlemen and children, nothing to offend the most refined taste." Jones knew that what the public wanted was "melodrama first, last and all the time." It was the clerks, he noted, and shop girls who poured into his little theaters, who were most thrilled by the melodramas.

The rise of nickelodeons "contributed to the formation of a new industry, which promises to assume large proportions. That is the manufacture of films for the moving picture machines. At first this industry was monopolized ... by a couple of Parisian firms. However, within the last few years, three or four concerns have been started in America, two of which are located in Chicago."[15] Mr. Edwards, in observing that the new motion picture industry would assume large proportions, could not have known how correct he was.

Motion pictures changed the lives of everyone with whom they came into contact. The nickelodeons appealed to clerks and shop girls because they were affordable and convenient. They also frightened people who saw young women going to the shows unchaperoned.

Couples frequented the shows, finding privacy in the dark. Potentially objectionable material was shown to anybody who could pony up the cost of admission, including children and immigrants. The new working class had money to spend on entertainment, and nobody seemed to be overseeing what they were watching. Chicago created the country's first motion picture censorship agency in response to middle-class fears. The fears would only build in the years to follow.

Kathleen's generation could not imagine a life without motion pictures. The films grew longer to accommodate maturing tastes, which was bad news for nickelodeons that charged a nickel a show: they depended on a fast turnover to make money. This situation was not helped by the Banker's Panic of October 16, 1907. "Banking Troubles Hit Stocks Hard," the *New York Times* declared.[16] There were bank runs, and banks began to close. The whole economy was rocked, and especially hard hit were the nickelodeons. The smaller electric theaters began to disappear towards the year 1908, forced out of business by the bigger houses that could better absorb expenses.[17]

4

Atlanta, Georgia, 1908–1911

Colleen summed up her childhood movements simply: "I was born Kathleen Morrison. I was also born a Yankee—in Port Huron, Michigan—but I lived most of my childhood in the South, first in Atlanta, Georgia, then in Tampa, Florida."[1] Much of what she recalls of her childhood is recalled without benefit of identifying the city. What is known is that, by 1908, the family had relocated to Atlanta, Georgia. Charles had a managerial position, one that he would hold for about two years.[2] Along with Grandmother Kelly,[3] they moved into a house at 301 Capitol Avenue near downtown Atlanta.[4] In the years 1908 and 1910[5] the Morrison family would have lived within the territory of the Shrine of the Immaculate Conception, which is probably where Kathleen went to school. Cleeve, before too long, would be headed off to boarding school.

Kathleen and Cleve made friends quickly. They were both outgoing and funny, and as they moved from one location to the next they learned how to fit in. They were well-read, their tastes running towards adventures. Among the projects she and Cleve embarked upon was an attempt to emulate the characters in the book *The Swiss Family Robinson*. With the aid of the boys from the neighborhood, they went about building a tree house. Though she was a slight girl, Kathleen hauled boards from the local lumberyard just like the rest of the boys.[6]

The second Morrison home in Atlanta was at 41 Linden Avenue, about a mile and a half directly north of their first Atlanta home.[7] The end of the 1909 was a busy one for the family. On August 14, 1909, Agnes left with her mother and the kids on a trip to Chicago to visit her sister. "Mrs. Charles Morrison, Mrs. Kelly and Kathleen and Cleve [sic] Morrison leave Saturday for a visit to relatives in Chicago." It might have been the first mention of Kathleen in print.[8] A few weeks later they were back—"Mrs. Kelly and Mrs. Charles Morrison have returned from Chicago"[9]—and they were visited by more Chicago relatives: "Mr. E. Elwyn Spencer,[10] of Chicago, is the guest of his aunt, Mrs. Charles Morrison, on Jackson Street."[11] Agnes's sister Beatrice came to town as well: "Miss Beatrice Stone will be in town for the auto races. She will be the guest of Mrs. Charles Morrison."[12]

It was in Atlanta where the acting bug began to express itself in Kathleen. The third Morrison house in Atlanta, at 240 N. Jackson Street,[13] provided Kathleen and Cleve with something they had not had before to aid them in their games: a car barn at the rear of the property, with a loft in the roof.[14] The unused space provided them with a ready-made stage. In November 1909, Barnum & Bailey's circus came to town with a parade.[15] The circus was an inspiration. Colleen and her brother created the "American Stock Company," and she and her brother Cleve put on shows for the neighborhood kids in their backyard and in the loft of the garage at the back of the Jackson Street home.[16] She was "hero, villain, playwright and director."[17] Neighborhood kids played the parts of clowns, Kathleen and

Cleeve (left) and Kathleen Morrison, at about three and five (courtesy Judy Coleman).

Cleeve were the acrobats and assorted pets were the caged menagerie. By advertising that the circus would exclude boys from the audience they assured a full crowd of curiosity seekers.[18]

The family had its share of hardships, as Charles had been struck ill in early 1910. A newspaper item would later report: "Mr. Charles Morrison, who has been ill at home on Jackson Street, is better."[19] Within a month he was recovered enough to travel.[20] Cleeve and their cousin Jack Stone were struck ill next. This, too, made the news: "Masters Cleve [sic] Morrison and Jack Stone are convalescing after scarlet fever."[21]

While in Atlanta, Kathleen discovered motion pictures. They were hard to avoid, with theaters popping up in every neighborhood. Kathleen developed a taste for adventures. In *Silent Star* Colleen wrote she watched Grace Cunard and Francis Ford in the *Lucille Love* series at the Bijou theater in the same breath as she mentions Tampa, and seeing Mary Pickford or Marguerite Clark or Francis X. Bushman at the Strand Theater, but neither city possessed a Strand and Bijou theaters at the same time.[22] Atlanta did possess a Bijou Theater at the corner of Cone and Carnegie Way.[23] The theater was just over a mile from the Linden

Avenue and N. Jackson Street houses, and she might have seen movies there. There was a "Grand" theater in Atlanta, but not a Strand.[24] Wherever she watched her favorite motion pictures, once she discovered them she was smitten. Between motion pictures and the plays she put on in her backyard, her urge to act out stories grew.

The American Stock Company, however — at least in its Atlanta incarnation — was a short-lived affair, as by mid-1910, the family was on the move again. Grandmother Kelly had moved out of the North Jackson house in advance of the relocation[25]; Charles had left the managerial position to become a traveling salesman.[26] The *Atlanta Constitution* made note of the move: "Mr. and Mrs. Charles Morrison and children and Mrs. Beatrice Stone leave today and make their home in Warren Pa."[27]

Warren, Tampa, Chicago and "Some Pumpkins," 1910–1916

> Some Pumpkins: A term in use at the South and West, in opposition to the equally elegant phrase "small potatoes." The former is applied to any thing large or noble; the latter to anything small or mean.
> — *Dictionary of Americanisms: a glossary of words and phrases usually regarded as peculiar to the United States*, by John Russell Bartlett, Little, Brown and Co., 1889, page 626.

In Warren, Pennsylvania, Charles Morrison worked as a traveling salesman, living at 107 S. Irvine Street,[28] on a block dominated by the Jacobson Manufacturing Company. Given the industrial nature of the area and the short duration of his stay, the rest of the family probably stayed elsewhere. The city was the home of the Piso Pocket Almanacs, published by E.T. Hazeltine, full almanacs that could be carried in one's pocket. They were perfectly doll-sized, and would have fascinated Kathleen.[29] By 1911, the Morrison family was reunited again, and had moved south to Tampa, Florida.

When they arrived, the town was transitioning from a sleepy port to a center of commerce. Construction on the Panama Canal had begun a few years earlier: "Nearest to Panama of all the adequate Atlantic Coast ports of the United States is Tampa.... She has her boats in commission. And her port is in readiness to receive the vessels of the seven seas and all that therein is."[30] It was a prosperous city and Charles was drawn to prosperous cities.

Their home was a few blocks from Tampa Bay itself, at 215 Magnolia Street,[31] near the corner of Magnolia and Platt. A quick run south on Magnolia Street past the fire station on the corner and she and Cleeve could be in the water of Tampa Bay. The Morrisons' stay in Tampa was the longest and most

Kathleen (left) and Cleeve Morrison, photographed on the occasion of their first communion, Tampa, Florida, May 1911.

stable yet for the family. Kathleen would come to think of Tampa as her home town. She was enrolled in the school at the Convent of the Holy Names, and on May 28, 1911, she received her First Communion at Sacred Heart Catholic Church in Tampa. She and Cleeve posed for a studio photographer, both in fine white clothes: Kathleen stared straight into the photographer's lens, displaying her most serious expression. Cleeve may have attended Holy Names as well before he was off to school on his own.[32]

While at the Holy Names Academy, Kathleen received piano lessons. She showed enough of an aptitude for her parents to imagine a career as a concert pianist for her. Kathleen had other ideas. She wanted to be a motion picture star. The most famous motion picture actresses at the time were the embodiment of American beauty, semi-mythical figures with titles. Florence Lawrence was the "The Biograph Girl." Florence Turner was "The Vitagraph Girl." Mary Pickford was "The Girl with the Golden Curls." Kathleen, in contrast, had grown into a skinny, gangly girl with very long, straight dark red hair. She was a tomboy and she still loved the outdoors and water. Besides swimming in the bay itself, she would sometimes catch the TECO streetcar with Rosa Galvin, who was in her class, and ride out to Sulphur Springs for an afternoon of fun.[33]

Kathleen learned to cry at will, practicing on the streetcar, from time to time eliciting the concerns of fellow passengers. As the importance of motion picture personalities grew, so did Kathleen's interest in them. Magazines dedicated to motion pictures and their stars were just becoming popular. *Motion Picture Story Magazine* had begun publishing in February 1911; in December it ran its first star interview.[34] Six months after *Motion Picture Story Magazine* was first published, *Photoplay* appeared on the scene.[35] Newspapers were dedicating space to the films and their casts. In school, Kathleen read the magazines when she should have been paying attention to her studies. On weekends she still staged productions in her backyard with a cast of local neighborhood children. There was a car barn in the backyard,[36] facing the alley behind their house. When a neighbor had taken delivery of a stand-up piano, Colleen managed to talk the delivery man into delivering the empty box into her own back yard,[37] and it served as a proscenium stage. The American Stock Company was reborn (possibly with a new name, according to one newspaper clipping: "Using a stage made of boxes, the founders — she and her brother — called themselves 'The Hyde Park Stock Co.' Charging a penny a couple, they still made 50 cents").[38]

She continued to write and direct and star in her plays, always acting the part of the hero. Edith Gibbons (Mrs. W.O. Kinnebrew) always played the part of the heroine because of her beauty. Edith Allen believed Kathleen would be famous and had an idea that if she tagged along, she might be famous, too.[39] Edith Gibbons and Angie Allen (Mrs. Willard Casterline) were Kathleen's "unsuspecting pupils," trying out Kathleen's interpretive dances, which were "very *a la* Isadora Duncan."[40] When she was not appearing on her backyard stage, Kathleen was in the darkened theater[41] catching the latest films.[42] In 1912, the serial *What Happened to Mary* was released simultaneously with the serialized story of the same title published monthly in *Ladies' World* magazine. Directed by Charles Brabin, it was the first of the motion picture serials. Kathleen followed the serials with enthusiasm. Sometimes after the matinee, she found her way to the soda counter at Hutto and Schoenborn's in hopes of seeing "Bert Leighi — or another of the Hazel Burgess Players — eat ice cream. Bert was Kathleen's hero then."[43]

With the coming of summer the humidity shot up. The Gulf waters that keep Florida's temperatures uniform throughout the year also served to freight the air with humidity: "it is well known that the air of the Gulf of Mexico is extremely humid. Heavy dews are

Left to right: Cleeve Morrison, Marie McRea, Edith Gibbons, Mildred Gibbons (front) and Kathleen Morrison. The children were photographed at the corner of Magnolia Avenue and Platt Street, Tampa, Florida, ca. 1914 (courtesy Joseph Yranski).

deposited on the peninsula of Florida, particularly in summer; tropical floods of rain fall."[44] Between the days of wet-blanket humidity that could sap the enthusiasm of even the most energetic child, frequent storms would sweep in from the Gulf.[45] The boomers brought gusts of wind and rain and even hail and lightning. A string of summer storms could make a season of misery for Kathleen, who could find herself confined to the front gallery watching the rain turn yards and sidewalks impassable with mud. When it was impossible to play outside she lost herself in her favorite motion picture magazines. Kathleen was growing restless to do something about her dreams.

Chicago had higher summer temperatures but lower relative humidity, so whenever Aunt Liberty and Uncle Walter sent the invitation, Kathleen was happy to visit. "I adored going, if only to watch the fights."[46] Walter was bombastic. Charles thought he was nuts.[47] Liberty was a match for all her husband's bombast. They were both loud and energetic, and their explosive fights often ended with either laughs or tears, the tears followed by proclamations of undying love. Liberty Howey, née Board, née Kelly, was "large and handsome, like the statue of the same name," and she came from good social stock.[48] Kathleen thought she was one of the most beautiful women in the world, a standard of beauty, just like Kathleen's mother, Agnes. Kathleen wondered what had happened to her that she was so plain in comparison.

Lib and Walter's arguments were loud and dramatic, epic opportunities to "try out their vocabularies." They were small dramas for Kathleen to watch, each as exciting as any film or play.[49] At times they would argue over Kathleen; Liberty doted on her, calling her the "child of her soul," while Walter would reply she was the "child of his imagination." It made Kathleen feel like "some pumpkins." They both adored her.

For Kathleen, Chicago held other attractions. There was baseball for example; having grown into a tomboy, Kathleen loved to watch and play the game. Chicago was home to the White Sox/Cubs Rivalry, which always made for exciting entertainment. But more importantly was Chicago's position as the virtual center of the growing motion picture industry.

With the organization of the Motion Picture Patents Company in 1908, Chicago attracted the independent motion picture movement. Several antitrust importers and exchanges were located there. According to the *Baltimore Sun*, in 1907 "it [motion pictures] engages the efforts of thousands of men; it involves the exchange of thousands of dollars a day. And yet a year ago it was unknown."[50] Even before the Motion Picture Patents Company, Chicago's importance to motion pictures began with George K. Spoor, the box-office manager at the Waukegan Opera House, who helped Edward H. Amet to develop the Magniscope, a motion picture projector. Amet sold his interests in the device to Spoor. Spoor partnered with Gilbert M. Anderson, soon to be known onscreen as Broncho Billy Anderson, and they created the Peerless Film Manufacturing Company. After a name change, the studio opened its two-block production plant in 1908 at 1333–45 W. Argyle St. in Uptown, Chicago.

Besides the Essanay Studio, Col. William Selig had a studio in Chicago, at Irving Park Road and Western Avenue. Carl Laemmle opened his first nickelodeon in Chicago in 1906. The American Film Manufacturing Company — the Flying "A" Studios — was founded in Chicago. The American Vitagraph Company also had an office there. William Foster started Foster Photoplay Company to produce race films in Chicago. Bell & Howell was founded in the city. Chicago was a transportation hub. Railroad lines from every corner of the country came into the city. Film crews could send their film to Chicago via train, where it could be processed and edited. Completed films cold be struck in Chicago and distributed.

When she was in Chicago, the motion pictures were all around Kathleen.

5

Chicago and Tampa, 1911–1916

Between the years 1911 and 1916, the motion picture industry had undergone a series of changes that would mark the end of its pioneer days and point in the direction the industry would take. With Edison's Motion Pictures Patents Company (the "Edison Trust") chasing after the independents, many production companies moved farther afield to avoid the prying eyes of the MPPC. Cuba and Florida became winter capitals of motion pictures, but it was the moderate and year-'round sun of Southern California that attracted the most attention. Nestor Company built a full-time studio in the Hollywood district of Los Angeles. Carl Laemmle founded Universal Pictures Company. Jesse Lasky formed the Jesse L. Lasky Feature Play Company with Samuel Goldfish (later Goldwyn) and Cecil B. DeMille. Adolph Zukor founded the Famous Players Film Corporation. Mack Sennett formed the Keystone Film Company with its studio in Edendale. Paramount Pictures was founded to release the films of Jesse Lasky and his Famous Players, one of the first nationwide motion picture distributors.

The MPPC agreed to keep their actors unbilled. The independents, however, banked on the popularity of their actors. Before long, the relative anonymity of motion picture actors gave way to unprecedented fame. Even actors from the so-called "legitimate" stage had not achieved such fame, an actor could only be at one place at a time. Film of an actor could show in a dozens of cities. Actors became the draw for films. The first custard pie was thrown into an actor's face, initiating a standard shtick for motion pictures for decades to come. Mary Pickford signed a seven-figure contract with Adolph Zukor. D.W. Griffith's *The Birth of a Nation* was released, an epic at three hours with a ticket price of $2. Thomas Ince introduced techniques of mass production so that his studio could crank out unheard of numbers of film while maintaining their quality. And most importantly, William Fox's fight against the MPPC was a success. In 1915 it was declared illegal as a monopoly.

Motion picture palaces were popping up in cities around the country, and even the classiest venues were showing motion pictures. The Cort Theater in San Francisco showed them with regularity. The theater's assistant treasurer was a young man named John McCormick, whose family moved to the city from Seattle in around 1912. John was a smart young man, talkative with grandiose ideas about the potential of motion pictures, but prone to episodes of melancholy.[1]

Chicago, 1916

Kathleen's campaign to get into motion pictures was not planned. There was no structure to it. She expressed her love of the medium, and her conviction that she would someday be immersed in it. She knew nobody involved in motion pictures. Nobody in her family had ever been involved in films or theater. She might enter a beauty contest, but she knew she was no great beauty. Her conviction that she was destined for fame was the sort of thing her at which family rolled their eyes. Her friends wished her luck but there was nothing they could do. There was no opportunity to take concrete action.

For a time the Howeys lived at 4161 Sheridan Road in Chicago.[2] The Northwestern L ran right by their house at grade. The streetcar passing outside the house could have provided Kathleen, if she wished to take advantage of it, with easy access to the Essanay studio, which was less than one and a half miles distant from the Howeys. Hop on at the Buena Station, and two stops later hop off at Argyle.[3] The Argyle Street station was at 1118 West Argyle. Essanay was at 1333-1345 West Argyle. Later, when the Howey residence moved to a smaller apartment at 4942 Sheridan,[4] the route would remain the same. Later she would say "The old Essanay Company had a studio in Chicago. It was a long way from home, but I could reach it after school by the street car."[5]

In late 1916 the Essanay Company released *The Prince of Graustark*. There is a brief scene during a party at the home of the Blithers, where several maids are visible. For a moment one maid appears on the screen. Many viewers who see this maid are struck by the fact that she is the spitting image of Kathleen Morrison.[6] The film was made in Chicago, during the summer.[7] Though she stated in *Silent Star* that she first appeared in motion pictures in 1917, it's still a tantalizing possibility that she might have managed to appear, if only for a moment, in Essanay films before then.[8]

Even if not, in an indirect way, all the hoping and wishing paid off. Aunt Liberty knew of her wishes, and so one day suggested to Walter that he might do something for Kathleen. Walter knew D.W. Griffith; he had helped him get *The Birth of a Nation* past the Chicago censors. Griffith owed him. Walter allowed he might be able to cash in a few chips with Griffith. As she told it in *Silent Star*, when Walter got Griffith on the line and told him he had a niece who wanted a start in the motion picture world, Griffith sighed and complained "not a niece!"

Tampa

The long, continuous ring of the telephone in the Morrison home in Tampa meant the call was long-distance. Charles answered it and the rest of the family, including Cleeve and Kathleen, fell silent. Long-distance calls often carried bad news that could not wait to be delivered by post, and required immediacy and details a telegram could not convey. Charles announced it was Walter, calling from Chicago. He was quiet as he listened to Walter's voice through the background hiss. At first he was bewildered, repeated the unbelievable news that Kathleen had been given a six-month contract with D.W. Griffith. Agnes took the telephone and instructed Walter to explain everything to her. From where she listened, Kathleen's heart pounded as she awaited clarification.

At last her mother hung up and explained that Griffith owed Walter a favor. Walter had cashed in his chips for Kathleen.

The family hastily convened a conference to discuss the matter. Charles opined that when she graduated, there would be plenty of time for Kathleen to try her hand at motion pictures. Her mother objected, pointed out that this might be Kathleen's only opportunity and those six-months in California could be no worse than six months of the measles. If she kept up with her lessons, then she could return to school after her six month experiment and hit the ground running.

Kathleen could not go to California alone; it was out of the question. California was uncharted territory to the family. The family could not relocate just for Kathleen, and Agnes could not act as chaperone as six months away from the family would be too much. That was when stern Grandmother Kelly stated that she would accompany Kathleen to California. Kathleen broke out in tears.[9]

Within a few days, after packing and making all the necessary arrangements with Lib and Walter up north, Agnes, Kathleen and Grandmother Kelly were on the train headed northward.

Chicago

Uncle Walt and Aunt Lib welcomed Agnes and Grandmother Kelly and Kathleen, but informed Kathleen of a hitch: she would have to be tested to make sure both eyes photographed the same. Motion picture film was orthochromatic. One product of this color sensitivity was that actors with blue eyes photographed with irises so light they looked white. The fact that both Kathleen's eyes had photographed the same in still images in the past was no guarantee they would record that way on motion picture film, under the glare of bright motion picture lighting. Kathleen would be tested at Essanay.

At the Essanay Studios Kathleen met Helen Ferguson,[10] the youngest actor on the lot. The impression Helen Ferguson gave with her description of meeting Kathleen was they had spent considerable time together before Kathleen went before the camera.

> [Charles] Babille brought a girl to me with long red curls, her name was Kathleen Morrison and she was 14 years old, he told me. Since I was the youngest at the studio and she would be the next youngest, I should take very good care of her. We would draw pictures of theatres — she had to have an Irish name, so she would take the name of her grandmother, Mary Moylan. I had to have any other name but Helen Ferguson — I chose Jewel Farnum, after Dustin!
>
> One day someone said they were going to shoot a film of Kathleen Morrison to send to D.W. Griffith. By now they had converted some of the offices upstairs so we no longer had to stand up to do our makeup. They allowed us to go into rooms with windows, and they gave us a place for makeup and Kathleen sat next to me, clutching my hand. Anyway, they were going to shoot this film, and I knew what it meant to her. I walked back and forth on the stage, asking God to please let it be, let her get to work for Mr. Griffith. Harry Beaumont shot it.

Possibly Kathleen's test was shot on the tail end of some film under production. She asked the director if she would have to cry during the test. He said to go ahead if she felt like it.[11]

The studio was a loud place. Other films were in production, men in workshops hammering away at their benches, machinery at work. It was a clangorous atmosphere. Helen noted:

Well, there was a buzz around the studio, as there always was when something had happened. I hoped it meant that Kathleen had done well. When I saw her, her eyes were all red. She had been crying. She had been told to act jealous so she cried. I asked her "How did you cry?"

She was crazy about Charlie Chaplin and Lillian Gish. So she said, "You know how I love Charlie Chaplin, and you know how I hate spotted neckties? Well, I thought of Charlie Chaplin wearing spotted neckties and I cried!"[12]

Overnight the film was processed, the reel sent to editing to be divided up into scenes, ready to be cut together into the final product, and the test of Kathleen would have gone under the loupe for inspection. There was a difference in the darkness of her eyes, but not enough to be obvious. They photographed acceptably. With that judgment, the contract was signed by Agnes for Kathleen, and Kathleen's dreams of a Hollywood career officially began.

6

November 1916

It was Tuesday, November 21 and in Chicago, the California Limited[1] was due to leave the station at eight sharp.[2] Walter handed Kathleen's mother a newspaper and gave Kathleen a letter to read on the trip before the all boarded their Pullman car. It was past sunset when the train pulled out of the station and headed southwest.

As the party settled into their berth, Kathleen read Walter's letter: "Hollywood, where you will now be living, is inhabited by a race of people called Press Agents. The studios pay them a lot of money to think up stories about the players under contract and to persuade the editors like me to print their stories. So the moral of this letter is: never believe one damned word you ever read about yourself."[3] The newspaper Walter had given her mother sported a minor squib about the new actress named Colleen Moore.[4]

Once the lights of the city had slipped past, there was little of interest to Kathleen outside the window. The moon was in its last quarter, so there was little to see. The world was dark. Colleen wrote that she spent hours staring at her contract in disbelief until her grandmother told her she would wear the ink off the paper if she kept at it. Grandma Kelly took the contract and Colleen never saw it again.

They left Illinois well past midnight, into Missouri and arrived in Kansas City after daybreak. Breakfast was in the dining car. While it had been warm early in the month, cold weather had reasserted itself in the last few days. The prairies are known for dramatic weather, but Colleen wrote nothing of the weather or the vistas. The *click-clack* of the car's wheels on the rails counted off the minutes to her arrival in Los Angeles.

They passed through Emporia and Newton, passed into Colorado and stopped at La Junta, where just over two years earlier the Triangle Film Corporation was formed.[5] Their route took them through Albuquerque and Williams and Ash Fork. In California they headed southward through the Cajon Pass.[6] The train pulled into the La Grande Station[7] just past two in the afternoon.

Luggage in hand, the party went to the lady's waiting room to await Mrs. Brown,[8] who worked for the studio as a sort of combination truant officer/manager. Upon her arrival, Mrs. Brown told them she would take Agnes and Grandmother Kelly to their bungalow near the studio, and Colleen to the studio itself. Looking down East 2nd Street the group of women could see the taller buildings of downtown Los Angeles, some buildings as tall as 12 stories.

From the station they drove to Fountain Avenue. Fountain was within quick walking distance of the studio. Visible over the roofs and trees were the crumbling walls of Babylon, an old set from *Intolerance*, now left to the elements.[9] To the north loomed Mount Hollywood, and beyond it lay Carl Laemmle's Universal City. A mile to the east was Silver Lake Reservoir, adjacent to Edendale, where Mack Sennett had brought the Keystone Company of New York Picture Company and settled in the old Bison plant. Vitagraph was near the reservoir as well. Many studios were within a short distance.

At the bungalow, they unloaded their luggage, and then Colleen went with Mrs. Brown to the studio.

The Triangle Fine Arts Studio was on Sunset Boulevard, about two blocks from Fountain. It was a collection of shacks and makeshift buildings thrown up on a weed-covered lot, all set at odd angles.[10] When the studio began to increase production to meet their quota for Triangle, two new stages had been added.[11] When they ran out of real estate, they tacked second stories to existing buildings. Open stages were in the process of being glassed in and electrified. The place was a hive of activity, with the smell of sawdust and pine tar in the air. Mrs. Brown took Colleen to the offices of Frank Woods, the manager of production, who ran the studio while Griffith was away.[12] Triangle cranked out several films a week.

Woods was the head of the scenario department, which produced stories around the clock. He made sure the paperwork for Colleen was in order and that she was on the payroll at the agreed-upon $50 a week.[13] He suggested that Mrs. Brown see if she could scare up Chester "Chet" Withey, the director. Their new talent might be suited to one of his films.[14]

From Wood's office Mrs. Brown took Colleen out to the court in front of the studio and left her to acquaint herself with some of the stock company. The young actresses congregated together to chat and gossip. It was just like every new school Colleen had ever been to, aside from the makeup and costumes. The only actress she recognized right away was Bessie Love, though she would learn the names of the rest and make friends with many of them in time. Of the group, blue-eyed Mildred Harris was the old pro. Just days shy of her 15th birthday she had started out in child parts, appeared in a slew of films by Francis Ford and Thomas Ince, followed by parts in the Oz series of films. She had eventually graduated to adult roles and, like many in the group, she had appeared in *Intolerance*.

Colleen listened in on the gossip circulating through the group. The most conspicuous thing about all the girls was that they were strikingly beautiful. They were the ideal of womanhood in America, as beautiful as required by the unforgiving lens of the camera. Colleen was not statuesque, did not have the wasp waist or S-curve silhouette of a Gibson Girl. She was slim and gawky. Her hair was too straight and fine to pile atop her head in a bouffant and would not keep a Mary Pickford-style curl for very long. Her complexion was freckled. She knew then that it would not be easy for her. If she managed to become a star it would not be on her looks alone. That knowledge bred her determination.

Pauline Stark, one of the girls, asked Colleen if she was going to attend the school on the studio grounds. Because many of the performers were underage, the California compulsory education laws required a school to provide instruction.[15] Colleen said that she was going to have a tutor, to which Pauline replied that she was going to miss out on a lot of fun. The school was a real hoot.[16]

The gossip shifted from subject to subject: who liked whom in the studio, who was nice and who wasn't. Bobby Harron liked Dorothy Gish.[17] Dorothy was always talking about Harron. Lillian was the more reserved of the two Gish sisters, very private and professional. She never spoke of her private life. There were catty remarks about Carol Dempster, a young dancer who caught Griffith's eye and had been throwing herself at him since she had been cast in *Intolerance*. Lillian had seen Griffith's attention turn to Carol, and everyone knew she had taken it personally.[18]

After a time Mrs. Brown returned and retrieved Colleen, and told her she would be sharing a dressing room with Mildred Harris. She took Colleen to Chet Withey, a young man who had four films under his belt as director, ten times that number as an actor. He was one of those talents who did a little bit of everything at the studio. He gave Colleen the once-over and allowed that she would do. She could play the city girl in his upcoming production. Colleen was cast in her first credited part.

The film was going to be a five-reeler. Robert Harron was a popular actor. He often played the part of a quiet and soft-spoken youth, roles not so distant from the man's own personality. The fact that Colleen knew his name added to her mounting excitement.

The dressing rooms were atop a long building. Mildred was vivacious and chatty and, from her and Mrs. Brown, Colleen got an idea of what she would need for supplies on Monday. The studio would provide nothing. It was the responsibility of every actress to be ready for the day's work.

7

The Bad Boy,
December 1916–January 1917

Monday morning at 7:30, Colleen showed up at the studio with her makeup kit.[1] Her dressing room was bare. First she applied her makeup. Sitting before a mirror with her hair tied up, she would have applied a coat of cold cream to her face, getting it right up to the hairline, extending down her neck and shoulders, keeping it out of her eyebrows. Then she would have carefully rubbed it all off with cheese cloth and applied a gob of skin-colored greasepaint to her cheek, spread it carefully with her fingertips until her freckles disappeared beneath it. Then she applied some gray paint under her cheekbones, blending it in with the skin-toned paint. Some eyeliner, using it sparingly, then powder over it all. Then a second layer when the first layer was absorbed by the greasepaint, and maybe a third.[2]

After makeup, there were steps she needed to go through before she could appear on camera. Colleen was shown the ropes: where to find the call sheet for the day's work, where to pick up her paycheck at the end of the week, which buildings were stages, which were the factories that turned out sets, and so on.

Like any other industry, there were standards and procedures, with bean counters keeping watch over it all. There were many steps to be passed through before the idea could start filming. From the initial idea, a story would have to be written. From the story a scenario had to be created, which would cover the cast of characters, synopsis of the story, scene plots and the continuity.[3] From the continuity, it could be figured out what sets would be needed, what costumes, what extras. Would new sets be needed, or could old ones be redressed? How many cameras would be used? All the details of production. Colleen wrote of early films being made in a slapdash manner, but by the time she arrived in Hollywood those days had largely passed.

The film Colleen was to be in was *The Bad Boy*, written by Woods and Chet Whithey. The story, in short is of a resentful young man who falls in with a bad crowd and is eventually redeemed through the power of a good girl. Monday turned out to be a sunny, mild day. No rain clouds on the horizon, and none expected.[4] Colleen was still not ready. She would need appropriate attire. In *The Bad Boy* she was cast as a soubrette, so she was sent to Madame Claire,[5] head of the costume department, to be measured and dressed in an appropriate costume.

Once everything for the day's shoot had been collected, the group rolled out of the studio. The location for the day was Sawtelle, a small town between Hollywood and the ocean. She might have hitched a ride in a car with some of the actors, or with some of the crew on a truck hauling the props, or even taken the Pacific Electric trolley. The sight of costumed actors, sometimes carrying props, on streetcars or along the sidewalks was not an uncommon one in those days.[6]

7. The Bad Boy, *December 1916–January 1917*

They were shooting at the Soldier's Home, a complex of red-roofed, double-storied buildings reminiscent of old Southern mansions.[7] The grounds were landscaped into gardens. Nearby was the cemetery.[8] Once there, the crew went to work. The actors went to work getting into costume and touching up their makeup while the actresses would have gone to work setting their hair in curlers.[9] Colleen might have chatted with Mildred as she worked, looking to distract herself from the anticipation. Mildred was a sweet girl, quick with a smile and a bit flighty,[10] an image she cultivated. She had been turning men's heads since she had begun playing adult roles, wearing adult outfits, playing adult parts. She projected innocence and naiveté. Her sweetness, or at least her youth and inexperience, showed in her performances.

Youth was what people wanted to see. Motion pictures were new and vital, and audiences wanted heroes and heroines who were young and vital as well. It was not uncommon for very young actresses to play roles well beyond their years. A few wrinkles in a young man's face could be overlooked. Not so with women. As Colleen later wrote, "Only the youngest, clearest, most wrinkle-free skins could stand up to the scrutiny of closeups under their [Klieg lamps and Cooper-Hewitt lights] harsh glare."[11] Youth was worshipped.

Mary Miles Minter was marketed to the public almost entirely on the basis of her tender age: "Beautiful, the world's most charming and most youthful star."[12] That year, in *Dimples*, Minter played an orphan who had a wealthy boarder fall in love with her. In *Dulcie's Big Adventure*, she was a southern lady who comes to California to land a wealthy husband, but her true love follows her and eventually ends up at the altar with her. In *Lovely Mary*, it is a land speculator who falls in love with her, while in *Youth's Endearing Charm* she wins the affections of a young millionaire. All of this when Minter was only 14.

In *The Bad Boy*, Mildred, as Mary, played the sweetheart of Bobby Harron, who was nearly a decade older. Colleen, as Ruth, was the more sophisticated woman who tries and fails to seduce him. That was just the way the industry worked. The audience wanted to believe that through film something like eternal youth could be achieved.

Robert Harron played Jimmie Bates in *The Bad Boy*, the anti-hero who started off full of pranks and mischief. When his father runs out of patience, he beats Jimmie. Angry, Jimmie runs away and spends a few years on the road until he is pinched on a larceny rap. When released from prison he falls in with a bad crowd that plans to rob his home town bank. The bank, as fate would have it, was where his father works. By chance, Jimmie runs into Mary, his old sweetheart, and the sight of her prompts him to reform. He tries to back out of the heist but the gang forces him to go through with it. Because he has seen the righteous path he thwarts the plan, ends up in jail, escapes and, after being nursed back to health by Mary, he captures the bad guys and wrangles a confession from them. After being hailed as a hero, Jimmie reconciles with his father and lives happily ever after with Mary.

Studio portrait by Evans of LA, 1917. The inscription reads: "Colleen Moore made a personal appearance for me at the Miller Theater in L.A. selling candy in the lobby for the Red Cross. A charming girl of 17."

Once she was ready — costumed, hair in rag curlers and waiting for the call to prepare for her scene — Colleen would watch the crew at work. Men arranged big reflectors to bounce some of the sunshine at the actors and fill in the harsh shadows cast by the sun overhead. The director watched over everything.

Harron's acting was subdued, without most of the posturing and mugging Colleen remembered from earlier movie heroes. His gestures were smaller, his expressions more natural and intense. The style made an impression on Colleen. Mary Pickford had the same subdued style of acting. Silent film acting required an economy of style and an ability to include a maximum of information into a minimum amount of action, but too much looked silly onscreen.

At last Colleen was told her shot was next. She released her hair from her rag curlers. Chet would have explained what Colleen's character would be doing and thinking. It was not his style to push actors in front of the camera and bark orders at them through a megaphone. As he wrote of his approach, "I know from experience and observation that the camera will record the thoughts of a person absolutely.... The camera keeps grinding ceaselessly and misses nothing."[13] In other words, think it and the camera will see it. Believe it and the audience will believe it. Convince the audience that what is going in front of you is real.

When all was ready, Chet sat off to one side of the camera, called "Camera!"—and David Abel, the cameraman, started cranking the camera. Then Chet called "Action!" the cue for the actors to begin the scene. Colleen reacted to Bobby's emotions and followed Chet's direction. At one point a still photographer aimed his camera in their direction and exposed a frame just as Colleen's eyes flashed towards Chet. That image made it into her autobiography 51 years later, an illustration of how she said she got through that first day: just listening and taking direction as it was given.[14] And after a few seconds in front of the camera, her first take was done. Colleen went back to fix her hair and touch up her makeup and wait for when she was needed next. In all, Colleen estimated her part in this first film required no more than four days.[15]

Regardless of whether she was called for on the set or not, Colleen was at the studio every day. Some days she followed the production out on locations. Besides rural locations, the production took advantage of the city's densely developed center as well. The robbery scene for *The Bad Boy* was staged in the Hiberian Bank in early January. According to the *Los Angeles Times*, "Chester Withey, director, went to one of the largest banks in the city the other day and arranged for the use of the bank."[16]

Off the set, out of the studio, life had begun to settle into a routine. Colleen's mother had found a new home on Virgil Avenue,[17] and they had moved out of their temporary lodgings on Fountain Street. The new home was about a half-block closer to the studio. Each morning she was up early and off to work on foot. Sometimes she would meet Carmel Myers outside the entrance to the studio, and they would talk before going to work.[18] Inside the studio she would check to see if she was needed for that day's shoot. If not, she watched and listened. Colleen liked to keep busy.

Sometimes her grandmother came to call on her at the studio at the end of the day and they would walk home together. Colleen would tell her grandmother what had happened that day at the studio, what she had learned, how she had intended to use her knowledge. She had other parts coming her way. Frank Woods, who was in charge, liked her.[19]

7. The Bad Boy, *December 1916–January 1917*

Colleen had lessons in the evenings with her tutor, a weekly package of lessons from the convent having arrived for her to study. She found free time every so often. As winter overtook Southern California, she and Carmel Myers would occasionally go to the Bimini Baths, an outing doubtless reminiscent of her trips to the Sulphur Springs in Tampa.[20] Built over a natural hot springs near Third Street and Vermont Avenue, it was set beside a ravine "nestled in the eucalyptus groves surrounding the hills beyond the Westlake oil fields, it is out of the sight of most men."[21] Water bubbled out of the earth at 112 degrees, just the thing to fight off the chill of a stiff breeze blowing off of the Pacific Ocean. California winters are, at worst, mild compared to the snows and cold of the East and the hurricanes of the South, but they were still cold enough to draw huge crowds to the baths.

The Bad Boy was released on February 18, opening in Los Angeles at Clune's Broadway Theater to good reviews, the movie teamed with a Triangle Komedy *The Telephone Belle*. Triangle advertising touted the film as "The real story of a real American boy."[22] Colleen and her grandmother—and maybe her mother, if she was still in town—watched the film at Clune's, Colleen watched her performance[23] with a critical eye, examining her scenes to see what she would do differently the next time. She didn't like her profile, her nose, the way her red hair photographed jet black; all that time spent on curls and they could hardly be noticed. She saw the angles that worked for her and those that didn't; saw that if she dropped her chin towards her chest it gave her a double-chin; that if she faced the camera directly she could notice the different gray-values of her mismatched eyes. Better to keep at an angle to the camera so the difference wasn't so noticeable. She made a mental note of every detail and filed it away for future use.

Associated First National Pictures

Thomas Tally of Los Angeles and Turner and Dahnken of San Francisco set out to organize prominent exhibitors into an organization to exhibit films on a franchise basis. The organization would act as the go-between for motion picture producers and exhibitors. Member exhibitors would show the films first, and then redistribute them through existing or created circuits. Some 29 exhibitors joined the organization, and by the middle of 1917 they became the First National Exhibitor's Circuit, Inc. The members subscribed for shares of stock and received an exclusive franchise to exhibit films in a geographic territory. Though the organization purchased films for exhibition, it also began to sign talent so that they could secure enough films for the exhibitors.

The system was a direct threat to Famous Players-Lasky Corporation and Adolph Zukor, who had come up with the block/booking system that forced exhibitors to take films in a package, so that they would have to take films they didn't want in order to get the films they did. It set up a war between the two organizations that would last more than a decade.

An Old-Fashioned Young Man *and* Hands Up!, *January–April 1917*

> Every fourth person you meet nowadays, it seems, has at some time during his young life fallen victim to the movie-acting microbe. Like the sufferers from many other disorders, he comes to California to seek the cure. The remedy, however, does not lie in antiseptic sunshine or sea-purified breezes, but it requires a regular job — or the lack of one. Mostly it is the lack of one that kills the germ, but the process is not pleasant.
> — "Getting into the Movies," March 11th, 1917, *Los Angeles Times*, pg. III.

When Colleen was interviewed by studio publicists, refinements were made to the story her uncle had concocted; these misstatements that would appear throughout her career. The first big announcement of Colleen's debut in the industry had appeared in the January 20 issue of the *Moving Picture World* on page 384, a two-paragraph squib that gives the Colleen Moore story in its embryonic form:

> The Most recent addition to the Triangle-Fine Arts Company is Colleen Moore, a pretty Irish maid from Chicago, who will be given roles that were designed for Mildred Harris before it was decided to send Miss Harris east with Douglas Fairbanks.
>
> Miss Moore was sent from the Windy City to Los Angeles by a well-known director of the Fine Arts Company, who met her at a social function and was so favorably impressed by her beauty and personality that he recommended her to the managers of the Fine Arts. She is a graduate of a Southern convent and is an accomplished musician.

Before long Colleen was decorating her dressing room and at work on her next film,[24] at the time called *A Young Gentleman of the Old School*. This film was another adventure, the gentleman in question an honorable man in contrast to Harron's previous anti-hero. The film was to feature Sam De Grasse, Loyola O'Connor and Colleen, among others. This time Colleen had a featured role, though a largely passive one. She was the prize awarded to Harron after surviving his perils. It was a good place to be in her second film with Triangle.

In the movie, Harron plays Frank Trent, the titular young man with an old-fashioned reverence for the fairer sex. Frank travels to the city to take a job as aide to the corrupt Senator Briggs (Wilbur Higby). It is an election year, and Frank learns that Briggs is going to ruin the reputation of Mrs. James D. Burke (Loyola O'Connor), Higby's opponent, with a story that Mrs. Burke's adopted daughter Margaret (Colleen) is in fact, her illegitimate daughter, born out of wedlock. It was the sort of devious behavior that Frank hates, and so he quits his job, determined to disprove the smear. In New Orleans, Frank obtains records proving the adoption of the infant Margaret after her parents were killed in a train wreck, but Briggs sends his own men to intercept Frank. Much of the action of the film comes with Frank's efforts to evade his attackers. When Frank returns home he discovered that his father, James Trent (Thomas Jefferson), was once Mr. James Burke, the husband who had left Mrs. Burke. Cleared of all suspicion, Mrs. Burke wins the election and is reunited with her husband. Through his bravery, Frank has won Margaret's love.

Two weeks after Colleen's initial mention in the *Moving Picture World* was another mention of Colleen in connection with *A Young Gentleman of the Old School*,[25] with a whole paragraph refining her story: "Mr. Griffith saw Miss Moore in Chicago during the production of *Intolerance* at the Colonial theater. The following day, accompanied by her mother, Miss Moore was en route for Los Angeles. The second day after arrival at the coast studios she was cast as one of the leading characters for a Fine Arts-Triangle play."[26]

7. The Bad Boy, *December 1916–January 1917* 35

The film is set in the South, some portions set in New Orleans. For Colleen this was to be another sophisticated city-girl role. Once work on the set was completed, a portion of the cast of the film left for location work. "A trip from Los Angeles to New York via El Paso, New Orleans and Washington D.C., is to be undertaken this week by director Lloyd Ingraham, and the principals taking part in the Triangle production, *A Young Gentleman of the Old School*, featuring Robert Harron. A number of scenes will be staged at El Paso, New Orleans, and Washington, with the final ones being shot in New York."[27] The choice to take the cast of the film on location was an expensive proposition. Outwardly, things at the studio seemed to be going just fine. Actor Elmer Clifton had been promised to direct *Her Official Fathers*. Kenneth Harlan had come to the studio from the stage.[28] After Harry Aitken had sold off the Triangle exchanges, there was a new infusion of cash.

However Griffith's epic *Intolerance* turned out to be a spectacular failure. The film had not been released under Triangle's auspices. Expecting the same sort of emotional experience as they had had with *The Birth of a Nation,* the executives walked out of *Intolerance* with

Inside page of Triangle pamphlet for *An Old Fashioned Young Man*, 1917. Colleen is second from left in the lower left photograph (courtesy Joseph Yranski).

dazed expressions on their faces, as if they had been pole-axed in the dark. The failure cast a shadow over everything connected with Griffith, including Triangle. Rumor had it that Griffith was broke.[29]

Unbeknownst to Colleen, while her career was just starting to take off, the studio was on a downward slump. With the production of *An Old Fashioned Young Man* (the release title of "A Young Gentle of the Old School") on location, Colleen joined the production of *Hands Up!*[30]

In *Hands Up!* Colleen played the daughter of a railroad magnate; sophisticated city-girls were becoming her forte. The film would be Colleen's first real western, and this one came with a pedigree. It was based upon a story by Al Jennings, the "ex-bandit, ex-convict, politician, motion-picture actor and evangelist," as the *Los Angeles Times* called him.[31] This film required some horseback riding by the principals. Prior to being cast, Colleen was asked if she could ride a horse. Knowing she might not get the part if she said no, she said yes. How hard could it be? The first scenes to be filmed involved outdoor stunt work,[32] for which the cast and crew headed out for the Santa Ynez Canyon. When it came time to mount her horse, Colleen did her best to hide her inexperience. The actor playing the head bandit saw her.

"Girl, have you ever been on a horse before?"

"No," she admitted, and asked him not to tell anyone. She wanted to keep the part.

The bandit instructed her to hold on tight to the horn of the saddle. When the cameras started to roll, he'd smack the horse on the rear, and it would charge up the hill. Hold on, he told her; he'd help her dismount when they got to the top of the hill.

When the cameras began to roll, the bandit smacked the horse on the rear and it took off like a shot. Bouncing in the saddle, the horn proved not to be substantial enough for her to hold onto. She wrapped her hands around the neck of the horse and held on for dear life. The bandit approached her as her horse rounded the top of the hill, and he reached out and pulled her off her horse by her waist. The bandit was was Monte Blue, would go on to earn his own fame.[33]

In March, a rumored change in the motion picture industry came to pass: "D.W. Griffith, the master picture producer, has severed his connections with the Fine Arts Film Company and with the Triangle. This announcement has been expected for some time, but it was not until yesterday that the definite news was received."[34] It was expected that Griffith, out of town at the time, would return soon. Instead he headed off to Europe. He would soon begin work on *Hearts of the World*, at the suggestion of the British War office, perhaps in hopes of encouraging American participation in the war. Colleen realized things were going to change for her one day after standing in line to pick up her paycheck in its yellow envelope. Right away she noticed the regular yellow envelope had been replaced by a blue one. Inside was a letter: "We regret to have to dispense with your artistic services," it read, and for a moment Colleen felt elation: artistic services ... her efforts had been recognized! It took a moment before she realized that the studio regretted dispensing with those talents. Colleen got the boot.[35]

8

April–December, 1917

After she had been given her walking papers, Colleen had shown them to her grandmother, fearing that Grandmother Kelly would tell her that she had given it a good try, but perhaps a career in motion pictures was not in the stars. Instead, upon looking at the letter, her grandmother said: "Now, my dear, not a word of this to the family. I have some money — enough to take care of us until we see this thing through."[1] Colleen had barely started to work; there was no sense in packing up so quickly. And besides, there was the matter of the contract. It had time before it expired. She should go back, look into the matter.

Buoyed, Colleen returned to the studio.

Frank Woods remained in his office. The studio, once a hive of activity, had become quiet with the departure of Griffith. Grace Kingsley reported that while the Fine Arts Studios "wait for a new master, the hollow echoes are about all that one hears out there. However, Frank Woods and Mary O'Connor still remain to attend to the finishing up of certain pictures in such matters as subtitling, cutting, etc."[2] Frank kept Colleen on at the studio, and told her that the contract would be honored.[3]

With Griffith out of the country, Eli Clark Bidwell was managing the studio for him. With Frank's recommendation that Colleen be kept on the Griffith payroll, she might be assured another six months' employment. She had proven herself a dedicated to all aspects of the industry. A fact Colleen discovered early was that good acting alone would not make her a star. The most important work would happen away from the cameras. The film industry was a business, and to be successful she would have to be a businesswoman and sell herself as a product. She had seen the value of hard work within her own family. Her father had spent years in banking, chasing opportunities, and it had worked to give her a comfortable life. She knew that, in addition to all the skills that would add verisimilitude to her acting, she would have to become her own press agent. Her family still called her "Kathleen," which reinforced the fact that "Colleen Moore" was an invention. So she launched into a campaign to sell the brand name "Colleen Moore." Other actresses would find the behind-the-scenes work boring or tedious, but not Colleen. Over the years she would work the crowds, and make personal appearances. She did not shy away from portrait sittings, nor did she avoid promotional activities. This dual nature was not lost on people who knew her, and interviewers often commented on how she seemed to be, by turns, a light-hearted little girl and a woman wise to the ways of the world.

This was an attitude that would not fade even when she achieved fame at First National, when vacations were seldom about rest and relaxation, but story meetings, portrait sessions, interviews, costume fittings, tours and personally meeting the various franchise holders.

So for Colleen, the world of motion pictures was an all-encompassing venture.

While Griffith was in France, he decided he would shoot his film with the war as the background. He sent for his most valued people: Robert Harron, the Gish sisters, and many members of his stock company.[4]

Colleen was not among those sent for, so she remained in California. Unwilling to remain idle, she went to Eli Bidwell looking for any clues as to her future disposition. Bidwell was in almost daily contact with Griffith's lawyer, Branzhaf, in New York. She also set about looking for work elsewhere. Rupert Julian of Universal offered her a role in his latest production. She accepted, expecting no problems getting released temporarily from her contract. She went to John A. Barry,[5] who agreed to release her from the contract for five weeks, and included the information to Bidwell in a telegram. "Huck and Colleen off payroll this week," he wrote. It was the first week of August.[6] Colleen went off the Triangle payroll, for "five or six weeks with Universal Blue Bird beginning this week."[7]

Julio Sandoval (The Savage), *August 1917*

"Colleen Moore, Bluebirder," said the *Moving Picture World*. "Colleen Moore has been added to the galaxy of youthful beauties of the Bluebird West Coast studios.... Miss Moore was assigned by Production Manager McRae to the Rupert Julian Company ... where Director Julian has started production upon a new Bluebird Photoplay entitled *Julio Sandoval*."[8] The film was retitled *The Savage* and was made in the foothills of the San Bernardino Mountains, near Big Bear Lake. Monroe Salisbury would star. He was a big man who looked as rugged as the surroundings.[9]

Julio Sandoval (Monroe Salisbury), a feral half-breed, is taken by Marie Louise (Ruth Clifford), who recently returned to her home town from the big city. Lizette (Colleen), another half-breed, loves Julio, but he barely notices her. Marie is engaged to Captain McKeever of the mounted police. Sandoval is ruled by his passions, and so when he encounters her in the forest one day, he carries her to his cabin on the mountain top. However, after the abduction, he is struck by a bout of mountain fever. Marie Louise takes pity on the man who had kidnapped her and nurses him back to health. Several days pass. When the townspeople realized that Marie Louise has vanished, a posse is organized. Back in town, Lizette becomes jealous upon realizing that Marie and Julio have vanished at the same time. When the outlaw Joe Bedotte tries to woo her, she tells him she might be willing to go with him if he kills Julio.

When the posse arrives to rescue Marie, she tells the party that she had gotten lost on the mountain and Julio saved her. They all return to town to discover that McKeever has been captured by Joe Bedotte. A grateful Julio goes to the mountains to rescue the officer from the outlaws, but dies in a shootout during their escape.

The work took only two weeks. Colleen returned to the studio with three weeks of leave left, but nothing to do. She began to visit Bidwell, who felt concern for her. He mentioned her in a letter on September third to Banzhaf:

8. April–December, 1917

> What shall we do about little Colleen Moore? She is a little girl Mr. Griffith "found" in Chicago about the first of the year and sent out here. She has been drawing $50.00 per week ever since the studio closed, except for two weeks just recently when she worked in a picture for the Universal "Bluebird."
>
> I did not include her in my requisition while she was away, and when she returned I understood that she still has some "interiors" to take at the studio; but I was mistaken and she has been out of work for two weeks just passed and at the end of this week will have been idle three weeks. At $50.00 a week this of course would be $150.00.
>
> I understood from Mr. Barry that Mr. Griffith wanted to retain her, and I am taking this means to explain the matter so that you can decide what to do about sending her salary. I overlooked it a week ago, and am writing now instead of telegraphing in order to give the details. She is a clever little girl (seventeen years old I believe) and has made good in all the pictures she has played in.[10]

A little less than a week later Colleen had a meeting with Bidwell. The second half of that morning's telegram to Banzhaf reflected her state: "Miss Moore in to see me again per my letter third she has been idle three weeks and now appears anxious about salary."[11] Just over a week later Bidwell received the following reply from Banzhaf: "Will advise about Colleen Moore."[12]

This did not sit well with Colleen. On September 22, Colleen walked into the telegraph office and shot off a message to Banzhaf (in the standard clipped form of telegrams):

> Recently I paid off Mr. Griffith's pay roll two weeks to work in another picture and relieve Mr. Griffith. Since then Mr. Bidwell says he has received no money for me. Have not been with salary five weeks. Can you help matters? Mr. Barry knows about my engagement.[13]

Less than a week later Banzhaf instructed Bidwell to pay Colleen $100 on account, and that he would further advise him after an interview with Barry.[14] In October, Bidwell telegraphed Banzhaf a standard report, including a note, "Colleen Moore again inquiring about money says she is broke."[15]

At the end of the month Bidwell included Colleen's plight at the end of another telegram: "Please advise about Miss Moore as she claims six weeks due her at fifty." That would have been $300.

In April the *Los Angeles Times* reported that Griffith was expected back in the next six weeks: "The news that Mr. Griffith is to return to California to continue his photoplay productions is the first definite that has been vouchsafed regarding his plans since he went to Europe."[16]

A week later came this item:

"It is definitely announced this week that arrangements have been made whereby the Fine Arts productions will come under the personal supervision of Thomas H. Ince, and will be put on at the Culver City studios."[17] Some at the studio were drifting to other venues: "Mr. and Mrs. Frank E. Woods leave today for New York, where a number of flattering offers await Mr. Woods's consideration in the picture field. He wishes thoroughly to look over the ground before finally deciding."[18]

That same month before Colleen's six-month contract expired it was renewed by John A. Barry,[19] who had been recently elected secretary of DWG Incorporated. When Griffith had returned, sets were built to finish work on *Hearts of the World*. Perhaps as much to keep Colleen active as to meet his "discovery," he sent word for her to pay him a visit.[20] She found him a tall but unassuming man in a rumpled brown business suit. She was offered a bit part in *Hearts of the World*, that of a terrified girl who tries to set her alarm clock forward, reasoning that if time can be made to move faster, the battle around her would pass. She poured her soul into those few seconds, feeling her "golden hour" had arrived, and went home that evening satisfied. Some months later, when she saw the film herself, she wept when she discovered the scene had been left on the cutting-room floor.[21]

If nothing else, by December the Triangle account books recorded that Colleen had received her pay.[22]

9

Selig Polyscope, 1918

With the end of her association with Griffith, Colleen visited the Selig Polyscope studio, where there were plans in the works to adapt the poems of James Whitcomb Riley to film.[1] Col. William Selig had been one of the pioneers of motion pictures. At a point he had owned three studios: his studio in Chicago, his Edendale studio and the studio on Allesandro Street. By the time Colleen was put under contract, Selig's fortunes were waning. In 1916, Selig had sold his Edendale property to William Fox and moved production to the Allesandro studio, onto the grounds of what would become the Selig Zoo.

A number of factors had contributed to the decline of Selig's fortunes, not the least of which was the end of the Motion Pictures Patents Company, or the "Edison Trust." Selig had been a founding member. Selig's conviction that the future of motion pictures lay in two-reelers made it difficult to compete with the end of the MPPC. According to a newspaper report "Col. Selig is firmly of the conviction that the demand for short subjects is rapidly increasing.... 'Motion picture theatergoers are discriminating. They want the best. The time for stretching a two-reel story into a five-reel feature has gone by. The public will no longer tolerate the padding.'"[2]

An event that would have a devastating effect on the country as a whole, and especially on the motion picture industry, was the outbreak of Spanish Flu in the United States. Motion picture theaters would be emptied of their audiences, leaving studios with a backlog of films. The disruption would shake many companies to their foundations. It did nothing to help Selig.

By the time Colleen arrived, Selig was beginning to dedicate himself to bigger productions.[3] The company was looking to film all the Charles H. Hoyt comedies,[4] it was reported. *A Hoosier Romance* was to be one of his features, directed by Colin Campbell. "The minute motion pictures loomed up," he said, "I knew there was nothing else on earth I wanted to do so much as direct them."[5] As to his directing style: "'I am boss,' said Mr. Campbell calmly. 'I don't believe in the divine intuition of actors. They don't as a rule know. They need to be shown. I show them."[6] Colleen had been directed to Colin Campbell when she arrived at the studio. The director took one look at her and asked: "Are you related to Lib Howey?"

"Yes, she's my aunt," Colleen said.

Colin nodded and said, "I thought so; you have the job."[7]

A Hoosier Romance, *June 1918*

Based on the poem by James Whitcomb Riley, the scenario for *A Hoosier Romance* was written at the La Salle Hotel in Chicago, typed up on the back of La Salle Hotel stationery.[8] In the film, Colleen played Patience Thompson, a long-suffering girl who lives with her greedy and distant father, Jeff Thompson (played by Thomas Jefferson, a tongue-twister if ever there was one), on their farm in Indiana. When John (Harry McCoy) asks her to marry him, her father is enraged. Instead, her father selects an old but wealthy widower (Frank Hayes) for her so as to secure his family fortunes. With the help of a kindly squire (Edward Jobson) and his wife (Eugenie Besserer),[9] John hides in the Thompson home on the day of Patient's nuptials. Walking down the aisle, Patience runs out of the room and seems to flee the scene on a horse. While the search is on for the runaway bride, Patience and John marry.[10]

The interior work was done at the Selig studio at Eastlake Park. Working at the Selig Zoo was a new experience for Colleen, who remembered that after hours the zoo staff would let the lion and tiger cubs and various other young animals play on the grass. Colleen liked to play with the tigers; she thought it was great fun. It was a magical place to her,[11] though not entirely without problems. There was friction.

After *A Hoosier Romance*, Selig's Chicago office had arranged a contract for Colleen to play in *Little Orphant Annie*. Colleen's grandmother had instructed her that if she was offered $50 for a job, she should ask for double, the idea being that nobody would offer the maximum they could afford in their first bid. They would always low-ball, so Colleen should always ask for double. It was a strategy that had paid off so far. With Selig, Colleen had been under the impression that she was to be paid $150 per week. The contract that Selig's Los Angeles manager, "Mr. MaGee" (James L. McGee)[12] had shown her was for $125. This was a misunderstanding, McGee insisted. Since Colleen was still a minor, he said, the corrected contract had to be mailed off to Agnes for her signature. Later, Colleen discovered the contract sent to Agnes had been for $125 a week, without the promised correction. Colleen had been cheated out of $25, and she was livid.[13] At a point there was a lull in work at the studio. Selig Polyscope was going to resume production on the West Coast "on a big scale"[14] at their studio near Eastlake Park.[15] There was plenty of confusion at the studio and it was unlikely that anybody had drawn a very good bead on what the future held for them. Colleen, a newcomer, was worried.

The studio added another layer to the myth of Colleen's path to stardom: "Director Calls Colleen Moore Readymade Star," the promotional materials for *A Hoosier Romance* declared, stating she had been a student at the Lakeview High School at Chicago when Campbell saw her portrayal of "The Unruly Pupil" in a school production of Julia Crathorpe's *The Cornhuskers*. He "knew that he had discovered a jewel."[16] First Griffith had discovered her, now Campbell staked a claim.

Little Orphant Annie, *July–August 1918*

Little Orphant Annie was originally written by Gilson Willets as a straightforward adaptation of Riley's poem, with some additional details derived from Riley's *Where Is Mary*

9. Selig Polyscope, 1918

Alice Smith, his account of the girl brought to his childhood home to care for his family. However, the story grew with each new draft. Annie was described as "tall for her age, thin, gaunt, spindle ankles, awkward, gawky, slender wisp of a girl." She is barefoot and half-starved, a "soul warped by the brutality and terrors" that she suffered at the hands of her Uncle Tomp. "Her hair (in the first scene) is ragged and unkempt.... Altogether, Annie is a winning and lovable character. She is sad-eyed, weird, a little gypsy, mysterious, an elfinish figure. She rolls her eyes when she tells her spooky goblin stories."[17] She sees visions of the goblins from her stories, a characteristic that would make its way through all the drafts and onto the screen.

Production had started back in December 1917, with exteriors being shot in the San Francisco Bay Area. Their arrival in Pleasanton warranted a mention in the local paper: "That Pleasanton is just the spot for motion-picture work is once more emphasized by the fact that the Selig Polyscope Company ... selected the town as the place to put the finishing touches on a film to be known as *Little Orphant Annie*.... A company of 13 arrived in town Thursday and completed their work Saturday morning."[18]

The *Livermore Echo*, in an article reprinted from the *Pleasanton Times* for December 13, 1917, stated that the Rose Hotel in Pleasanton had received thank-you letters from members of the Selig Polyscope Company.[19]

Lobby card from the Selig Polyscope film *Little Orphant Annie*, 1919, with Colleen as Annie, unconscious in Eugenie Besserer's arms. Eugenie would appear again with her, ten years later, in *Lilac Time* (courtesy Judy Coleman).

In *Little Orphant Annie* Colleen plays the little orphan girl who told stories of "gobleums." The film is framed as a story told by poet James Whitcomb Riley to a group of children. Riley appears posthumously, thanks to the fact that he had been filmed by the Selig Polyscope Company for the Inter-State Historical Pictures Corporation, which had commissioned Selig to produce a film about the state. Portions feature Riley telling the story of Indiana to a group of children.[20] Annie charms the children of the orphanage with her stories until her uncle Tomp is made to claim her. On his farm, she is forced into hard labor for her uncle and aunt. Big Dave, a neighboring farmer, witnesses their abuse. Annie sees him as a knight in armor. Big Dave tells the kindly Squire Goode and his wife, who take Annie off Tomp's hands. In the Goode home, Annie tells the children her ghost stories. As she does so, she sees her aunt and uncle among the gobel-ums. The characters of her stories haunt her, but she finds relief with Big Dave, who has fallen for her. When Dave joins the army, Annie fears the worst and sees him off. When her aunt and uncle learn that Dave has been killed in battle, they rush to the Goode house and gleefully tell her. Annie becomes ill, believing that the gobel-ums have taken her Dave. Surrounded by the Goode family, she seems to die. But then the camera returns to where she had seen Dave off. In the street, seeing the vision of life without Dave, she collapses. Squire Good finds her and carries her home, assuring her she has only had a bad dream.

In September, Colleen wired Selig in Chicago and asked to be released from her contract, but permission was not forthcoming. She had been negotiating with another company, but upon learning that Selig intended to keep her, she dropped those negotiations.

By the end of the year things were shutting down at the Selig plant. Nobody knew what would happen next. Colleen became worried that she was about to be dropped from her contract. In October, she wrote to Selig and appealed to him for information and pleaded her case. Colleen was clearly in a near-panic as she wrote the letter:

October 17, 1918
Dear Mr. Col. Selig,

I thought I would write to you because nobody here knows anything—and if they do they don't tell me—and I want to know if you will please tell me what your intentions are regarding my future. I wired for a release from my contract a month ago and you refused it—I then dropped negotiating with this other company. Now Mr. McGee tells me I can have it and you do not intend taking up my option up, as I was told you would—I read you intend to produce again. Is this true? Of course I only know what I read, I do not know what Mr. McGee has written you or how things have been represented to you—What I want to know is do you intend to use me in your forthcoming productions?

You see I am puzzled, because I don't [know] what you really mean—one day I am told to go and the next to stay.

I hope you liked *A Hoosier Romance* and *Orphant Annie* and I surely enjoyed making them, especially the latter.[21]

Colleen wrote that she hoped he would be coming west, as she was anxious to meet him. She also asked for a two-week release from her contract for a trip back east. Less than a week later she was writing to Selig again. Something had transpired in that time that left Colleen even more panicked than before, as can be seen in the many underlined words.

October 23, 1918
Dear Mr. Col. Selig,

Please do not ["not" triple underlined] listen to the awful tales that I do not want to work for as I want to do good work. It is untruthful. ["untruthful" underlined]. Because I do ["do" triple underlined] and I have always wanted to finish the Riley works — it is just everything has been a series of misunderstandings and gossip and I want to make them and please don't let anyone else — please. I love Mr. Riley and *Orphant Annie* is my ["my" is underlined] child and so is Patience — I lived those parts. And they were successful ["successful" is underlined] every notice was good. And please let me make the rest. Let the other girls do any other pictures but leave the Riley ones to me — please.

All the misunderstandings about ulcers was too bad and things have been wrongly represented to you — that's one reason I want to go East, to see you and straighten things out myself ["myself" is double-underlined]. But I cannot afford to go and not received my money. I didn't know you would care, as I do nothing but loaf, and go to school now.

I wish you were here yourself it's so much nicer to do things right with the head instead of a lot of managers and telegraph wires.

So please Mr. Selig wire me and tell me I can do Mr. Rileys works — why I must know them all by heart — and I am studying them with my tutor now. And please don't believe the horrible things I heard were said to you — and can't you come west — the trip would do you good — and oh! I do want to see you ["you" is underlined] yourself. And I honest truly will work so hard ["hard" underlined] — I always do — I can't do otherwise because I live my parts — please tell me I am to play them — and let me continue being the Riley girl.[22]

Less obvious in her letter than her concern for missing pay or loss of work is her wish to continue being the "Riley girl." Like the "Edison Girl" or "Vitagraph Girl," Colleen understood that being known as the "Riley girl" would carry with it cachet of association.

Little Orphant Annie was released in December, and became a popular film. One critic wrote "Colleen Moore will divide honors with Thomas Santschi in *Little Orphant Annie*. She was a lovely and unspoiled child the last time I saw her. Let's hope commendation hasn't turned her head."[23] The Selig Polyscope Company fared worse. It went belly-up and once again Colleen found herself unemployed. Her mother had joined her grandmother and her in California. Her father and brother would soon join them. Colleen's work schedule was crowded, though she would still find enough spare time after work to watch baseball games in Washington Park.

10

1919

Colleen had redoubled her efforts to find work and ended up in several overlapping productions. It was an itinerant existence for Colleen. Motion pictures had grown in size so that feature productions were the standard. The studios still turned out the short two-reelers as programmers to fill in the space between feature attractions, but features were the future.

At the newly built Ince studio in Culver City, Colleen landed a role opposite Charles Ray in a baseball film called *The Busher*. While Selig's organization had been in decline, Ince's studio was a going concern. Charles Ray was one of Ince's biggest stars.

The Busher, *January–February 1919*

"It has been a long time since we have seen Charles Ray in a really suitable part.... It [his next film, *The Busher*] is the country type of picture, with Mr. Ray as the baseball wonder of the local team."[1] Charles was a youthful-looking man who specialized in simple, unassuming farm-boy characters. There was comfort for audiences in characters unfazed by the turmoil of social change in the country. *The Busher* would be directed by Jerome Storm, who had directed several of Ray's most popular films. An actor named Jack Gilbert (later known as John Gilbert) was cast as the heavy, Jim Blair.

Charles Ray was the attraction of the film: "The public will probably never tire of Charles Ray. To date he has played the same part innumerable times and each time he is delightful." There was an emphasis on authenticity in the production: "Baseball experts testified that *The Busher* was true to the diamond."[2] It was tough, physical work and it took its toll on Ray, whose arm gave out on him at a point due to his strenuous pitching in the film.[3]

Once Colleen's work was finished for *The Busher* she went to work on her next film without a break. This one was for Fox Films and she would appear opposite a new and popular leading man, Tom Mix.

The Wilderness Trail, *February–March 1919*

The secretary of the Chamber of Commerce of Flagstaff had gotten a telegram on February 3, 1919: Mr. Tom Mix will arrive in Flagstaff Tuesday night or Wednesday morning for purpose of making arrangements for production of several pictures around Flagstaff. Any courtesy you may extend to him will be greatly appreciated.[4] In Flagstaff, upon reading the telegram sent by producer Sol Wurtzel, Mr. A.A. Johnston suggested Mix delay his arrival, as two feet of snow had left conditions in the Flagstaff area poor. The reply was that Mix was looking for snow.

The Squaw Man was said to have been filmed in Flagstaff, Arizona. Hollywood productions returned from time to time for the spectacular scenery. Tom Mix was returning.[5] Since the end of the war the mood of the country had changed. The Old West shows were in decline, Buffalo Bill Cody died in 1917 and nobody had assumed his mantle. Tented shows were vanishing while motion pictures were on the rise. America's future looked vibrant, and tastes turned towards more vibrant characters. Tom Mix fit the bill with his breezy, moral characters and exciting productions filled with stunts.

Tom had been shooting films in and around Prescott, Arizona, since the Selig years with the lumpy, rippled Granite Dells or Watson and Willow Lakes as background, but for *The Wilderness Trail* he was looking for something different. He turned to the small town of Flagstaff.[6] The film was to be an adventure set in the far North, with Tom playing the part of Donald MacTavish, new head commissioner of the Hudson Bay Company in the Canadian Northwest. Colleen would play Jeanne, daughter of his rival, who is in love with MacTavish's son. As often happened to Colleen's characters in those early days, she is abducted, her life in danger.

Colleen had a crush on Mix: "Tom was a tall, handsome man, part Indian — and proud of that, too — with a slim no-hips figure and a face tanned to leather by the sun. He had strong jaw lines, a large, slightly hooked nose, ebony black hair, and brown eyes so dark they were almost black. In my love scenes with him I nearly swooned away." She wrote that Tom considered her a little girl, and that he was more interested in Colleen's mother, but that was fine by her. She just wanted to be around Tom. She'd listen to him tell stories for hours.[7]

Tom arrived in Flagstaff with his wife on February 4. President L.C. Riley of the board of trade paid them a visit and, learning that Tom was an Elk, the "two journeyed to the local lodge rooms, where great things were going on." He was well enough pleased with conditions in town that he wired for the rest of the company to leave right away for the city.[8]

In Prescott, word that Mix had picked Flagstaff for his next film was met with disappointment, but the papers there still followed the antics of Mix's troupe: "Six valuable Malamute dogs have been brought from Alaska, while a tribe of Navajos, numbering over 50 are to figure in this act." There was to be a hand-to-hand fight to the death with a bear, among other spectaculars. "thrilling scenes were being pulled off in the streets of that city and environments, in which many cowboys are participating."[9]

There were about 40 men and women, 20 horses, a half-dozen malamute dogs and a bear named "Theda Bara" (Bear-a), along with various props and equipment necessary to turn Flagstaff into an outpost of the far North. Common laborers and carpenters were lined up by the town to support the production. The cast and crew took over the Commercial Hotel with the blessing of the manager, Mr. Prochnow.[10] Colleen stayed there with her mother.¹¹ A month later the *Los Angeles Times* would report the Commercial Hotel had been renamed the Mix House, with a sign atop the entrance, reading:

> Mix Café.
> Tom Mix Manager.
> Operated under the Personal Super-
> vision of Mr. Mix.
> All Complaints must be made in per-
> son to Mr. Mix.
> Between the hours of 8 and 9.
> In the back yard at 15 paces.
> (Leave name of next of kin.)¹²

At sunup on February 11, they were at work in front of the old Pierce property on Railroad Avenue, leaving by noon for Greenlaw's mill. When not at work they might be found

Glass slide advertisement for Fox Film Corporation's *The Wilderness Trail*, 1919, with Colleen in Tom Mix's arms (courtesy Joseph Yranski).

in the dining room of the Commercial Hotel, where individual tables had been replaced by two long row tables and meals prepared by a cook from Los Angeles were eaten home-style.[13] Or else they might be found showing off outside: "When Tom Mix and his troupe were making scenes for *The Wilderness Trail* they would put in from eight to ten hours on location in the snow-covered land.... When they returned to their hotel, however, the cowboys just played.... When the fever to use their guns came on they would move out to the open spaces and shoot at bottles or cans or rocks." Tom saw Sid Jordan smoking a cigarette. Tom said, "Turn around, Sid, and I'll shoot that cigarette out of your mouth."

Jordan turned sideways and Mix "cut the cigarette in two" with his Winchester. "Mix invited one of the local Native Americans to stand in for Sid, but as he took up his place where Jordan had stood, fear got the better of him. He cried, 'Don't shoot! I can't stand it!'"[14]

Colleen was fascinated by the cowboys. They were full of stories and liked to put on shows. One day the animals got loose and put on a show of their own: "Theda Bara, the Fox bear, got tired of the limited view of life obtainable from the coral and broke loose. A Malemute dog and one of the ponies joined her, and together they trotted down to the far end of Beaver street.... The absence of the trio of adventurers was discovered at the Bennett stables ... and a posse started a pursuit.... It took eight men three hours to get the animals safely back to the stables."[15]

By the end of the month, work on the film was completed. Tom left town Sunday and on Monday night, February 24, a Pullman passenger car and baggage car were pulled onto a siding so equipment and props and people could be loaded, leaving the town's streets quieter and a little more subdued than usual.[16]

Once interiors were shot in Los Angeles and the film was finished and edited, William Fox viewed it and considered *The Wilderness Trail* a "fine picture."[17]

Devils Have Their Friends (The Man in the Moonlight), May–July 1919

From Fox Films, Colleen was back at Universal. She was going to be reunited with her leading man from *The Savage* in a film with the working title *Devils Have Their Friends*,[18] written by Elliott J. Clawson and directed by Paul Powell.[19] "*Devils Have Their Friends*, the new Monroe Salisbury vehicle, which took the star and his big company to Big Bear in the San Bernardino Mountains, has brought them back to Universal City to take interior scenes under Paul Powell's direction. Colleen Moore is playing opposite Salisbury."[20] *The Man in the Moonlight*, the title by which the film would be released, was another story set in the Great North, the mountains of Southern California standing in for Canada. Salisbury would play Rossignol and had an unusual take on the French-Canadian villain in the film, dressed as "a South American gaucho in a flat black hat, black poncho, open shirt, and beads. To complete the characterization Salisbury kept a cigarette dangling constantly from his lips."[21] The story, however, would revolve around the imperiled romance between Colleen's character and her fiancé, and around the doomed love of Rossignol.

Louis Delorme (Arthur Jasmine) is a wayward youth who ends up in prison with the notorious Rossingnol (Salisbury). A few years later, as the story begins, Louise's sister Rosine (Colleen) is about to marry Sergeant O'Farrell (William Stowell) of the Royal Mounted Police when three mysterious strangers show up in town: two men and a woman. O'Farrell gets word that Louis and Rossingnol have busted out of jail, so he postpones the nuptials to apprehend them. One of the strangers approaches Rosine and tells her he can take her to the whereabouts of her brother if she can first guide them through the "road of death." She does, and at the end of the trail they find a cabin. Louis is not there, however. The taller stranger reveals himself as Rossignol. When she faints, he drags her to the cabin's bed to hypnotize her. Louis, the other stranger, warns that the police are following. Rossingnol has Louis hide with his sister in the brush. The woman, who loves Rossingnol, stays with him and he is shot dead. O'Farrell resigns his position and leaves with the reunited Rosine and Louis. In the United States, O'Farrell marries Rosine.

While the story is as exciting as the standard-issue western, it also has the elements of a tearjerker, with a tragic villain who dies in the arms of his true love, elements the writers doubtless thought would appeal to women in the audience.

"While encamped in Bear Valley County of southern California, miles from the nearest ranch, director Paul Powell lamented the lack of variety in the next evening's dinner menu; "beans and beans, and beans." Monroe Salisbury volunteered to run to the closest ranch to buy a chicken. However, the rancher he approached was not willing to part with any of his chickens.

When Salisbury returned, however, he had a chicken ready for roasting. That evening Powell, while biting into his chicken, came across a small round pellet: buckshot. When he asked Salisbury why the chicken was peppered with buckshot, Salisbury explained "That buckshot was meant for me."[22] Work on the film was done in mid-July; "Final scenes for *Devils Have Their Friends* with Monroe Salisbury as the star have been taken on Mt. Baldy under the direction of Paul Powell."[23] The company wasted no time rushing the film through the process of post-production. By the end of July, the film had been released.

The Egg Crate Wallop, *July 1919*

Colleen's reunion with Monroe Salisbury was followed by a reunion with Charles Ray and director Jerme Storm. The *Chicago Daily Tribune* reported: "That cunning little Colleen Moore has been engaged to support Charles Ray in his coming picture. It is said that this picture will contain one of the greatest ring battles ever screened."[24] The film was to be entitled *The Egg Crate Wallop*. "Jerome Storm, who directs Charles Ray in Paramount pictures produced at the Thomas H. Ince Studio, has arranged, during the time he has been directing the youthful star, nearly every kind of contest from a baseball game to an auto race." Commenting on the trend, Ray said, "I suppose next time it'll be a boxing bout."[25]

He was right. Storm went about finding a sparring partner for Ray: "Reports from the athletic club and from some who tried out indicated that Charlie had an awful wallop. Six bruisers quit before a real game one was finally found."[26] As before, Charles was the simple young man in an athletic role, starting off as the Jim Kelly, assistant to railroad freight agent Dave Haskell (J. P. Lockney). Through lifting egg crates into railroad cars Kelly develops strong arms. He is in love with Dave's daughter Kitty (Colleen) and jealous of city boy Perry Woods (Jack Connolly). Woods steals $2,000 from the station safe. The currency has been marked, and when Jim sees Dave with some of the marked currency, he confesses to deflect crime from Kitty's father. He flees for Chicago and finds work as a training assistant in a boxing gym due to his impressive "egg crate wallop." In a bout, Jim takes the place of a boxer who was planning to throw a fight. His opponent turns out to be Woods. After five punishing rounds, Jim knocks out Woods. When Jim finds some of the marked currency on Woods, he reveals Woods to the authorities as the real thief and returns home to Kitty as a hero.

To keep the film as authentic as possible, the boxing scenes were shot as realistically as they could be: "The fistic duel between Charles Ray and Jack Connolly, which goes five rounds to a knock-out, is declared to be the fastest, most exciting mill ever picturized. Ince built a genuine prize fight arena and stadium at his studio for the 'punch' scenes.... To give the proper atmosphere, about 500 fight fans were hired as 'extras' to sit in the bleachers; hired at $5 a head and professional players were used at a cost $4,000 for the day.[27] For two days they watched some of the liveliest pugilists in the country in action, and most of the 'spectators' agreed it was the softest job they ever had."[28]

Common Property, *July 1919*

Colleen returned to Universal for *Common Property*. Elliott Clawson, who had written *The Man in the Moonlight*, had written *Common Property* as well; both films were directed by Paul Powell.

It was a timely movie, with a story suggested by recent events. In the wake of the October Revolution in Russia, banks were nationalized, private bank accounts seized, wages were fixed and control of factories handed over to the soviets, America fell into a "Red Scare." In Washington, a Senate committee, investigating Bolshevism around the world were treated to the story of the Saratov decree. As read to the committee, the decree dated March 15, 1918, stated: "Social inequities and legitimate marriage having been a condition of the past which served as an instrument in the hands of the bourgeoisie, thanks to which all the best species of all the beautiful women have been the property of the bourgeoisie, which has prevented the proper continuation of the human race." In short, to correct things it was proposed to abolish "possession" (by marriage) of women between the ages of 17 and 32, exempting them from "private ownership" and declaring them the property of the entire nation. The Anarchist Saratov Club was to have domain over their distribution. The women were to be issued an allowance. Those who were pregnant had four months off from their duties, and women with more than five children were exempt.[29]

It was scary stuff: a socialist revolution which potentially threatened to spread across the world. Into the mix was added American troops in the form of the Allied Expeditionary Force, Siberia, sent to Russia by President Wilson. The idea of American troops fighting back against the "Red wave" made for a good story.

The idea formed the basis of *Common Property*. It was a fast production, filming having commenced less than a year after most of the events that inspired the story. The lead was played by Robert Anderson, as Paval Pavlovitch, who brings his new American wife back home to Russia. The men of the town covet her. Nell Craig played the part of the wife, Anna Pavlovitch. When the decree is handed down nationalizing all the eligible women of the town, townsmen file claims for both she and Paval Pavlovitch's daughter, Tatyone (Colleen). They are rescued by American troops.

Motion Picture News reported: "The final scenes in *Common Property*, a drama of Russian Nationalization of women, is being made at Universal City."[30] The same news was repeated a week later.[31] By the end of the month, the photography was in the can. It would take until October before the film was released, and in an odd attempt to take advantage of lingering fears of Bolshevism and to generate interest in the film, an unusual publicity campaign to promote the film was started in Los Angeles. Posters had been pasted up on walls and fences around the city that read "proclamation. On and After November 30, 1919, all women between the ages of 18 and 37 are hereby declared to be 'common property.'"[32] The proclamation was signed by "Ivan Ivanoff, Bolsheviki Minister." The *Los Angeles Times* stated, in an article entitled "Press Agent Stirs Storm," called it a crude stunt to advertise a motion picture. Most of the posters had gone up in the Russian quarter, creating no end of aggravation and indignation among the city's women, who inundated the police with complaints. Recent Russian immigrants, aware of the events back in their home country, feared the same fate was being visited upon them. The police chief gathered together a squad of "I.W.W. hunters" who went about tearing down all the posters they could find. A press agent was discovered to be the perpetrator and was dragged into court—all splendid publicity, he thought—and was fined $5. Those frightened and offended by the stunt would have preferred the press agent be run out of town.[33]

The Wilderness Trail was released on July 6 and distributed by the Fox Film Company. It was followed less than a month later by *The Man in the Moonlight*.

By August, Colleen was faced with her first break in months, as reported in the *Los Angeles Times*. To relax, she spent time every afternoon in Washington Park: "She is an ardent baseball fan and can make as much noise as anyone."[34] But the prospect of a break was short-lived.

Colleen had begun to notice a trend in her roles. Her last few characters were all essentially damsels in distress. If her roles stayed the same, then she would be stuck where she was. The publics perception of Colleen Moore would have to change if she wanted to expand her horizons. As things were, she was going nowhere.

11

Discovering Comedy

Any chance Colleen might have had for a vacation was shot when two contracts came her way. "Two long-term contracts have been submitted to her [Colleen], both attractive, and she will sign one in the next few days."[1] No details were given, but it was possible they were offered once Colleen had realized her recent roles were variations on the same type of character. She was perceived as suitable to a specific type of role, such as the orphan, the waif, or the young, suffering mother. She knew she had to expand her repertoire.

There had been a recent trend in the selection of actresses for dramatic roles. Betty Compson, who "used to romp through Al Christie comedies" had been cast of late in dramatic roles. "I think the exodus began with Gloria Swanson, who used to cavort in Keystone comedies and who now emotes under the Lasky banner; then Clarine Seymour, who used to dazzle in Pathé fun features ... was discovered by D.W. Griffith, after which she rang the bell as Cutey Beautiful in *The Girl Who Stayed at Home*." Mary Thurman, one "of the loveliest misses who ever inhabited a bathing suit," who was equally at home in drama, and Alice Lake who used to ham it up with Fatty Arbuckle's comedies, was now doing drama.[2]

Colleen had a single-note resumé, all drama. It was the comediennes who were landing the dramatic roles. While at work on *The Egg Crate Wallop*, she had been involved in some physical comedy and the director had been dissatisfied with her timing. She knew that, to succeed as an actress, she had to be capable of doing anything the director asked of her. That meant she needed comic training. If, Colleen thought, comic training led to better dramatic roles, so much the better.

There were three major comedy producers from whom Colleen might find the experience she needed: Hal Roach, Mack Sennett and Al Christie. Hal Roach was distributing his comedies through Pathé, but he had been handicapped by Pathé's financial problems and the explosive injury to Harold Lloyd, his most popular comedian, who lost several fingers and injured his eyes in a stunt gone awry. Roach faced the possibility that his best known comedian might not act again. That left Roach out of the running,[3] so the choice was between Sennett or Christie.

Sennett's style of comedy tended towards heavy slapstick. Belly-laughs and knockabout comedy were the order of the day. Christie's comedies were of a more civilized flavor. The two contracts offered Colleen in August might well have been from both Sennett and Christie, leaving Colleen to decide between the two. Of the two, Sennett was the better known, the virtual king of comedy.[4] His comedies were fast and physical, and Colleen was game for anything. The problem was the Sennett Bathing Beauties; Colleen might have to prance before the camera in a revealing swimsuit.[5]

There were bathing beauties at the Christie lot as well, but Christie had a better reputation, and Colleen had already earned a degree of name recognition. As she recalled "I felt ... I must have some comedy training to round myself out, to learn.... I went over to the Christie Comedy Company, to Mr. Christie, and I said: 'I'd like to come and work for you.' Well now, I was coming along pretty well then, and an actress then who, when they reached the spot I had, wouldn't want to go to Christie Comedies. It seemed like a backward step. So he was delighted. He said: 'We would love to have you.'"[6]

Colleen approached Charles Christie, who handled the studio business, about joining the company. She knew that going from drama to comedy was a step down in the hierarchy of motion picture roles, but she needed the training. The Christie organization would benefit from the presence of a respected dramatic actress. They struck a deal for Colleen to come to Christie for $200 a week. In *Silent Star,* Colleen wrote that they had a verbal agreement, something she stated in later interviews: "We had an agreement, and the agreement was that that they would pay me so much a week and yet I could rent myself out if I wished. But I could keep the difference."[7] The Christie brothers encouraged her to look for work outside their studio. When the big role she needed came along and she became famous, they would have bragging rights that they gave Colleen her start.

The Cyclone, *October 1919*

Colleen had another film to make for Fox. Tom Mix had wanted Colleen again, as long as Agnes was going to come along. For this film, Tom took the company to Prescott. Like Flagstaff, the area was no stranger to motion pictures. In some ways it was like an old frontier town; the hotel was false-fronted with a balcony overhanging a wooden sidewalk. "Prescott was born in a gold pan and cradled in the first rude rocker with which the shining golden grains were sifted out of what are now its streets and thoroughfares."[8] By the time of Colleen's arrival with the Tom Mix troupe, the town had grown. The city had a profusion of elegant Victorian homes. In 1900, the city had been struck by fire that had "practically demolished the business section of the town." The destruction turned out to be a blessing in disguise, because "from its ashes were built the modern business blocks that set the metropolitan stamp on the new city."[9]

As in *The Wilderness Trail,* Colleen was keen to learn any new skill she could. Cowboy star Buck Jones was along on the production[10] and he taught Colleen a number of skills. She learned how to roll a cigarette one-handed and learned to use the lariat. Others gave her riding tips. As she recalled, "They taught me to rope and ride and I had a good time."[11] The location work in Prescott went smoothly, and Tom was pleased with the cooperation he received. In October, he showed his appreciation to Prescott and Yavapai County for the hospitality the town had shown him by appearing in the Northern Arizona State Fair. "He and his famous horse, Tony, led the parade, Mix saluting with his big white hat and flashing his famous smile.... Later, Mix headed up a contingent from the Fox Film Co. in a show called Range Pastimes that has the fair audience buzzing."[12] Tom's name appeared in a variety of capacities in the programs of the fair published in the paper daily, both as guest and as judge of events: "The Northern Arizona state fair held during October was a decided success. The Tom Mix aggregation of the Fox Film Company was an attraction, and aside from enlivening the program, they will perpetuate the doings of the fair, due to their having photographed many of the events."[13]

11. Discovering Comedy 55

Tom Mix and Colleen are pictured in a lobby card for Fox Film Corporation's *The Cyclone*, 1920 (courtesy Joseph Yranski).

When the location work completed, the company returned to the back lot of Tom's studio in Edendale, dubbed "Mixville" by the folks who worked and lived there. Interior scenes and the more complicated stunt scenes would be shot there. The site had been equipped not only with all the props necessary to represent any western scene, but was run like a working ranch. "Mix has been acquiring a new string of fine horses, and new stables are being built at Mixville, the Mix ranch not far from Hollywood. It is at this ranch that Mix makes many of the scenes in his pictures. He has had there a hundred head of cattle and sixty head of horses; but the constant arrival of additional animals has necessitated an extension of quarters."[14] Working at Mixville would have been exciting for Colleen with the array of characters in residence at the lot, and the skills on display.

One stunt for *The Cyclone* required the construction of a massive set for an over-the-top rescue of the sort that could only happen in a Tom Mix film at the time. "When Director Cliff Smith made arrangements for the filming of *The Cyclone*, he consulted some of the best contractors in the vicinity of Mixville, Cal., regarding the erection of a building that was to house a Chinese den."[15] The building was open on one side, consisting of a flight of stairs that ran up the set four stories; the stairs were breakaways, rigged to collapse when Tom and Colleen, atop Tom's stunt horse for Tony, climbed them. The walls were made of chicken wire and plaster, so that there would be a suitable amount of debris and dust sent crumbling on cue without injuring them. After the collapsing building, there was a picture window of breakaway glass to be jumped through by the pair and their horse. It was all pure excitement to Colleen.[16]

Christie Comedies

The excitement of Mixville stood in contrast to the more urbane atmosphere of the Christie Studio. Christie specialized in polite, situational comedy. Al Christie, who was in charge of film production, was well liked. He was "unlike any other Hollywood film mogul. He was a nice guy. There was nothing crude about him. He was gentle. He was kind. He liked beautiful women."[17] He had an eye for what made people laugh, and ran the studio in a genial way.

"Live, Love, laugh, Labor and Be Happy" is his studio motto. "And anyone who can't live up to the studio motto," says the producer, "had better pack his make-up and costumes and leave."[18]

Certain comedy players were doing scenes in Griffith Park, a lunch box paradise for California week-enders. Said Al Christie to Eddie Barry, "Eddie, in this scene you go over to that girl sitting by the tree and put your arms around her. Then her escort gets mad and hits you an awful wallop—"

"But, Mr., Christie," said Eddie, "that isn't an actress by the tree, that is a tourist."

"I know," said Al, "the blow will be quite natural on the young man's part. It will be a corking scene."[19]

At first Colleen may have thought she would pick up the nuances of comedy timing quickly, if her quotes are to be believed. "Colleen Moore has just started work as the lead in a Christie comedy, but will make only one picture.... 'Never in my life,' says the popular young actress, 'have I done any comedy, and I felt that I really needed the experience if I would be completely equipped for my work.... I shall be in comedy for a little less than three weeks, but I believe the training will make it a responsible experience for me'"[20] In fact, Colleen would be in comedy for considerably longer.

Christie Studio

The Christie Studios had a long history. In 1909 Al Christie shot his first film in Hollywood for the Nestor Studio, which was owned by Centaur Film Company of Bayonne, New Jersey. Nestor had taken over the Blondeau Tavern at the corner of Gower and Sunset in Hollywood: "The first pictures made here were taken on the shady side of a barn, the eaves of the barn serving to hold one end of the diffusing system made up of bed sheets sewn together."[21] The rear garden of the roadhouse became Nestor's back lot, the tavern became the office. Within months, more than a dozen film companies leased land along Sunset Boulevard.[22]

Nestor was taken over by Universal in 1912,[23] and Al Christie had worked with them until 1916 when he and his brother, Charles—who strictly handled the financial end—struck out and created the Christie Film Company. They leased the old Nestor plant, but Christie's needs were outstripping the utility of the facilities as they existed. By the time of Colleen's arrival, change was underway with the row of dressing rooms being demolished and replaced with larger and more spacious quarters. "The open air stage is now the full length of the Christie grounds, extending from Gower to El Cerito. The enclosed stages have been increased in size, and additional lighting facilities have been added to the electrical department."[24] The studio was about to transition from short films to features, and a popular actress like Colleen would help sell their features.

A Roman Scandal, *September–November 1919*

Colleen would head the cast of her first Christie production. "According to reports, the plot involves the burning of 'Rome' and such characters as the historic Nero, Brutus, Cassius, etc., the whole theme, of course, being burlesqued from the Christie comic viewpoint."[25] The film was *A Roman Scandal*, a spoof on the theatrical aspirations of a young soon-to-be housewife who would not marry her fiancé until she made a splash in the local theater scene; and the local scene was of a decidedly rural bent. When the actors go on strike, Colleen gets her chance to star, and the local actors watch from the audience. In some ways the film was a reflection of real life: the audience of the play watched Colleen's character struggle with drama, while the audience of the film watched her struggle with comic timing. It was training that would prove invaluable in the near future.

Though it was a hilarious film, in *A Roman Scandal* Colleen's part was essentially played straight. Her character was an amateur actress who wanted to experience the theatrical world, and was ready to delay marriage until she achieved fame. Straight was the only way to play the character. The humor was in the timing and the reaction to the chaos around her. Timing was essential in Christie's type of humor. Pratfalls brought laughs for Sennett, but for Christie the payoffs came after the build-up: "In analyzing even the wildest sort of 'slapstick' comedy, you will invariably find at least a trace of fundamental drama."[26] The drama, in Colleen's case, was her character's honest belief that she was in a serious drama while disasters mounted backstage and her fiancé suffered the embarrassment of being dragged into the disaster.

Suspense in drama is relieved by catharsis; in comedy, by humor. The zaniest sorts of chaos may occur, but it is through the hero or heroine of the film that the audience experiences it. By the end of her first film with Christie, it was evident to Colleen that she still had not nailed down her comic timing. Her part had been mostly passive. Colleen was having fun, her smiles were natural and unforced, but she still felt mastery of timing evaded her.

The construction at the studio did not slow down production. It continued "amid the din of hammer and saws, concrete mixing machines, hoisting derricks and what not."[27] There was still time for fun between the construction and production work: "The gangs at the Christie studios were invited at the ranch of Charles H. Hastings where a barbecue was served. Everybody spoke a piece or sang a song, and there was a lot of cutting up. Everybody had a good time, and Al Christie lost his hat."[28] There were Christmas celebrations as well, staged for the benefit of the public, though of a decidedly Southern California flavor: "With the warm sand of Venice taking the place of a carpet of snow, and with Santa Claus dispensing presents in a bathing suit, the entire Christie comedy studio celebrated an old-fashioned

Christmas in advance, on the beach the afternoon before Christmas." A Christmas tree in the sand and airplane dropping confetti completed the scene. "Several thousand people crowded the beach where the unusual Christmas celebration was held, and it is estimated that more than 2,000 visitors from the East took photographs of the bathing suits." Present at the festivities were many members of the Christie troupe, including Fay Tincher, Bobby Vernon, Earl Rodney, Dorothy Devore, and Colleen Moore.[29]

With the completion of *A Roman Scandal*, an announcement regarding Colleen's next step was made: "Colleen Moore, who was introduced to comedy in Christie's *A Roman Scandal* ... has been secured[30] for a further engagement by the Christie company and will be featured in another of their two-reel feature comedies."[31]

The Devil's Claim, *December 1919*

Pretty, popular Colleen Moore was an asset to the Christie troupe, and her image had appeared in the studio's promotional materials. The December 6 edition of *Motion Picture News* featured an ad running across the gatefold: "*A Roman Scandal*, featuring Colleen Moore."[32] Colleen's appealing photograph was on prominent display. *A Roman Scandal* was released at the end of November.

Colleen was free to farm herself out to work for other studios. So she went to work at the Haworth Pictures Corporation, which had been established by Sessue Hayakawa in 1918, in part a reaction to his dissatisfaction with Jesse L. Lasky Feature Play Company.[33] In the film *The Devil's Claim* Colleen played the part of Indora, Persian lover of Sessue Hayakawa's Akbar Khan, who is a successful author who draws the inspiration for his books from his affairs. Rhea Mitchell, as the American Virginia Crosby, vows to bring Khan back to Indora. A portion of the movie becomes the dramatization of the story Kahn is writing in serialized form, and from there it only gets stranger. However, Colleen — using some distinctive mannerism and with her hair parted in the center — made a very convincing Persian.

Her Bridal Night-Mare, *December 1919–February 1920*

Colleen's second Christie two-reeler would be *Her Bridal Night-mare*, a comedy of errors, mistaken identities, chases, and her character's futile attempts to end her nightmare through suicide. Mary (Colleen) is a bride whose wedding-day dreams are thrown asunder when a jealous suitor hires a local pickpocket to steal the groom's suit. In the first of many cases of mistaken identity, the groom is arrested in his skivvies by the police while the pickpocket, in Jack's suit, has free reign of the party. The spurned suitor tells Mary her groom has run off, and she is so distraught that her love has eloped with another woman that she wants to end it all. In the meantime, the groom has escaped the local jail in a stolen police uniform, only to be ratted out by the failed suitor. Jack is incarcerated and released multiple times while the jealous suitor manages to have him re-arrested. And so it goes; situation upon situation building up the tension Al Christie wrote about, until the outlandish resolution.

At the beginning Mary is played straight; her performance might have been lifted from any of Colleen's earlier roles. But the action gets moving quickly, and Colleen is pulled along. For this film, Al Christie takes advantage of her expressions and reactions. The sight of Mary in gown and veil and with her bouquet in hand attempting to end it all by stepping in front of fast-moving traffic, only to have the drivers steer around her, is a striking one. She happens upon the pick-pocket who has cleaned out her wedding reception, and hires him to kill her. She discovers his stash of the wedding gifts he has stolen from her reception and finds a note from her groom-to-be. When she realizes she has not been abandoned, she discovers a new desire to live; only now she must evade her would-be assassin. There is a chase, a number of near-misses between Jack and Mary, and a newly repentant pickpocket who returns his loot and saves the day.

Throughout the film Colleen displays a physicality that would become one of her hallmarks in later years. She was placed front-and-center in Christie's promotions, so there was no doubt her work was seen as more than satisfactory. "After viewing the rushes of *Her Bridal Nightmare*, the response was good."[34] She was learning, but she was not yet finished with Christie.

The year 1919 had been brought major changes for both the nation and the motion picture industry, changes begun years earlier by players who had no way to foresee the results of their actions. The "Volstead Act" passed Congress, and the road to its passage had been paved the Pure Food and Drug Act of 1906. The Pure Food and Drug Act, in turn, followed the publication of Samuel Hopkins Adams's investigative series of 1905 in *Collier's Weekly* entitled, "The Great American Fraud." Adams's writing led indirectly to Prohibition, and Prohibition would create the circumstances wherein Colleen's role in *Flaming Youth* would prove a star-making turn. Samuel Hopkins Adams created that character. Later, F. Scott Fitzgerald would claim, "I was the spark that lit up Flaming Youth." In a way, he was wrong. Samuel Hopkins Adams, writing under a pseudonym, would fill that role.

In the motion picture world, Harry Cohn, Jack Cohn and Joseph Brandt formed C.B.C. Pictures, which would eventually become Columbia. The Warner brothers released their first films. Associated First National, in August 1919, resolved to organize a unified national distributors' exchange with a single management to remedy its haphazard collection of independent exchanges and lack of centralized control. In November, it organized Associated First National Pictures, Inc.[35] Adolph Zukor, head of the Famous Players-Lasky organization, and First National were in a virtual state of war, and their race to acquire theaters shaped the industry. Vertical integration of the industry — where the same company ran the studio, distributed the films and owned the theaters where the films were exhibited — was acting to choke the creativity of the artists. In response, Charlie Chaplin, Mary Pickford,[36] Douglas Fairbanks and D.W. Griffith came together to launch United Artists. The *Los Angeles Times* suggested this was at least in part, a reaction to the "war" between Adolph Zukor and First National.[37] "My God," Richard A. Rowland (of Metro Pictures Corporation) is believed to have said, commenting on the creation of United Artists, "the inmates have taken over the asylum."

12

"Dry Land; That's All."

1920

Overnight America became a dry nation and possession or recreational drinking of alcohol made lawbreakers out of millions of citizens. An underground economy popped into existence with a whole new counter-culture that would provide the backdrop for a new category of motion picture drama.

Prohibition hardly touched the Hollywood film industry, which had enough money to secure a steady flow of liquor. With the end of the war, Hollywood's dominance of the world's film market was assured. Colleen was not affected because she did not drink, and there were other matters to occupy her mind: "Emphatic denial is made by Colleen Moore, Christie comedy star, of a report being circulated through the East of her engagement and approaching marriage to a wealthy Angelino." The man was never identified, and Colleen denied the rumor. "'I cannot guess who or what started this story,' Miss Moore declares. 'If there were a shred of truth in it, the report would be circulating in my home town of Los Angeles. I am wedded to my art, if you will excuse the expression, and that is the only wedding I contemplate for a great many years to come.'"[1]

She had caught the eye of at least one wealthy Angelino: Al Christie. Colleen referred to him as "Mister Al." When they were together talking and playing jacks, Colleen would notice smiles on the faces of the crew. Al was an older man and not a bad catch. Still, Colleen could not get past the difference in their ages. It was enough that she could not stop herself from addressing him as "Mr. Al."

One afternoon Christie visited Colleen's dressing room. He put an arm around her and told her she was a very nice girl. She knew where he was going with the comment, and spoke up before he could continue.

"You've been so good to me, Mr. Al," she told him, "if you were my own father I couldn't like you more."

Deflated, he managed to cover by telling her she was a nice girl and he hoped she never changed. It was, she wrote, the first time she had "mistered" a man to deflect his attentions.

> Chic Sale's picture debut is to be made under the auspices of Al Christie at the Hollywood Studio of the Christie Film Company.... While in New York recently Charles Christie, the business head of the Christie Company entered into a contract with the Exceptional Pictures Corporation to produce the Sale feature comedy which is to be

12. "Dry Land; That's All."

released by the Robertson-Cole Company. No expense is to be spared in making the production."
—"Plan Chic Sale's Premier," *Motion Picture News*, vol. 21, no 9, February 21, 1920, page 1904.

Charles "Chic" Sale was a vaudevillian who specialized in rural caricatures, a "rural protean comedian" as the *New York Tribune* termed it.[2] His various characters included Jefferson Sapp, Jr. the "rube railway station agent." He also played an "ancient and asthmatic Bazoo."[3] They were the sorts of cornpone impressions that would form the basis of his characters in the completed *His Nibs*. In December 1919, Sale signed with Robertson-Cole "for a long term."[4] The first of what was expected to be a series of pictures was to be based on Irvin S. Cobb's short story "The Smart Aleck" from the *Saturday Evening Post*.

The Christie Company had also acquired the screen rights to *So Long Letty*, a popular Broadway musical comedy from Oliver Morosco and Elmer Harris, for $50,000.[5] With a popular stage comedian in the company and a popular musical waiting to be developed, the Christie Company was preparing for bigger and better things.

When Dawn Came, *January–April 1920*

While the Christie Company was putting together its plans, Colleen was reuniting with her *Little Orphant Annie* director Colin Campbell. "Production work has just started on an eight-reel super production of the newly organized Hugh Dierker Photodrama Producing company,"[6] it was announced in January. "Colin Campbell ... is handling the megaphone, and Colleen Moore has the leading role.... Miss Moore's part is that of a blind girl. To properly prepare herself ... the star took into her home for an entire week a blind girl. The two were together practically all the time." Colleen spent a week with her subject to prepare for the role.[7]

"Colleen Moore has been suddenly elevated to special honors," it was reported in *Motion Picture Classic*, forgetting for the moment Colleen's roots in feature-lengthed films, "and is doing an seven-reel feature, the biggest thing ever handed out to that bright little gossoon....

Miss Moore was out on location at the celebrated San Juan Capistrano Mission, half-way between Los Angeles and San Diego, and sent lots of snapshots to her studio friends from that interesting resort. San Juan was pretty well destroyed by an earthquake in 1812, and only part of the mission has been restored, although the beautiful and quaint old cloister garden still offers splendid 'shots' for the camera.[8]

Colleen and L.C. Shumway in *When Dawn Came*, for Cosmopolitan Productions, 1924. Portions were shot on location at the San Juan Capistrano mission (courtesy Joseph Yranski).

The film, called *When Dawn Came*, it has "a Catholic theme and prominent portions of it were filmed at the San Juan Capistrano mission. Robes used by the priests in the picture are the property of Franciscan fathers and were used 500 years ago in Spain."[9] *When Dawn Came* offers a glimpse of the mission before it had been restored, broken arches and ivy-grown walls, "there is an old unused confessional box and an equally old bier for the dead."[10] The film featured some realistic aspects of Colleen's performance, down to the detail of her blind character wearing flat shoes.

The film was finished by April,[11] though it would not be released by the Producers Security Corporation until near the end of the year.[12]

Charles "Chic" Sale and The Smart Aleck (His Nibs), March–May 1920

> Colleen Moore will start Friday as leading woman for Charles (Chic) Sale in his first motion picture venture.... Miss Moore recently finished as Sessue Hayakawa's leading woman in *The Bleeder* [working title for *The Devils Claim*], and is enjoying a short rest.
> —"Colleen Moore in 'Chic' Sale Picture," *Los Angeles Times*, February 28, 1920, page III4.

Colleen started *The Smart Aleck* with Charles "Chic" Sales in early March 1920, overlapping with her work in *When Dawn Came*. Though the film was being made by Al Christie, he was under contract with Robertson-Cole. *The Smart Aleck* would be her second Robertson-Cole film.

At the same time, the Christie studio was acquiring property in the neighborhood in order to expand: "The first acquisition is three acres on Selma Avenue, on which a big new stage is being built and also a street scene for a new special production which will introduce Chic Sale as a star under the Robertson-Cole banner."[13] The street scene was, of course, for *The Smart Aleck*, and it was where "a large amount of action ... takes place."[14] Initially a straight forward production with a simple story, the film would turn out to have a complicated and mysterious production history.[15] *The Smart Aleck*, by Irvin S. Cobb, was a story of a small-town wit that travels to the big city and finds himself out of his depth. Sale would star as "The Boy" and Colleen as "The Girl." As originally planned, the story could have been lifted from a Charles Ray film, though with Sale's comedic spin on the story. In its finished form however, as *His Nibs*, it would depart from anything suggested by Cobb's original story.

By May, Colleen's work on the film was completed, though the film itself would not be finished for several months. Colleen had several other projects to occupy what little free time she had. A campaign had been started by the Forest Service (and various municipal organizations) to clean up highways and picnic grounds in California. Signs reading "Help Keep the Mountain Clean" were to go up throughout the state. Colleen was pictured beside one of the signs, waving a warning finger at the camera.[16] A month later the Pasadena chapter of the Red Cross, along with the Automotive Club of Southern California, started posting first-aid kits at major intersections. Colleen was not only photographed with one of the kits,[17] she also became the face of a "No Hats Summer" club which had enlisted some five-hundred high-school girls. "There is nothing better for the hair than sun and air, and a few weeks without a hat will provide a good treatment for the scalp as well as the profiteers."[18]

All that, plus she was in negotiations with Marshall Neilan for her next role.

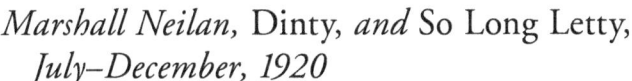

Marshall Neilan, Dinty, and So Long Letty, July–December, 1920

> Colleen Moore is the cleverest of the young stars. Her middle name is Noylan.... If they don't spoil her she's going to be quite somebody some day.
> —Mae Tinee, *Chicago Daily Tribune*, May 23, 1920, page 23.

Marshall Neilan was one of the rising stars in Hollywood. He made a name for himself directing Mary Pickford and his whimsical, offbeat approach to direction seemed a perfect complement for her film persona. He had created his own company, Marshall Neilan Productions, and was vice-president of Associated Producers,[19] a group he helped establish.

He loved a good time, loved to spend money and was generous with his people. Once, when finished with scenes set in a ballroom, the "producer acted as host, retaining the orchestra used in the scenes, and a dinner dance was given."[20] In the increasingly regimented atmosphere of Hollywood, his devil-may-care attitude was unique and increasingly out of place.[21] While his generosity with his friends and employees earned him their loyalty, his flippant attitude and disregard for authority also earned him powerful enemies.

During the filming of his film *Go and Get It*, Neilan saw potential in the character of Dinty O'Sullivan, played by Wesley Barry: "After a course of training by Mr. Neilan, the boy made an instantaneous hit in his first prominent role."[22] Neilan created a story around Barry's character and called the film *Dinty*. He would need someone to play the part of Dinty O'Sullivan's mother.

Colleen went to audition for the part of Doreen O'Sullivan, a young mother who had come to America to join her husband.[23] Neilan was impressed enough with Colleen to meet her salary demand. Colleen's asking price for work outside of the Christie Studio was $500 a week, $300 over what she got as salary from Christie, but she had asked Neilan for $750, and he granted it.[24] She thanked him and called him "Mr. Neilan."

"Hey, Irish!" he said as she was leaving. "My name is Mickey Neilan, Mickey ... don't ever call me Mr. Neilan again."[25]

Go and Get It, the film that had introduced the character of Dinty O'Sullivan, was shot under the working title of *The Harbor City Mystery*, and had wrapped in early June. Preparations began for *Dinty*.[26] Much of the exterior work was to be shot on location in San Francisco, which required the cast and crew to go north.

Colleen's work on *Dinty* was scheduled before *So Long Letty*, sometime before the end of June, but with every announcement of the production's status in *Motion Picture News*, the start date was pushed back. This would allow Colleen more time to finish her work on *Dinty*.

In between all the excitement of working with Marshall Neilan and location work in

San Francisco, the rest of Colleen's family had relocated to California. Colleen's had become enough of a success that the rest of the family moved to California to be there with her a fact that made the papers: "Colleen Moore has brought all the members of her family from the east to Hollywood and set them up in happy domestic abodes."[27] They moved to 1119 Grand View Avenue.[28] Cleeve had been enrolled in the Gardner School for Boys and Girls, but before long he would join his sister in motion pictures.[29]

> Marshall Neilan feels that he has another "find" in Colleen Moore, the little actress, now appearing opposite Wesley Barry, in the first Neilan production, featuring the boy actor. Miss Moore has already had considerable screen experience.
> "I consider Colleen Moore one of the big possibilities of the future.... Above all things she is just as natural a born artist as little Wesley Barry is. She presents a type that in itself cannot help but prove popular with motion picture patrons."
> —"Neilan Likes Work of Colleen Moore," *Motion Picture News*, vol. 21, no. 23, May 29, 1920, page 4492.

The part of Doreen O'Sullivan was custom-made for Colleen: Doreen had arrived in San Francisco only to discover that her husband had died. As a single mother she labors to bring up Dinty. In the end, Doreen succumbs to tuberculosis. A dramatic role for Colleen, even if she was bed ridden for most of the picture; it had become one of her strengths, the ability to register suffering so vividly on the screen.

In less than a month it was being reported that Colleen Moore "expects to finish with *Dinty*.... This will give her a short vacation before she starts work on the Christie film adaptation of *So Long Letty*."[30] Her vacation would be just over a week, though complications arose. In early June, Neilan had traveled to New York for a conference of the "Big Six," the Associated Producers, for which he was vice president. It was expected that he would be away three weeks, but the plans changed and work on *Dinty* was suspended.[31] "Colleen Moore, who has a leading role, is scheduled to start next Tuesday as one of the principals in the Christie film version of *So Long Letty*. This may cause further delay on *Dinty*, as the company must make a trip of three days to San Francisco for scenes in which she is featured."[32]

Almost midway through June, Al Christie was still casting parts for *Letty*. The start of production on *Letty* continued to drag on due to scheduling conflicts. "Practically everything is in readiness for filming of *So Long Letty* by the Christies for Robertson-Cole," J.C. Jessen reported in *Motion Picture News*, "and director Al Christie will probably start the making of this within the next two weeks. At the present time director Al is busy with the making of a two-reel comedy."[33] For her role as Grace in *So Long Letty* Colleen made a change in her appearance: "And now Colleen Moore is a blonde! No, not a mail-order blonde. She hasn't done anything to her tresses. She has merely bought a wig, which she is wearing in her role ... [as] one of the wives in *So Long Letty*."[34] Finally, in the middle of July, it was reported that the actual filming had begun with the entire cast assembled for the first time.[35]

So Long Letty is the story of Harry Miller (T. Roy Barnes), a party boy who is married to Grace (Colleen), a devoted homebody. Grace has more in common with her neighbor Tommy Robbins (Walter Hiers). Tommy's wife is Letty (Grace Darmond), who lives for fun. Harry Miller pitches the idea of a wife swap to Tommy. Each divorces his wife and remarries his neighbor's wife. The wives catch wind of their idea and come up with a

Walter Hiers and Colleen in *So Long Letty*, Robertson-Cole, 1920. The interior arrangement of the set did not match the exterior of the bungalow used in the film.

counter-proposal. They suggest a week of platonic trial marriages, each with the other's spouse. The wives have already decided to make the husbands' lives miserable by behaving as the other does. Grace becomes careless around the house while Letty becomes a doting homebody. The husbands eventually return to their respective spouses.

In July, Neilan had returned to take his cast and crew to San Francisco.[36] He would make several trips to there, looking for the correct atmosphere and enjoying the hospitality of the city, which was notorious as Hollywood's party town.

The Smart Aleck remained in a dormant state while Chic Sale was in New York.[37] Colleen took some time to join a group of Hollywood notables on a trip to Oakland for the city's First National Day. They arrived in Oakland where they were met by a reception committee and escorted to the Hotel Oakland for lunch, then an afternoon parade.[38] "Entire East Bay District Invited ... to the doings at the First National Day," the *Oakland Tribune* trumpeted. Also scheduled to be present were Al Christie, Charles Ray, Wesley Barry, King Vidor, and Marshall Neilan.[39]

When the Christie brothers accepted Colleen into their troupe, they had encouraged her to look for work outside their studio. So when Neilan's offer for *Dinty* came along, she took it. Her work in the film paid off. Neilan offered her a contract, and the Christie brothers told her to take it. She would be paid "one of the largest salaries ever paid a young star."[40]

13

August 1920

In August the 19th Amendment to the United States Constitution was passed, guaranteeing women's suffrage. Coupled with the presence of women in the workplace, the amendment would fundamentally alter the perception of women in American society and bring them greater visibility. In the motion pictures, independent young women became visible as a type. The word "flapper" entered the language, and the women they represented, young and bold, became increasingly identified with changing times. In *So Long Letty*, it was Grace Darmond who had played the independent modern woman. Colleen had played the old-fashioned homebody.

In *Dinty*, Colleen was playing the homebody again, in this case the dying mother. *Dinty* wrapped up shooting off the coast of California: "Marshall Neilan made the final scenes for *Dinty* at Catalina Island where with all members of the cast a number of aeroplane stunts were staged. The principal supporters for Wesley Barry who plays the title role are Pat O'Malley, Colleen Moore, [and] Marjorie Daw."[1]

In signing her contract with Neilan, Colleen was assured dramatic roles and a higher profile. Back at the Christie studio, work continued with *So Long Letty*, which was in the post-production stage: "Colleen Moore, one of the principals, has in her support in this picture two of her relatives. Both her brother and a cousin make their screen [debut] as extras."[2]

The Smart Aleck was undergoing a transformation. Test audiences had probably not liked the finished product. Chic Sale was known for his many caricatures. Appearing simply as "The Boy" might have been unsatisfying. The burlesque of a country boy adrift in the city might not have appealed to an audience either. The unspoiled country boy was a favorite character type and the audience might not have appreciated the burlesque. Rather than jettison everything, a means of salvaging the film and creating more roles for Sale was conceived.[3]

There were no such doubts for *Letty*: "Al Christie ... believes the cast [of *So Long Letty*] which will be seen in this comedy-drama ... is one of the best ever assembled."[4]

The Sky Pilot, *September–November 1920*

Between productions, Colleen had been studying French, or at least "enough of the language to play in a French picture."[5] She had also studied Shakespeare and horseback

Top: King Vidor (second from left) and Colleen on location in Truckee for *The Sky Pilot*, Cathrine Curtis Corporation, 1921. Below, Colleen and King (at right) on location in Folsom preparing for stampede scene photography. Cameraman Ira H. Morgan can be seen in pit with camera (courtesy Judy Coleman).

riding, and planned to take classic dance with Theodore Kosloff. Colleen also found time for "partying around with a certain handsome dark young man," but those plans would have to wait.[6] Once she signed with Neilan, he loaned her out to fellow Associated Producers member King Vidor. Vidor was another up-and-coming director with a list of successful films who hand built his own studio, Vidor Village, in Santa Monica, with advance money from First National.[7] The first film to be made at Vidor Village would be *The Sky Pilot*. The expense of location work would tax the organization and complications in the production would eventually break the organization.[8]

The Sky Pilot was not a typical western story. It was about a preacher forging a collection of people into a community through his actions, not his ideals. It was a film that rejected rigid morality. Vidor wanted the audience to be enriched by his film, and his approach was to look towards what the audiences needed, not what they wanted: "The public is 100 percent human and 99 percent clean. Some of the world's greatest literary masterpieces are simple and clean.... It stands to reason that photodramas can be simple, different and clean.... The producer who forces smut on our mothers, our sisters and our kiddies through the screen, without showing the shame and the wrong of it, is a poltroon and a coward."[9]

The film was being produced by Cathrine Curtis. She was a "tall, handsome and dynamic female," according to Vidor.[10] A shrewd speculator, she saw *The Sky Pilot* as an opportunity to present a story with character and a message.[11] "Miss Curtis has succeeded in putting into execution her plans for the making of pictures informed with high ideals, marked with sincerity of purpose, distinguished for beauty of theme and endowed with literary qualities that shall invest them with universal appeal."[12] Her goals and those of King Vidor's dovetailed nicely.

Vidor was convinced that Colleen was the only actress who could play the part of Gwen,[13] and he had approached Neilan about a loan out. When Colleen first met Vidor, she had no idea he was the director of the film. She wrote about him as a youthful-looking man whom she thought to be about her own age, an assistant director perhaps, certainly not the co-owner of his own studio. She signed on with the production.

Work was started at the studio by September before venturing out on location.[14] *Motion Picture Classic* ran an interview with Colleen, mentioning her work in *Dinty*.

> She ... becomes a mother and, old and careworn, dies. This is the kind of character part Miss Moore loves to do. She hates a simple ingénue role.... Asked if she could ever leave the screen, her brown eyes flash and she will tell you vehemently:
>
> "I should say not! There's something about it ... gets in your blood ... I can't even stand a vacation away from the studio.... Work, in and around the studio, and out on location, is the only absorbing thing in my life. I'm not happy when I'm not working."
>
> Miss Moore is ably backed up by a jolly mother, a business-man father and an adoring, young seventeen-year-old brother, Cleeve, who is just now in love with a different girl every day.[15]

While she disliked the "simple ingénue roles" they were still her bread and butter. Her role in *The Sky Pilot* would be a little different in how she was first seen by the audience — on horseback, riding like an old hand — and in her rescue of the male lead early on, but in the end it would essentially end up an ingénue role.

Cleeve Morrison has makeup applied by his sister, Colleen, circa 1921 (courtesy Joseph Yranski).

"King Vidor's company is to make the first scenes [of *The Sky Pilot*] ... and will journey thither in the few days."[16] Colleen had been to the hills many times before. Motion picture companies on location brought economic opportunity, and the Southern Pacific railroad was quick to jump on the bandwagon. Southern Pacific had opened a "location bureau" in Los Angeles in 1916 to assist the studios. Every time a locomotive with the words "Southern Pacific" painted on the tender rolled through the screen, it was free advertising.[17] Vidor availed himself of the railroad's services for the California portion of the location work in the city of Truckee and on Thursday, September 30, the cast and crew for *The Sky Pilot* "left for Truckee ... whence they will go to Salt Lake City, then on up to Canada.[18]

"As there is to be much riding in the feature, Miss Moore has been exchanging the comforts of her new Cadillac limousine for the back of a rough old rangy horse, but she said yesterday she felt she was still in the kindergarten riding class."[19]

The crew went to work erecting town sets across the Southern Pacific tracks opposite the hotel, including a frontier town with saloons and store fronts and gambling dens. The crew stayed in the Southern Pacific Hotel and relied extensively on the help of the hotel's Mr. Wilbur Maynard. Colleen's arrival, in particular, afforded the local townsfolk an opportunity to make some extra cash: "Residents of Truckee, Cal., have been doing a flourishing business of late in old-fashioned wearing apparel that was even out of date in Truckee." Before the Vidor troupe had shipped out for Truckee, "Colleen Moore spent two days purchasing at Los Angeles second-hand stores her wardrobe ... but the apparel was not exactly to her liking.... So she let the word go out that she was in the market for old clothes, the older the better. Immediately the natives repaired to their attics and dug deep into their trunks. The result was a flood of ancient garments."[20]

Set in the Canadian Northwest, a preacher (John Bowers) receives a rough welcome from the cow folk in a small town where he has come to preach. During his first sermon gets into a fight with Bill Hendricks (David Butler), foreman of the Ashley ranch and ends up getting tossed out of town. Afterwards, the two become friends and the preacher works on the ranch. His life is saved by Gwen (Colleen), but her father (Harry Todd) kicks the preacher out of his cabin, having lost is faith. Over time the locals gain a grudging respect for the preacher, who proves to be just as tough as they are. Out of respect they build him a church. Later, the preacher saves Gwen from certain death in a cattle stampede. She lives, but is crippled. Gwen's embittered father and a band of cattle rustlers, whose plot against the Ashley ranch is thwarted, set fire to the preacher's church. In the effort to save the preacher, Gwen recovers the use of her legs, and her father regains his faith.

While the cast and crew were at work in the wilderness, Cathrine Curtis had secured distribution of the film through First National.[21] That was one small worry out of the way, but certainly not the last. The worst was yet to come, in the form of the weather.

The film took place over the period of a season, with scenes set both

King Vidor, Colleen and snowman having fun on location in Truckee for *The Sky Pilot*, Cathrine Curtis Corporation, 1921.

in the sunshine of summer and the snows of winter. Shooting the summer scenes with the carefully constructed village set went smoothly, but after a few days of shooting, the cast and crew awoke one morning to find the ground blanketed with snow. "We went up to Truckee to shoot," David Butler recalled to Irene Kahn Atkins.[22] "When we got there it snowed — for the first time in sixty-five years, they said."

It was very bad timing for Vidor, whose story called for less blizzard-like conditions than what he found.[23] There were still several days' worth of shooting ahead of them that required sunny skies and snowless conditions. The end of the movie called for the destruction of the sets by fire during a snowstorm. They could torch their sets in the snow, but they would have to be willing to re-erect a village set from scratch when the weather cleared up. The cost of rebuilding, however was prohibitive.[24] Grace Kinsley, reporting a message sent by Colleen about the shoot, wrote: that "the story has changed to include a blizzard." Colleen, Grace wrote, was "having a lot of fun learning the gentle art of skiing."[25]

"The company lay idle, for the scenario called for sunshine, with never a mention of snow. Days passed into weeks, and the snow only grew deeper. Each day King Vidor studied the script.... Finally someone hit on an idea: 'Why not,' he inquired of the producer, 'change the scenario. Where the script reads "sunshine," substitute "snowstorm!"'"[26]

They shot what scenes they could, hoping the weather would clear up enough to complete their summer scenes. When they weren't shooting, they were waiting restlessly. Sometimes they organized baseball games on Truckee's main street. At night they organized vaudeville acts to entertain them. The people of Truckee couldn't understand it; all those people sitting around, waiting for the snow to pass and melt. Every day the inactivity ate into the production's budget. In desperation, Vidor organized an effort to manually remove the snow from enough of the ground surrounding the sets to complete their scenes. Then Mother Nature rewarded their efforts with sunshine and clear skies.[27] They waited for the bad weather, but it was not forthcoming.

"Then the snow stopped after about two weeks," David Butler described, "so we went down to Folsom to shoot a roundup of cattle."[28]

The stampede scene was a real corker, due in no small part to the willingness of the star to get in harm's way; the scene had originally been shot with a dummy, but the results had been unconvincing. Bowers volunteered to do the scene himself.[29] "In *The Sky Pilot*, all inside views were shot in the studio, most of the big outdoor scenes, which include the thrilling cattle stampede, in which John flowers, as *The Sky Pilot* rescues Colleen Moore, were shot at Walright [sic], Canada, and amid the gorgeous mountain scenery at Banff, Canada, while Truckee, California, at the summit of the Sierras provide most of the deep snow scenes."[30] "Then we went back to the studio — near Fountain Avenue and Vermont — a little bit of a studio — built sets and shot there. When it snowed again, we went back up to Truckee."[31]

The second trip to Truckee was near the end of November, just after Thanksgiving. The big day had been postponed so that people could enjoy the holidays with their families, but afterwards it was back off for the wilderness.[32]

Lacking the snow needed for the scenes of the destruction of the village sets, Vidor sent to Sacramento for a railroad car full of salt, which was distributed where needed. The sets were then burned.

13. August 1920

In spite of the problems with the production, Colleen and King got along well. There was camaraderie among the cast and crew, owing to their isolation. With the nearest movie theater an hour's sleigh ride away, the company created shows to entertain themselves. Colleen and Vidor worked out a mind-reading act based on a series of verbal clues to tip off the partner guessing what a hidden object was. King was intelligent and dynamic; Colleen, well-educated and funny. They both loved motion pictures. They were comfortable around each other and enjoyed each others' company, wrote each other notes, made their own codes, like children in school.[33]

In one interview printed in the *Los Angeles Times*, they are quoted as finishing each other's sentences like an old married couple. The writer compared their conversation to brushstrokes of a painter:

> King Vidor and Colleen Moore told me in duet of an exciting ride they had in a cutter coming back from location. That is, Vidor told the story and Colleen supplied what she called the necessary "splotches" of color.
>
> "It was an old-fashioned cutter," said Vidor, "with a high dashboard. We were coming along the road just at sundown —"
>
> "Yes, it was a beautiful sunset," tinted Colleen.
>
> "And right in front of us was another sleigh, and —"
>
> "Yes, it made such a pretty soft silhouette against the sun," pastelled Miss Moore.
>
> "And as I turned out to pass the sleigh, which was stalled —"
>
> "It made me think of the sleighs I saw in Michigan when I was back there," backgrounded Colleen.
>
> "The road was very steep toward the side, and all of a sudden —"
>
> "I saw a big mud puddle right in front of me," splotched Miss Moore.
>
> "'The cutter tipped over and Miss Moore and myself both sprawled"
>
> "In the mud puddle."

The horses continued on, Vidor left Colleen in the puddle to chase after them, successfully. Returning to the puddle, they were rescued by Dave Butler, who gave them a ride back to the hotel. The writer had some poetic words to describe Colleen, whom he said, was "still just a wee wisp of a child — with hair soft as the moss in the glen, and eyes that are like the shadows of the Kilarney lakes where the sunlight glints through — she has already brightened many important pictures with her presence."[34] The same basic story found its way into another story printed a month later, from the troupe's supposed adventures in one of its two Canadian locations: Wainwright, Alberta.[35]

The location work came to an end by the end of November.[36] At last, they returned to Los Angeles.

14

November 1920–March 1921

While work on *The Sky Pilot* continued, *So Long Letty* was just being completed. "Particular attention is being given to the art effects, these being done by E.G. Klein, of the Christie art staff, and Harry Barndollar."[1] The film was released on October 17, 1920. *Dinty* was released at the end of November by Associated First National. "Simultaneously with the release of *Dinty*, Woolworth and other stores ... will place on sale a little book on the life of Wesley Barry."[2] In addition to the Barry book, there would be books on the rest of the stars. Available for ten cents, Colleen's edition of The *Little Movie Mirror Books* offered a story of her life and career, along with photographs, including one of Colleen and her mother and grandmother, and another with Colleen and her collection of dolls. "Slender, lithe and with the bounding stride of the danseuse, Colleen is a charming personage, strange admixture of romantic girlhood and understanding womanliness."[3]

The Sky Pilot was completed in mid–December. "In this photoplay of the Canadian Rockies he [Vidor] infuses ... an elemental strength, a native vigor that conduces to a tonic quality, symbolizing the wild, wide places where man contacts the mountains, the great trees, the animal kingdom, and sleeps on the naked earth beneath the canopy of the sky."[4]

The year ended on a low note for Colleen, in a hospital bed recovering from tonsillitis.[5]

With *Dinty* being released by First National and *The Sky Pilot* soon to be released by First National as well, Colleen's photographs passed across the desk of publicist John McCormick. He'd been in Hollywood for a time and had worked recently with director Raoul Walsh on his film *The Deep Purple*. Miriam Cooper, Walsh's wife, had starred in the film. Bessie Waters,[6] an acquaintance of Miriam's, was an extra on the film. John met her and sparks flew. John had an idea for a beauty contest and proposed that Raoul give the winner a part in one of his films, and that Miriam give the winner acting lessons. Entrants had to fill out a coupon printed in newspapers and return them to John with an 8 × 10 headshot: a panel of experts would select the winner.

Entries poured in from around the country. Miriam announced the winner — none other than Bessie Waters. It did not go over very well with Miriam, who saw it as a dirty trick that had cheated other aspiring actresses out of a chance at fame. She had Raoul fire John.[7]

John, "who never made a nickel by singing, but receives a stipend for beating an 'Underwood,'"[8] bounced back. He had moved on to First National and was a rising star.

The Lotus Eater, *January–April 1921*

While Colleen recovered from tonsillitis, Marshall Neilan was planning his next few films. Albert Payson Terhune's *The Lotus Eater* was scheduled for production.[9] "Miss Moore is awaiting Marshal Neilan's return from the East. Two producers are seeking to borrow her for the feature role in their productions, but no decision can be given until Mr. Neilan returns."[10]

Mickey returned in early February,[11] but less than a week later Gertrude Bambrick, his wife, filed for divorce. Neilan had married the actress in 1913, and she had charged Neilan with desertion. Neilan had lately been seen with the actress Blanche Sweet on his arm.[12] He was asked about it over the telephone. "What is it people always say in a case like this?" he asked. "I believe they always declare they have nothing to say." He was to leave the next day for New York, and it was possible he would not return until he had filmed a story in Miami, Florida.[13]

Neilan was not the only one with romantic entanglements:

> Wooed by cable!
> Just think of receiving a proposal of marriage and an offer of a fortune seven thousand miles away.
> Miss Colleen Moore is the beauty so originally implored.... Making love over the cable may be an ordinary thing; but making a proposal of marriage 7,000 miles over cable to someone he never saw outside of a screen is new, we'll say. The high cost of cablegrams is barrier for the swift pace of love.
> The love adventurer is a man of London, England. The cablegram is the first step in the marriage quest."—*Morning Republican* (Mitchell, South Dakota), February 23, 1921, page 6.

Marshall Neilan left for the East with his troupe to begin work on *The Lotus Eater*.[14] Colleen traveled in the company of her mother, as she always did for location work.[15] The film would feature John Barrymore, one of America's foremost actors, as well as one of Neilan's drinking buddies. The trip to New York was necessary because Barrymore refused to come to California to work on the film.[16]

As Colleen traveled eastward, *The Sky Pilot*, was previewed. "Final studio run of *The Sky Pilot* ... was shown Monday evening January 24, to Associated First National representative Sol Lesser," *Motion Picture News* reported.[17] "Mr. Lesser expressed himself as more than pleased with the production."[18] The following day the edited print and negative were shipped East.[19]

The Lotus Eater would be photographed mainly on a yacht, a tropical island and in New York. The film was about Jacques Lenoi (Barrymore), son of an eccentric millionaire, who had lived his life aboard a ship and was ignorant of the world. When his father dies and he is exposed to the civilized world. He immediately falls for the first woman he meets, gold-digger Madge Vance (Anna Q. Nilsson). His failure to acquire his complete inheritance doesn't sit well with his new wife. While on a dirigible excursion, Jacques ends up stranded on an island where shipwrecked survivors of earlier expeditions live together in an ad hoc society led by "The Dean" (Frank Currier). Though he longs for his wife back home, Jacques falls for island native Mavis (Colleen). When he finally manages to leave the island and return to New York, Jacques finds Madge has taken up with a wealthy broker. Both Jacques

John Barrymore and Colleen on location in Florida for *The Lotus Eaters*, Marshall Neilan Productions 1921. Barrymore is shown in the short toga costume that Colleen so admired him in (courtesy Joseph Yranski).

and the broker appeal to her, but the gold-digger elopes with a count. Jacques returns to Mavis and finds happiness.

In New York the troupe lingered long enough to secure transportation south to Florida. Agnes Morrison decided to let Colleen go on to Florida unescorted, and let her travel to locations without chaperone from then on. She was old enough. Before the troupe traveled south, there was time to enjoy New York. *Motion Picture Magazine* ran a story on Colleen that played up the wide-eyed, innocent aspect of her public persona: "The Unsophisticated Colleen," by Frederick James Smith.[20] "Colleen Moore is positively the most unsophisticated movie favorite we ever met." The writer had met Colleen at the Algonquin, where she was described as being in awe at the sights of the metropolis, in awe of the subway, which she called "the underworld." They had arranged for a lunch interview and Colleen arrived accompanied by Agnes. She was excited both about the upcoming film and her visit to the city. She'd seen Broadway all lit up, planned to make the ascent up the Statue of Liberty, and to the top of the Woolworth Building. Frederick Smith had admitted he'd never done either in spite of his many years in the city.

When the interview began in earnest, Colleen said that she was struck by all the tired faces she saw in New York, people who looked worried. She discussed her favorite author — Hitchens — and how she had started reading Ibsen and Tolstoy, but that "Mamma Morrison" made her hold off on reading them until she turned 20. She was going to take up Shakespeare, and Emerson was her favorite philosopher. She liked her roles in *Dinty* and *The Sky Pilot* and *Little Orphant Annie*, preferring the last one most of all. She liked New York but she hoped she didn't have to stay for long.

"You don't like it?" we ventured.

"Well, no-o-o," she admitted. "There's too much hurry and not enough air or rest or space. I like the west."

While she would come off as a guileless innocent in the story, she was, in fact, enjoying a sudden flare of attention, tasting life as a "social butterfly" for the first time.[21] When Agnes returned home to Los Angeles, Colleen had her first real taste of freedom, and the responsibilities of an adult.

Neilan chartered a steam yacht from Frank Bowne Jones[22] and proceeded to head south by train with the troupe while the yacht sailed on ahead. "*The Lotus Eaters* ... certainly suggests tropical foliage — that is why this triumvirate (Neilan, Barrymore, and Anna Q. Nilsson) and the rest of the company have left for Florida by rail to Palm Beach and Miami — and then a cruise along the coast on a private yacht, to film the Southern exteriors of this story which marks the return of Barrymore to the screen."[23] The first stop was Palm Beach where they set about scouting locations. "The Everglades Club received a visit from John Barrymore and various members of his staff yesterday ... as the company hopes to obtain permission to stage a few scenes of Palm Beach life here."[24]

Aware of Barrymore's reputation as the royalty of the theatrical world, Colleen was intimidated by performing with him. In addition to his stellar reputation, he was a handsome man. In their scenes they wore Grecian tunics. Barrymore's was short, and Colleen felt he cut a fine figure. Every evening he'd change into swimming trunks and dive off the mast of the yacht into the ocean to swim, and Colleen would watch. Her first scene with Barrymore was a love scene. When the cameras started grinding, Colleen froze, overwhelmed. It took Neilan's kidding to get her to relax for the scene, but Colleen was never quite comfortable with Barrymore. He helped her, offered her advice, smiled and complimented her, but his reputation was still too intimidating.[25]

Both Barrymore and Neilan were pranksters, and the upper crust of Palm Beach did not appreciate their antics. They were informed by the community that it would be appreciated if they moved their production to points south.[26] They moved on to Miami, where one newspaper reported: "John Barrymore and about 25 of his fellow actors who have been immortalizing Miami, at least until several thousand feet of film have been worn out, will leave Sunday for New York."[27]

Director Marshall "Mickey" Neilan, Colleen's director and friend. Photographed by Donald Biddle.

The Lotus Eater's problems were mostly delays from the spotty attendance records of the star and director, who would go drinking and not return for days. Though a heavy drinker, Neilan needed his sleep to be sharp on the job. Barrymore seemed immune to sleep and exploited Neilan's weakness. He would telephone Neilan whenever he estimated the director had just gotten to sleep. One night during the filming of *The Lotus Eater*, Neilan was sleeping off the evening's drunk and received a telephone call in his hotel room. Calls in the middle of the night were not unusual for an important movie director who might have to deal with disasters at any time of day or night. Neilan would answer the telephone, groggy with sleep, and Barrymore would conduct his crank call with a disguised voice, posing as whatever character he thought might get a reaction out of Neilan. Once Barrymore had posed as Hawley Harvey Crippen, once as Diamond Jim Brady, and once even as a hooker.[28]

One night Neilan answered the telephone. A voice asked for Mr. Marshall Neilan. Neilan, suspecting Barrymore, told the caller he was a cretin and told him to get the hell off the line. The surprised voice on the other end claimed to be William Jennings Bryan, hoping to speak to Mr. Neilan. Neilan told the caller what he could do to himself, hung up and had the hotel operator block all further calls to his room that night. It was not until sometime later that he was introduced to a woman at a social event. The woman turned up her nose at Neilan and walked away. It was explained to him that the woman was Ruth Bryan, and that her father, William Jennings Bryan, had tried to call Neilan about a potential film, when Neilan had been so insulting.[29]

The company was due to leave for their return trip to New York on Sunday, March 27.[30] Barrymore had a commitment to return to the stage, and a new born daughter in New York. Colleen was certain Barrymore had not been impressed by her work until he approached her about playing the ingénue role in *Clair de Lune*, a play his wife had been working on for years. Colleen had to decline at Neilan's insistence, as he had plans for her.

Interiors for *The Lotus Eater* were shot at the old Biograph studio in the Bronx. Barrymore worked between rehearsals and performances of *Clair de Lune*, which opened on April 18.[31] When they were not working, Neilan showed Colleen New York, took her to parties and set her up on dates. She lived the life of a genuine celebrity.[32] Chic Sale had brought her backstage to see his performance.[33] There were plenty of plays, shows, lights and dates. There were also offers to leave motion pictures for the stage, Barrymore's offer for a part in *Claire de Lune* first and foremost, but there had been reports of others: "Colleen Moore ... had a narrow escape from taking up permanent residence there [in New York].... She was seriously considering two offers of stardom made by New York producers."

New York itself had been less exciting than the trappings of fame. "Colleen Moore ... the Glad Girl is home sick. She has written to a Hollywood friend that the excitement of the metropolis is thrilling her but the winter snow chills her heart. Better a bungalow in Hollywood than a mansion in New York."[34] The big city also had an effect on the romantic lives of its citizens.

> Colleen Moore, pretty little leading woman ... doesn't like New York. She has very definite opinions about the place and is not afraid to express them. Among its other handicaps she declares it is a city that fairly stifles romance.
>
> "Twenty years from now the only young men and women between the ages of 15 and 25 who

will allow themselves to remain in New York will be the hopeless anti-marriage advocates," is Miss Moore's statement. Miss Moore made a rather minute inspection of New York upon a recent visit ... her conclusions were drawn with due care and consideration. The pretty little Irish miss didn't even smile when she said it. She was in the deadliest of earnest.

"I mean it," she continued. "Twenty years from now you won't be able to hold young people in New York for any kind of money."[35]

The taste of fame was enough to make Colleen think. Her goal was to be a famous actress. She had not yet achieved the kind of fame she had imagined for herself. When she returned to Los Angeles, she returned to a life as another popular actress with a moderate following and a degree of name recognition, but she was not the household name she had always imagined for herself.

15

April–June 1921

In April, *When Dawn Came* was given a big kickoff by Hugh Dierker. "He has arranged a large symphony orchestra, will stage a beautiful prolog and will include in the program several added features." The movie was said to combine "high-class society drama, thrilling melodrama, a human drama of the slums, a beautiful love story, a tense drama of the underworld, and a spectacular historical production."[1]

The premiere was at the Trinity Auditorium which had opened as a Methodist church complex with theater, hotel, and restaurant in September of 1914.[2] "L.A. Lambert, the manager of the Trinity, has secured the Ladies' Columbia Symphony Orchestra, with Mme. Frances Knight as conductor.... Genevieve Gilbert, dramatic soprano, will be the soloist.... Miss Dorothy Volkey, classic dancer, will appear in her newest dance creation."[3] The premiere was to serve as the debut of the Trinity as a motion picture house. L.S. Shumway and James O. Barrows were to appear in the prolog of each performance and the film was said to have "incorporated a new photographic process ... which is said to have created a sensation at every showing."[4]

Elsewhere, the announcement was made of the signing of former Metro director Wesley Ruggles to direct a film version of *Slippy McGee*.[5] "Telegraphic advices carrying this information were received yesterday from Oliver Morosco, who is now in New York."[6]

Colleen's return to Los Angeles had been accompanied by accounts of her adventures in New York and Florida. "Having been shipwrecked off the coast of Miami and having been engaged once, but looking as if both experiences had merely freshened her up and done her good, lovely little Colleen Moore came home from New York yesterday after an absence of five months." The wreck happened six miles off the coast of Miami while Neilan and his company, including Barrymore, were sailing in their yacht back towards the mainland after shooting scenes on a small island off the coast. A storm blew the yacht onto a coral reef, beaten by the waves until it nearly tipped over, and then the tide went out, leaving the yacht high and dry. Neilan left for the mainland on a gas-powered launch. He found help and a hydroplane with which to get everyone off the yacht, but by the time he returned the tide had come back in and the yacht had slipped off the reef and into deep water. "'Everybody sat up all night,' declared Miss Moore, 'while the yacht ground and spun around on the rock.'"

In New York, "There wasn't a theater of a fine café ... that didn't receive Miss Moore's patronage, she declares." She gained 13 pounds during her stay, she said.

There was an engagement as well, Grace Kingsley hinted, involving another mysterious man, this one from Canada. In her teasing way, Kingsley declared: "Oh well, it's all over now, so why talk about it?"[7]

Upon her return from New York, Colleen found herself on loan to the *Slippy McGee* production.[8]

Between her return from New York and her departure for location work on *Slippy McGee*, Colleen played the part of Wild West barmaid in an only-in-Hollywood benefit called the Actor's Fund Festival, described as "a dazzling array of talent, beauty and costumes." It was not the first time Hollywood had contributed to the fund; in 1916 the Motion Picture Campaign for The Fund hosted a Roman spectacle production of *Julius Caesar*.[9] With Roman legions in costume and hundreds of dancing girls in the spectacle, the cast were headed by William Farnum, Tyrone Power and Douglas Fairbanks.[10]

The 1921 spectacular opened on June 4, and for the price of admission visitors were treated to a million-dollar performance by an array of stars in costume, prowling the Hippodrome stadium in Beverly Hills.[11] "Besides the array of feminine beauty, exquisite costumes, and talent, and the scores of sideshow attractions, practically every available member of the screen and speaking stage professions will be on hand to do his or her share in making the occasion memorable."[12]

There was a rodeo presided over by the industry's best riders, a Roman Derby chariot race, a parade of screen comedians and clowns, vaudeville shows, exhibits and fireworks. "The vast bowl of the stadium was circled by side shows and concession booths, while mingling in the concourse were hucksteresses, some in Parisian frocks, some in riding habits, and some harem trousers." Mabel Normand was a guide pointing out such features as Sid Grauman's Million Dollar Beauty Show with orchestra; Mrs. William DeMille's art studio; caged authors (trained and untrained) presided over by Rupert Hughes; and Charlie Ray's country store with Ray as the bumpkin clerk. Charlie Murray had a '49er camp complete with bathing beauties. The Blue Law Street was patrolled by Al Jennings. Madam Elinor Glyn, in Egyptian costume, played a charlatan giving psychic readings.[13]

Colleen, as barmaid, served mugs of near-beer. "Would you pay a dollar or five for a drink of near-beer? The answer to this is, 'Yes, when Colleen Moore is the barmaid.' Near-beer is worth whatever you may pay for it when Miss Moore hands it over with a smile and a merry glance."[14] It was the sort of role that was expected of Colleen: working class. Nobody expected glamour or fashion from her. The times, however, were changing, and people were looking for sensation. The thought had occurred to Colleen that she had reached as high as she was going to in the film world.

While Hollywood's elite were having fun at the festival, John McCormick was back in New York on business, enjoying himself somewhat less than his pals back in the land of sunshine and motion pictures. "Wireless messages bring the information that he got a boil and an ulcerated tooth. Outside of that he is having a wonderful time."[15] He was moving up from his position as First National's western press representative to western representative for First National. "Mr. McCormick is expected to arrive in Los Angeles on Saturday of this week from New York. In his new capacity Mr. McCormick will succeed Sol Lesser."[16] The announcement had been made at a dinner held in his honor in New York; while there, he had begun a campaign to fight "slanderous gossip" against the Hollywood community, which "is morally far above the average."[17] On June 7, he took up his duties in his new office.[18] With the new job came new responsibilities and pressures. From time to time John was known to take a drink, Volstead's best efforts notwithstanding. Once in a while he would disappear and turn back up a day or two later, sharp as always. He was a young man, though, and everybody took a drink once in a while. Nobody thought twice about it.[19]

A gun-toting Colleen as Wild West barmaid at the Motion Picture Benefit of 1921. The nation had just begun its experiment with Prohibition, so "near-beer" was all that Colleen could legally serve (courtesy Joseph Yranski).

Slippy McGee, *June 16–July 25, 1921*

The story *Slippy McGee, Sometimes Known as the Butterfly Man* was that of a hardened city criminal, injured in the commission of a crime, who finds he must recover in an old-fashioned rural village. With time his wounds heal and he undergoes the requisite transformation from criminal to honest, hard-working man through both the kindly graces of the town and the influence of a young woman, Mary Virginia Eustis.[20] Set in the fictional southern town of Appleborro, George Shryer suggested the production consider shooting on location in Natchez, Mississippi.[21]

Natchez had recently hosted a film production and was ready for more. Located on the banks of the Mississippi, the city was surrounded by hilly terrain. "Approaching Natchez from upstream, the river makes a long sweep or bend and takes a direction nearly at right angles to the bank, then turns in another bend to follow the direction of the high ground."[22] Besides the town proper there was Natchez Under-the-Hill on the margin of the Mississippi, the commercial center. Once upon a time, Natchez Under-the-Hill had a reputation for "licentiousness and dissipation,"[23] but by the 1920s the reputation, as well as the district itself, was disappearing. "The low ground of 'Natchez-under-the-hill,' having been located in the bight of the bend, was eroded until it nearly all disappeared, barely space enough remaining for one street on the side-hill between the water and the bluff."[24]

Natchez-on-top-of-the-hill had managed to avoid the worst of the Civil War, and many antebellum mansions survived. The geography and climate had been perfect for the cultivation of cotton, and the crop had brought great wealth to the city. The mansions were "testaments to their success."[25] In the last decade, however, hard times had been visited upon Natchez with the loss of river traffic to the railroads, and the arrival of the boll weevil. The hard times had given the town character: "It kept a loveliness owed to oak and chinaberry trees lining its streets, and to honeysuckle and wisteria vines holding together its rotting fences."[26]

The book had a canning factory where Appleboro's Polish inhabitants worked. Natchez had opened a canning company the year before.[27] The fictional Appleboro had "the usual shops and stores, even an emporium or two, and street lights until twelve, and the mills and factory."[28] Natchez had its own Main Street crowded with automobiles and stores like M.M. Ullman's, Benoist Brothers, Burns Shoe Store, and others.[29] Appleboro had "river trade and two railroads tap our rich territory to fetch and carry what we take and give."[30] Natchez had a railway station on Broadway near the end of Main,[31] the Mississippi River, and Natchez Under-the-Hill. The parallels were uncanny: "Slippy Magee [sic] is Story that Could Have Happened Here," declared a headline in the *Natchez Democrat*.[32]

Wesley Ruggles, the director, had said, "We might have substituted Natchez in our studio, but I was determined to get realism above all things." Ruggels declared that he would be "pleased to answer through the columns of your paper any questions that aspiring scenariotists or budding directors might wish to ask."[33]

Shooting for *Slippy McGee* began on June 16 with exteriors of a local residence and scenes inside the Institute Hall. Wesley Ruggles' secretary had given word that the Institute Hall shoot would represent a town meeting and that extras would be needed.[34] For the next several weeks it would be common to see mentioned in the *Natchez Democrat* that a crowd of people would be needed for a given scene.

Colleen's work did not start until after the 18th, which left her with two days to enjoy the town. The company had been guests at the dances of the country club and at many local events.[35] What struck Colleen was the hospitality displayed for the production, the many invitations extended to them. "We were almost too busy to work," Colleen said, "what with the dinners and dances, teas and picnics."[36]

As the attractive new girl in town, she drew the attention of the local men, as well as a man who had gone to Natchez looking for her, as claimed by Grace Kingsley: "There was a young lawyer — but pshaw, nothing came of it after all, so why harp on the theme, even if he did move clear up from Atlanta to be near the young lady." Who the lawyer was, Kingsley never said. "[Colleen] will admit those southern boys are breathlessly fast workers — that they tell you you're pretty and call you an angel the first hour, and propose to you the next."[37] The attentions of the local boys, on top of the glamorous social scene of New York just a few weeks before, made the time seem almost enchanted.

> "Romance, mystery and adventure are in the air.... It is simply thrilling to be down here among the scenes and the people who have always had a romantic interest for me,)" writes the chic Colleen.... "And the men are wonderful — such sweet manners and masterful ways; the women too take more time to indulge in the delightful pastime of making themselves utterly charming and their hospitality is simply delightful.
>
> "Imagine being taken into a garret filled with the feminine clothes and jewels and fans and, handkerchiefs worn by the southern belles before the war. Such lace — it is like the thinnest of

cobwebs and the linens and brocades are simply wonderful.... I adore the people here; they have taken us all to their hearts and while I came down expecting to have a little rest—I have more engagements than I had in New York."[38]

The children were all beautiful, Colleen said, and the girls all pretty and well-dressed. "Since I have been here a great many of the dears have been to see me, bringing me little

Screen Stars To Appear In Person Tonight at Baker-Grand

THE MOROSCO FILM COMPANY, ASSISTED BY LOCAL TALENT WILL PRESENT-IN ORIGINAL

VAUDEVILLE ACTS

"QUEENIE"—Slippy Magee's Dog Assisted by Mr. Peerson.

MISS YORKE

MISS COLLEEN MOORE

BURKE, MONTGOMERY, KENDALL AND DIX.

PIE EATING CONTEST.

MISS CONNER AND MISS BRETHAUPT

RUGGLES OAKMAN AND LLOYD

OAKMAN AND LLOYD

O'MALLEY AND DE GRASSE

Advertisement for the vaudeville show put on by the *Slippy McGee* company for the people of Natchez, in the *Natchez Democrat*, June 1921.

gifts, and I cannot say just how much I appreciate this."³⁹ Local girls took to wearing their hair in an approximation of the hairstyle Colleen had imported from New York, dubbed the "Colleen Curl" by the locals.⁴⁰

The company was kept busy with the production and their social schedule: "No effort has been spared by the people of Natchez to make all of the members of the *Slippy Magee* [sic] Company ... feel at home," as the production got into full swing, "If all the invitations were accepted, the members of the company would have little time for anything else."⁴¹

After Colleen's first day of work, the company was invited to a swimming party. They had been invited by Mr. Joseph Serio to attend the Turtle Lake celebration on the evening of Colleen's second day at work.⁴² Plans had been made for the company to get involved in local charity work. There would be a costume ball for the benefit of the Volunteer Fire Department, tentatively planned for July 25, and a show at the Baker Grand Theater to benefit the municipal swimming pool project. The show, a vaudeville act, was an idea hatched between Ruggles and Wheeler Oakman.⁴³ In the vaudeville show at the Baker-Grand Theater,⁴⁴ Colleen was the headliner as the third act, after "Queenie," Slippy's dog,⁴⁵ (who had the Deuce Spot on the bill) and Edith Yorke. The name "Miss Colleen Moore" was, by far, the largest print in the ad, intended to draw the biggest audience.⁴⁶

Wesley Ruggles managed to find the time to deliver his promised columns to the *Democrat*, offering insights into the workings of the motion picture industry, expressing the fact that besides the actor and director, the rest of the crew was extremely important to film production. "It is with all personal depreciation that I say the cameraman is next to the director in actual importance.... The wardrobe mistress clothes thousands of people annually, and always knows just what is the 'proper' thing for the occasion.... One other important office in the studio is that of the studio manager. This is purely an executive capacity which is usually filled by a man who has long experience in the commercial world."⁴⁷

The weather was mostly favorable except towards the end of their stay. In addition to the work in and around Natchez, the company went further afield for various scenes: the St. John Lake in Louisiana and the small town of Washington, near Natchez, which, in Colleen's opinion, was so old-fashioned that she "expected every time she looked around the streets to see ladies in hoopskirts stepping out of the houses."⁴⁸

The whole city was involved with the production: "Three young society misses, Katherine Healy, Bardell Wheeler and Frances Smith, played bits." It was possible that they might find their way to Hollywood, according to Colleen: "Mrs. Mary Connor, a society woman, played a part, and she ran away with her scenes.... And I wore the dear old lady's wedding dress in a scene!"⁴⁹ Judge Will Foster played the part of Judge Mayne.⁵⁰

Music to set the mood of a shot was often performed by "Negro orchestras."⁵¹ Liberal prices were being paid for butterflies, resulting in nearly every kid in town chasing the insects, looking for a bounty.⁵² George Healy was an extra, his second "Hollywood" job after his stint as an extra in *Heart of Maryland*, his second job for hard cash.⁵³

While the city itself was electrified, electricity was not available at all locations.⁵⁴ "Some of the homes have retained the old kerosene-lamp chandelles, and to photograph the interiors it was necessary to string miles of electric cables to the special Morosco generators furnishing power to the batteries of lights."⁵⁵ There was no film processing in the vicinity, so negatives were shipped to Los Angeles overnight, processed and returned as soon as possible to determine if reshoots were needed. And, on occasion, there was rain; the planned shoot of the opening sequence of the film, showing the title character "Slippy" McGee robbing a bank, had to be delayed because of a passing storm that threatened the electrical equipment with dampness.[56] On July 19, a fight scene was postponed because the necessary film stock had not arrived. The scene was reschedule and needed "thirty or forty men on hand dressed in working clothes to be in the scene as spectators of the fight."[57] This request was modified three days later to "all white men who may be interested."[58]

During their stay, Colleen's film *So Long Letty* made a swing through the local theater. Colleen went to see the film, accompanied by Wesley Ruggles. The pair watched the film in secrecy, hidden in the audience in the dark, before the announcement was made of her presence. She put in an appearance on the stage, to loud applause.[59]

By the end of July it was getting time to wrap things up and return to Los Angeles. "Oliver Morosco Company Will Leave Natchez Monday," the *Natchez Democrat* stated, noting that "during the time that the members of the *Slippy Magee* [sic] company have been here, many Natchez people have come to know them personally and form friendships that will not soon be forgotten." A letter from Louis Keppler, Morosco business manager, was printed thanking the city for their welcome and the hospitality during their stay: "The whole company feels like we were one big, grand family of the most charming, clean cut people."[60]

"Director Wesley Ruggles and members of the *Slippy McGee* cast are expected to return from Natchez, Miss., the latter part of this week to complete the Oliver Morosco feature at the Mayer Studio.... William Foster, a prominent judge, was "kidnapped" by Ruggles to play a judge in the story."[61]

Between New York and Natchez, Colleen experienced exactly the sort of fame and recognition to which she had always aspired.

16

Censorship

As motion pictures worked their way into American society, audiences were drawn to glamour, urban sophistication, exoticism, and sex. Some said motion pictures were following the trends of the day, but there was a widening opinion that they were a corrupting influence and Hollywood was a den of immorality. After the Volstead Act, a number of controversies originating in Hollywood underscored this view. America's Sweetheart, Mary Pickford, had been seeing Douglas Fairbanks for years. On March 2, 1920, she divorced Owen Moore. Within weeks she married Fairbanks.[1] In September 1920, Olive Thomas died in France, likely an accidental death but there were questions surrounding the circumstances. Many attributed the fast and loose behavior of Hollywood's celebrities to a libertine atmosphere, and before long a movement was afoot to rein it in.

In 1921, the New York State Legislature established an independent commission to censor films. The industry objected but Governor Miller signed the bill because "it was the only way to remedy to what everyone concedes has grown to be a very great evil."[2] "[Philadelphia] Mayor Moore announced today that a censorship over theaters and motion picture shows would probably be established."[3] Chicago was taking action against violence in films: "Motion pictures portraying criminals at work have been barred in Chicago…. The order became public when three youthful robbers, who were sentenced to the state reformatory at Pontiac, said their crimes had been inspired by a 'crook' moving picture."[4]

"'Now that the saloons have been put out of business these professional reformers look upon the motion-picture industry as their natural prey,' Mr. [W.A.] Brady declared at a luncheon given by Chicago motion-picture men and women here today."[5] A. T. Poffenberger, writing in *Scientific American*, declared: "Wrongly used and not carefully guarded, [motion pictures] might easily become a training school for anti-Americanism, immorality and disregard for the law."[6]

Voices were being raised in support of curtailing Hollywood's glorification of sex and violence.[7] A vocal swath of rural America looked with

Colleen and her father, Charles Morrison, at a baseball game, probably in Washington Park, circa 1921. The ballpark was demolished in the 1950s (courtesy Joseph Yranski).

alarm at the highjinks that emanated from such cities like Hollywood and New York. Colleen had returned to Hollywood to find herself surrounded by that atmosphere. Being an actress, she might easily find herself a target of rural America's ire. She had been haunted by stories of flirting romances with a string of unnamed men,[8] the most recent of which made it seem men were falling at her heels. "They say Colleen Moore is trying to decide between a New York millionaire and a movie hero. Which would you take, girls?"[9]

In her comments that New York was not her cup of tea, she had managed to distance herself from her more cosmopolitan contemporaries. It acted to shore up her image as a wholesome young woman. That perception, however, was a double-edged sword. Being so identified placed her in a rut. In the Chicago papers, she was the "Glad Girl of films," and nice girls could only go so far in the industry.

In July, *Photoplay* magazine ran a poem/editorial on Colleen:

> Colleen Moore said/She would Wear
> A Red Hat. I Watched/The Red Hats Go By.
> I Counted/At Least Twenty-six when
> I Saw Colleen — and/She Wasn't Wearing a
> Red Hat at all. /It was Green.
> She is Irish. /You Can't Help liking her.
> She's So Young that/She Wants to Play
> Old Ladies, but/Mr. Neilan
> Won't Let her./She Likes
> Ripe Olives,/Director Mickey,
> Adela Rogers St. Johns, /Riverside Drive, and
> John Barrymore. /But
> She Loves California, and/She Wants to Go Back.
> They all Do — someone/Should Write a Song about It.
> Colleen is Playing opposite/John Barrymore Now — and Now
> Her Uncle is Going /To Print her Picture
> In his Paper. He is/A Newspaper Editor, but
> He Always Said to her, /"You'll Never Get your Name
> In my Paper until you Really/Make Good."
> Colleen Has. /And she'll Keep Right On —
> She's Just that Kind of a Kid.[10]

In it one can read her aspirations: "She Wants to Play/Old Ladies, but/Mr. Neilan/Won't Let her." Colleen had begun to chafe against her rut. In New York and Natchez, she had been a celebrity. She might break out of that rut if she were willing to try something risqué, but then she had to worry about being caught up in the backlash against the corrupting influence of Hollywood. And she had to worry about what her grandmother would think.

Goldwyn, Rupert Hughes, and The Wall Flower, *August–September 1921*

Marshall Neilan Productions had been releasing its films through First National, but the contract was due to expire. First National was unlikely to renew it, so Neilan suggested to his people that they move on while the getting was good. He directed Colleen towards

Goldwyn and recommended her to Rupert Hughes.[11] Neilan had seen *The Old Nest* and was reportedly so impressed that he had written to both Samuel Goldwyn and Rupert Hughes. To Goldwyn he commented that the film stood apart like "radium from other minerals." To Hughes he wrote, "I think your story the most human document that so far has been produced on the screen."[12]

Hughes, a popular writer, had become increasingly involved in film production. His latest offering was *The Wall Flower*, and the main character — a young, introverted woman who was required to blossom before the cameras — was reported to be a difficult part. Who could play it?

> Have you a little Wall Flower in your home?
> If so, there's a good job waiting for her, provided she is a most unusual Wall Flower.
> The reason is that Rupert Hughes has written *The Wall Flower* for Goldwyn, which has such a type for a heroine. She must be pathetic and sad at first, but must later blossom out into a thing of beauty and charm.
> So difficult is the role to cast that tests have been given to a dozen or more actresses in the film colony.... It will mean all the more credit to the actress who is finally chosen for the part.[13]

Colleen had wanted a starring part and had resolved to hold out for such an offer, but took the part when Hughes offered it to her. The role called for an actress who was not classically beautiful, but who could pull off ordinariness and beauty in turns. It meant that once again she would play the good girl, but at least this time, a good girl with a twist. It would also mean, once again, that her character would be injured in the course of the story, which was nothing new.

> In *Little Orphant Annie* ... she died of a broken heart.
> In *When Dawn Came*, she was blind up to the closing scenes.
> In *Dinty*, Marshall Neilan's recent triumph, she was bed-ridden in much of the picture and finally was called by death.
> In *The Sky Pilot* ... she was supposedly seriously crippled.[14]

In *The Wall Flower* she would have a taste of roles to come. The plain girl transformed into a sophisticate would become her specialty. Soon Colleen would be all about transformations.

Colleen gave an interview to Grace Kingsley, during which she waxed romantic about Natchez. "Society women vied with each other to get us to use their houses," Colleen said in the interview, pointing out that arguments would break out between homeowners. "When we used one house and didn't use the other it caused a social split.... I don't suppose Natchez society will ever be the same again."

Kingsley quoted Colleen: "Society women were delighted to get their old mammies into the picture, too. A mammy, 90 years old, played my nurse." Besides parties, Colleen had done a survey of the local mill workers and their lives. The local society girls, descendants of those who used to watch over the slaves, had taken to watching over the welfare of the white mill workers. Because of child labor laws, the youngest kids were not yet at work in the mills and were "pale, hollow-chested, undernourished and subnormal mentally in many cases." Housing conditions were getting better, but there were still families that lived "twelve to fourteen in a room." During the production, Colleen threw a party for the factory children: "Of course, our boys kidded the negroes who acted with us a good deal.... Wheeler

Oakman sent a crowd of them one rainy day to all the hardware stores in town hunting for mythical 'sky hooks.' They took it all in good part, though, when they discovered the joke was on themselves."[15]

The story cast the city in a provincial air that rankled some of her Natchez hosts. A letter by A.N. Ryan ran in the September 4th *Los Angeles Times* as a rebuttal to the Kingsley story. He wrote that his feelings of Colleen's recollections and emotions "ran the gamut, I might say, from the sublime to the ridiculous, and from justifiable anger, at the unpardonable misrepresentations to hilarious merriment at Miss Moore's loquacity and peculiar mental ability to misconstrue southern hospitality as a species of tomfoolery."

Mistakenly referring to Kingsley's preamble to the interview, he opined: "Miss Moore states that 'the people don't see a bunch of actors but once in a blue moon,' implying that her bunch were real bona-fide actors, possessing genuine histrionic talent, and not the absolute automatons that nearly all movie actors are." He was displeased that she seemed to be acknowledging their hospitality in one breath while in the next mocking it. "Natchez, with it's beautiful and cultured woman, it's gallant men, and surroundings of picturesque beauty is famed in song and story for its unstinted hospitality, but for that hospitality to be accepted and used to the fullest by an inappreciative recipient, and then, at a safe distance to be traduced and gibed at, is indeed a glaring illustration of ill-breeding." He concluded that he sympathized with her "apparent inability to restrain her loquaciousness, and general tendency to use the slangy idioms with which movie life seems replete."[16]

The rebuke might have hurt were it not printed just a few weeks after meeting John McCormick.

Colleen had been selected for the leading role in *The Wall Flower*, described as the most difficult part ever written by Hughes, but "Miss Moore is said to have come through the screen test preceding the selection, with flying colors.

"Richard Dix has been selected to play opposite Miss Moore. Shannon Day has also been engaged for a part in this picture."[17]

The role marked the first of several for Colleen with Goldwyn under a four-film deal.[18] It was Sam Goldwyn who suggested that Colleen let her hair grow long again. The role had the potential to help her career, given the way her character was to bounce between plainness and beauty. The idea of women making changes and gaining social status was a new and appealing one.[19]

Rupert Hughes's interest in films stemmed from his wish to see his writing correctly adapted to the screen. He had taken to motion pictures right away, pushing cameramen and directors to do things his way, having ordered at one point a scene that required six exposures on a single length of film.[20] He wanted to get it right, just as Colleen did. The two would get along well.

Censorship

In late July, a course had been charted for resolving the issue of film censorship: "A member of every censor board in the country will arrive at Universal City on August 15 to go into action with Universal directors to straighten out the tangle of hokum which has surrounded the censorship question since it started."[21] Hollywood showed them the old razzle-dazzle. Members of the official censor boards of several American and Canadian cities arrived in Los Angeles as guests of Carl Laemmle. They had a full schedule for the week, starting Monday, when they would be treated to a lunch at the Universal studio, a tour of Universal City, a trip to Santa Monica, sea bathing and a barbecue. For the evening they were scheduled to be guests of the Emanuel Presbyterian Brotherhood at a meeting "of particular interest to those concerned in censorship." Tuesday was for tours of studios, followed by a motor trip through Pasadena and a sneak peak at Stroheim's *Foolish Wives*. Wednesday started at Universal City for an animal circus and was scheduled to end at the Sunset Inn for an event hosted by Priscilla Dean.[22]

Colleen played her part in the events. "When these august persons [members of the various censor boards] arrive, they may be surprised at the modesty of the California beaches, for there are plans on foot to have all the bathing beauties and screen stars wear 'censorship bathing suits' during the stay of the censors on the coast." A photo of Colleen in a swimsuit that covered her from neck to ankle accompanied the story. "Colleen says her bathing suit will be passed by the censors whether her pictures are or not."[23]

Neilan invited Colleen, by way of her mother, to the Sunset Inn the evening after the August 17 event. He wanted Colleen to join him and his fiancée Blanche Sweet, because he had a man for Colleen to meet.[24]

The Sunset Inn, August 18, 1921

> [The Sunset Inn] is called that way because it don't start until sunset and then tries to double for the sun all night. It blazed with orange lights, and as we stopped in front the orchestra broke out into a fresh effort. From the row that it made I could easily imagine some well-known star was playing the traps as per usual.[25]
> —*Laughter Limited*, by Nina Wilcox Putnam.

The Sunset Inn had a reputation. The Pastor G.L. "Golightly" Morrill opined, "The Inn was conducted with a cafe attachment where the attachment was more for liquor than solids. No matter who owned or leased it, it was alleged the devil ran it as a house on the road, that is, a road house."[26] Even if the liquor did not flow, the music did. "The real cutups go to ... the Sunset Inn on the road to Santa Monica, miles from Hollywood."[27]

Colleen had been there in spite of her later insistence that her date with John and Neilan had been on the occasion of her first visit. "Colleen Moore, who with Richard Dix, won a cup at the Sunset Inn for dancing, has deserted the jazz haunts."[28] The story was dated November 20. From Grace Kingsley's stories, one might believe she had a fully booked social calendar.

> Colleen Moore was entertained by two handsome dark men, out there [at the Cocoanut Grove at the Ambassador Hotel] the other night, one of them a sort of "ex." And oh, that wicked Colleen!
> "What is your favorite color?" she asked one of them.
> "Why blue!" answered the dark young man, delightfully flattered. "Why?"
> "Oh," said Colleen demurely, "I just wanted to tie up your love letters with that color ribbon before I put them away forever, that's all!"[29]

Who was seeing whom had long formed a basis of back-fence gossip since the day they made the first back fence. With the increased familiarity the public felt with the personalities of the motion pictures, there was a demand for more such stories.

Marshall Neilan picked her up Thursday night. He was driving and was accompanied Blanche Sweet. In the backseat was John McCormick with another woman.[30] Introductions were made, and Colleen climbed in back. It had been a pleasant drive out to the Sunset Inn.

John McCormick was over six feet tall and slim and handsome, with blue eyes and fine dark hair slicked down on his scalp. Colleen was attracted to him. He had an outgoing manner. He was sharp and enthusiastic and unabashedly attracted to her. He spoke quickly and assertively.

Inside, they danced. While on the floor, without preamble, he confessed that he was in love with her and asked her to marry him.

She laughed. "Call me up in the cold gray dawn, and tell me that."

"I will," he said.[31]

His birthday had been the day before, he told her — his 27th, and he knew hers was the next day. They must marry. Three days in a row to celebrate. What else could it be but fate?

They had plenty to talk about that evening, sharing a common interest in motion pictures. All aspects of motion pictures interested Colleen, and so talk of the business end would have appealed to her. He was a natural-born salesman and could talk a blue streak on any subject. He was charming and assertive. That night he made her the center of his universe, and such unabashed attention was irresistible.

The next morning, bright and early, the telephone rang. Colleen answered. It was John: he asked her if she remembered him.[32]

She certainly did.

"It's the cold gray dawn, and I love you. When are you going to marry me?"

She had no answer. He asked her to dinner that night. She said she was having dinner with her grandmother.[33] John told Colleen to bring her grandmother along. Then a bouquet of flowers arrived from John, with a note wishing her a happy birthday. A half-hour later the first of a series of 19 telegrams that day arrived. Read in order, they told a fairy tale, ending with the requisite "and they lived happily ever after." Between the telegrams, flowers and candy were delivered; an organ grinder with a dancing monkey arrived to deliver birthday wishes, and a carton of chewing gum was delivered with a funny jingle written on the wrapper of each stick.[34]

John's pursuit was enthusiastic. That evening at dinner neither he nor Colleen touched their dinners. John talked; Colleen listened. Her grandmother liked him. Only an Irishman could be so creative. When Colleen's family met him, they liked him. Clearly, Colleen was smitten. His talk of marriage became more firm, a foregone conclusion so far as John was concerned. Grandmother Kelly was in favor of Colleen marrying John. Agnes wanted Colleen to slow down.

Censorship

Whatever accommodation might have been reached on film censorship was scuttled when the Roscoe Arbuckle story broke. A lovable comedian seemed transformed overnight into a leering monster hellbent on orgy and rape. "Girl Dead after Wild Party in Hotel," the front-page headline of the *San Francisco Chronicle* screamed.[35] "Arbuckle Dragged Rappe Girl to Room, Woman Testifies," the *New York Times* reported on its front page. "'I've waited for you five years, and now I've got you,' Arbuckle declared, Mrs. [Bambina Maude] Delmont said, adding that he locked the door.... When she heard her [Virginia] screaming she became alarmed." Readers could only imagine the worst after Delmont described the lolling, dopey smile Arbuckle displayed when he finally opened the door.[36] With sensational testimony like that, and with the Hearst papers and especially Colleen's own uncle, Walter Howey, fanning the flames, the stories multiplied.

Arbuckle was a big man, and presumably a man of gluttonous appetites, a man capable of anything. He became a focus of attention for those convinced Hollywood was a den of inequity. Grotesque stories of Arbuckle's exploits and sensational stories of Hollywood's craven habits circulated. Eventually vindicated, the assumption that he had done something terrible had even followed him to the grave.

17

August 1921–December 1921

It was Colleen's birthday and at one party the birthday girl spent a portion of the festivities attempting to evade two of her guests: the "ardent" Rush Hughes, son of Rupert, and Tom Gallory. They threatened to kiss her 20 times, once for each year, and Colleen had to dodge them that evening.[1] When the partying was over, Colleen went to the Goldwyn Studio, the Pickford-Fairbanks lot on the corner of Formosa Avenue and Santa Monica Boulevard, where *The Wall Flower* was days into production.[2]

There were problems at the studio. The country had just come out of a recession, a post-war adjustment from war-footing to peacetime that had run from a peak in January 1920 to a trough in July 1921. Goldwyn's overall film production was running light, and so they began to distribute the material of several small producers.[3] Eminent Authors went through a period of financial strain when Rex Beach left. Rupert Hughes remained with the studio as a director as well as a writer.

Colleen would be billed in the film as a featured player, but her role was still the starring one, her character bouncing from plainness to beauty.[4] She had gone light on her makeup in the early scenes, allowing her freckled complexion to show. She combed her hair back so that her ears were more prominent.[5] In the later scenes, she had returned to her customary makeup, her complexion looking as smooth as usual, and she sported a more modern coiffure. In the story, Idalene Nobbin (Colleen) is a wall flower, ignored by her mother and brothers. At a dance she is asked by a popular athlete to dance but afterwards she becomes the victim of a practical joke that leaves her mortified. She tries to end her life by throwing herself under a car, but survives, albeit with two broken legs. She is found by society girl Pamela (Gertrude Astor) and her friend Walter Breen (Richard Dix). They take her home to care for her. Learning of Idalene's fears that she will die alone as a spinster because of her lack of social skills and grace, Pamela takes her under her wing. From there it becomes a Pygmalion story as Pamela slowly transforms her though manners and clothes and lessons on the finer points of society into a lovely woman. Throughout the process, Walter finds himself attracted to the new Idalene. At a party thrown by Pamela as Idalene's debut, Idalene's former tormenters are shocked. Walter proposes to her. Idalene has fallen for him, but she turns him down out of loyalty to Pamela, whom she discovers is also in love with Walter. Pamela, however, denies her feelings in favor of Idalene, paving the way to her happiness.

As Idalene Nobbin, Colleen acquired her share of bumps and bruises. "While working in a scene at Goldwyn, Colleen Moore cut her arm severely on a fragment of broken glass. The injury was not serious, and Miss Moore has been able to continue in her roles."[6] When not getting sliced up, she was suffering from sunburns: "Colleen says she doesn't mind the burn — but the way she got it! Funny thing is that most girls would be tickled to death to get it the same way — emoting for the screen under the sunlight arcs, instead of playing about the beach. But then, as the little actress herself philosophized while making up as *The Wall Flower* ... 'It isn't what people have that they want. It's what they haven't.'"[7] Not all of her injuries were real. "Colleen Moore Reel Accident Victim," declared one story in the *Los Angeles Times*. "Colleen Moore, captivating little screen actress, was run over by an automobile recently. Yes, really; no, reely. The car passed over, but she wasn't hurt a bit.[8] The director and his associates are keeping the process a deep secret."[9]

By the end of September Colleen's work on the film was done: "Recently finished productions [at Goldwyn include] ... *The Wall Flower*."[10] Rupert Hughes was impressed enough with Colleen's performance that it was reported, in early October, that he was already at work writing a story specifically for her.[11] The new film would be under way before November. "The complete cast for Rupert Hughes' story *Sent for Out*, under the direction of Al Green, includes the following supports for Colleen Moore: Mary Warren, Farrell McDonald, Florence Drew and Kate Price."[12] Ralph Graves had been selected as the male lead,[13] and Kathleen O'Connor had a role as well.[14]

There were several productions already underway at the Goldwyn studio, while *The Wall Flower* was in the post-production stage: "Rupert Hughes new play, *The Wall Flower*, is receiving finishing touches in the laboratory."[15] One of Colleen's performances from the year before was about to have its long-delayed premier as well. "Exceptional Pictures Corporation announces that the premier production, *His Nibs*, starring Charles 'Chic' Sale, will be given at the Grand Ballroom of the Hotel Astor, New York, on Thursday evening, October 6th." Among the parts Sale plays are "'The Boy,' who plays the hero of *He Fooled 'Em All*, a thrilling drama of the fight for fortune and a girl which is interpolated with *His Nibs*."[16] The final form the film took was to frame the original spoof, *He Fooled 'Em All*, with a new story centered on a film projectionist showing the film that featured Sale playing several parts. *He Fooled 'Em All* became the film shown in the theater, and Sale, as Theo. Bender, narrated the action for the audience, not only allowing him to give commentary on the stock melodrama of the time, but on his own performance in that film.

Goldwyn Pictures, looking for publicity, combined with the *Chicago Daily News* to announce a contest intended to attract the interest of the average film viewer:

> Judges have been announced for the photoplay contest of the Goldwyn Pictures Corporation, in co-operation with the *Chicago Daily News*, the most expensive moving picture scenario contest ever held. At the close of this contest will be awarded $30,000 in prizes to the writers of the thirty-one best scenarios entered. It is dedicated to the belief that amateur scenario writers, with proper advice and encouragement, can produce quantities of strong, vivid stories and real life scenarios that will give stimulus to the work of establishing moving pictures as one of the great American contributions to art.
> Prizes arc offered as follows: First prize, $10,000; ten second prizes, each $1,000: twenty third prizes, each $500. Goldwyn will produce the first prize winner as a big special production. The judges will be Samuel Goldwyn, D.W. Griffith, Charles Chaplin, Norma Talmadge, Mary Roberts Rinehart, Rupert Hughes, Gertrude Atherton, Gouverneur Morris and Amy Leslie."[17]

Sent for Out (Come On Over), November–December 1921

With the contest underway, the cast for Colleen's next film, *Sent for Out*, was being settled on. Ralph Graves, having recently married, had just signed a new contract at the Goldwyn studios and was slated to be Colleen's male lead.[18] A film better suited to Colleen's persona at the time could scarcely be imagined. She would play the part of Moyna Killiea, whose sweetheart, Shane O'Mealia (Graves), emigrates from Ireland to the United States, leaving her in the care of the elderly Bridget Morahan. Once he establishes himself, he assures her, he will send for her to join him. Shane lives with the Morahans in New York, but he has difficulty keeping a job and raising a stake with which to send for Moyna. He is often seen with Judy Dugan. As the film progresses, it looks more and more like Shane and Judy have become involved, while back in Ireland, Moyna has grown forlorn waiting with her mother to hear from her beloved. Michael Morahan, the family patriarch in New York, longing to revisit his home country and bring over his elderly mother, Bridget, travels back to Ireland. He is so pleased with Moyna's caring for his mother that he brings her back to America with him. At hearing his announcement, Moyna dances a jig with childlike pleasure.

Believing Judy and Shane are engaged, Moyna flees the Morahan house into the night. Moyna ends up in the Bronx, lost in a strange and busy metropolitan space completely alien to her rural experiences. Lost and confused, she seeks refuge in the first park she finds. Delia

Kathleen O'Connor, Ralph Graves, and Colleen in a publicity image from *Come On Over*, Goldwyn, 1922. Directed by Alfred E. Green, who would helm some of Colleen's most popular films, including *Sally* and *Irene* (courtesy Joseph Yranski).

Morahan puts a call in to her police-officer brother, and the whole Irish community acts to find her and bring her back home. In the meantime, the Morahans manage to pull some Tammany Hall strings in the form of Danny Carmody, who has made good in railroads, to get Shane a stable job. The family is invited to dinner at the Carmody home. Newly dressed in a modern gown, Moyna is still distraught with Shane's secretive behavior and the belief she will be abandoned by Shane in favor of Judy. At last, it is revealed that Shane has managed to get Judy's drunkard father to take a pledge of sobriety before a priest, explaining the secrecy. Understanding at last, Shane and Moyna are united and all the dinner guests begin to dance the dances of the old country to the music of an old piper brought in just for the occasion.

Portrait of Cleeve Morrison, ca. mid–1920s (courtesy Judy Coleman).

The film presented a stagey view of the modern Irish existence in America. It had at its root the established first generation welcoming the new generation into their homes, and the new generation working hard to fit in. Colleen portrayed the unsophisticated woman, longing to join her sweetheart in the new world, but rejecting the clothes and finery she is given in favor of her simple clothes and ways. "Particularly entertaining is the Irish jig competition in a luxurious home between two older women, girlhood friends in Ireland, who do a breakdown, even though one of them is now a society matron and clogs in silk and sigh French slippers."[19] Colleen had shown off her skills at dancing the Irish jig. She had become an accomplished dancer of late but turned to an authority for help with her jig — Grandmother Kelly.[20] It was thanks to her grandmother that Colleen, as "Irish as the Blarney Stone," was able to "revert" to a charming brogue.[21]

Work on the film went quickly, with a few delays courtesy of the occasional botched take by two of the film's stars: "Monte Collins and Kate Price are charged with holding up production at the Goldwyn studio. They keep Al Green and Colleen Moore laughing so at their talks of 'twenty years ago, when we played in variety,' that no work is done."[22] Filming had wrapped by December: "Sent for Out" and *Hungry Hearts* have been finished."[23] As the photography was being completed, the *Saginaw News-Courier* reported that Colleen's family was taking the last steps, severing itself from the old business connections to the East and setting up shop in the West as her father gave up most of his business interests to join Colleen in Hollywood.[24] Cleeve, who had gone to school in Santa Clara and was living there, was due to return for the holidays, and there were relatives coming from out of town. "Colleen Moore, is all excited because her brother is coming home from college, an aunt and uncle are coming from New York, and grandmother is already here to make the Yuletide merry."[25] All this combined with the entry of John McCormick into her life doubtless added up to a merry holiday season.

1922

The new year began with a racy rumor about how Colleen's private life intersected with that of Rush Hughes's: "A reported romance between Colleen Moore and the son of Rupert Hughes is now reported to be 'off.' Son has gone back to college and the pretty Colleen Moore is merrily playing about with another boy."[26] The "other boy" was, presumably, John McCormick.

Rupert Hughes continued his professional relationship with Colleen. "Goldwyn has purchased the screen rights to another one of Rupert Hughes' humorous short stories ... entitled *The Bitterness of Sweets* ... [it] has to do with an ambitious but poor young girl who often does not have enough to eat. The Goldwyn editorial and scenario departments believe that they have material in this Hughes short story for another motion picture comedy masterpiece."[27] The writing staff at Goldwyn had grown during the previous year. "Carey Wilson[28] has been added to the [Goldwyn] scenario staff."[29] *Sent for Out* was renamed *Darlin*,[30] but it didn't stick. It was renamed again to *Come On Over*.[31]

While no cast had initially been announced for the new film by late February it was the general expectation that once again Colleen would assume the lead.[32] News of Colleen's engagement to John McCormick broke in February. "Although the young lady denied it repeatedly, rumors are nevertheless busy to the effect that Colleen Moore will soon be the bride of John McCormick, well-known motion picture man. Miss Moore is wearing a diamond ring, the gift of Mr. McCormick, although she stoutly says she will not wed any one for a long time yet."[33] She denied the engagement publicly, but had

> confided to intimate friends that she intended to marry the picture man. Mr. McCormick, too, has, in confidential moments, let it be known that he expects to marry the beautiful young picture star.
>
> Devastating indeed, will be the word of her engagement to Miss Moore's many admirers, as she is personally one of the most popular stars in the business, possessing a charming Irish wit, as well as much beauty, tact and charm.[34]

Colleen was very slowly building towards the recognition to which she aspired, a fact acknowledged by a group of motion picture press men who came together with the idea of finding the actresses who would become the next really famous talent. "Film Press Men Plan Big Frolic," was the headline, the first to mention of which stars were to be honored. "Predicting that they will become the 'stars of tomorrow,' the press agents have named a baker's dozen of film girls who will be officially presented to the public under that prophecy at the frolic."[35]

The Western Associated Motion Picture Advertisers had been formed in 1920. The association was concerned with many issues, but none attracted attention like their proposed frolic. If nothing in Hollywood attracts more attention than a pretty girl, then 13 pretty girls would cause a riot. The frolic was planned to celebrate their future. The studios saw the value in having their young stars touted as the next big thing, and so backed the idea.[36]

The event in March was under the personal direction of Roy Leek. The plans and logistics for the event were being worked out by a committee of the public relations organization headed by John McCormick. An animated feature of the event was to be shown. A newspaper of the event was to be published during the proceedings, lampooning many of the guests.[37] The hoopla surrounding the Frolic only grew as the date neared. A motion picture was to be created of the guests. The raw film would be rushed from laboratories directly back to the frolic where it would be viewed by the guests. Douglas Fairbanks and Mary Pickford, freshly returned from New York, along with Charlie Chaplin, were to attend.

Colleen was among that first class of actresses. Adela Rogers St. Johns picked Colleen out for especial notice: "Of them all, I found the most honest enthusiasm, the most confident praise and prediction behind Colleen Moore." Colleen and Adela were friends, but Adela reported the enthusiasm for Colleen's prospects did not stop with her own opinion. Rupert Hughes called her "wax to mold but marble to retain." He was impressed with her ability to portray the complete spectrum of emotions demanded of her. "She met every one of these demands with intuition, enthusiasm, and perfect technique." Marshall Neilan had high praise as well: "Although hardly more than a child, she has the accomplishments of a veteran of the drama at her fingertips."[38]

Studio portrait of Colleen, ca. 1922, by Evans of L.A. Compare this image to the 1918 portrait, also by Evans.

In mid-March, *Come On Over* was released, beating *The Wall Flower* to the theaters, just in time for St. Patrick's Day. Lowes State theatre in Salt Lake City featured a full-sized cutout of Colleen superimposed with the title of the film before the ticket office. A miniature of the Statue of Liberty was perched atop the ticket office "enlightening the world." Two arches were erected over the entrances, each decorated liberally with shamrocks. Irish flags were strung above the entrance on wire. Shamrocks were painted on the glass doors leading inside.[39] The Capitol Theater in New York advertised it: "All Irish week. The presentation by Rothafel will be as sweet as a song of Erin and you'll welcome it as you would the green grass of springtime. Mother, father, sister, brother—the whole family—*Come On Over*!"[40] In Chicago, Mae Tinee gave it a frothy review written in pidgin Irish accent, describing the film as the product of the imagination of a man sitting in a sunny window seat with his pipe in his hand imagining the perfect scene. "It's cuddlesome and mirthful with a tear in its eye. It's as homey and satisfying as the odor of fresh baked bread."[41] At the Merrill in Milwaukee, the management gave their promise that "this 'peach' of a picture has the punch of a shillelagh, the sweetness of an Irish rose — and fun fresh from the 'ould sod.'"[42]

The film was well received, as was Colleen's performance. She was riding a wave of positive publicity. The motion picture community had proclaimed her a powerful actress with a great future. The country adored her. She was in demand.

In spite of all this, she was still not a star.

18

The Bitterness of Sweets (*Look Your Best*), March–May 1922

The expectation that Colleen was to appear in *The Bitterness of Sweets* was confirmed as stories about the production were reported. "Antonio Moreno," it was announced, "has been engaged by Goldwyn to play the lead."[1] The lengths to which Colleen would go for her new role were reported with interest: "Colleen Moore, who weighs 110 pounds, has just been ordered to weigh in at 98 for the first scenes of *Bitterness of Sweets*.... But that isn't the half of it. The little leading woman must then raise her poundage to 118 — more than she has ever owned in her life. You see, the picture calls for a thin heroine who grows plump. Miss Moore is reducing by rigid diet. She will be fattened at a milk farm near the Culver City studio. Life is one trial after another for the 'movie' queen."[2]

This time Colleen was to play Perla Quaranta, "daughter of Little Italy," who was given a place in impresario Carlo Bruni's (Antonio Moreno) "Butterfly Act" after the departure of a "Butterfly Girl" who had grown too fat for the trapeze. While in the show, Colleen befriends the high-wire man, Krug, but rejects his advances. In return, Krug sabotages the wire to convince Bruni that she has gained too much weight. Seeing through the ruse, Bruni assaults Krug, and is arrested and jailed. After a month, he is released with a new act brimming in his mind, just waiting to be produced with Perla as the star. In the end, the two marry.

Colleen in costume for *Look Your Best*, directed by Rupert Hughes, Goldwyn, 1923 (courtesy Judy Coleman).

The film is set in a vaudeville house, with dance to be featured again ... ballet this time instead of Irish jigs. "Miss Moore is studying classic dancing with Theodore Kosloff.... "I can stand on my toes," declared Miss Moore yesterday, 'and I've learned all kinds of poses — $1 poses, $40 poses, and, oh, everything down to 10-cent poses.'"[3]

18. The Bitterness of Sweets (Look Your Best), *March–May 1922*

Colleen and Antonio Moreno in a scene from *Look Your Best*, directed by Rupert Hughes, Goldwyn, 1923 (courtesy Judy Coleman).

Antonio Moreno took dance lessons, having "taken to dancing like a Spaniard to bullfighting."[4] In addition to the regular cast were the smallest pony in the world; a monkey with "human understanding"; Blanche Payson, six-foot-four, the largest woman in pictures; Billy Fletcher, five-feet tall, as a clown; a team of blackface comedians; and six butterfly girls selected by Mr. Hughes as the most beautiful in filmdom.[5] Hughes had to interview upwards of 500 women to winnow the field down to the six chosen. Among them were Monica Bracken, daughter of an accomplished sculptress (a friend of Hughes, as it turned out) who studied under Isadora Duncan.[6] Even after the film was completed, Hughes would continue to test the butterfly girls on the theory that they were of such pulchritude that they should be recorded on deathless celluloid, provided their talents were anywhere near their looks.[7] One of the acts staged for the movie involved hoisting the butterfly girls in harnesses so that they might appear to fly through the air while Colleen performed her dance number.

By the end of April the film was being edited.[8] "In all probability Rupert Hughes new Goldwyn photoplay *The Bitterness of Sweets*, featuring Colleen Moore and Antonio Moreno ... will not have any subtitles. "Mr. Hughes is now editing the film and proposes doing away with all subtitles, if it is at all possible, or, failing that, to use them so sparingly that they will scarcely be noticeable."[9] As the film was being edited, Colleen's next role was already mapped out.

May 1922

> It seemed to me no vanity
> Was here, but earnest and sincere
> The eyes that looked at me.
> This was no up-stage mood, but a girl, verging on womanhood
> Who, like a rose, and without pose,
> Offers her best, gives herself as she is,
> Craving a rose's place among our memories.
> —"An Interview in Verse," by Hallett Abend,
> *Los Angeles Times*, June 11, 1922, page III15.[10]

The Wall Flower was released before Colleen went to work on her next film, and like *Come On Over*, it was well received: "For those who enjoy a sparkling comedy, brilliant titles and mayhap a little weep or two, *The Wall Flower* is recommended."[11] One reviewer wrote, "If they continue to give her more roles of this sort she will achieve a very high place for herself among film comediennes. And, moreover, a unique place. Because nobody ever has struck exactly that quaint, charming, amusing, teary quality before."[12]

In spite of the good reviews, Colleen was not yet a star. She could deliver an excellent performance, but she was still only seen as the ingénue. Audiences were looking for characters to whom they could relate. That category of independent young woman known as the "flapper" was becoming the rage, and it was not a type with which Colleen was associated. She

Colleen in a lobby card from *The Wall Flower*, directed by Rupert Hughes, Goldwyn, 1922.

18. The Bitterness of Sweets (Look Your Best), *March–May 1922*

Two portraits of Colleen while under contract with Goldwyn, both photographed by C.S. Bull.

sported modern looks and enjoyed the cosmopolitan life whenever she visited New York: "Jim, the doorman at the Hotel Ambassador, daily opens the door for dozens of America's favorites. Colleen Moore is a frequent visitor there."[13] Even so, she was mostly seen as the unspoiled Irish lass. It was a product of the split between the woman, Kathleen Morrison, and the actress and persona on the screen, "Colleen Moore." Kathleen the woman was a young modern. Colleen the persona was an innocent girl.

She had adopted a more modern look and attitude, though tempered by her family's values. "At first glance, one decides that her hair is bobbed," wrote Gordon Gassaway in an interview for *Motion Picture Magazine*. "Her mother once told me that Colleen would never be allowed to bob her hair, come what might ...." However, her hair *looked* bobbed. "It's only camouflage.... I tuck it under!"[14]

The woman and the persona often intersected. "Are you a flapper?" Gordon Gassaway asked while interviewing Colleen — wondering, "if the F. Scott Fitzgerald influence had penetrated to the homes of our favorite"— and her reply was: "Well, I don't roll my stockies, I don't swear — much, I do not smoke cigarettes or a pipe or anything. I don't drink cocktails, and you know that mother won't let me bob my hair, so I guess I don't qualify."[15] Though she was a modern woman, she valued family and old-fashioned values. She recognized the characters she depicted on the screen and the "Colleen Moore" persona she projected to the world as distinct from herself, but often the character and the woman shared the same qualities. The Colleen Moore flapper, when it came into being, would be quite a different creature from all her sisters.

Her next scheduled film for Goldwyn was exactly the type of role with which she was most associated, the story coming from November's scenario contest. The selection of the final batch of stories had involved spirited discussion and debate between judges "scattered in various parts of the country.... Right up to the last day the matter of the first prize was in doubt, but in the final voting the $10,000 check went to Miss Lavina Henry, nom de plume for Miss Winifred Westover, of Appalachia."[16] The winning story was entitled *Broken Chains*.

It would be an elaborate production. "The preliminary work has begun. Carey Wilson has been assigned as supervising editor."[17] Allen Holubar was brought in from Associated First National for the project.[18] Colleen was selected to portray the heroine, the very first cast member chosen.[19] She had been out of town when the selection was made.

After *The Bitterness of Sweets*, Colleen had disappeared to Soboba Hot Springs. While hiking she encountered a rattlesnake. Fortunately a young man escorting Miss Moore killed the reptile." When the announcement of her selection for *Broken Chains* was made in *Motion Picture News*, a photograph accompanied the article. It was a portrait of Colleen in a backlit portrait with an uncharacteristically sophisticated gown and hairdo. Her expression was very serious, projecting a new and more sophisticated image.[20] The photograph might have been part of her attempt to recast Colleen Moore in a new light, and to expand her horizons.

Unfortunately her more modern appearance in public was not finding its way into her film roles. Perceptions were slow to change. Facing another damsel-in-distress role and knowing she had until the 20th to prepare for *Broken Chains*, she signed on for another film that had a more modern theme.

Colleen in a scene from *Affinities*, Ward Lascelle Productions, 1922 (courtesy Judy Coleman).

Affinities, *June–July 1922*

The film would be squeezed into her schedule before *Broken Chains*. It had the provocative title of *Affinities*, a Ward Lascelle film that would be lighter fare than Colleen's last few roles, with a more daring subject: "There won't be a dull moment over at the Ince Studios in Culver City if Ward Lescalle has anything to say

18. The Bitterness of Sweets (Look Your Best), *March–May 1922*

about it…. Initial scenes were shot yesterday on location at Balboa. Sets are being built at Ince Studios for the interiors, which will be made next week."[21] The movie came from a short story by Mary Roberts Rinehart. Told from the point of view of a young woman named Fanny, it took a look through her eyes at relationships between men and women and husbands and wives. Ferd was chummy with Fanny: "He never made love to me or anything like that, but he understood me thoroughly…. It is absurd, now that it's all over, to have the others saying he was my affinity or anything of the sort. I never cared for him."[22]

Once again Colleen was teamed with John Bowers from *The Sky Pilot*, and the story mirrors *So Long Letty* insofar as there is a theme of wife swapping. Colleen plays the part of Fanny Ilington, the wife of Day Ilington (Bowers), an avid golfer who spends much of his free time at his golf club. Fanny feels neglected by her husband. At the same time Ferd Jackson (Joe Bonner) feels neglected by his wife. Both Fanny and Ferd commiserate with each other and so, in a fit of boredom, they go to an "affinity" party.[23] In the end, Fanny discovers her husband secretly feeling neglected, attending an affinity party of his own with Ferd's wife. They reconcile, and all is forgiven. While the action in the film is played for laughs, there is still the undercurrent in the story of easy temptation. A modern part, with a modern subject, exactly the sort of role Colleen would need if she was to change her public perception.

Portrait of Colleen, ca. 1922.

The work on the film went quickly, the photography being finished in about a month. "The negative is in the Ince Laboratory for autumn release."[24] The film was quickly assembled and headed for the screen. "The Symphony Theater is dolling all up" in preparation for the film, Grace Kingsley reported. "A new orchestra is being installed, and a dance prologue will be a feature of the program."[25] In spite of the preparations, not everyone was impressed by the result: "The picture is not expertly made; the early scenes are rather shoddily photographed, but the wife's dash for home in a 'borrowed' auto is throughout filled with bright touches of humor…. Colleen Moore is in the picture, and while her character is not typically sympathetic, her doing of it is very pepful, which evens the score."[26] The writing, in the form of the intertitles, brightened the picture: "Those subtitles! They are a string of sparklers in themselves." For example: "A woman always rehearses a quarrel with her husband, that's why she usually wins." Another reads: "It's no fun being affinities if we're going to quarrel just like married folks." Comment was made of Colleen's versatility in the role; how well suited for it she seemed in spite of her persona: "That astonishingly versatile young actress Colleen Moore, again makes you feel as though nobody else could possibly have played that young wife except herself."[27]

Broken Chains, *June–August 1922*

In his "Interview in Verse" in the *Los Angeles Times*, Hallett Abend asked Colleen about her roles of the past and where she saw her career going. Her answers as reported, put into poetic verse by the author, reveals her hopes for her part in *Broken Chains*:

> "I queried when
> She will abandon cutie parts; if then
> Her youthful mannerisms will be cast
> Aside with all those tricks that in the past
> Have helped to stardom. "Soon, I hope," she said
> And as she spoke she raised her head
> Almost defiantly it seemed to me
> "You see, I hope to do
> Some work that's fine and true.
> I've tried being Irish and Italian,
> A proper miss, a tomboy ruffian.
> In *Broken Chains*, with Alan Holubar
> Directing (my next part) I travel far.
> And play a wife's part. I've a child, as well,
> In this new play. I hope — but you can't tell."[28]

"There was some hesitation," it was written, "about giving Colleen the lead in the picture because her role to date has been comedy-drama, and *Broken Chains* is powerful. But those who know Miss Moore argued she was neither a tragedienne nor a comedienne, but an actress." Any misgivings aside, it was expected that this was the part that would "make" Colleen in Hollywood.[29]

Carey Wilson had become so interested in the basic story that he wanted to write the continuity himself to assure all the enthusiasm he felt for it made it into the final form. The film was planned to go into production around May 15,[30] but it would be June before photography began. A cast was chosen and locations were scouted in the wilds at Huntington Lake, and plans were made to shoot in the redwood forests of Santa Cruz.[31] "Santa Cruz, Calif., home of the giant redwood trees, deep gorges and magnificent scenery has been chosen ... for *Broken Chains*.... Allen Holubar director, Cedric Gibbons, art director, and other members of the studio staff have just returned south from Santa Cruz.... The first scenes, however, will be interiors and photographed at the studio, where several elaborate settings have built."[32]

Santa Cruz had been used for location work in the motion pictures for years. A frontier-style town had been built for motion pictures in the Boulder Creek area called Poverty Flats.[33] The outdoor set "is no ephemeral creation of the stage-carpenter, but a solid, log-built village of over two dozen dwellings, stores, offices and saloons — a typical mining camp set up for photoplay 'scenery' at a cost of a thousand dollars."[34]

In June, Malcolm McGregor was chosen for the part of the male lead.[35] Work commenced with shooting of interior scenes.[36] Once interiors were completed, the cast and crew went afield to work on the exteriors. While shooting in Santa Cruz, Holubar was assisted by Nat Salmon, with Byron Haskin in charge of photography.[37]

In the movie, the wealthy Peter Wyndham (Malcolm McGregor) is useless in attempting to prevent the theft of Hortense Allen's (Claire Windsor) jewelry during a home invasion

18. The Bitterness of Sweets (Look Your Best), *March–May 1922*

robbery. A butler attempts to intervene and is shot in the process. Unable to face his cowardice, Peter heads west for a job, working at one of his father's lumber mills. In the meantime Mercy Boone's (Colleen) newborn child has dies, devastating the young mother. Boyan Boone (Ernest Torrence), her husband, is callous towards her loss, the child nothing more than a nuisance. He is the local thug, and works with a band of ne'er-do-wells. When Mercy attempts to escape her husband, he meets Peter briefly at the station, but Boyan returns her to his cabin where he chains her up. Peter finds her and unlocks her chain, and they begin a stealthy romance, their time together limited by the alarm clock kept within earshot that calls Mercy back to her chains before Boyan can learn that she is enjoying a degree of freedom. He does learn, however, and proceeds to beat up Peter. Peter, in time, has to summon the strength and bravery to fight him for the honor and freedom of his beloved.

> Miss Moore was asked how she made such a difficult role as was assigned her in this picture appear so thoroughly convincing and natural.
>
> "That," was her reply, "is indeed a compliment. There is a technique about everything that is done on the screen, and the highest form of technique is to make the audience forget that there is any technique at all."
>
> "One never learns all there is to be known of technique.... I am still learning, I know, and expect to keep on learning until I retire. I believe I am learning faster, too, than I ever did before, and in this belief I find true reason for happiness and optimism."
>
> "Crying for me was always easy. For some it is very, very hard. Probably the things that are hard for me are easy for others — that is merely the difference between different people."[38]

Photography was done by mid–August and Holubar went into the editing room.[39] With the end of her work on *Broken Chains* came the end of her contract with Goldwyn.

19

Forsaking All Others, September–October 1922

"Forsaking All Others" was a short story by Mary Lerner that had been published in *Collier's Weekly*.[1] Touching on the subjects of youth and temptation, it was a natural for adaptation to the screen. "*Forsaking All Others* ... will be made an all-star [Universal] Jewel production, to be directed by Emile Chautard. Colleen Moore has been engaged for the lead, while other roles are being cast, gradually."[2] Emile Chautard was a French film director, actor and screenwriter who had come to America to work at the Éclair American motion picture company at Fort Lee, New Jersey. Fire had destroyed the Fort Lee facilities, so Chautard had moved on to other companies.[3]

Production on *Forsaking All Others* began in mid–September with Cullen Landis starring opposite Colleen.[4] Also among the cast was "June Elvidge, who used to be a star when vamps were popular."[5] The story was described as unusual in that there were no heavies or

Crew, musicians, Rupert Hughes (center, with cane) and Colleen in costume for *Look Your Best*, Goldwyn, 1923. Colleen holds her makeup kit in her lap (courtesy Judy Coleman).

19. Forsaking All Others, *September–October 1922*

villains in the traditional sense. "Although the two character roles, played by June Elvidge and David Torrence, function as the 'heavies' by guiding the action through mistakes and accidental interference."[6] The film was about Mrs. Newell (May Wallace), family matriarch and overprotective mother of Oliver (Cullen Landis). Convinced that Penelope Mason (Colleen) is not good enough for her son, she strives to keep them apart, finally managing her goal when she fakes a sickness and convinces her son to accompany her to a resort for her health. Oliver, however, turns his attentions towards a married woman, Enid Morton (June Elvidge). Her husband (David Torrence) is suspicious of what is going on between his wife and Oliver. When Mrs. Newell realizes her solution could result in scandal, she convinces Penelope to win her sweetheart back, which she does.

June Elvidge and David Torrence had to finish their parts quickly so that they could move on to their next project, *The Power of a Lie*.[7] A week after they finished, Chautard finished the rest of the photography.[8] Colleen scrambled to her next job. "Having just finished a series of pictures for Goldwyn, she is now moving her belongings to the Vitagraph studios, where she will be starred in *The Ninety and Nine*. Miss Moore will have as her leading man Warner Baxter. Vitagraph is planning to make *Ninety and Nine* a big special and extra attraction."[9]

The Ninety and Nine was an interesting choice to follow up *Forsaking All Others*: it would be an old-fashioned drama to follow a fast, modern story.[10] *The Ninety and Nine* was a morality tale based on a Bible hymn. They couldn't be more different. In one interview, when Colleen was asked if she was a flapper, she opined that she thought she did not qualify: she was not vulgar enough; she did not have the vices; and her mother would not approve. She was, at heart, a good girl. In another, printed in the appropriately titled periodical *The Flapper*, she would embrace the flapper ethic:

> "Why," said Colleen.... "Why, I'm a flapper myself!" Colleen is twenty-one, correct flapper age, at any rate — but somehow, until she mentioned it, I really hadn't cataloged her as precisely that.
>
> "A flapper," Colleen went on, with wisdom, "is just a little girl trying to grow up — in the process of growing up.
>
> "She wears flapper clothes out of a sense of mischief — because thinks them rather 'smart' and naughty. And what everyday, healthy, normal little girl doesn't sort of like to be smart and naughty?
>
> "Little Lady Flapper is really old-fashioned; but in her efforts not to let anyone discover that her true ideal is love-in-a-cottage, she 'flaps' in the most desperately modern manner.
>
> "Left to her own devices she would probably dance and flirt just as girls have always done — but honest, I don't think she'd wear her skirts so short!
>
> "She likes her freedom, and she likes to be a bit daring, and snap her cunning, little manicured fingers in the face of the world; but fundamentally she is the same sort of girl as grandmamma was when she was young.
>
> "The chief difference is that she has more ambition, and there are more things for her to wish for, and a greater chance of getting them.
>
> "She demands more of men because she knows more about their work.
>
> "She uses lipstick and powder and rouge because, like every small girl, she apes her elders.
>
> "She knows more of life then than her mother did at the same age because she sees more of it.
>
> "She knows what she wants and what she is what she is doing, all of the time — and she meets life with a small and an eager, ardent hope. She's a trim little craft and brave!
>
> "The flapper has charm, good looks, good clothes, intellect and a healthy point of view. I'm proud to 'flap'— I am!"[11]

It was an analysis of the flapper that was optimistic. In Colleen's view, the flapper was just a phase, the same stage girls of all previous generations went through, only informed by a modern world that moved faster than it had in the past. The new generation had borne witness to the horrors of modern war — mechanized war machines, chemical weapons of mass destruction, pointless death in trenches for a few dozen yards of territory — and found the old ideals left a spiritual gap in their lives. They lacked the certainty of earlier generations, and so they rebelled.

Colleen's view of the flapper, as expressed in that interview, presented a middle-of-the-road perception, one that had not quite taken hold in the popular imagination yet. Sometimes change is slow.

First National, 1922

Sometimes change is abrupt. In June, Richard A. Rowland had been brought over to the First National organization.[12] They had been having problems keeping up with the demand for quality franchise films. While it had been intended that each First National subfranchise holder had to take the motion pictures First National distributed under its franchise, there were pictures that were excluded from this arrangement and distributed on what was called the "open market plan," whereby the picture was first offered to the subfranchise holder. If the holder did not wish to contract for it, the company was free to sell it to another customer. Through this arrangement the company ended up selling franchise pictures to franchise and nonfranchise holders, expanding the number of "open market" pictures.

Several large producers releasing their films through First National did not like the idea of selling their pictures under franchise, preferring the open market plan. They felt their films were being used to help sell cheaper films, and thought the exhibition rate assigned to their films was inequitable. Most producers suspected the others had gotten better deals. Jealousies arose,[13] and films were increasingly sold in the open market plan, which, in turn, resulted in the difficulty of securing enough films for the franchise plans. This led to the push to get into the actual production of films, in addition to their distribution.[14]

By mid–1922, it was known that First National would move towards producing films, rather than simply distributing them. Grace Kingsley had reported on a committee appointed by First National to explore the issue, as announced by Sol Lesser, consisting of Richard A. Rowland, J.D. Williams and C.L. Yearsley. Their charge was to "select, consider and recommend to First National for production, stories, books, stage plays as well as artists and directors."[15] Before long, however, the company had drifted towards the notion of actual film production; it was a move resisted by J.D. Williams, one of the founders of First National:

> J.D. Williams ... has presented his resignation to the directors in session here [New York], says Louella Parsons in the *Morning Telegraph*. His resignation has been accepted and Richard A. Rowland, who has been associated with Harry O. Schwalbe for six months, has been appointed to the position left vacant by Mr. Williams.[16]

J.D. Williams had started First National with Thomas L. Tally and had been an advocate of keeping out of film production. With his resignation, it was evident that views had shifted.

The Ninety and Nine, *October–November 1922*

> I say unto you, that likewise joy shall be in heaven over one sinner that repenteth, more than over ninety and nine just persons, which need no repentance — Luke 15:7, *King James Bible*

The American Vitagraph Company had not been having a good year. An influenza outbreak had hit the studio hard: "About 60 percent of the employees are on the sick list."[17] It had been an important studio in the years before the First World War, one of the original ten companies in Edison's Motion Picture Patents Company and one of the first American companies to set up distributorships in Europe, but its fortunes had dwindled. With the disruption of the war, they lost foreign distributors. It had embraced big pictures, and the productions of its biggest star, Larry Semon, were getting bigger all the time.[18] By the end of the year, W.S. Smith, the organization's vice-president and treasurer, would announce that the studio was concentrating on large specials. Those productions would be under the direction of David Smith.[19]

Before then, David Smith would first direct *The Ninety and Nine*. In looking for good material, Vitagraph went back into their archives. They had made a version of *The Ninety and Nine* in 1916, a Vitagraph Blue Ribbon Feature. The 1916 production had been adapted from a 1902 stage play by Ramsay Morris. The play had been based on the hymn *The Ninety and Nine*,[20] which had been, in its own turn, inspired by Luke 15:7. The play concerned the redemption of a fallen man (the single sheep, "Far off from the gates of gold") while the rest of the town stood idly by (the other ninety-nine "that safely lay/In the shelter of the fold").

A feature of the play had been a mechanical effect to create illusion of a locomotive for the audience.[21] The play was about the refugees of a forest fire huddling in the momentary safety of a railway station. They await a rescue train, but there is none in sight. Only Tom Silverton knows how to operate a locomotive, though he is the town drunkard. With the encouragement of his sweetheart, Ruth, he manages to summon the courage to rescue the town. For the 1922 motion picture, the story would acquire new complications.

The casting was completed in early October, and hundreds of potential cast members were auditioned to find the perfect players.[22] Among those chosen were Colleen, Gertrude Astor, Warner Baxter and Aggie Herring.[23]

In keeping with Vitagraph's policy of elaborate productions, Smith would make *The Ninety and Nine* on a big scale, with an eye towards realism, knowing that his audience would notice any attempt to skimp on production values. "So keen is the desire of David Smith ... that his pictures be studies in realism that it has been suggested that he be rechristened 'Realistic' Smith.... [He] spares no expense in making his pictures, because he realizes the public is now so discriminative that faked shots, double exposures or double prints are easily detected."[24]

In Smith's version of the motion picture, Tom Silverton was given a back-story. He was a wrongly accused man, only momentarily slipped from the path of righteousness. He begins the film as Phil Bradbury (Warner Baxter), who is engaged to society girl Kate Van Dyke (Gertrude Astor). However, Kate falls in love with Mark Leveridge (Lloyd Whitlock). When there is a murder in the Van Dyke home, Bradbury is the primary suspect. He leaves before he can be arrested and heads for the out-of-the way town of Marlow where he takes the name Tom Silverton. Living under his new identity, he appears to be a simple drunkard to the rest of the townsfolk, but Ruth Blake (Colleen) tries to sober him up, and for her efforts and concern she is ostracized by the rest of the town. Even her father disowns her, leaving her mother, Tom and the village half-wit as her only friends. When Kate and Mark come to town, they spot him, but before he can make his escape a forest fire erupts and surrounds the town. The stationmaster refuses to allow the only locomotive to carry the townsfolk away, as he believes it would be suicide. Tom, however, knows how to operate a locomotive, but if he displays his skills by undertaking the job of rescuing the town it will reveal his identity to the detectives who are looking for him. He chooses to operate the locomotive and pilots the train and townsfolk out of the danger of the raging fire, and in the end he is exonerated of the crimes he was falsely accused of committing and is able to settle down with Ruth.[25]

Many extravagant scenes were shot for the film: "The big thrill is the rescue of an entire countryside from the fury of the flames, as the forest fire races towards the surrounded town."[26] While working on preliminary scenes in the forests surrounding the mountains of the Sawtooth Range in Idaho, a real fire had erupted in the upper slopes. The locals knew that David Smith, with his large troupe of extras and firefighting equipment, would prove invaluable in helping extinguish the fire. Never one to miss a unique opportunity, Smith and his cameraman, Steve Smith, Jr., worked their way up the mountainside to shoot as much of the conflagration as they could. The blaze was quickly contained thanks to the surplus of available people to fight it, and the material shot at the site of the fire was worked into the film.[27]

By November, photography had been completed for the film: "Director David Smith has completed and turned in for revision the first of Vitagraph's big, twelve special productions, *The Ninety and Nine*." Completion of the film did not mean Colleen would have much of a rest. In November she moved on to her next production: "Colleen Moore would have to be twins to keep any busier or to accept all the parts offered her. She completed *The Ninety and Nine* for Vitagraph, under direction of David Smith, one day recently and the next day reported for the leading role of *The Nth Commandment*, the Fannie Hurst story which Frank Borzage is directing for Cosmopolitan. They're working at the Ince studios."[28]

In December, the films *Forsaking All Others*, *The Ninety and Nine*, and *Broken Chains* were released a week apart each ... on the 10th, the 17th, and the 24th. They were produced (respectively) by Universal, Vitagraph, and Goldwyn Pictures. *The Ninety and Nine*, had been turned around after less than a month of editing and post-production. Reviews of Colleen in the film were good, though *The Ninety and Nine* seemed to be the product of a different era: "Colleen Moore is engaging but acting the part was quite evidently a strain."[29]

Colleen's career had failed to gain traction. After five years in the business, she had hoped to be a star.

20

The Nth Commandment, November–December 1922

By November, it was known that Colleen's next film would be *The Nth Commandment*,[1] a Cosmopolitan Production. William Randolph Hearst created Cosmopolitan Pictures with Adolph Zukor in March 1919. Paramount distributed the films Cosmopolitan produced, and through Cosmopolitan Zukor had access to film rights to stories that appeared in Hearst's magazines. Colleen's uncle Walter Howey had worked for Hearst and was his friend. That connection helped her land a part in the film. She contracted to make two films with Cosmopolitan, *The Nth Commandment* and *The Daughter of Mother McGinn*.

Colleen returned to Culver City to work at the Ince Studios on *The Nth Commandment*. "Frank Borzage is at work on *The Nth Commandment*, from the story by Fannie Hurst."[2] For this film Colleen would have a costar with a familiar last name: "Colleen Moore and James Morrison head this cast."[3] A report circulated that Colleen and Morrison were related: "Colleen Moore and James Morrison discovered while working in *The Nth Commandment* that they are distantly related. Their fore-fathers hailed from County Down, Ireland."[4]

As production was getting underway, two of Colleen's previous films were receiving finishing touches. "Avery Hopwood, playwright, has written the titles for the First National release, *Slippy McGee*, produced by Oliver Morosco." It would be a December release.[5] Rupert Hughes's film *The Bitterness of Sweets* underwent a title change to *Look Your Best*.[6]

The sets for the film were elaborate, including the department store interior recreated on the stage down to the minutest accoutrements, and a supper club set designed by Stephen Goosson, built with a 60 foot dome that sported a large chandelier.[7] By December, the bulk of the photography had been completed.[8] "Frank Borzage is at present completing the last of his productions for the Cosmopolitan company, *The Nth Commandment*."[9]

Colleen in a scene near the end of *The Nth Commandment* (courtesy Judy Coleman).

Sarah Juke (Colleen) works as a department store counter girl and dresser in the unmentionables section of the Mammoth Department Store. Her sweetheart is Harry Smith (James Morrison) from the wrapping department. Harry wants to move up in the organization, but he is ill (the illness is never stated but is probably tuberculosis). Jimmy Fitzgibbons (Eddie Phillips) is attracted to Sarah and comes between Harry and Sarah on the night he intends to propose to her. As a result Harry and Sarah split. Jimmy takes Sarah to dinner at a Chinese restaurant, where Sarah's naiveté in the ways of the world are apparent. After a kiss, she assumes she and Jimmy are engaged. When Jimmy discovers that Harry is sick, he realizes Sarah might pass on the condition. Rejected by Jimmy, she returns to Harry. It is not a solid foundation for their marriage.

Sarah and Harry end up in a tenement apartment with a child. They want to move to California, but Harry has not moved out of the wrapping department due to his lingering ill health. Because of that, they cannot afford to relocate. On Christmas Eve a friend from the department store, Angie Sprint (Charlotte Merriam) appears on the scene with Jimmy in tow. Jimmy has become a successful Broadway songwriter. Sarah's embarrassment at her small abode is apparent. Jimmy apologizes for his behavior and they reconcile. Later, after Angie and Jimmy leave, Harry discovers that Jimmy was in the apartment. They argue and Sarah leaves to seek out the dazzle and excitement of Broadway.

While on the town with Jimmy, Sarah convinces him to buy her gifts. At a supper club, Jimmy dares her to dance for the crowd, and entices her with $100. She succumbs. Later, he dares her to climb into a fountain, offering her $200. Again, she submits. She says she will run away with him, but she needs to collect her things from her place. Jimmy takes her home, but she leaves him waiting on the doorstep with a taxi meter running. Upstairs, she places the gifts Jimmy enticed her with under the meager Christmas tree. Meanwhile, out on the street, Jimmy realizes she's given him the old heave-ho. He leaves.

When Harry wakes up, Sarah shows him the $300. It is enough to move. Near the brink of death, Harry seems to understand what she has done. The film ends with Colleen and her child in the doorway of a bungalow in the California sun. Interestingly, Harry is nowhere to be seen.

It was a risky film with risky subject matter for the time. Sarah runs off with a fast crowd to dupe Jimmy out of some loose cash for her husband. She sells herself to Jimmy with the promise that perhaps things will develop further between them. She sells her dancing to the crowd for money. The audience thinks she has succumbed to corruption until the very end. While she has rejected the lights and glamour and Jimmy, she still led him on. "It just don't seem fair for you to have to do it all for us," Harry tells her near the end, and she tells him everything's fair in love. By implication, she would be willing to do whatever circumstances required of her.

The moral ambiguity of the film's message aside, the early scenes presented the audience with a preview of a Colleen that would become prominent in the near future, insofar as she displays well-sharpened comic timing and facial expressions that would serve her well with First National. The Colleen Moore that would become world-famous was on display, waiting to be discovered.

First National

Richard Rowland replaced J.D. Williams and immediately made moves to change the business model for First National. "Mr. Rowland points out that Associated First National is, first of all, a distributing organization absolutely devoted to keeping the market open to the independent producers of motion pictures.... 'It is true that we may produce some pictures in accordance with certain ideas, formulated by our directors at the recent meeting, but such production will take the direction of assisting producers of promise to enter production rather than for our company to build up a vast organization and studios and itself become a big competitor in the production field.'"[10]

Eventually, Rowland said, First National would become a big competitor in the area of production, but at the moment they were staying small.

Early 1923

> I had no idea of originating an American flapper when I first began to write. I simply took girls whom I knew very well and, because they interested me as unique human beings, I used them for my heroines.
> —*F. Scott Fitzgerald in His Own Time: A Miscellany*,
> by Matthew Joseph Bruccoli and Jackson R. Bryer,
> Kent State University Press, 1971, page 265.

By the early 1920s anything a woman or man did that did not fall within the neat orthodoxy of acceptable behavior was deemed flapperish, and while deplored, modern youth was also viewed with fascination. Fitzgerald's *This Side of Paradise* had piqued the national curiosity towards modern youth. His 1922 *Tales of the Jazz Age*, with its cover by John Held, Jr., only whetted the appetite for more. Held's illustrations of coquettishly leggy women and ping-pong-ball-headed collegiate men helped define the look of the age, the confidence and sophistication of the new young set that was both worldly yet inexperienced.

The questioning of morality had become an overarching theme. *The Age of Innocence*, by Edith Wharton, was an examination of morals and assumptions of the upper-classes in New York in the 1870s. In Sinclair Lewis's satirical *Main Street*, the free-spirited female protagonist set about reforming the backwater small town of her husband, the inhabitants of which are depicted with vicious, sharp humor. D.H. Lawrence's *Women in Love* had attracted controversy for its sexual subject matter. Many books' authors were "devoting whole chapters to the 'flapper' and her masculine playmates.... All agreeing in the presentation, as a visible and audible part of 'society,' of young girls who ought to be in the Bedford Reformatory and of young men who not many years ago would have been soundly thrashed by the first father or brother who learned of their behavior. "If these pictures of 'high life' are accurate, the novelists, in painting them in full detail, are performing a duty, not committing the crimes charged against them."[11]

In January 1923 the publishing company of Boni & Liveright, at 61 West 48th Street, published *Flaming Youth*, by the mysterious "Warner Fabian," pen name for the author whom the publishers insisted was one of America's foremost literary voices. His or her identity was not released at the time of publication, which added to the cache of the book. In fact, it was a pseudonym for Samuel Hopkins Adams. Adams said he had based the book on the diaries of "a young friend." The story was told from the point of view of an older man, the family doctor, recording the events that whirl around a family after the death of the mother.

The Frentiss family lived an unorthodox lifestyle, not at all what the American public expected of the upper classes. There were parties and drinking and petting. Before she died, the mother kept a younger lover who would turn his attentions to Patricia, taking on the role of an older lover. The father has his own floozy. Patricia Frentiss, the youngest of the Frentiss daughters, was the center of the book. The book showed the younger generation not only doing all the horribly inappropriate things the public thought, but enjoying it.

It went through 16 printings in 1923 alone.[12] In March, First National snapped up the rights to *Flaming Youth*, the "celebrated Warner Fabian novel, which can be found in any 'Six Best Sellers' list" for $14,000.[13] "*Flaming Youth* ... in all probability will be filmed in time for release early next season."[14]

April Showers, *February–March 1923*

Originally entitled *Sunshine Alley*,[15] *April Showers* would bring Colleen to the Mayer-Schulberg Studio (formerly the Selig studio). The latest tenant was Schulberg, who had set up at the studio with Louis B. Mayer: "B.P. Schulberg has gathered around him a staff of experts for the making of Preferred Pictures that is not to be excelled in any studio.... Preparations of scenarios are under the supervision of Eve Unsell, one of the foremost screen writers in the industry.... According to a recent announcement made by Schulberg, Olga Printzlau ... has been engaged to write the script for *April Showers*, Tom Forman's[16] next production."[17]

Portrait of Colleen, ca. 1923.

In an announcement that certainly couldn't have thrilled Colleen, Schulberg declared an end to the "star system," and that he would sign no more big stars. "Featured players, yes, he says.... The best pictures are being made with players picked for the parts, instead of roles being suited to stars willy-nilly."[18] Photography on the film was underway in early February,[19] and it (as well as several other Preferred Pictures) had been booked by the Moss, Keith and Proctor theaters in New York City.[20]

The film was another Irish story. Following *The Nth Commandment*, a modern story, *April Showers* would be a more old-timey, romantic story. It was billed as having "the 'all-Irish-all-star' cast,[21] in which Danny O'Rourke (Kenneth Harlan) is the son of a police officer who was killed in the line of duty. Danny is eager to join the police force but he fails his exams, disappointing his mother (Myrtle Vane). The failure causes him to neglect his sweetheart, Maggie (Colleen), whose father (Tom McGuire) is a lieutenant on the police force. His attentions turn instead towards Miriam Welton (Ruth Clifford), a society girl who is doing settlement work. When Danny's sister, Shannon (Priscilla Bonner), is arrested for shoplifting, Danny has to turn to boxing to save her. He works his way up the ranks towards the championship, only to find out that the fight has been rigged. Danny fights anyhow and he is beaten, but it is discovered that a mistake had been made on his exams and he actually was eligible to join the police force after all.

The film had designs on being an "Irish *Humoresque*," hoping to connect itself indirectly to Frank Borzage's earlier and popular film, *Humoresque*, which had been equal parts soap opera and a depiction of the Jewish community of Manhattan's Lower East Side in the 1920s. To create an Irish atmosphere, Tom Forman "summoned for this preferred picture all the McGuires, O'Rourkes, O'Briens and Caseys on the books of all the agencies in Los Angeles to act as extras."[22]

To prepare for his boxing scenes, plans were made to recruit some of the best trainers available for Kenneth Harlan.[23] "Johnny Wilson,[24] middleweight champion of the world, probably will fight his next ring battle exclusively for the camera. His antagonist, according to present plans, will be none other than Kenneth Harlan, idol of the feminine theatergoer." Harlan was training with "Kid" McCoy[25] and "Doc" Leach Cross,[26] who had "groomed six pounds" off the actor already.[27] McCoy was of the opinion that working in films was a more satisfying use of his talents than either of the two activities he'd engaged in recently — pugilistic and domestic battles.[28]

The boxing scenes were among the last to be shot, with the climactic moments scheduled to be filmed during the first week of March. "The final scenes, which take place in a prizefight arena ... which those who have been watching the rushes declare to be the best of Forman's directorial career."[29] About the time work on the film ended for Colleen, she had some fun with her brother. Diving into the cold water at the Crystal Pier on March 11, Colleen won a bet with Cleeve; he wagered her three theater tickets to a pair of gold stockings that she wouldn't dare jump in. She did, and she won.[30] Tom Forman was still at work editing the film.[31]

Broken Hearts of Broadway, *June 1923*

"Colleen Moore has completed *April Showers*, which she says will be her last film engagement before her marriage to John McCormick."[32] Though Colleen looked forward to wedded life she was still dissatisfied with her career. Her attempts to make herself over in a more modern style had not paid off. For Colleen the change in look and style, from long hair to short and new ritzy outfits, was in part a bid to show she was capable of breaking out of type. Doubtless, John had his hand in the re-engineering of his fiancée's image. He was aware that public perception of an actor had as much to do with casting as anything. People still looked at Colleen as the melodramatic actress with the potential for light comedy, but nothing truly earth-shaking. She had had successes, even great successes, but the breakout role she needed had eluded her.

With a few months to go before her wedding, Colleen took another role, this time with Irving Cummings Productions, for whom she was to play the part of Mary Ellis in

Broken Hearts of Broadway, a story about a small-town girl who comes to New York to make it big on the Great White Way. Her story, told in flashback—by a cab driver (Tully Marshall) to Creighton Hale and Kate Price—was part melodrama and part murder-mystery. Mary Ellis shows up in town and lands a spot with a chorus line, befriending Bubbles Revere (Alice Lake) and neighbor George, a songwriter. Bubbles is a gold digger, happy to take advantage of a pair of amorous show owners, but Mary has started to fall for George and remains loyal to him. She rejects the advances of the show owner and swiftly finds herself without a job. George manages to come to the rescue. He secures her a job dancing and singing in a Chinese cabaret. One night after a fight with an audience member, Mary is falsely accused of the murder. George straightens things out, and afterwards writes a production based on the events that befell Mary. He then casts her as the star, and the show is a hit, making Mary as famous as she had hoped to be.

It was a light story with Colleen doing little aside from projecting her own lovable persona for the audience. She played the piano a bit, danced a few steps, wore a few costumes, but did little else. Even so, it was a different sort of part for her, and these story of an actress who found fame had its appeal for Colleen.

The film was released in the middle of the year after the writer of the original play gave his stamp of approval. "James Kyle MacCurdy, well-known New York playwright, is in Los Angeles to approve the completed production of *Broken Hearts of Broadway* made by Irving Cummings from an adaptation by Hope Loring and Louis D. Lighton of Mac-Curdy's stage play of the same name."[33]

One night, John knocked on Colleen's door. Agnes answered and saw that he looked antsy, like a man with a secret. He needed to talk to Colleen first before he could tell anyone else his secret. She accompanied him outside to his car and they drove around the block. First National, he told her, had decided to get into production of motion pictures. The board of directors had decided to sign up eight young actors with star potential. It could be her big chance; he told Colleen he was going to campaign to get her signed as one of the eight.

His campaign started the next day, using a variety of clever stunts to bring Colleen's name to the attention of each member of the board.[34] They told him the decision had already been made to sign her.

Colleen laid out some specific conditions for her contract, relayed to Richard Rowland by Earl Hudson via telegram on April 5:

> Transportation hotel meals while on location for self and chaperone who is her mother all personal appearances by mutual agreement stop no member of cast to be filled in type larger than used for her name stop she be mentioned first in every cast or reference in advertising publicity to cast for her picture stop she to provide three changes wardrobe each production including one evening gown Gems [First National] provide wardrobe requirements beyond this point and all wardrobe in costume pictures stop she to be given only leading parts no second leads or bits stop Gems has right to story selections stop Gems has right to lend her other productions but only for leading parts and not at less than she received from us under contract and furthermore with provision that she receive fifty percent of difference between amounts gems pays her under contract and amounts received her services other producers....

Right from the start Colleen was letting the studio know she was to have leading roles, and nobody else in the production was going to have their name in larger-sized type then hers in any advertising. She would have her say in what personal appearances she was going to make and would not be lent out to other studios for anything less than leading parts. She knew her potential value to the studio and was laying down the law. Earl Hudson recognized this:

> I believe we should begin starring her after *Flaming Youth* and perhaps one more picture consequently these conditions seem fair stop suggest contract become effective May first or immediately completion her present picture after that date but not later than May fifteenth please advise me whether these conditions satisfactory

Richard Rowland agreed with Earl's assessment and passed down word that she should be signed, laying out the terms of her contract:

> Kindly draw up a contract immediately between this company and Colleen Moore for her to appear in productions to be made by us, and also the right to farm her out to our producers or outside companies as long as we farm her out to productions of highclass, and on the standard with her usual line of productions and befitting her position as an artist.
>
> The contract is for a period of three years. We are paying her $800, guaranteeing fifty weeks for the first year, an option of $1200, guaranteeing fifty weeks the second year, and an option of $1700, guaranteeing fifty weeks the third year.
>
> Kindly get this contract out as early as possible. In the mean time I have advised McCormick to consider the matter closed.[35]

"Colleen Signs on the Dotted Line," proclaimed *First National Franchise*, the house magazine for the company. Pictured with her was John with Richard Walton Tully and Earl J. Hudson.[36] The *Los Angeles Times* noted "Miss Moore's first appearance is scheduled for the title role of *The Huntress*, which is to be directed by Lynn Reynolds and which will go into production on the 15th." Her second film would be the highly anticipated *Flaming Youth*, to be directed by John F. Dillon.[37] Dillon was paid $10,000 to rewrite the story and to direct the picture.[38]

First National had also purchased rights to another controversial book, *Black Oxen*.

Colleen's roles would be starring roles, just what she was looking for. John also moved up in the organization, signing a new contract that made him assistant to First National's production supervisor, Earl Hudson, earning $750 a week.

The Daughter of Mother McGinn (Through the Dark), May–July 1923

Colleen had a second film to finish for Cosmopolitan Productions before she could go to work for First National. *The Daughter of Mother McGinn* was based on one of the Boston Blackie stories. "Boston Blackie" had originally been a character in short stories by Jack Boyle. The various stories had been collected into the 1919 book, *Boston Blackie*. He was a safecracker and jewel thief in his original incarnation, a hardened criminal. Work on *The Daughter of Mother McGinn* began in May.[39]

Boston Blackie (Forrest Stanley) has just escaped from San Quentin and is headed for Mother McGinn's (Margaret Seddon) house, which she runs as a refuge for criminals. Along the way he saves her daughter, Mary McGinn (Colleen) from a runaway horse. Mother

McGinn has been running a boarding house so that she could afford to send Mary to an expensive private school. Having been saved by Blackie, Mary decides to return the favor by, helping him evade the police and delivering him to Mother McGinn. Mary discovers through Blackie that her father, now dead, had been an inmate with Blackie in San Quentin. When detectives reveal her background to Mary's school, she is expelled.

Mary falls in love with Blackie and tries to reform him, joining his gang in an act that dramatizes the consequences of his deeds. With Mary's encouragement, Blackie chooses to return to jail and complete his sentence so that when he is released there will be nothing to interfere with their marriage.

It took about a month to shoot the film, including portions that were shot on location in San Francisco. It completed Colleen's commitment to Cosmopolitan, but didn't quite free her from the production of the film. There had been problems resulting in re-shoots, and perhaps a change in director.[40] "In making added scenes for the Cosmopolitan Production, *Daughter of Mother McGinn*, at the Hollywood studios, Director Paul Powell is up against a real problem. All of his principals, including Colleen Moore ... are working in other productions and Powell has to do his shooting nights — not night, but on those rare occasions when he can get all of his cast together at the same time."[41]

In mid–October, it was reported that work had, at last, been completed on the film.[42] A month after that would come news that the film had been shipped off to New York and was in the process of editing.[43]

Colleen went to work on *The Huntress*. Without a studio of its own, First National leased space on the United studio lot. "Probably no other motion picture studio will present more activity this summer than that scheduled at the United Studios. Eleven production

Colleen as Mary McGinn, and Forrest Stanley as Boston Blackie in *Through the Dark*, directed by George Hill, Cosmopolitan Productions, 1924 (courtesy Judy Coleman).

20. The Nth Commandment, *November–December 1922*

companies are making their headquarters there.... First National alone is placing five companies on work at the United."[44]

It was at about the start of production on *The Huntress* that John disappeared for the first time.[45] Colleen went into a panic. She called his friend, George Landry,[46] who told her not to do a thing. "I know where he is, and he's okay."

Since George would tell her nothing more, Colleen hung up and waited.[47]

Two days later John reappeared with a couple days' growth of beard, bloodshot eyes and shaking with delirium tremens. The sight of him frightened Colleen. There had never been any drinking in Colleen's family. She had no experience with weekend benders or hangovers. The drinkers she knew like Marshall Neilan never looked as bad as John did at that moment.

Colleen in a publicity portrait, wearing her disguise to join Blackie's gang in *Through the Dark*, Cosmopolitan Productions, 1924.

Agnes seemed to have been expecting him. She sent John to the Athletic Club (where he had been living), telling him not to come back until he had straightened himself out. When he was gone, she sat Colleen down for a talk. She had been hearing stories that John was an occasional but heavy drinker, and told Colleen that perhaps it would be a good idea to put off the engagement. Marrying John meant marrying his faults, and being a drunkard was a difficult fault to live with.[48]

John's plight awakened Colleen's protective side. She wanted to help him, and together they could defeat it.

When John returned to the house that evening, he was cleaned up, shaved, hair slicked back. When he asked to speak to his fiancée alone, her family gave them the privacy he wanted. In the living room there was a fire in the fireplace, and they sat in front of it. John stuck a poker in the fire. When Colleen asked what had happened, he had no answer. John did not understand it himself. When she asked why he had been drinking, he told her that their marriage, only a few months away, seemed too far off to stand.

Her mother, Colleen told him, wanted her to break off the engagement.

He drank, he told her, because he was not sure if she loved him. Jealousy or insecurity. Colleen assured him that she *did* love him. John withdrew the poker from the fire, pulled up his sleeve and laid it to the skin of his arm, burning himself.

Colleen screamed.

After a moment he told her: "This is to remind me, every time I look at this scar, how close I came to losing the only thing that matters in my life — you."

It would not happen again, he told her. She believed him, and the engagement would remain on schedule.

21

The Huntress, May–July 1923

The Huntress was a mix of romance, comedy and western. Colleen was to play Bela, a white girl raised among Indians, determined that she will find a white husband and physically hunt him down. Bela was a flapper in buckskins.

Once the director, Lynn F. Reynolds, had selected all the exteriors,[1] work on *The Huntress* began at the United studio lot,[2] a sprawling plant with five closed stages and an exterior lot with street sets. At about 40 acres overall, many individual companies worked there.[3] The interior scenes were shot first and the cast and crew departed for location work. At Convict Lake, crews had built outdoor sets in mid–May so that all would be in readiness at their arrival.[4] From the lake the cast and crew traveled to Bishop[5] for two weeks of shooting.[6]

June and July are warm months on the valley floor, but the higher one travels in altitude, the colder it becomes, with a 3.6 degree drop per every thousand foot rise in elevation. Often at the higher elevations, even in the summer, the temperatures can dip very low.[7] Colleen described the temperatures not only as cold, but freezing.[8] The *Inyo County Register* bears out this claim, noting: "The weather in the mountains has been disagreeable and delayed the production work."[9] The cast and crew lived in a summer camp unsuited to the low temperatures. Pine log cabins with inch-wide gaps between the logs could not keep out the cold. Smoky oil lamps and small wood-burning stoves provided insufficient heat.[10] Colleen had to travel miles to a hot spring to take a bath. The Keough natural hot springs were eight miles out of town and very likely where the troupe went.[11]

Colleen's cabin had a small stove, and the prop man would have to build a fire in it for water, and for Colleen to unfreeze her makeup. The food was horrible and Colleen survived on raw eggs and crackers, but it was all very exciting.[12] The locations were beautiful. "They had to shovel their way into Twin Lakes as the snow had not left sufficiently to open the road." From there they moved to Silver Lake, where they were working in mid–June.[13]

The production was being shot on land of the

Colleen in a publicity portrait from *The Huntress,* First National, 1923 (courtesy Judy Coleman).

120

local Native Americans — Bishop Paiutes — with many of the locals working as extras, dressed as motion picture Indians and getting paid $6. One day the townsfolk in Bishop were treated to a surprise: "Residents of Bishop, California, had visions of Piute Indians last week when 35 braves, in war paint, descended on the peaceful town." At first the sight seemed a curiosity. "Then when they headed for the First National Bank, the fears grew to intensity. 'The Indians have turned bank robbers,' thought the citizens.

"But they were all wrong.... They had come there to cash their salary checks which they had received for playing parts on *The Huntress*, a First National picture starring Colleen Moore, now being taken in the Sierras, a few miles from Bishop."[14]

Snitz Edwards, who played the character of Musq'oosis, Bela's friend in the film, gave the local Indians a barbecue, and milk was furnished to the children by the company. Colleen learned from Big Tree, who played a part in the film, how to say, "I do not want a husband" in the Iroquois language. "Nita wha gam juh!"[15]

Flaming Youth, *July–September 1923*

With the end of filming for *The Huntress*, Colleen went straight to work on *Flaming Youth*. It would be a controversial film. In the book *Flaming Youth*, the central character, Patricia Frentiss captured the reader's imagination. She was wild and reckless and her behavior mirrored that of the young women of the day. Translating her story into a motion picture would be tricky. Many subplots could not be touched, but the basic story of a young girl in danger of losing her innocence and her rescue at the last possible instant was a tried-and-true formula. An actress was needed who could embody girlish innocence and wonderment at the adult goings-on, and then become a girl who partakes of those goings-on. Colleen was the natural choice. She had been playing variations on the part for all of her career. She threw herself into the part.

Patricia was a modern woman, and modern women wore short, modern hair styles. So Colleen began her transformation with her hair. The story she told was that she and her mother — who was once reported saying Colleen would never be allowed to bob her hair — had chopped off her long hair in a fashion inspired by one of Colleen's China dolls. With that act, the famous Colleen Moore pageboy bob was born, launching countless bobs around the world.

The truth is a little more complicated. Colleen's hair was already getting short. She had admitted to wearing a faux bob hairstyle, with the bulk of her hair rolled up in back, under shorter cut hair. When she signed with First National, the role of Patricia Frentiss was in the contract. When she cut her hair, it was not a desperate act to get the part but to look right for the role. In fact, the July *Boston Traveler* had reported that Colleen had bobbed her hair earlier for comfort in *The Huntress*. That part required her to wear a wig with long braids.[16] For *Flaming Youth*, she cut it shorter still. It was not yet the Dutchboy bob for which Colleen would later become famous, but it was not very far in her future.

> This week saw the beginning of production of *Flaming Youth*, a photo play which promises to mark an epoch for its type.
> —"Work is begun on *Flaming Youth*," *Oakland Tribune*,
> August 12, 1923, page W-2.

Production started in July.[17] Elliott Dexter was reported to have a "prominent" role.[18] Myrtle Stedman was cast in the role of Mona, family matriarch.[19] Some society personalities were drafted into the production: "Mrs. Mary Louise Hartje Woods, granddaughter of John L. Scott, will make her debut on the screen in *Flaming Youth*."[20] Even with production barely started, the film was already so famous that even society bigwigs wanted parts: "Another of society's favorites ... is Lady Bancroft, widow of the late Sir Stanley Bancroft.... Lady Bancroft, who chooses to be known as Patricia Prevoss on the screen, has the role of a dancer in *Flaming Youth*."[21]

There were beauty contests offering parts as prizes. The film promised more than its share of skin and sin and beauty: "Dorothy Dial of Dallas, Texas, who won a contest for having 'the most perfectly formed figure in the Southwest,' is one of the many Hollywood beauties who have parts in *Flaming Youth*."[22] Beauty contest winners from around the country flocked to the set for their moment of fame: "Miss Gladys DePoy, winner of a beauty contest in Logansport, Ind., has received a trip to California.... After two weeks Miss DePoy will go to the United studios to work in *Flaming Youth*."[23] They even came from overseas: "The latest contest winner to invade Pictureville is Doris Stone, the English girl who won the *London Daily Mirror* contest as the 'most petite girl in the British Isles'.... Miss Stone was engaged by First National soon after arriving on the coast and was given a part in *Flaming Youth*.'"[24]

Colleen and John McCormick getting their marriage license, August 17, 1923.

"Several score of Hollywood's prettiest girls ... have been given parts in *Flaming Youth*." They would be in ballroom and pool scenes.[25] Even Colleen's brother, Cleeve, was cast as a swimmer in the pool scene, his diving skills put to use.

A few weeks prior to their wedding, John and Colleen motored west towards the beach, walking the last length to the shoreline.[26] John endowed Colleen with a nickname: Alanna.[27] Colleen was contented, looking forward to married life.

The next night John disappeared again. This time Colleen kept

Colleen applies makeup to her mother, Agnes, ca. 1923 (courtesy Judy Coleman).

the fact from her family and friends. When asked after John's whereabouts, she said he had gone north to visit his parents. He was gone three days, and when he returned he told her a yarn. He had fallen asleep on a yacht in San Pedro, where he and some friends had gone to take publicity stills. While asleep they set sail, and it had taken him that long to get

Carmelita Geraghty and Colleen, photographed by W.F. Seeley of L.A.

back. Colleen did not believe him—the story being "full of holes"—but she did not call him on it. She chalked it up to pre-wedding jitters.[28]

On August 17, Colleen and John obtained a marriage license at the courthouse. The wedding would be August 18, two years after their first meeting. As Western Representative for Associated First National Pictures, John was "one of the best known motion-picture executives on the west coast." The wedding was played up in the press for all it was worth, with the *Los Angeles Times* referring to it as the culmination of a "film idyll."[29] They were

Colleen and John McCormick, wedding photograph, 1923 (courtesy Joseph Yranski).

married at the Catholic Church in Beverly Hills, St. Thomas, in the sacristy, due to John's being an Episcopalian and Colleen a Catholic. The Reverend M.J. Mullin presided over the ceremony. Carmelita Geraghty was the maid of honor; Earl Hudson was the best man, and present as guests were Adela Rogers St. Johns and her husband, Ivan (head of *Photoplay*); McCormick's parents; Colleen's parents; Colleen's aunt and uncle Mr. and Mrs. Walter Mitchell; Earl Hudson's wife; Cleeve and Mary Kelly.[30]

"The wedding trip [for John and Colleen] has been postponed until after the completion of *The Swamp Angel*, in October, when the couple will go east to New York and other Atlantic Coast cities.... Mr. and Mrs. McCormick will be at home at 869 South Bronson Avenue, Los Angeles after September 1."[31] Before their move, Colleen and the family had been living at 1231 South Gramercy Place, having moved there from the Grand View Avenue home.[32]

That evening, at their wedding supper, John proposed a toast to Charles and Agnes. He downed his glass of champagne in one gulp. He chased it down with a second. Colleen thought it bad manners but said nothing. Retiring to a house rented for them by Colleen's mother, Colleen and John were greeted by a cook/housekeep with a bottle of champagne and two glasses. Colleen had a few sips. John polished off the bottle. The more he drank, the louder he became. His face became slack, and he announced to her that on their wedding night he was drunk. He cried and groveled, made a show of his regret, and then suddenly his mood shifted and he became a braggart.

Shocked, Colleen ran to her room and locked herself in. Later, when she ventured to look at him again, she found him sprawled out on the floor in his pajamas, out cold, a drained bottle of Scotch nearby.[33]

The next morning Colleen discovered John was missing. She returned to the studio, all smiles, and covered for John. Her story was that John had seen his parents to the train station.

The scene to be filmed that day was one where Patricia walks down the stairs of her home after a night's debauch. She would be shocked at the sight of the drunken human wreckage. Among them was Patricia's still-drunk father, working his way through a tune on the piano. She drew on personal experience for her reaction.

Later that day John arrived, all smiles, like nothing had happened. Colleen considered having the wedding annulled, but decided against it. She would give him another chance. When they arrived home, Colleen found that John had tied balloons to every table and chair with messages inked on them, declaring how sorry he was. She was delighted. When John came into the room, he told her he had considered shooting himself when he realized how he had jeopardized their marriage. He showed her a gun, and she screamed, seized it from his hand and threw it away. He then gave her a gold pendant with the words "Love Never Dies" engraved on it.[34]

Colleen in scene from *Flaming Youth*, the film that would finally bring her fame (courtesy Judy Coleman).

John had managed to work his way back into Colleen's good graces, and Colleen had managed to protect John from the consequences of his drinking. It was a pattern that would be repeated throughout their marriage.

The Huntress was released in August and the initial reviews were not kind. The *Los Angeles Times* reviewer had problems with the preview cut. Too many scenic shots ("which will draw a lot of delighted gasps from a lot of audiences, but which have no dramatic value in the picture whatsoever"), Lloyd Hughes's acting ("he overacts terrifically"), and bland titles spoiled the picture.

A scene the reviewer found touching was intended to be comedic: "Miss Moore blows upward a feather drooping into her eyes. But how she blows it! She does it in a way which eloquently shows what she could have done with the rest of the picture — had it been there to do."[35] Another reviewer, watching another preview, was not impressed with Colleen's characterization, though he allowed it was not her fault: "At no time is she Indian in character.... The fault is not so much Miss Moore's as it is Lynn Reynolds,' whose directorial craftsmanship is not up to his usual standard. Hence while *The Huntress* will make a passable program feature, it adds nothing to Colleen's screen prestige."[36]

The Huntress was just the appetizer. The main attraction would be *Flaming Youth*. The book, after its release, had been serialized in *Metropolitan Magazine*, increasing its exposure. The advertising for the film was linked to the fortunes of the book. Boni and Liverlight, the publishers of *Flaming Youth*, pushed the limits of what could be published. In an early and ingenious example of product placement, Colleen's character of Patricia in the film would be seen reading the book *Black Oxen*, simultaneously advertising the book and the upcoming movie. In the movie *Black Oxen*, Clara Bow reads *Flaming Youth*.

Sets for the film were closed to the public, the result of a bystander's exclamation while watching a dramatic scene being shot. "Lordy, ain't she lovely," exclaimed a "dear old lady from Council Bluffs," in voice that shattered the mood.[37] The closed set only piqued the public's curiosity.

Colleen and John McCormick, 1923.

Work on the film ended in late August, with a break of about two weeks between *Flaming Youth* and her next film, *The Swamp Angel*. During their brief respite, Colleen and John took a trip to the Grand Canyon with Richard A. Rowland and Sam Katz, who were headed back to New York from Los Angeles,[38] with plans for the real honeymoon on hold.[39] For Colleen, vacations meant more work: promotional work, publicity photographs, and all the things necessary to make sure she was in the public eye.

There was a stop in San Francisco, where Colleen was escorted by Mayor James "Sunny Jim" Rolph. "San Francisco turned out riotously for the famous girl." At the train station she was whisked through crowds behind a phalanx of motorcycle police to the mayor's office. She was a guest of honor at a banquet of the Ninety-First Veterans. Dressed in a tailored uniform that sported major's insignia, she presented Colors to the Division and "captured the outfit single-hearted."[40]

Colleen's next role would be one to which she could relate. "The active girl — the athletic girl — the war heroine — the flapper — the queens and romantic figures of the past.... All have had their day on the screen. But one has been neglected — the 'tom boy' of the street. But this type is now to be immortalized and the task has been placed on the shoulders of Colleen Moore, who portrays such a characterization in her latest featuring vehicle *The Swamp Angel* ... being directed by Clarence Badger.[41] By late October the film was in production.[42] *Flaming Youth* was being prepared for release, and its debut would be one of those only-in-Hollywood extravaganzas.

First National

In September, a contract had been executed between First National and its inactive 1919 subsidiary, "Associated First National Theatres, Inc.," changing the name to "First National Productions, Inc.," and stipulating that it would produce pictures that would be distributed by First National Pictures, and that First National Pictures would pay First National Productions for their expenses.[43] First National had officially entered film production.

22

The Swamp Angel (*Painted People*), October–November 1923

The third film in Colleen's contract with First National was *The Swamp Angel*, directed by Clarence Badger. It was the story of Ellie Byrne (Colleen) and Don Lane (Ben Lyon), the children of glassblowers who grew up together as friends in a rundown neighborhood on the wrong side of the tracks. Don has a longtime crush on the wealthy Stephanie Parrish (Charlotte Merriam) while Ellie admires eligible bachelor Preston Dutton (Joseph Striker). They take separate paths as Don moves to the big city to find fame and fortune and to make a big enough mark to attract the attention of Stephanie. In the meantime, Ellie goes to work for a famous actress. In a few years' time Ellie finds herself on the stage, a famous actress in her own right, and engaged to Preston. Don, however, is still struggling. Ellie writes a play based on her life in the neighborhood, which is edited and rewritten by Don. Through his reworking of the play—which opens in their home town—he achieves his own fame and attracts the attention of Stephanie. However, Ellie discovers that Preston is only interested in her money, and Don breaks up with Stephanie. When Don and Ellie return to their neighborhood they realize that they love each other.

In the film, Colleen had the opportunity to play baseball. After multiple rehearsals of a scene in which Colleen was to knock the ball out of the park, she struck out. Hoping to inspire her, Clarence Badger went ahead with the scene. Three pitches resulted in three fly balls, but afterwards, during a scrub game with cast and crew, she could not come within a mile of the ball. Colleen was quoted as saying: "The grinding of the camera sometimes works miracles."[1]

The set of *The Swamp Angel* hosted a notorious collision of worlds, as Colleen clashed with Clara Bow, who had a part in the film. Clara had won the 1921 Fame and Fortune Contest in January 1922. "She is very young, only 16. But she is full of confidence, determination and ambition." Her arrival in Hollywood was announced in the papers: "Clara Bow Due Today to Work for 'Maytime,'" the *Los Angeles Times* reported on July 20, calling her an "18-year-old high-school athlete, who joined the ranks of the successful few who entered films by way of magazine beauty contests."[2] Clara had seen motion pictures as a means to escape a broken family, so for her, success in motion pictures was more than just a goal—it was a means of survival.

Clara was working on two films back-to-back: *Black Oxen* and *The Swamp Angel*.[3] *Black Oxen* had finished in mid–October. In the film she played a defiant teenager in pursuit of the film's hero (Conway Tearle), who at first finds her flirtations to be annoying and often threatens her with violence. Clara's character, Janet Oglethorpe, would respond to the threats by suggestively asking, "Do you promise?" It was a part better suited to her personality

22. The Swamp Angel (Painted People), *October–November 1923*

than that in *The Swamp Angel*. The vivacious Clara had been poorly cast. During one scene, close-ups were slated for Colleen. Clara suggested close-ups of herself as well, as she was playing the sister of Colleen's character. What followed is a matter of speculation. It's been said that Clara suggested that she and Colleen switch roles. Supposedly Colleen objected to Badger,[4] who acquiesced. For her part, Colleen simply wrote that after two days of work on the film, Clara declared to her that she didn't like her own part, and that she wanted Colleen's.[5] After that, she returned to Paramount.[6]

At the end of the day the sets were struck and Clara returned home in a rage, determined to leave the production. She went to a doctor and demanded he perform a sinus operation on her. No notice was given to the studio. She came back from the doctor with her face in bandages. It would take weeks for her to recover, and there would be no way to rearrange the shoot around her. Her part was recast, her scenes reshot. It was the sort of stunt that Colleen would have found unthinkable.[7]

The stunt turned out to be the smart move for Clara as Victorian parts were not her forte. The popularity of *Flaming Youth*, when it was released, opened the floodgates for young women to be saucy, vital, turbulent flappers. With the success of *Flaming Youth*, Clara found her niche.

Premiere and Tour of Flaming Youth, *November–December 1923*

Flaming Youth was released in November. On the West Coast, it made its debut in San Francisco.[8] On the East Coast it opened in New York at the Mark Strand Theater and was part of an elaborate show.

1. PRELUDE
   MARK STRAND SYMPHONY ORCHESTRA
      CARL EDOUARDE, Conductor
      JOHN Ingram, Associate Conductor
2. MARK STRAND TOPICAL REVIEW
   Pictorial News of the World, presented
   as fast as modern equipment can deliver.
   (at 2:00, 4:00, 5:52, 7:25 and 9:25 P.M.)
3. PROLOGUE TO *FLAMING YOUTH*
   (a) "First, last and Always" ... Davis-Akst
      Mark Strand Symphony Orchestra
   (b) "Swinging Down the Lane" ... Isham-Jones
      Hurtudo's Royal Marimba Band
   (c) Tango "Capricho"
      Mlle. Ruarke and M. DeVilla
      Assisted by the Royal Marimba Band
   (d) "Loves Sends a Little Gift of Roses" Openshaw
      Ruth Arden, Soprano
   (e) "No, No, Nora!" ... Fiorito Erdman
      1. Solo. Mlle. Klementowicz
      2. Trio. Mlles. Rivlin, Hickson & M. Bocrmann

3. Solo. Mlle. Hickson
   4. Solo. Mlle. Rivlin
   5. Ensemble. Mlles. Bawn, Dickson, Loraine,
      O'Donohoe and Mahurin
   6. Grand Finale
         Anable Bourmann, Ballet Master
         Scenes designed by Henry Dreyfus
      (at 2:10, 4:06, 7:35 and 9:35 P.M.)
         Program subject to change
         without notice
4. Associated First National Pictures, Inc., presents
      FLAMING YOUTH
   From the novel by "Warner Fabian" featuring
      COLLEEN MOORE
      (AND CAST)
5. ODDS AND ENDS
      A compilation of Interesting Short Subjects
      (at 3:50, 5:46, 9:15 and 11:15 P.M.)
6. ORGAN SOLO
      PERCY J. STARNES, Mus. Doc.
      RALPH S. BRAINARD (Organists)[9]

With the release of the film, the trajectory of Colleen's career radically changed, and the perception of the younger generation changed with it.

"Threatened with an injunction prohibiting the showing of the film *Flaming Youth*, A. P. Desorrneaux, manager of the Strand Theater [in Wisconsin] this afternoon held a pre-showing of the picture at which judges, police officials, city officers, education department heads and members of women's clubs were asked to be present." A telegram protesting the film had been sent to F. J. Fitzgerald, manager of Milwaukee National Pictures Corporation, on behalf of the Public Opinion committee, the Madison Women's club, the Madison Parent-Teachers' association and the League of Women Voters. Desorrneaux voiced his willingness to substitute another film if *Flaming Youth* was found objectionable, but he was reminded that he had contractual obligations to show the film.[10]

Seattle theater manager Leroy V. Johnson had been arrested for exhibiting the film because of its "objectionable behavior," the warrant signed by George Bouckaert, chairman of the Seattle Board of Theater Censors.[11] In Hackensack, the showing of the picture created a storm of protest. "Members of the Women's Club here were given a private showing ... prior to its public exhibition ... and [they] declared that 'it is not a fit picture for young people to see.'"[12]

Most found the film to be more smoke than fire. Though shot as a serious drama, many took the film as a comedy or burlesque, which served as a redeeming quality for the film. "The success of the picture is phenomenal, inasmuch as it followed a long, long trail of mediocre and tawdry productions detailing the sins of us young wild people.

"'As long as you [Colleen] played sweet, wistful young girls you were just one more leading woman,' the exhibitors reason with her, 'but since you have played Pat in *Flaming Youth* you are a sensation.'"[13]

Flaming Youth was planned to be followed by a promotional tour by its star that was

22. The Swamp Angel (Painted People), *October–November 1923*

played up as a belated honeymoon.[14] It was more about work than pleasure. Colleen would make personal appearances in cities around the country and visit the various prominent First National exhibitors. The exhibitors, Colleen knew, were her bosses.

It was reported that First National had a sequel to the film planned called *Flaming Wives*[15]: "An innovation in screen production is promised by Earl J. Hudson, production manager of First National, who just left New York for California to complete arrangements."[16] The February 10 *New York Telegraph*, picking up on the theme suggests that *Flaming Wives* will be a worthy successor to the successful *Flaming Youth*. However, little information was given about the planned film, other than that it will be a First National Special, and that the identity of Warner Fabian will not be revealed.[17]

Helen Klumph suggested Colleen's next film be *The Demi-Virgin*, a controversial play from 1922 that had been called "immoral, obscene and shocking to the sense of decency of even the most abandoned" by Assistant Corporation Counsel John Lehman in New York.[18] For the film the studio commissioned Madam Frances to design a wardrobe to make flappers around the country weep with envy.[19]

The tour stopped in Atlanta, one of Colleen's childhood homes, where the city embraced her. On November 27 they arrived at Terminal Station and were greeted by Mrs. Alonzo Richardson (president, Atlanta Better Films Committee) and a host of friends including Mr. and Mrs. Sig Samuels, Mr. and Mrs. Willard C. Patterson and C.R. Beacham, local branch manager of Associated First National Pictures. Besides Colleen, the city claimed John as their own, giving an invented biography of his days in Atlanta[20]: "He lived in Atlanta six years, attended grammar school here and won boyish fame as the batboy for the Cracker team who kissed the bat Heine Groh used before he went to Philadelphia and broke up a world series."[21]

In New York they were the toast of the First National organization. Some 75 representatives of the press and members of the motion picture industry gathered for a festive luncheon at the Ritz-Carlton on Tuesday, December 11, to meet Colleen. It was a "*Flaming Youth* Luncheon" with two pajama-clad, bobbed-haired ladies serving monogrammed cigarettes. Colleen gave a speech to the gathering.[22] Copies of the book *Flaming Youth* were distributed to all the guests. Warner Fabian was rumored to be in attendance, but the mysterious author was not revealed.[23] Publicist Harry Reichenbach was toastmaster.[24] In his toast, he suggested that the newlyweds would return to California and live in the sets of *Flaming Youth*.[25] John McCormick said he was told to deliver the goods, and he delivered them in the form of Colleen.[26]

After New York was Chicago. On December 17, they dined at the Blackstone Hotel and, when interviewed, Colleen opined that she did not think marriage detracts from a woman's success, but adds to it: "That is, if you are happily married." Colleen said she loved all things that went into making a home, though she would hardly call herself domestic. "Besides being western representative ... Mr. McCormick confesses to being his wife's manager and boss."[27]

From Chicago, they left for Minneapolis on the maiden run of Northwestern's "Million Dollar Special."[28] There was a stop in Grand Rapids, where it was reported they picked out new furniture for their new ten-room home. She arrived in Minneapolis on Wednesday for an 11-hour stay in the city as the guests of Messers Finkelstein and Ruben.[29] In the afternoon there was a screening for club women of *Flaming Youth*, introduced by Colleen.[30]

They then made a "Flying Visit" to Boston. Colleen was the guest of honor at a luncheon given for her at the Copley-Plaza by the local First National people.[31] John was reported as stating that Warner Fabian would write another story expressly for Miss Moore's use, to be called *Sailor's Wives*.[32]

Before the end of the year, on Christmas Eve, December 24, the tour returned to Los Angeles. "Met at the station by professional friends who braved an unusually early hour to pay tribute to the couple, Miss Moore and Mr. McCormack were driven directly to their new Windsor Square home (the Rossmore home) which they now occupy for the first time."[33] It had been a successful tour but it had left Colleen dissatisfied. She had still hoped for an opportunity to talk to John as her husband, not her boss.

That night, after trimming the Christmas tree, they went to bed. The next morning Colleen woke up. John was gone. She searched the house, checked with the help. His car was gone, but nobody had seen him leave. So she waited. When he returned, driving the car back into the parking lot, the front end was smashed in. Colleen was horrified. John stepped out of the car, gestured to the wrecked front end and announced that it was her Christmas gift. In spite of her anger, she laughed. John promised it would never happen again, and they returned inside. Among the gifts she received was an Irish terrier puppy from John. He told her they should go to the Desert Inn in Palm Springs. It was a dry establishment, and Colleen knew he was trying to make a show of avoiding temptation. She wanted to believe that the episodes would pass.

When John drank, he was unrecognizable. He was loud and dull and glassy-eyed. When his benders passed he looked hungover, but he had his wit. He knew what to say to diffuse Colleen's anger, and it always worked. She would forgive him and give him another chance. But the episodes of drinking were not isolated incidents. They happened with a rough degree of regularity. Several weeks sober, and then he would snap.

23

The Perfect Flapper, January–April 1924

Through the Dark, which had started life as *The Daughter of Mother McGinn*, had been released in early January, and benefitted from the sudden publicity surrounding Colleen and *Flaming Youth*.

With her popularity still high, First National moved to capitalize on it. Before the end of January, *Painted People*, formally entitled *Swamp Angels*, was released. One review wrote that *Painted People* was merely a series of close-ups of Colleen Moore's face, but "the whole story is told on her swiftly changing and mobile face, and she has so many of these will-o'-the-wisp moods that to me she is endlessly delightful." Furthermore, the reviewer said: "Amazing child this Colleen! But while she may if she wishes make a tremendous name for herself in comedy, I feel that she has a talent of yet a higher order—a whimsical humor."[1]

Her next film was being pushed towards production, but the grueling schedule took a toll on Colleen and she ended up for a break in a sanitarium taking a milk cure.[2] "Of course, being a star means a lot of responsibility.... I don't believe it would worry her if she had to make three pictures at once and prepare for another one at the same time. But furnishing her new home ... is enough to send anyone to a sanitarium, isn't it?"[3]

The break was rejuvenating enough that she was ready for work without missing a beat. Billed as reuniting the individuals responsible for the success of *Flaming Youth*, the story appeared in *Ainsle's Magazine* as "The Mouth of the Dragon," by Jesse Henderson. "What kind of girl do I have to be to be the kind of girl the fellows want me to be?" was the epigrammatical theme. In fact, many of the people responsible for *Flaming Youth* had moved on to their next projects. The story was renamed *The Perfect Flapper* and news that it was beginning production spread quickly. "*The Perfect Flapper* is getting shot. Filmatically speaking.... In other words, Colleen Moore has simply begun work in her next picture."[4]

Sydney Chaplin (Charlie's brother) was brought into the project, Earl Hudson would produce it, and the writers were Joseph Poland as scenarist and Marion Fairfax as editorial director. It was tied to *Flaming Youth*, with emphasis on Colleen, who was billed as the "*Flaming Youth* Girl." In *Painted People*, Colleen would up the flapper ante. "You see, the flappers that Colleen portrays do rather go to the limit," Alma Whiticker wrote. When asked if Colleen knew any of any girls who behaved like the ones she portrayed, she answered, "Yes, I do. I certainly do.... High school girls, college girls—at parties, oh, any time. You see, I have a young brother, and he tells me things."[5]

In the film, Colleen's Tommie Lou Pember was looking to outshine those around her. She throws a costume party which starts off as a dud, but the party picks up steam when one of the boys spikes the punch with some rotgut liquor. Tommie's brother-in-law Dick Trayle (Sydney Chaplin), dressed as Romeo, unknowingly shares a few glasses of adulterated punch with Tommie, dressed as Juliet. They end up drunkenly playing the balcony scene of *Romeo and Juliet* at the local roadhouse. The resulting scandal infuriates Tommie's sister (Phyllis Haver), Dick's wife, throwing their marriage into disarray. To divert everyone's attention, Tommie talks the family lawyer, Reed Andrews (Frank Mayo), into playing the role of her sweetheart. Tommie, of course, is secretly in love with Reed, and believes that, to keep his attention, she must mimic flapperish ways. Reed, on the other hand, is disinterested in her immature behavior, but before long realizes she is only putting on an act. They end up living happily ever after.

Helen Klumph had suggested after *Flaming Youth* that Colleen film *The Demi-Virgin*, so that they might push the limits of debauchery and degenerate behavior even further. Instead, *The Perfect Flapper* topped its predecessor in stunts and adventure. One scene, a party set in a house being relocated, was achieved "by the construction of a cantilever truss floating on a central pivot." Built upon a cast-steel ball six inches in diameter, the set had a maximum rock of six feet. "This seems a bit of work for 'The Foolish Flapper.'"[6] The scene was inspired by a party that "recently actually occurred in Hollywood."[7] Even with the stunts, the film retained the requisite degree of bared skin, a "vast expanse of backs and arms and legs and torsos on view."[8]

Tommie's efforts to attract the attention of a potential mate form the basis of the story, and laid the foundation for the archetypal flapper for which Colleen would become famous. She was the good girl who plays at sophistication for a time, and eventually returns to her true nature when she meets the right man. This formula made it possible to depict a myriad of shocking antics to draw in an audience while at the same time insulating Colleen's character from the seamy aspects. Mistaken identities, disguises, and misperceptions would form the standard complement of plot complications to many of Colleen's roles, which would turn out to be flashy Cinderella stories set to jazz.

As in *Flaming Youth*, Cleeve had a role in *The Perfect Flapper*. The newspapers reported that he had worked in the business department of First National with John McCormick when he had tired of his duties. He told McCormick that he wanted to become an actor. McCormick told him to go ahead, and Cleeve secured his part in *Flaming Youth*. His work in the film was so good that, as a reward, he was given a part in *The Perfect Flapper*. True or not, Cleeve would pop up in many of Colleen's films.

Between appearing in Colleen's films, Cleeve was a competitive swimmer, having dropped out of Santa Clara University in May 1922, four units shy of completing his Preparatory Department program.[9] He competed in the "Ambassador Hotel plunge," a swim and dive meet, and won in the low-board diving contest for the Hollywood Athletic Club.[10] This led to Cleeve winning the Southern California diving championship. "He has a score of trophies, and is now in hard training to compete for the Olympic elimination."[11] A few days later he moved on to the two-day Olympic tryouts at Brookside Park, Pasadena.[12] Colleen was there rooting for her brother. "After the results were announced Colleen and Cleeve put on a real emotional scene that far surpassed any the beautiful screen star ever did for the camera." In the plain high diving, Reggie Nickerson of Pasadena edged Cleeve out by one-tenth of a point.[13] From there, Cleeve and Lee Jarvis, both of the Hollywood Athletic Club, went east to Indianapolis for the final Olympic tryouts. Cleeve was slated to take part in the ten-foot board fancy diving contest.[14]

In June, when Cleeve qualified in the final swimming and diving Olympic tryouts for the southwest district, Colleen would postpone the beginning of her next film long enough to accompany him to the train, which he would take to the National tryouts at Indianapolis.[15] In the end, he did not make the team.

The Perfect Flapper was completed towards the end of April, one of a series of films from First National, including *Lilies of the Field*[16] and *For Sale*[17] that were characterized as "society dramas."[18] This marked the end of the first 50 consecutive weeks of Colleen's May 18, 1923 contract. Since she had signed, she had become a very hot property and she was given the option on an additional year at $1,200 per week.[19]

The Perfect Flapper was released on May 25th, 1924. In the *Chicago Tribune*, Mae Tinee gave it a favorable review, stating it "has its truths, its moral, its merry moments, and it's sad ones." If the film has its exaggerations, one can "forgive them, for on the whole, you have been entertained and not caused to think too much."[20] The *New York Times* was less impressed: "Colleen Moore ... is entirely satisfactory in her portrayal of the unsophisticated girl who subsequently imbibes too much knowledge. However, in this instance she does not have the opportunity she had in *Flaming Youth*.... John Francis Dillon, the director, might have done a lot better by this production, and so might the title writer. Miss Haver and Miss Moore are the only outstanding players in this film."[21] The *Washington Post* felt it followed its own course in its examination of the flapper: "Colleen Moore is indeed the perfect flapper. There is not another artiste who could duplicate her charming performance ... which, incidentally, transcends both her part in *Flaming Youth* and ... *Painted People*."[22]

In the end, the film did not quite match the popularity of *Flaming Youth*.[23]

Counterfeit (Temperament, Flirting with Love), May–July 1924

There had been rumors that First National might move production to the East coast. Some studios were convinced that the future of motion pictures remained in the West, while others thought production should move back East. Technology allowed films to be shot on stages dressed to look like any locale, and they could be shot indoors in any weather. Production was no longer tied to California's good weather.

Richard Rowland favored a move back East. He was "such a strong advocate of producing in the East so that the office executives can readily get in touch with production managers that his studio staffs are to be brought to New York." Cecil B. DeMille of Famous Players-Lasky Corporation had decided to make his next film at the Astoria studio.[24] These moves, some thought, signaled a potential exodus of film production back East.

For the moment, First National's productions remained on the West Coast, where Colleen's next film would be made. The story came from an unpublished novel purchased from LeRoy Scott: "It is *Counterfeit*, and Conway Tearle will be seen in the leading masculine role. The star has a unique role as a temperamental actress who becomes a vamp to 'get' an enemy."[25] Again, mistaken identities and a main character posing as something she was not would form the basis of the story.

Counterfeit would be one of two "laviash productions," along with *Single Wives*, another of the stories of "modern society" that First National had found so profitable. As Gilda Lamont, Colleen would play an actress who had worked her way up from a factory to starring on the legitimate stage. Her climb would be interrupted by bad timing in the form of a local psychiatrist, Wade Cameron (Conway Tearle) "alienist, playwright, and busy little protector of public morals."[26] The doctor, who headed the Better Plays Committee orders her risqué play, *The Lost Kimono*, shut down. Seeking revenge by gaining access to his private life, Gilda poses as a mental patient with amnesia and a split personality (a counterfeit patient), maladies irresistible to the doctor, who has seen neither the play nor Gilda on stage. Cameron puts her under observation, during which she falls for the doctor. As this transpires, the doctor pitches his own play to the theater's manager Franklyn Stone (Alan Roscoe), who is facing financial hardship owing to the original closure. Cameron suggests his amnesiac patient play the lead. The manager agrees, but he plans on presenting the play — a straight drama as proposed by the doctor — as a comedy. Along the way, her plan would lead to a series of "exciting and romantic experiences."[27] Gilda is recognized by the audience as a casualty of the doctor's earlier ban and they expect some biting criticism from her, but to preserve his reputation she feigns the symptoms of the memory loss and personality disorder she had earlier displayed for the doctor. In the end, she ends up with the doctor.

Colleen was kept busy by her popularity away from the camera as well as in front of it. She participated in a Perfect Flapper's Ball: "A dancing contest for girls only will be a feature of the 'perfect flapper's ball'.... Girls will dance together in the contest, showing the independence of the modern flapper, who does not need a mere man to dance with her. Colleen Moore ... will judge the contest and present prizes." E. G. Bond of the Biltmore was to be there cutting hair into the Colleen Moore bob before the dancing audience.[28]

While women everywhere were looking to emulate Colleen's hairstyle, she was looking to change it. She knew she would need a new look for her next role. "Hairdressers are doing all sorts of things ... but as yet nothing satisfactory to the star has been achieved.... Colleen had promised a big red apple to the person who gives her the best suggestion."[29] To portray the actress in *Counterfeit*, recently renamed *Temperament*, she would trade in her simple bob for something more elaborate.

Temperament itself would be a large and elaborate production. Some of the larger sets had to be built at the Clune Studios, across the street from United Studios where the film was being shot.[30] By mid–July it was being reported that *Temperament* had been renamed yet again, this time settling into the title *Flirting with Love*.[31] It was described as a departure from Colleen's flapper roles: "She had to break away from these [roles] some time and so she decided to do it now."

"Colleen Moore. The '*Flaming Youth* Girl,' the acknowledged perfect flapper of the screen, had turned her back on hoydenish flapper roles for the time being. In *Flirting with Love*, the comedy drama of stage life ... she demonstrates that she is just as much at home in parts calling for emotional dramatic acting as she is in roles of lighter vein."[32]

Colleen was aware that her newfound fame was built largely upon the popularity of her characterization in *Flaming Youth*, and the similarity of her characters in her following films to her original flapper role. It was, she realized, the formula that First National had settled on for her. The problem was that, even if her films were different in details, they were largely the same roles. She had just broken out of one rut; she did not want to end up in another. "I became frightened for fear the public would keep on associating me with flapper roles and that I would never break away from this type. I have always wished to be versatile and make each part quite different from the last."[33] The demand for flappers, she knew, would eventually end.

As an antidote, Colleen wanted an old-fashioned drama. First National had already purchased the latest book best seller, and Colleen lobbied for the lead role.

So Big, *July–October 1924*

So Big, by Edna Ferber, had a strong following.[34] The book was an unlikely hit, a story without a real plot. At a time when fiction was exploring such themes as sex and disillusionment, *So Big*'s protagonist was a 19th century woman, strong and long-suffering. She possessed strength, but she did not threaten the social norms of her day.[35]

Colleen wanted to play Selina, the protagonist, but given the degree to which the readers felt a loyalty to the character, First National[36] was reluctant, even though she had played hard-working and long-suffering mothers before. Her image, as promoted by the studio, was youth-oriented and modern.

Eventually, First National gave her the part.

The news was perplexing to some; perfectly natural to others. One film enthusiast who was identified merely as "Jazbo" in his or her letter to Mae Tinee wrote:

> If the casting of Colleen Moore as Selina in Edna Ferber's *So Big* is causing as much discussion everywhere as it is around this little old neck of the woods, it must be by way of becoming a national topic.
>
> Not that we love Colleen less, but we love Selina more. We think Miss Moore, in her line, is unexcelled, but can you, by the wildest stretch of your fancy, picture her doing that classic, beauty-loving, soul starved Selina?

Later, the writer suggested that the audience, upon seeing Colleen in calico dress sitting atop a vegetable wagon would howl with laughter.[37]

The publicists made the most of the Colleen's new role: "No more flappers!"[38] They were a thing of the past. The public wanted more than soda-pop romance. The audience wanted real drama, and real

Frankie Darro as young Dirk DeJong and Colleen, in a scene from *So Big*, First National, 1924 (courtesy Joseph Yranski).

drama it would have. "*So Big*, Edna Ferber's amazing cross-section of a woman's heart, will be Colleen Moore's first starring vehicle under the new honor bestowed by First National whereby she will hereafter 'star' in her own right."[39] To guide the production First National brought in a director known for his human touch: Charles Brabin.[40]

Brabin had originally headed *Ben-Hur* until the newly formed Metro-Goldwyn decided to start over and replaced him with Fred Niblo. June Mathis placed the blame for the unsuccessful location shoot in Italy squarely on Brabin.[41]

> Miss Moore left Hollywood for a complete rest in preparation for her next characterization in *So Big*. The part she is to portray in this story is considered her most emotional character to date, and Colleen has decided she will be fit when the director calls "camera" on the first scene.
> —"Flashes; Colleen Moore Please Write," by Grace Kingsley,
> *Los Angeles Times*, July 10, 1924, page A9.

Work began on the film at the end of July,[42] one of two big productions just started at the United Studio under the supervision of Earl Hudson. "Ben Lyon, heretofore Miss Moore's screen lover, plays her son."[43]

The book takes its title from the nickname Selina Peake gives her son Dirk. Selina begins life as the daughter of a Chicago-based gambler in Chicago who, in spite of his itinerate ways, manages to instill in his daughter love for the simple things in life, as opposed to the superficial trappings of wealth. She becomes a teacher, and during her stay on the High Prairies in the vicinity of Chicago, she encourages her student Roelf Pool to explore the things that interest him. He leaves the farm for France. Selina then marries Pervus (John Bowers), a Dutch farmer. They have a child named Dirk. When Pervus dies, Selina takes over the farm to provide a means for Dirk (Ben Lyon) to follow his dream of becoming an architect. Dirk, faced with the temptations of the city, becomes a rich stockbroker living an empty life. His drive to make money disillusions both his mother and his artist girlfriend, Dallas O'Mara (Phyllis Haver). When Roelf Pool returns from France as a famous artist, he and Dallas fall in love and, realizing this, Dirk is left to ponder his life from the vantage point of a sumptuous city apartment that seems cold and empty.

Publicity portrait of Colleen, in costume as Selina Peake, from *So Big* (courtesy Joseph Yranski).

One problem with the book was that, as Ferber herself put it, it was a portrait of a character without much plot. The story takes place over the lifetime of Selina, around whom all the events revolve. Changes were made to the basic story, writing Roelf out to simplify things. Dirk was made a more attractive character. He remains an architect instead of becoming a stockbroker. It's Dirk who leaves

Dallas after he meets Paula, a more alluring woman. In the book, Dirk is left a casualty of the empty, materialistic society he had embraced, a definite down note on which to end the story. In the movie, Dirk returns to his mother, reconciling with her, and is reunited with Dallas.[44] Colleen's Selina is more flapperish than the book version, with Selina offering to find work to support herself and her father when he finds himself insolvent, and later reacting angrily to her husband, Purvis, when he berates her for dancing in a field.[45]

Colleen was surrounded by a cast that was both famous and familiar to her, including numerous former co-stars. Milla Davenport, once known as "the shapeliest woman in vaudeville," had been given a part. "Veteran playgoers who remember Miss Davenport in the halcyon days of her stage popularity will be slow to recognize in the fat, Dutch cook of *So Big* the sylph-like dancer."[46]

In order to keep her thoughts in the proper mindset of the aging Selina, Colleen insisted there be no modern music played on the set. When filming her previous few films, there had always been jazzy, upbeat music played to set the mood. This time the mood Colleen wanted was more somber. The orchestra leader was told to search for material from the 1890s to play. Charles Ray had told Colleen once to find someone upon whom to base her characters and study them in their smallest habits, so as to create the small eccentricities and habits that give a character verisimilitude. Secretly, Colleen studied Grandmother Kelly. So complete was her impersonation, she would write, that she could not shake it for weeks, seeing her co-stars and friends from the viewpoint of a much older woman.[47]

24

Sally

Before Colleen finished *So Big*, it was announced that she would have a flapper role waiting for her: *Bobbed Hair*, by June Mathis,[1] who had returned to the states and in August had been signed to First National. *Bobbed Hair* offered a return to the formula that had worked for Colleen, with a heroine pursued by two suitors, entangled with bootleggers, wild parties and fights. Colleen did not want a return to formula.

In October, the issue returned of whether First National would produce its films on the East Coast or West, with the story circulating that First National would depart for the East, making room for Cosmopolitan Productions at the United studios.[2] "The first removal of a moving picture corporation from Hollywood, Cal., to New York was witnessed at the LaSalle Street Railway Station today.... In the First National Productions party were sixty-five, including directors, a supervisor, editors, scenario writers, electricians, secretaries and a lot of minor office help.... The special train also carried films, said to be valued as $2,500,000...."[3] Soon, it was speculated, the "great, lonely and often deserted old Biograph studio in the Bronx is once more to echo with the hollow laughter and constant hammering that symbolize movie making."[4]

All the speculation came to an end when M.C. Levee of United Studios, who had been in the East on business, returned to Los Angeles with news that production in the West, not the East, would surpass previous levels. "'The bulk of the pictures for First National will continue to be made in Los Angeles, reports to the contrary notwithstanding.'"[5] John McCormick chimed in on the question by announcing "a production program that definitely set at rest stories ... that First National was contemplating an 'exodus from Hollywood.'" While there would be two units producing in New York, McCormick said, "The bulk of production, as always, will be in Los Angeles."[6]

On November 28, 1924, it was agreed to amend Colleen's contract of May 18, 1923, so that retroactive to August 25, 1924, Colleen's salary would be increased by $800 a week, bringing her salary up to $2,000 per week. The second option was raised to $2,500 per week.[7] Colleen's work on *So Big* was completed before the end of November and the film was slated for a December release.

Sally

Written in the 1700s, "Sally in Our Alley" was a popular song that inspired a play of the same name. The play, a musical comedy, opened August 29, 1902, and ran for 67 performances. It told the story of a good-hearted Jewish girl named Sarah, but called "Sally" by her family and friends.⁸ The play was the basis for a 1916 film wherein Sally McGill (Muriel Ostriche) is taken from her city slum to the country. A young man falls in love with her, much to the displeasure of his girlfriend, who arranges to have Sally returned to her alley. The man, smitten, follows and they are eventually united.

The 1902 play also inspired the Ziegfeld show, *Sally*.⁹ The image evoked by the phrase "Sally in our alley" set the scene when Zeigfeld, Kern and Bolton and Wodehouse first put together ideas for a vehicle for Marilyn Miller. The musical had been an instant success. The public sensed that *Sally* would be something special, a hit of the first order. "Mr. Errol is at his best," wrote the reviewer, and Miller, whose "sprightly dancing and tonic freshness has enchanted us all.... She is singing as never before."¹⁰ Songs in the play included "Look for the Silver Lining," "The Lorelei," and "You Can't Keep a Good Girl Down."

As a vehicle for Colleen, *Sally* was the polar opposite of *So Big*. June Mathis was busy preparing the adaptation of the musical *Sally*,¹¹ and the studio looked towards the original play to find the talent to support Colleen. "Leon Errol arrived yesterday to undertake his part in the film version of *Sally*."¹² The best talent would be bought in for the film. Carlo Schipa, brother of opera singer Tito Schipa, would play the part of Sascha, the "darkly romantic" violinist at the Alley Inn.¹³

Portrait of Colleen, in costume for *Sally* (courtesy Joseph Yranski).

Al Green was selected to direct *Sally* and he brought his own gag man, Mervyn LeRoy, who gave up continuing engagements on the stage to work on the film. To retain the atmosphere and "rollicking pace," he surrounded himself with musical comedy men to "provide that intangible, imponderable, but tremendously important thing called 'atmosphere.'" At the piano was Harry Seymour. Carlo Schip accompanied on violin obbligato. From time to time Louise Dresser and Jack Garner stopped by. The set of *Sally* had become a gathering place for musical comedy performers.¹⁴

In the movie, Sally (Colleen) is adopted out of the orphanage by Mrs. Du Fay (Louise Beaudet), who teaches dance. Hard times hit and Du Fay loses all her students. Sally finds work as a dishwasher at the Ally Inn cafe, run by Pops Shendorf (Dan Mason). Sally meets the Duke of Checkergovinia (Leon Errol), a European nobleman fallen on hard times and working as a waiter. She also meets Blair Farquar (Lloyd Hughes), a wealthy society man who frequents the cafe. Blair catches Sally's eye. Sally has dreams of a better life, and knows her dance skills are her means to succeed. When given a chance to dance at the cafe, she is a hit. She acquires an agent who has her pose as a famous Russian dancer. While performing at a reception held by Mrs. Ten Broeck (Myrtle Stedman) she runs into Farquar, who falls in love with her. She rejects his affections, knowing that when she was a lowly drudge she was not good enough for him.

Her performance at the ball is magnificent and she enjoys the adulation of the audience until the moment is ruined and the ruse revealed by Pops, who has followed her to the soirée. He exposes her as his dishwasher and she is banished from the Farquar home. One of the guests at the reception, however, was Florenz Ziegfeld, who signs Sally to dance in the Follies. She becomes a star, and Blair eventually convinces her to reconsider her rejection of him. In the end she decides to marry him.

For the production, a gown was designed by Mme. Francis of New York. Once it had been established after *Flaming Youth* that movie goers paid attention to Colleen's film fashions, marketing of fashions and cosmetics became tied nearly all of her films. Wardrobe became very important, unlike the days when she was making *Slippy McGee*, when she was looking for hand-me-downs. Mme. Francis's gown had become the subject of much gossip around the studio, and when the gown had been hung up in Colleen's dressing room, all the extras on their lunch break gravitated in that direction to catch a glimpse. When Colleen herself approached her dressing room, one of the extras, acting as a spokesperson, informed Colleen that they all wished to see the gown. By that time a sizable crowd had gathered, blocking traffic. With the help of a watchman to perform crowd control, extras were admitted to the room a handful at a time to admire the gown.[15]

The new man on the set, Mervyn LeRoy, had worked with Al Green on the film *In Hollywood with Potash and Perlmutter*, inventing gags. Green was so pleased with LeRoy's work that he invited him to come along as he moved up the ladder in the movie industry. Given $500 a week and film credit, LeRoy was eager to follow, with only one condition: "That title — 'gag-man,'" LeRoy told Green. "It doesn't do anything for me, and I know my mother wouldn't like it. It sounds like I'm in charge of choking people."

Green asked what title he wanted. LeRoy told him: "Comedy Constructor."

Sally would be a lively film. Mervyn LeRoy had rigged a gag so that Colleen could dance the hopak as well as a "born and bred Cossack." A harness was set up and she was suspended from piano wire that was handled by a man in the rafters. The filming of this stunt coincided with a visit to the studio of the backfield of Notre Dame's 1924 football team, called the Four Horsemen. When the orchestra struck up the tune for Colleen, the man in the rafters handling the wires lost track of what was happening, so taken was he with the famous football quartet. He pulled on the wires when he wasn't supposed to, and Colleen went sailing through the air, over the heads of the players.[16]

LeRoy met Colleen on *Sally*. He came up with a gag to liven up a dishwashing scene with Colleen and Leon Errol. LeRoy had Colleen throw a washed dish out of the frame. It would return boomerang style to Leon, who caught it. After the scene was shot, Colleen gave LeRoy a hug. From then on, the two were cinematically and personally inseparable. Mervyn proved a sympathetic listener, and Colleen knew she could talk to him about John's drinking episodes.

Colleen, John, Mervyn, Lloyd, and June Mathis would form the basis of the Colleen Moore unit at First National.

Mervyn LeRoy, comedy constructor, film director and friend of Colleen, photographed by Elmer Fryer. The inscription reads: "For Colleen, here's looking at you with all the admiration I have in my heart" (courtesy Judy Coleman).

25

The Desert Flower, February–April 1925

> Out of one cast and into another.—"*Desert Flower* Held Up by Colleen Moore's Injury," *Reading Eagle* (PA), March 8, 1925, page 25.

So Big was released in December. In Chicago, Mae Tinee had described it as a "good demonstration of what makeup can do to a girl." Colleen was as good as anyone could be in the role, and the supporting cast was "effective after the fashion of a Greek Chorus," but since much of the film was "concerned with the older Selina, it seems .... that an older woman would have been better in the part. I can imagine Norma Talmadge, for instance, getting away with it."[1] For the most part, Colleen was liked. Mordaunt Hall wrote, "Colleen Moore, the young actress who has attained no mean success ... delivers an astonishingly fine performance."[2] Though Colleen's performance was well received by the critics, the studio wanted to see her in a jazzier role.

In December 1924, First National had purchased the rights to a play called *The Desert Flower* for $25,000. June Mathis would adapt the melodrama for the screen.[3] The play seemed an unlikely choice; set in part in the desert with elements that were "just about the conventional ingredients of melodrama — a heroine taking watchful care of a baby (her stepsister, this time), a drunken stepfather, a final escape." The play was opened at the Longacre Theatre to mild reviews.[4] The Longacre was an inauspicious venue often avoided by producers. Built by impresario Harry Frazee, owner of the Boston Red Sox, he sold Babe Ruth's contract to the New York Yankees to raise money for his theatrical ventures. The result was the "Curse of the Bambino," which hovered over the theater. *The Desert Flower* had run 31 performances between November and December 1924. There was no obvious hook, such as popular tunes or musical productions, to draw in the audience.

There was, however, the basis of a story that was well suited to the persona that John McCormick was cultivating for Colleen. As adapted by June Mathis, the scenario had the requisite elements of adventure, hidden identities, a dash of humor and a pinch of pathos. It was, at its heart, a fairy tale.

"Colleen Moore has gone to the Mojave Desert.... The location is about forty miles west of Barstow.... The 'set' comprises a string of freight cars on a little-used siding far from human habitation. One of these cars has been especially rebuilt to resemble the box car home of the heroine, Maggie Fortune, stepdaughter of a railroad construction gang foreman."[5] The movie would reunite her with her director from *Through the Dark*, Irving Cummings.

In the movie, Colleen's Maggie Fortune lived with her abusive stepfather, Mike Dyer

Publicity photograph of Colleen on location for *The Desert Flower*, taken moments before the lurch that left her with two dislocated vertebrae (courtesy Joseph Yranski).

(Frank Brownlee) and infant stepsister in a railway car in a railroad construction camp, the car modified with various inventions to make Maggie's life on the rails easier. Life was hard. Noticing the escalating abuse of Maggie's stepfather, Mrs. McQuade (Kate Price) advises Maggie to leave the camp, which she does with her stepsister. On the way, they meet weak-willed alcoholic Rance, (Lloyd Hughes) who worked under Dyer. They end up in the mining town of Bullfrog. Maggie tries to make Rance quit his drinking, but nothing works. She manages to scrape together a grubstake so that he can take to the hills, prospecting. She hopes that while he is in the outdoors, doing honest, hard work, he will sober up and make a life for himself. When he returns to town he arrives at the same time as Mike Dyer, who has gotten into a fight with one of the townsfolk. During the fight a gun is pulled and it goes off, seemingly killing Dyer.

Rance, knowing that Maggie will be the prime suspect in her stepfather's shooting, confesses to the crime. At the same time, knowing the timing of Rance's return might cast suspicion on him, Maggie confesses to the shooting herself. The man who was fighting Dyer also confesses. Faced with three confessions and a mountain of paperwork, the sheriff declares the death a suicide. Rance reveals himself as the son of wealthy parents and asks Maggie to marry him, which she does. In the end, Dyer's shooting proves to be less than fatal. He was only wounded, and recovers.

The location work coincided with that year's Wampas Frolic. The fourth such frolic, it would feature the presence of the first three "crops" of baby stars. As a sign of recognition

25. The Desert Flower, *February–April 1925*

to one of the stars a trophy, the gift of Arthur J. Klein, was to be awarded to the one whose career had advanced the most since their recognition as a baby star.[6] Colleen was not expected to attend the festivities.[7] There was, however, an unfortunate change of plans. The Curse of the Bambino that lingered over the Longacre Theatre extended its reach to Barstow.

On February 4, a gag invented by LeRoy had Colleen's Maggie apparently bowing before an audience. When the camera pulled back it revealed that she was not bowing, but operating a railroad handcar. The crew and camera were set up on a short flatcar, to which the handcar was coupled. The handcar was hitched to a team of men with piano wire. When given the word, they were to pull the car forward. When the car was pulled, the handles would swing. All Colleen had to do was keep hold of the handles, and it would appear to the audience that Colleen was operating the car. After posing for a publicity photograph, the handcar lurched out from under her feet. She went over the side, landing on her head and neck.

Colleen stood up and brushed herself off and was ready to go back to work. She was bruised, but it seemed to be nothing serious. A stiff neck bothered her, with the curious effect that she was not able to keep her head straight. Her head wanted to nod to one side or the other. Some local cowboys suggested she take advantage of a local bone setter in the vicinity. Instead, Colleen returned to Los Angeles.

The evening of February 5 was the Wampas Frolic, and while her neck continued to bother her she still managed to attend.[8] "Colleen Moore has been crowned the 'Queen' of the 'baby stars'... [as] the 'baby star' of 39 chosen the past three years who has made the greatest stride to fame and stardom."[9] The trophy, however, had been misplaced. Upon her return to the studio, John was alarmed at the sight of her. They went to the Hollywood Hospital.[10] The smell of ether and Lysol "was as prevalent as the fragrance of flowers in a garden in spring."

Thinking it was just a stiff neck or some other minor problem, Colleen struck an indifferent attitude: "I marched boldly into the immaculately white interior of [the hospital] and smilingly said, with the unstudied indifference of sheer callousness 'Well here I am! What do we do next?'"

X-rays were taken. The doctor returned with another doctor and a nurse. They told her not to move her head, and explained that they would have to put her in a cast and immobilize her head. "A quiet-voiced nurse took me by the arm and led the way into a nearby nook. I was told to remove my garments and prepare to be placed in a plaster cast." From there she was led to another room where she saw "on a stand nearby the weirdest-looking assortment of knives and weapons these eyes of mine have ever beheld." A collection of surgeons and interns, dressed in white, awaited. Colleen was covered in a garment that covered her from her head to her waist. They cut holes for her nose and eyes, fitted an inch-thick felt collar around her neck and covered her in plaster and followed the plaster with a layer of bandages, winding her up like an "Egyptian mummy." According to Grace Kingsley, two of Colleen's neck vertebrae were displaced. Grace estimated she would need to recuperate for a couple of days.[11] It was more like a couple of weeks.

Colleen couldn't sleep sitting down, couldn't breathe standing up, and learned to twist her arms in new ways. She spent lots of her time in her garden learning to appreciate the California climate.[12] When the Klein trophy was found, it was presented to her at home, in bed.[13]

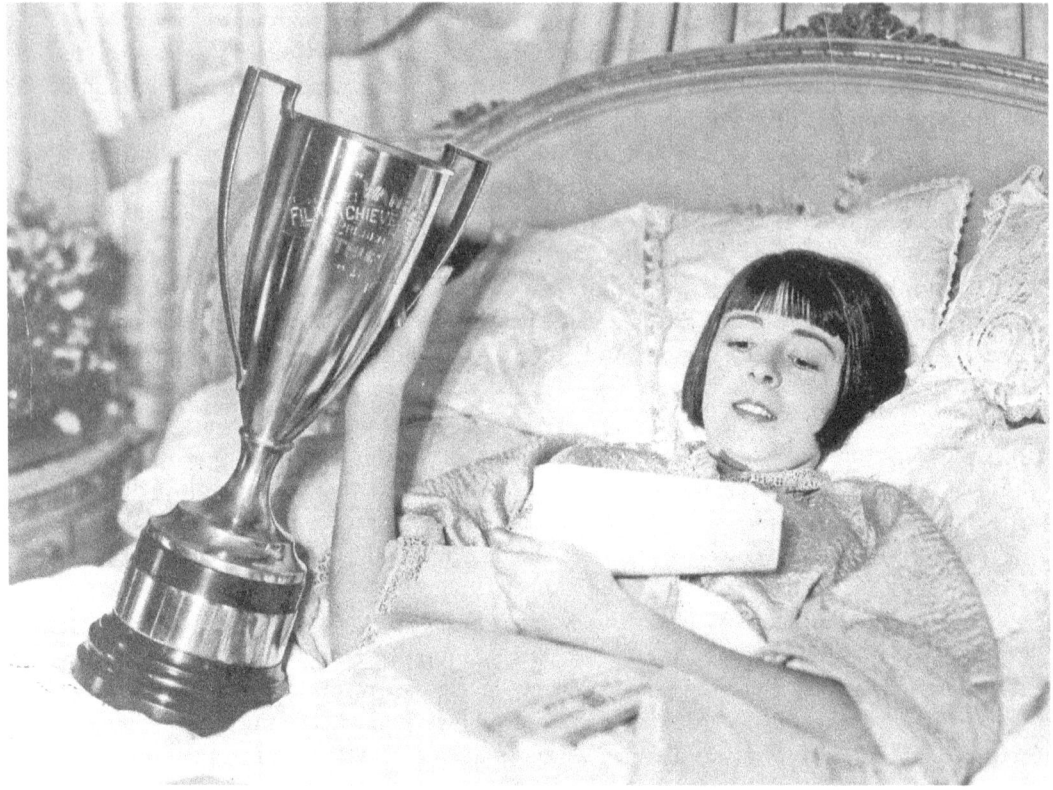

Colleen receiving the Arthur J. Klein award in bed, in February 1925. She is in her cast (courtesy Joseph Yranski).

Colleen was ordered to bed rest for six weeks. Production on *The Desert Flower* was halted. Once she was recovered, she had another tour to look forward, this time to Europe.

"I don't care such a lot about musty old castles and tombs of dead and gone people that you can't know the truth about, anyhow," Colleen said. What she looked forward to seeing most were "the Queens's doll house ... and the toy shops in Germany. Isn't that an awful confession for a married lady? But I really do.[14] 'If Queen Mary of England can have a doll's house, why not I?'" she asked.

Her father was busily at work on her newest doll house.

> It's a wondrous house — quite a dream house.... She is especially proud of it as he has never before made anything like it. It will be of Spanish architecture and there's to be a patio with a fountain, and a balcony with a tiny wrought iron railing.... The interior will boast a dining room furnished in old English style. The bedroom will be exquisitely furnished in Louis XIV period, and the entrance hall is to be strictly of the "grand mansion" type.
>
> Greatly pleased was Miss Moore with a gift of towels and bath rug for the tiny bathroom. Her initials were embroidered upon the tiny towels, while the bath towels were adorned with wreaths of embroidered flowers.[15]

Grace Kingsley wrote that, at home, John was in charge of the household expenses, and that he stayed up many late Sunday nights watching over the bills because such mundane worries distracted Colleen from her art.[16] The story painted a portrait of Colleen as a child-woman, playing with dolls while her husband ran the house.

25. The Desert Flower, *February–April 1925*

Colleen's fame grew, and so did the pressure on John to keep it growing. As the western representative of First National, he was the public face of the organization. If Colleen's career faltered, it would be a reflection on his abilities. As far as John was concerned, the Colleen Moore that the public knew was his creation. Colleen was becoming aware of this: Colleen Moore was a creature of the screen, a character of fiction. Kathleen Morrison McCormick was the actress who depicted her on the screen.

Kathleen, as her family still referred to her, was a very different creation from the carefree, spontaneous being the public knew. Kathleen was a hard worker, driven and smart. She looked like the average woman, with freckles and short red hair and two-different colored eyes. She wore everyday clothes and didn't care for fashion. The porcelain-skinned creature with black-lacquered hair on the screen was the Other Woman, coming between her and her husband.

The European tour would be as much about publicly as their long-belated honeymoon. After *Flaming Youth*, John had been busy concentrating on Colleen's career. Now, Colleen thought, she had reached the top. Perhaps he would take some time to appreciate all that they had accomplished. She looked forward to spending some time with her husband, talking with him as husband and wife, about their future.[17]

John was looking forward to the foreign location to work on a new vehicle for Colleen. Towards those ends, a play was selected for Colleen's next vehicle. It had not been a success on the scale of *Sally*, or even *The Desert Flower*, but it had as its central theme the conflict between young and old. "Israel Zangwill's play, *We Moderns*, has just been purchased by First National as a starring vehicle for Colleen Moore," it was reported. "Miss June Mathis, scenario editor, has gone over the play carefully and announced her opinion that it will serve as an ideal starring vehicle for Miss Moore."[18]

We Moderns was described as a "rather bitter comedy" about cultural and intergenerational differences as Israel saw them.[19] The conflict between young and old in the story harkened back to *Flaming Youth* and *The Perfect Flapper*.

John wanted a story lined up after *We Moderns*. Colleen and John met with June Mathis to discuss ideas. The studio was buying material to be adapted to film, and one particular property had them all enthused. John wrote Richard Rowland on March 7, 1925, "Colleen, June, and myself are all sitting on the anxious seat hoping to hear from you that *Irene* has been closed."[20]

The play *Irene* had run a total of 675 performances, and was a very popular play.[21] Four days later John wrote that Colleen was "tremendously enthused about *Sally* and doubly so over the fact that you are closing for *Irene*."[22]

With *Irene* added to her schedule, her schedule of pictures was reported as *The Desert Flower*, *We Moderns*, *Irene*, and *Clarissa and the Post Road*,[23] by Grace Sartwell Mason."[24]

After the passage of several immobile weeks, Colleen's cast was removed at the Hollywood Hospital. X-rays had shown that the vertebrae had returned to their normal position and her torn ligaments were healing. She faced another week in the hospital and a few additional days of rest, but to everyone's relief she could stand and walk and move.[25] She had to wear a leather collar to keep her head immobile at night, but, otherwise, she was ready to go back to work, which she did right away.[26]

The Desert Flower needed to be completed, and the announcement of the European trip, as well as the acquisition of *Irene* as a vehicle for Colleen had been made. "Colleen Moore is scheduled to finish work in her newest starring vehicle for First National, *The Desert Flower*, about April 20."[27]

At the end of March, *Sally* was released and was well received. After airing so many complaints about *So Big*, Mae Tinee had almost nothing but compliments for the actress and the movie: "She's a foundling. She's a gamin. She's a slavey." The film, in short, was a showcase of Colleen's versatility, and she "invests the title role with snap and charm. Her exquisite expressive little face is one you don't soon forget." The only complaint was that the film was too long. Helen Klumph proclaimed: "Manhattan Likes Colleen in *Sally*." The film was "one of those glorious successes that usually come but once to a player, if at all." June Mathis, she said, deserved much credit for reinforcing the original flimsy story for the film. "*Sally* is by no means a great picture, but it is an awfully likable one."[28] In Pennsylvania they thought "Colleen Moore makes this winsome child of destiny live upon the screen with all the fire, pathos and charm that marked *Sally*'s lengthy stage life."[29]

On April 20, Colleen's work on *The Desert Flower* was completed. *Sally* was a raging success. On that note, Colleen began her tour of Europe.

26

European Tour, April–July 1925

"Colleen Moore, Husband Start European Trip," reported the *Los Angeles Times*.[1] As they traveled, the newspapers followed their progress. The first stop was a brief visit with John's parents, before continuing north. The *San Francisco Bulletin* reported that Colleen had proven to be a "demure 'flapper.'"[2] From San Francisco they took the ferry east to Oakland, and from there they took the Overland Limited east. The *Omaha News* noted Colleen's presence there: "Colleen frolicked on the Union Station platform Sunday night during a thirty-minute stop."[3] From Nebraska they continued east to Chicago, where Colleen "stepped from the train at the Northwestern station that morning and did her daily dozen under the supervision of a flock of photographers.... 'Just like in the pictures,' said one woman. Everyone agreed."

In Chicago they passed the time at the Blackstone Hotel, visiting with a few of Colleen's acquaintances. "This is where I got my start," Colleen said. "I passed almost every vacation here working mob scenes. I believe I worked in more Essanay mob scenes than anyone else. Those were the days when every time my mother saw me wrinkle my face she would say to admiring relatives, 'See, she's a born actress.'"[4] The *Chicago Post* also printed those comments. "I used to think it was just wonderful. And mother thought so too. When the pictures were rushed she would come over every night and sit in the first row[5] and blink her eyes and say: 'Colleen, you're a great actress.'"[6]

After Chicago they headed to Washington, where Colleen and John were the guests of Mr. and Mrs. Harry M. Crandall.[7] They visited the presidential yacht, the *Mayflower*.[8] "Her Royal Highness, Colleen Moore, sovereign of Hollywood, the kingdom of Movieland," was what John Daly called her.[9] The *Baltimore News* reported that Colleen was expected to arrive in New York the next day.[10] Harold Lloyd and his wife, Mildred Davis, were in town, as were William Hart and Lloyd Hughes. Jack Holt was due in town soon. Alla Nazimova had been in New York, but had recently sailed for Europe.[11]

Snapshot of Colleen during her European tour, location unknown 1925 (courtesy Judy Coleman).

When Colleen and John arrived in New York they were greeted by a First National delegation led by Richard Rowland, and then Colleen was off to her lunch.[12] "Colleen may not know it, but she is to be invited to luncheon at the Algonquin to pay her own check. Yes, that's the way it's done, and the crowd that is being lined up to lunch with Miss Moore is going to permit her to do in Rome what the Romans do."[13]

"The party started with three or four friends and grew in proportion as the usual crowd who lunch at the Algonquin drifted into the dining room."[14] From New York, John and Colleen boarded the S.S. *Majestic* on May 2 and were on their way towards Cherbourg and Southampton.

The *Majestic* had pulled out of port four hours earlier than the S.S. *Leviathan*, her sister ship, but even before the gangplanks had been lowered to receive guests, passengers had begun to lay wagers on which ship would arrive first. Aboard the *Leviathan* was the wife of John McCormack, the famous tenor, for whom John McCormick (in print) was sometimes mistaken.

Besides Colleen, aboard the *Majestic* were other notable figures, including Countess of Lauderale; Vicomte de Sibour; Joseph Hoffman, pianist; and Serge Koussevitsky, Russian conductor. William Wrigley, of chewing gum fame, was also aboard.[15] One personality was the emir of Kurdistan,[16] having been "deported again."[17] He was bid a tearful farewell by the princess, who, prior to her entry into royal life, was Miss Kitty Speigel of Kentucky. The emir promised woe to the United States if the country did not do him justice.[18]

During the trip Colleen was a frequent visitor to the dining room, finding herself with spare time to eat and relax for the first time in a long while.[19] A radio telegram from the S.S. *Majestic* reported that Colleen had made three daily appearances at the dining room table every day so far.[20] Prior to beginning the trip Colleen had caught a head cold, but she still trouped on.

The *Newcastle Chronicle and North Mail* reported Colleen's arrival at Southampton on May 8.[21] Horace Judge, First National chief of publicity, staged a reception for them. The Tivoli played *So Big* in Colleen's honor. A few days later Ralph J. Pugh, managing director of British First National, held a banquet in honor of Colleen and John.[22] *Flaming Youth* had opened in England in late 1924[23] and was still playing in 1925.[24] The film was a phenomenon throughout the Empire: the *Times of India* ran a photo of her in early 1925 from the film.[25] Just as American youth had been affected by the war, so had youth in England. The year before, the Café de Paris opened in London. It had become the premier night spot for the upper set, and would remain synonymous with high society. In December 1924 it is claimed that a 17-year-old dancer from America named Louise Brooks danced the Charleston there. As in America, there was a fascination with the new, young set. American boys and girls had blazed the trail, and Colleen was the most visible face of that trail. Her movies were eagerly consumed.

"I wanted a rest," Colleen said. "Did I get it? Well, hardly!" Like her visit to Natchez, the European tour was chock-full of activities.[26] "The hospitality given us was simply charming. It was just one engagement after the other. Had the days been 48 hours long, we still

26. European Tour, April–July 1925

Left: snapshot of Colleen as she makes a personal appearance during her European tour, location unknown 1925. Right: Colleen and John McCormick, in London (courtesy Judy Coleman).

would not have found sufficient time to meet all appointments."[27] The stay in London was a little over a week. At the Savoy, on May 12, Colleen was the guest of honor at a "Dinner of Welcome." The menu included Florida Cocktails, Délicatesse Moscovite, Coupe de Tarrapine des Indes au Sherry, Crême Edouard VII, Carré d'Agneau de Dorset Bouquetière, and Pommes Nouvelles à la Menthe, among several other dishes. The menu only begins to represent the variety of dishes that Colleen and John were served during their tour of Europe.[28]

John had promised Colleen a vacation. Their initial visit to England turned into a succession of mobbed public appearances, interspersed with interviews. Colleen saw little of the city during that leg of their tour.[29] The queen's dollhouse had already been moved from the British Empire Exhibition. Madame Tussaud's Waxworks had burned down prior to her arrival in March. She wanted to take a taxi over Waterloo Bridge, but settlement of one of the span's supporting piers forced its closure.

England, on the other hand, saw plenty of her: "Colleen ... has charmed everybody by reason of her beauty and modesty. It is not often that stars of the first rank bear their honor so easily."[30] For John, it was exhilarating. Colleen had realized that John thought she was his invention, and he was responsible for her fortunes. Each reception and event was a personal triumph for him.

In Paris, she was a guest of honor, along with Alla Nazimova[31] and other First National notables, at a banquet on June 3 at the Restaurant Langer, Champs Élyseés. The menu was as much a celebration of First National's stars as the event itself and included items like Suprême de Sole Miltonn Sills, Poularde Rotie à la First National, Bombe Nazimova Friandises, and Corbeille de Fruits à la Colleen Moore.[32]

In Switzerland,[33] Colleen hoped for a rest but they ended up visiting a string of towns, including Lucerne, Geneva, Basle, Berne and Zurich. In Zurich, at the Café Huguenin, a small dinner party was held for Colleen and her husband; not the result of publicist, it was pointed out, but the result of fortunate happenstance, given their presence nearby at the Baur au Lac. Held in the upper floors, American and Swiss flags along with flowers decorated the walls and the table where some 30 people sat. That same night was the premiere of *So Big* at the Bellevue Cinema, where she was greeted by crowds.[34]

The screening of *So Big* was marred by the projectionist showing the reels in the wrong order while the orchestra played their score in the correct order, creating many mismatched scenes.[35] Switzerland was not all a disaster. Colleen and John acquired a St. Bernard dog named Max.

Colleen's ship arrived at Dun Loughaire Pier in Ireland on Monday June 15, and the couple was accompanied by Mr. Nerwood and Mr. Leslie of the First National organization. While in Ireland she was hailed as "Ireland's own Colleen."[36] In Dublin, she arrived to the opening of *So Big*[37] to discover a tremendous crowd awaiting her. She was there to promote *Sally* at the Scala and *So Big* at the Metropole,[38] and both films had been heavily promoted. Eight men with their faces blackened walked the streets with sandwich signs that read, "No wonder I look so black. I can't see Colleen Moore in *Sally* at the la Scala this week. Some 16 men in pairs — one tall and one short — roamed the streets with sandwich signs. The tall men's signs read, "I am so big. That is why I went to see Colleen Moore in *So Big* at the Metropole this week." The short ones of the pairs wore signs that read, "I am so small. That is why I went to see Colleen Moore in *So Big* at the Metropole this week."

Colleen, in Ireland, at Blarney Castle, kissing the Blarney Stone 1925 (courtesy Judy Coleman).

For the opening Colleen wore a salmon-colored dress with a green taffeta cape, covered with feather plumes in lighter green. She and John managed to enter and watch the film. After the showing, Colleen bowed from her box seat,[39] but as the theater started to empty she was told that the crowd outside had grown in size to a mob, and police had been called to control it. Urged to go to the balcony overlooking the street and wave to the crowds, Colleen and John thought that if they did, the throng might be satisfied and disperse. Beside her, John waved, too. He was elated by the crowds.

The crowd's refusal to thin out made it nearly impossible for the couple to exit out the front. The theater manager suggested another exit, but John would not have it. He insisted that they wade through the crowds to their car. The police cordon that was formed was insufficient to keep hands from reaching out for Colleen, grabbing and plucking at the feathers on her cape. They plucked the cape clean by the time they were in the car.[40] The size and enthusiasm of the crowds made news back in the Unites States. In Boston, the *Post* described a crowd of 10,000 people packing the streets to greet Colleen on the night *So Big* and *Sally* premiered: "Police reserves were unable to check the mobs determined to shake Colleen's hand."[41]

They left on June the 6th for another brief stop in Paris, and then back to London. "Gilbert Frankau, well known novelist, is giving a dinner in honor of the vivacious star, and next Thursday, Miss Moore will award the $5,000 prize that is being offered in the English girl's ambition contest in the new Gallery Theater, where on the same night the English premiere of *Sally* will be held."[42] The winners of the "Women with Ambitions" competition included Katherine Reeves (First Place), who intended to use her prize to learn to play the organ at her church; Enid Fielding (Second Place); and Maude K. Lures (Third Place). Colleen posed for photographs with Katherine Reeves and various other happy officials.

We Moderns, *June–September 1925*

Colleen went to work shooting exterior scenes for *We Moderns*. The plan was for them to shoot around important London landmarks like Buckingham Palace, Westminster Abbey, and the houses of Parliament. On June 24, the *Daily Express* reported, "A crowd collected round Nelson's Monument yesterday morning to watch a pretty girl repeatedly climbing over one of the lions and extracting a note from one of his nostrils.... She was Miss Colleen Moore."[43] The scenes depicted a scavenger hunt. What better excuse to have Colleen race from place to place? John supervised the shooting of the scenes. A car had been purchased for the scenes, and a special permit had been acquired for Colleen to drive it. The weather cooperated. Back in Los Angeles, sets were being built so that everything would be ready upon Colleen's return.[44] One set — an interior hallway representing the interior of a London home — was described as mammoth, occupying more than half of one of the huge United Studio stages; complete in every detail, even to adjoining room of the hallway, each with a complete interior.[45]

Jack Mulhall had been signed to play opposite Colleen.[46] T.D. McCord would be the cameraman, with Joe McDonald as his assistant.[47] "Every available space is being utilized for Colleen Moore's *We Moderns* sets."[48]

When the scenes shot in and around London were done and the car Colleen had driven was stored in the ship's hold, the couple left Europe aboard the *Berengaria* for America. Colleen had acquired a small household's worth of miniature furniture during the trip. A dinner was thrown for them on July 2, the final night of their voyage. The next morning they arrived back in the states to a welcoming committee. They were treated like returning royalty.

First National

"Fox Buys Interest in 120 Playhouses," The *New York Times* declared in July.[49] The theaters were part of First National's franchise for the western states, which were held by West Coast Theatres, Inc. West Coast Theatres had been built and controlled by the Gore

Colleen's reception in Los Angeles, on her return from her European tour. John McCormick is to the left. Note the banner in the background, bearing the name "The Owl Drug Company" below "Miss Colleen." Colleen's name was attached to a line of cosmetics and toilet items offered through Owl Drugs (courtesy Joseph Yranski).

Bros., Adolph Ramish, and Sol Lesser. Ramish had sold his interest in the organization to the interests of William Fox, giving Fox one-third control of West Coast Theatres. Fox attempted to purchase the remaining two-thirds, but the move had been deflected.[50] Still, possessing one-third interest in First National was significant.

———

New Contract, July 1925

"Colleen Moore Forms Own Production Unit."— Newspaper clipping, August 1925.[51]

Colleen and John settled into the Ambassador Hotel in New York, and negotiations began for Colleen's new contract. They went quickly, and on July 8 Richard Rowland advised Al Rockett that a new contract with Colleen calling for 12 pictures, starting with *We Moderns*. The films were to be produced on the basis of four films per year at a salary of $83,333.33 per picture, plus 25 percent of the net profits.[52]

Colleen would have the right to approve the material picked for her vehicles,

Colleen, in a candid moment, at the Barstow train station. Notation on back of the photograph indicates she was en route to Los Angeles, ca. 1925.

and approval of leading men, directors, continuity and cutting. If Richard Rowland ceased to be the company's production manager, her pictures would fall under the control of John. Her name was to be mentioned first in all First National advertising, except where Norma Talmadge's name was to appear, when Colleen's name would be second. She was to be advertised as the sole star of her productions. She was to be provided with wardrobe by First National, which would become her own once the picture had wrapped. Richard Rowland wrote her on that point: "All the clothes you use in your pictures you are permitted to retain for your own personal use but don't try and wear them all at one time or someone is liable to think you are just a new actress."[53] She would also be provided with a private bungalow.[54] The bungalow was, perhaps, of the greatest symbolic significance for her, given the bad luck she'd had earlier with dressing rooms. The press played the bungalow up as a surprise gift for her from John.

Colleen would have to keep her weight under 140 pounds, but the perks of her new contract were undeniable. The next day Rowland wrote to John: "In regard to the contract signed to-day between Colleen and First National Pictures, Inc., I beg to explain our understanding that while the terms are binding, the phraseology and clauses are subject to approval of your Counsel, who may change the same within ten days."[55]

On July 13, Colleen and John arrived in Los Angeles from New York. The next day Al Rockett wired Richard Rowland that McCormick had gone over the continuity of *We Moderns*: "We are of the opinion that first it is too long second that it does not come anyway near theme of original play nor does it resemble word picture Verse[56] painted to Model myself when we agreed to do story stop." McCormick explained that he and Colleen were never really sold on the story but consented because of Mathis's enthusiasm over its theme. Mathis had dropped the theme and so John felt it impossible to start shooting on July 20. Shooting would have to be postponed at least a week to get the story back to its original theme. "Also get Verse personal attention to script which I understand has so far been lacking. Stop our last picture in spite of box office success was bad one and you know well as I do next picture must be good and Model asks me to tell you she does not intend start in on any more stories on promises of their being doctored stop."

While there were problems with the treatment for *We Moderns*, the machinery of Colleen's production unit did not slow down. On July 15, Duncan Cassell wrote to Rowland that *Irene* was expected to follow *We Moderns*, and shooting was expected to start about October 15.[57]

"McCormick and Al Rockett were guests on Wednesday night at an informal gathering at the Hollywood Athletic Club, a sort of welcoming home dinner to McCormick and a good-by to Rockett, who left yesterday to take charge of his desk in First National's New York offices."[58] During the party it was announced that John had been promoted from western representative to general manager of West Coast productions. "In addition to supervising all productions for First National units, McCormick will represent the New York office of First National in its contact with independent producers."[59] From then on, John would be presenting all of Colleen's films.

27

First National, *Irene*

Colleen's contract was emblematic of the First National's approach to its stars. They paid their stars high salaries and their productions were becoming more expensive. While they still purchased most of their films from independent producers, it was an increasingly expensive proposition. The cost was passed along to the franchise holders. At the same time, more films were being released on an open-market basis. The open-market films were presented at a rental price that was higher than the franchise pictures. Franchise holders felt obligated to take poorer pictures, while the better pictures were sometimes priced out of their range.[1] One result was that the number of subfranchise holders began to shrink from 1,782 in 1923 to 1,034 in 1925.

In May, the organization took a blow when Nathan Gordon, one of the original franchise holders, sold his New England theater circuit—Olympia Theaters Incorporated—to Famous Players. Adolph Zukor won a victory in his war with First National with the transaction. It was the first in a series of events that would cripple the organization.[2] At the moment though things did not look so dire. First National obtained new capital from the sale of $2,500,000[3] preferred stock on the New York stock exchange on June 10.[4] Signing Colleen had been as much about assuring the future success of the organization as about keeping a currently popular talent.

The problems with the script for *We Moderns* were worked out and photography on interiors started on July 29. Colleen played Mary Sundale; the part of her brother was played by Cleeve (using the name "Cleve Morrison"). Mary is part of a London set called "We Moderns." She rejects her parents (Claude Gillingwater and Clarissa Selwyn) and their Victorian mores. She is fond of the young man they hope she will marry, John Ashlar (Jack Mulhall), but rejects him in favor of flamboyant Oscar Pleat (Carl Miller). Her parents warn her that her reckless ways will lead to trouble, but she ignores them. One evening her parents lock Mary in her room, but she escapes and engages in a treasure hunt that takes them around the city of London. She ends up in Pleat's rooms, but is found and rescued by John. Mary feels she does not need to be rescued and continues to associate with Pleat. She ends up at a jazz party held in a zeppelin. Pleat attempts to have his way with her, but an airplane collides with the zeppelin, sending the zeppelin flaming to the ground. Mary survives and is rescued by John, and, while in his arms, realizes that her parents had been right all along and decides to settle down with John.

It is almost the same story as *Flaming Youth*, with the action relocated abroad, and with Mary's behavior due to her association with the wrong people. Both Mary Sundale and Pat Frentiss are lured by a racier man (married author in *We Moderns*; jazz musician in *Flaming Youth*), both nearly lose their innocence to the advances of these men, both survive a life-threatening experience (zeppelin crash in *We Moderns*; drowning in *Flaming Youth*), and both realize that the morally upright men were the ones for them (Jack Mulhall's John Ashlar, the character being about 20 years older than the still-teenaged Mary; Milton Sills's Cary Scott, also being at least 20 years older than Patricia).

As work continued on *We Moderns*, the process of shaping up the next few films in Colleen's schedule had begun. The schedules announced were frequently works in progress, subject to change. "Colleen Moore's pictures are so in demand that they are chosen long, long before she can get to them. At present she is filming *We Moderns*.... And a more recent announcement adds, that after the completion of *Irene*, Miss Moore will screen the Tiffany Wells story *Shebo*."[5] On August 26, John wired Rowland that Colleen was "imbued with thought, wants to do character after *Irene* and asks that you read Burke's *Twinkletoes*[6] stop have given copy to Mathis read here stop find out what price held at and if available — if in your opinion not too heavy stop could change end and earlier part of story could be very light etc."[7]

Twinkletoes was a popular book by Thomas Burke, the story of a very young dancer in London's Limehouse district in the late 19th century who admires her father above all things. Chuck, a married prize fighter, is in love with her. Cissie, his wife, resents her. Lilac, a fellow dancer, is jealous of her and Roseleaf, who operates her dance hall, has designs on her. The story dwells on the crime-marinated atmosphere of the district. D.W. Griffith had made the successful *Broken Blossoms* a few years earlier using one of Burke's other Limehouse stories — "The Chink and the Child" — as the inspiration.[8] However, the story would need work.

Following *Irene* with a "character" story was part of John's strategy of staggering Colleen's types of films. This would spread out the genres of Colleen's films so that no single genre had the opportunity to become overexposed: drama (*So Big*); musical (*Sally*); comedy (*The Desert Flower*); flapper (*We Moderns*); and musical (*Irene*). If *Shebo*, a drama, followed *Irene*, then it couldn't be followed by another drama like *Twinkletoes*.

Work on *We Moderns* was finally finished on September 4, after 33 days of shooting.[9] Colleen would begin her two-week break before her next production was set to begin.

Irene, *October 19–December 22, 1925*

Colleen's break between films was short, occupied mostly with testing, owing to the planned use of Technicolor for the fashion show number. "For weeks Colleen Moore, with her cameraman, T.D. McCord, and a staff from the Technicolor studios, have been engaged in making tests."[10] The fashion show — the grand finale of the play and of the motion picture — would be far more elaborate than any party or stunt depicted in Colleen's previous films.

Rex Taylor completed the draft continuity for *Irene* by September 25.[11] John Francis Dillon had been suggested as director,[12] but the October *Variety* reported that Dillon was out and Alfred Green (who had directed *Sally*) was in. Production began on Monday, October

Kathryn (upper left), Colleen's maid; Sid Hickox (upper right), her preferred cameraman; Lucy (lower left), her hairdresser; and Dolly Beal (lower right), her stand-in (courtesy Judy Coleman).

19, with Alfred Green and Mervyn LeRoy as comedy constructor. LeRoy had been haunting department stores in the Los Angeles areas looking for inspiration for the film. At one department store, the house detective had become suspicious and confronted him. LeRoy told the detective that the only thing he was "lifting" was ideas.[13]

Irene was another story perfectly suited to Colleen's persona with its working-class roots, romance, mistaken identities, disguises, and the spectacle of choreographed numbers. October 28 was the opening of Colleen's bungalow. A "Spanish Type Bungalow" built by

P.J. Schulte[14] containing four rooms and bath,[15] it was erected at the corner of Avenue 2 and Avenue B, and First National was to keep the title to the building in perpetuity. Should First National move its production or if the lot ceased to be a motion picture studio, First National kept the right to remove the bungalow.[16] The housewarming was a star-studded affair. Norma Talmadge showed up in a brief outfit, having just come from shooting intimate scenes for *Kiki*; her sister Constance was there, along with Blanche Sweet and Bessie Love. Florence Vidor, Iris March, Ruth Roland, Clair Windsor and Virginia Valli also put in appearances.[17]

The bungalow made life easier for Colleen's hectic schedule. In the mornings, with a polo coat over her pajamas, she would be driven to her bungalow where her maid Katherine would have a bath and breakfast waiting for her. Her hairdresser would show up after breakfast. Often, the director would walk in to discuss the schedule for the day. Press agents would show up to discuss new publicity. By nine she was ready for work.[18]

The *Hollywood Citizen* gave a more detailed look at Colleen's daily schedule:

7:00 A.M.—Reveille
7:30 A.M.—Breakfast
8:00 A.M.—Leave for studio, read mail and dictate replies to secretary en route.
8:30 A.M.—Arrive at studio dressing room and makeup
9:00 A.M.—Report on set
12:30 P.M.—Lunch
1:00 P.M.—Siesta
1:30 P.M.—Back on set
5:00 P.M.—Projection room to see previous day's takes on the screen
7:00 P.M.—Home
7:30 P.M.—Dinner
8:30 P.M.—Read script for next day's work; answer letters; visit friends; read.
10:00 P.M.—Taps[19]

Colleen's schedule for the year was as hectic as her daily schedule. Four feature films a year was a breakneck pace for any performer. Harry Langdon was obligated to produce two feature films a year. Harold Lloyd and Charlie Chaplin produced only one a year each, and Keaton produced two features a year.[20] Colleen's films were elaborate, and *Irene* would set a new standard with the fashion show sequence. A multitude of gowns were designed and models were needed. "The task of selecting sixty beautiful girls has not been an easy one. All must be uniform in height and all must be able to wear gorgeous gowns like a shop window model."[21] In an interview, Colleen made sure to mention the girls: "Many of the girls are winners from beauty contests staged in New York and in other parts of the country. One fact is certain — they are all beauties."[22]

Colleen's outfits were hers to keep. She had not been very concerned with fashion in her personal life before, and many of the outfits would be too elaborate for her to wear in everyday life. However, Colleen was clever. Many outfits were trimmed in fur. The fur could be removed, sewn together and turned into fur coats. Colleen might not have much use for fancy gowns, but she could always use a fur coat.

In the screen version of *Irene*, the character of Irene O'Dare (Colleen) was an Irish lass looking for work. Her mother, Mrs. O'Dare (Kate Price), is busy taking care of the family while her father (Charles Murray) — who thinks "Old Crow is the Bluebird of Happiness" — spends his time happily drunk. Finding her way to New York, Irene lands a job making deliveries for a department store. At a delivery to the home of the wealthy Donald Marshall (Lloyd Hughes) she waits for an interior. Bored, she wraps herself in samples of silk. Marshall walks in on her and mistakes her as one of his mother's guests. Learning her true identity, he arranges for her to become a model in a new fashion designer's shop, instructing her and her friends to pose as society girls to boost the reputation of the shop. Irene keeps the nature of her new work a secret from her family. The proprietor of the shop, Madame Lucy (George K. Arthur), stages a fashion show for Donald's mother, leaving Irene in charge of the shop. At the shop, Donald insists she take part in Lucy's show. When Irene's mother finds out about the show, she crashes it. Donald's mother is taken aback that the models she thought were society girls were, in fact, commoners. Irene is angered at Donald's mother, and tells him she never wants to see him again. Donald, however, has the gift of gab and manages to win over Irene's mother. She takes Donald home, where he overhears Irene confess her love for him. He tells her he's fixed everything with the O'Dare family; they kiss and live happily ever after.

Progress on *Irene* was slow, with many delays due to occasional clouds and rain. Long shots of the Technicolor sequences were problematic. The production was eight days behind schedule, but everyone felt it was worth the effort. While Colleen worked on *Irene*, John worked on the matter of what film would follow. *Shebo* and *Twinkletoes* had been announced as among the candidates, but the decision had not been made. Several stories were under consideration. By November 18, the choice had been narrowed to *Shebo*, *Delicatessen* and *Daphne Goes Down*. With *Irene* so close to completion and Colleen's next vehicle still undecided, the unit could end up having to rush through the process of preproduction.[23] Aside from a few additional shots in late December and early January, photography on *Irene* was completed on December 22,[24] and the film went to June Mathis for cutting. A month later the film was shown to a test audience, to tremendous applause.[25]

The *Los Angeles Times* reported that *Shebo* and *Twinkletoes* had been "definitely determined" to follow *Irene*, both stories being ideal for Colleen. *Shebo* would be first, with Anthony Coldway at work on the script. Alfred Green would be directing.[26] Shooting would start on January 11.

The plan took a left turn when McCormick wired Rowland on December 11, bringing something he had seen in the newspaper to his attention: "There is a comic strip called *Ella Cinders*." It was, McCormick thought, the perfect vehicle to obtain for Colleen. Julien Josephson could work out the scenario and the film could follow *Twinkletoes*. Like *Sally* and *Irene*, the vehicle had the advantage of plenty of exposure. The strip was a modern retelling of the Cinderella story, with the heroine making good in Hollywood.

It was a story custom-made for Hollywood in more ways than one. *Ella Cinders* had begun life as a story pitched for a film. First, it was pitched to Paramount for Bebe Daniels by William Conselman and Charles Plumb.[27] They took the idea to other studios and nobody wanted to make it. As a last resort they turned it into a comic strip and bought space in the local paper. It had been picked up and syndicated, becoming popular before its potential as a source of a story was recognized. John decided to negotiate for the rights to the story. Before the end of the year, Cassell wrote to Rowland that *Ella Cinders*[28] would definitely be Colleen's next film following *Irene*, and it was hoped the film would go into production about January 18 with Alfred Green directing.[29]

28

Ella Cinders, February 19–April 6, 1926

> Samuel Katz, of the firm of Balaban and Katz, Inc., tonight refused to discuss the story that he and Adolph Zukor are planning to consolidate the motion-picture theaters of the country into one great company."
> —"Katz Refuses to Discuss Deal," *Los Angeles Times*, January 8, 1926, pages 1–2.

Samuel Katz's refusal to discuss the subject of a merger would shortly be overshadowed by the announcement that a major move had been made by Zukor towards consolidating a huge number of theaters under his control. In January, it became obvious that a major realignment of power in the motion picture world had taken place. "A gigantic motion picture holding corporation worth $1,000,000,000 is planned ... to own and operate the 3,000 first run motion picture houses ... the Publix Theaters Corporation, now managing 700 houses, will acquire ownership of these theaters valued at $200,000,000. The plan is to be financed by the public offering of stock. The Publix Theaters Corporation combined the management of the 200 theaters of the Famous Players-Lasky Corporation and the 500 of Balaban and Katz. Samuel Katz, who became president of the Publix Company, and Adolph Zukor, of Famous Players, announced that his company would henceforth concentrate on production."[1]

Through the acquisition of the Balaban & Katz chain, Zukor gained the services of Barney Balaban, his brother A. J. Balaban, and their partner Sam Katz. A few months earlier Zukor had hired independent producer B. P. Schulberg, who had brought Clara Bow, Donald Keith, Alyce Mills, Gilbert Rowland and director William Wellman with him.[2] With First National set to vacate their digs at the United Studio in favor of new real estate in Burbank, the Famous Players-Lasky Corporation purchased the lot as part of its "most ambitious program" in its history.[3] Zukor would move from the lot with the Lasky-DeMille Barn, but he would bring the barn with him.[4] There, the new studio would eventually expand to encompass Marathon Street itself.

The move towards consolidation did not sit well with everyone: "You can combine wealth and industries, but you can't combine brain-power. Any attempt made to stifle or kill individuality, originality or ingenuity deadens wit, leads to stagnation, kills a community or its people." So wrote the manager of the Palace Theater in Ohio's *Hamilton Evening Journal*. "Paramount may buy or build in Hamilton; they can't give you better entertainment nor more for your money than you have been getting."[5] It was a move that would considerably weaken the First National organization, which had been taking hits from Zukor for years.

28. Ella Cinders, *February 19–April 6, 1926*

The start of 1926 brought continuing speculation on Colleen's next film. "When Colleen Moore starts production on *Shebo*, the Tiffany Wells story ... it will be retitled *Miss Nobody*⁶.... John McCormick ... feels the original title does not give the movie fan the proper insight to the picture." The papers reported the next film had not been decided upon, but "a decision is to be made this week and work on the script is to be started immediately."⁷

Winifred Dunn completed her initial treatment for *Twinkletoes* after having toured San Francisco's Chinatown to get some local color.⁸ The story, however, would be problematic as a vehicle for Colleen if it were to stay true to its source material. In the book, the story is told through a layer of grime and a haze of opium smoke. The Limehouse district was as much a character as any of the people. There was an essential story that could be extracted from the haze, but extracting it while remaining true to the spirit of the book would not be easy. Winifred Dunn, however, was convinced it could be done, and would go to great lengths to assert this point as the treatment advanced through the next stages of development.

> After many conferences between Winifred Dunn, screen writer, June Mathis, editorial supervisor of First National Pictures, and John McCormick ... her [Dunn's] adaptation of *Twinkletoes* has been accepted.
>
> She will now proceed to the preparation of the continuity ... retaining all the color of the original Limehouse tale and building up the romance to lighten the soberness of the novel itself.⁹

Finding any romance would be difficult, given the romanticized, leering aspect of the narration.

Change was afoot for First National. The acquisition of Balaban and Katz had been bad news, but First National moved ahead with plans to build a new studio in Burbank. John McCormick stated, "The buildings will be erected in a most decorative manner and will be along Colonial, Spanish or Moorish lines."¹⁰ The Spanish style prevailed, given the location of the studio near the old California missions.¹¹ "The aim ... is to keep the old Spanish background throughout but within the exterior walls everything that is modern and complete for the making of motion pictures, will be installed."¹²

The construction was not John's main concern. He had a production schedule to oversee. In a letter to Rowland, he stated that he was going to move on with *Ella Cinders* in two weeks once the story was ready.¹³ He wrangled an additional year of employment for Mervyn LeRoy, the "youthful funster."¹⁴ On January 25, John requested that Rowland amend Colleen's contract to provide payment to her of $125,000 per picture. It was the beginning of negotiations that would last until March.

Ella Cinders started production on February 19, a straight comedy retelling of Cinderella. As in the comic strip, Ella (Colleen) is desperate to escape her evil stepmother and sisters¹⁵ and pins her hopes of escape on winning a contest for a part in a film. She has her portrait taken by the town photographer, but he snaps the picture at the moment she's trying to shoo a fly from her nose. The result is a funny face. The contest is a scam, and her portrait is chosen at random. Ella departs for Hollywood leaving behind Waite Lifter (Lloyd Hughes), her champion, only to discover that there is no part. Undeterred, she gets into the studio and tries to find a job. The story provided Mervyn LeRoy with ample opportunity for gags, from an "eye-exercise" optical effect to a cameo by comedian Harry Langdon.¹⁶ The film was a series of gags piled one atop the other. In the end, Ella wins fame and returns to Waite Lifter, the ice delivery man who always believed in her.

Set in Hollywood, the United Studio lot stood for Gem Studios. The director would be played by Alfred Green himself. The Gateman was Mike "Turkey Mike" Donlin, a baseball player "gloriously talented, but a showboat and a screwup."[17] It would be a very funny film, McCormick proclaimed, as "Miss Moore feels very much at home in the role, as she has enacted comedy parts in so many productions."[18]

Most of the first week, from the 19th to the 26th, was spent working out the gags before the cast and crew departed for Chino for location work.[19] Chino awoke one morning to find Colleen Moore had rolled into town.[20] While on location, Green thought some scenes "could be atmospherically strengthened by using some hundred 'extras' as natives of the place.... It came as a welcome relief in a humdrum existence and a really thrilling experience.... 'They felt flattered when asked to perform,' Green declared later. 'And when we offered to pay them — what do you think? — they scorned it!'"[21]

Most of the first week of April was ruined by cloudy weather and rain, but the studio was abuzz with work. "According to John McCormick ... every unit will be kept busy throughout the summer months despite the fact the First National organization is to move into its new home."[22]

In Pat O'Mally's weekly production letter of March 3, he indicated that it still had not been definitely decided on Colleen's next film. *Shebo* had been dropped, and the two new candidates were *Delicatessen* and *Twinkletoes*. Winifred Dunn was at work on *Twinkletoes*, with Julien Josephson on *Delicatessen*. Whichever story was chosen would go into production on about April 19.[23] Within a week John had settled on *Delicatessen*, and shooting was tentatively scheduled to begin on April 19 with Alfred E. Greene directing.[24] *Twinkletoes* was put on the backburner, but Winifred Dunn had become an advocate for the story, and her letters would be frequent and forceful:

My Dear Mr. McCormick:

I've hit on what I think is a very simple but effective solution!

If the picture is the father's — it is because of the great sacrifice he makes for Twinkletoes — thus winning for him, inevitably, a tremendous amount of sympathy.

Suppose — for argument's sake, he *is* a crook — has always been one, but hides the fact from Twinkletoes.... This would eliminate his becoming a crook to give her a chance....

And the characterization of Twinkletoes! Colleen IS Twinkletoes — oh please, please *please* don't discard it until we've analyzed it from every possible angle.

I *do* hope it will be possible for you to arrange a conference tonight. We'll make it very short and to the point —

Hastily but sincerely,
Winifred Dunn[25]

While Dunn fought for *Twinkletoes*, ground was broken on the new studio on March 28[26] and construction was underway by April.[27] Two days before the groundbreaking, John had completed negations for Colleen's contract. The contract of July 1925, calling for 12 photoplays from Colleen for $83,333.33 each, was canceled. Effective May 18, 1925, Colleen was engaged for 12 photoplays, now at $125,000 apiece.

John's increased responsibilities at First National led to new pressures. Colleen began to notice a pattern to John's drinking. He would be sober for weeks and perfectly fine. He was able to control the urge to drink. At social occasions he would drink ginger ale. Then Colleen would notice changes. John exhibited physical signs that signaled the onset of a drinking bout. John would become tense, strain visible in his lips. He'd take a drink, then he would disappear for days on end. Colleen was left making excuses for his absences. The spells started coming more often. Several weeks clean and sober, then he'd disappear. He'd return to her, shaking and weak, having subsisted on the nutritional value of his drinks alone. Sometimes he'd appear at her door; sometimes she'd get a telephone call that he had been found and was in a jail cell or hospital bed or hotel room drying out and waiting for Colleen to pick him up.

His drinking was beginning to affect her career. Her mother had already heard the stories of John's drinking, and stories had begun circulating around the studio. Given the hectic, 'round the clock production schedule of the studio and the simultaneous projects under his supervision, a drinking problem was the kiss of death. John would lose his job, and Colleen knew he was a proud man. It might be too much for him, and, in spite of it all, she still loved him. It left her frustrated, and so increasingly she dealt with him through harsh words and insults. He was ruining everything with his drinking, she'd tell him. All his plans to see Colleen Moore become famous would be for nothing if he couldn't stop.

The insults did not work; in fact they only made things worse. John simply could not control his drinking.

Delicatessen (It Must Be Love), *May 7–June 22, 1926*

> The picture ... is extremely spicy — but is not at all censorable, because the spice is of the delicatessen flavor.
> —"Colleen Moore in Spiciest Comedy," *The Bee* (Danville, Virginia) January 7, 1927, page 12.

Work on *Ella Cinders* was finished on April 6, about two weeks behind schedule. Winifred Dunn fought for *Twinkletoes*, and the start date for *Delicatessen* approached. The script had been delivered to M.C. Levee on May 1, and Levee wired Richard Rowland: "Script *Delicatessen* was delivered to me today which is one week ahead of starting date. This has never happened before in the history of First National."[28] Even with a completed script, the start date was pushed back into May ... May 3, then May 6, and finally May 7.[29]

With work on *Delicatessen* about to start, construction of the new studio was nearly complete. The studio would be run much the same way as the organization had been at the United Studio lot, with M.C. Levee as general executive manager and John McCormick supervising all the productions at the new plant.[30] The gates would be thrown open to the new studio at 7:30 A.M., June 15, a month early.[31] Not all facilities would be complete, but there would be enough to begin production. First National would vacate the United Studio lot. "First National units are scurrying around looking for quarters while they await the completion of their new studios." It was planned for Colleen and her unit to move to the Fine Arts Studio, where she had gotten her start in Hollywood.[32]

Delicatessen, however, would not be made there. It would be directed by Alfred Green, who was enjoying a streak of successes with Colleen. In the film, Colleen plays Fernie Schmidt, who lives with her parents in the rear of their delicatessen. The smells of the business — cheeses, sausages, garlic and pickled herrings — repulse Fernie, who dreams of removing herself from the environment and moving into a life with a more rarified. As in *Ella Cinders*, her character would live on the brink of poverty. Her father, Pop Schmidt (Jean Hersholt), has plans for his daughter to marry Peter Halitovsky (Arthur Stone), a sausage salesman, but Fernie is repulsed by the idea. At a dance, Fernie meets Jack Dugan (Malcolm McGregor), who tells her that he is in stocks, a paper-counter, and she falls for him. Because of her rejection of her father's chosen candidate for matrimony, Pop puts Fernie out of the house.

Fernie manages to find work as a counter girl in a department store. Luckily, the job is at the perfume counter. Jack, in due course, proposes to Fernie. Before she can give her answer, she is invited back home by Pop for dinner, at which time he announces he is going to buy a new home, removing himself from the back of the fragrant delicatessen. Peter is there and he proposes to her, but before she can reject him Jack appears on the scene, declaring that he has purchased a delicatessen business. Seeing that marrying Jack would return her to the life she wishes to flee, she finds herself resolved to the fate of marrying her father's choice of husband, Peter.

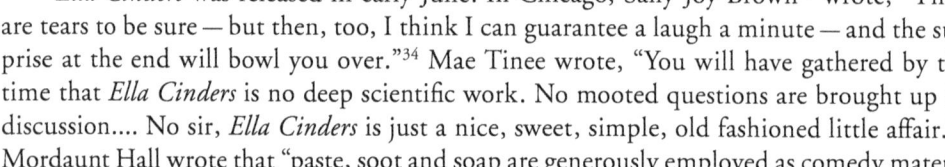

Ella Cinders was released in early June. In Chicago, Sally Joy Brown[33] wrote, "There are tears to be sure — but then, too, I think I can guarantee a laugh a minute — and the surprise at the end will bowl you over."[34] Mae Tinee wrote, "You will have gathered by this time that *Ella Cinders* is no deep scientific work. No mooted questions are brought up for discussion.... No sir, *Ella Cinders* is just a nice, sweet, simple, old fashioned little affair."[35] Mordaunt Hall wrote that "paste, soot and soap are generously employed as comedy material in *Ella Cinders*." In fact, throughout the film, Colleen threw herself into the gags with a relish few other actresses ever did. "This production will undoubtedly create plenty of laughter, for it is filled with those wild incidents which are seldom heard of in ordinary society."[36] The film was very well received.

Colleen's work on *Delicatessen*, renamed *It Must Be Love*, had ended on June 22.

First National Burbank Studio

The pride of the motion picture industry is the new First National Studio, in the city limits of Burbank, just over the hills from Hollywood. The studio is artistically landscaped with lawn, flowers and shrubs. It is the most complete studio, built from the ground up to meet the needs of modern motion picture production.

Planned essentially for the needs of today, it has also been constructed for the needs of tomorrow.... Every wall of each building in the studio is constructed to carry extra stories."

The statistics for the studio included 73 acres, with 20 covered by studio buildings and sets. Six paved streets, with corresponding alleys crossed the lot; six mammoth stages, with a total of 200,000 square feet of stage space dominated the studio; one star suite dressing-room building, and two mammoth dressing-room buildings were built to accommodate 2,000 players. A total of 27 permanent buildings housed the organization, with a total space of 347,160 square feet.[37] The star suite was Colleen's bungalow, relocated to the new studio from the United lot.

Work had continued on the studio after the gates had swung open, as many of the buildings were still incomplete. Colleen moved into her bungalow in June.

The new studio allowed First National to produce bigger, more elaborate films. Overall, First National depended less and less on independent producers for their product thanks to their expanded ability to produce their own films. The studio was recognized as one of the best producers of motion pictures, with some of the biggest stars in the business. They paid their stars high salaries to assure they would stay with the company. The combination of the bigger productions and higher salaries paid to the stars meant that the exhibitors of First National films were paying more. Bigger, more elaborate films meant larger exhibition values and, thus, higher rates to the exhibitors. At the same time, more First National pictures were being placed on the open market at the insistence of the independent producers. Big productions placed on the open market meant that franchise holders had to compete with non-franchise holders for them, resulting in the impression of franchise holders that they were obligated to take the smaller, less elaborate productions under their franchise agreements. The bigger productions were of no benefit to the franchise holders.[38] This situation was slowly weakening First National's position, along with the assaults of Zukor, though for the moment it was still the premier, ascendant motion picture studio.

29

Twinkletoes, July 26–September 15, 1926

For *Twinkletoes*, Colleen sported a new hair style. "Long golden locks[1] have replaced the trim Dutch bob.... Colleen will introduce two novel dances in the picture."[2] The film was reported to tell the "romances and adventures of a little Cockney English girl."[3] From that description one might expect a lively story along the lines of *We Moderns*. However, *Twinkletoes* was a drama based on material that was filled with crime and amorality.

The first step in rehabilitating the story was the director. "Charles Brabin [and Colleen] ... will actually go to work together once more today, this time in the production of *Twinkletoes*." Brabin's handling of *So Big* made him an obvious choice to direct Colleen in *Twinkletoes*. If anyone could find the human touch in the story, it was Brabin. The story would be dramatic and delicate, and would draw its humor from the spitfire behavior of Monica "Twinkletoes" Minasi as enacted by Colleen.[4]

On July 3, a story conference with Carey Wilson, John, and Colleen was held and some general topics were decided upon. They must have a "gorgeous introduction" of Colleen. At every opportunity, Roseleaf must stare at Twinks. They needed to "put in Chink atmosphere." A few scenes were finessed, such as Cissie learning of Dad Minasi's activities; Cissie's rage toward Twinks; the first love scene between Twinks and Chuck; and Cissie's decision to take action upon seeing them together.

Colleen wanted the "horse business" in the film, wherein Twinks strokes the head of the horse while she talks to it.[5] She also wanted the "violet prayer" scene, when Twinks lights a stick of incense and prays while knelt before freshly cut violets.[6] Finally, Colleen wanted the scene where Twinks toasts her legs: "When my legs begin to go, then there'll be an end of good things. All comes down to legs. Faces ain't no good. Look at Iris—awfully jolly to look at when she's undressed, but her nose ain't right. It's crooked. But if you're talking of legs.... You 'ave a look at 'ers when she gets up."[7]

John didn't like the idea of Roseleaf and Cissie as heavies. He preferred that Cissie be developed as the heavy propelling the action, and that Roseleaf serve as merely a background threat. He preferred Lilac to be a messenger for Roseleaf instead of his mistress. He wanted the Quayside Kids to feel the same disdain for Twink's adoration of her father as Lilac. In short, he wanted the audience to readily identify with Twinks

No specific ideas had been settled on for the ending.

Work on the film itself went ahead on July 26. The tone and story would generally follow the broad strokes of Burke's story. Still, there was one issue specific to the book that would have to be handled carefully: Twinkletoe's age and her role as the object of Chuck's long-simmering longing. Burke's book openly depicted young girls as objects of amorous urges. Young girls flitted, older men coveted them, and Chuck had been in love with Twinks for two years prior to the start of the story. Chuck is tortured by the fact. ("He tapped

Hank on the chest. 'What'd you say if you 'eard of a chap of twenty-nine in love with a girl of fourteen?'")[8] His was not the sort of high-minded love often depicted in films and books, or even the chaste love and devotion of Cheng Huan (the "Yellow Man") for Lucy (The girl) in *Broken Blossoms*, but a physical attraction for the child. He saw her as "a child as lovely and as insolently happy as a lyric ... bright curls foamed about her shoulders, and the black silk frock clung to her young beauty as though it loved her."[9] He "dared not dream of possessing her; of lacing arms about her; of pressing lip to lip; though every fiber of his being ached for her."[10] The sexuality dripped from the book, and even Twinks, while smoking opium and gazing at Lilac, had sensual thoughts: "Lilac was a dish of goblin sweetmeats which she could never reach. She wanted to eat her.... Her eyes closed ... she and Lilac flew away together."[11]

The language was carried over into the various treatments for the film, Brabin's treatments in particular.[12] While someone watching the film without knowledge of the book might not think about the ages of the characters, anyone familiar with the book would know Twinks was very young and Chuck was much older. For there to be the requisite Colleen Moore happy ending, Twinks and Chuck would have to get together by the end. Cheng Huan's love for Lucy in *Broken Blossoms* was unconsummated. In the book, Chuck and Twink's relationship was also unconsummated, as Twinks takes her own life by the end. It was the logical end to a girl who had seen her whole world collapse around her in one night. Her father is a criminal, her lover a murderer, and her friends are jealous. A happy ending would diffuse the drama. Colleen's characters had died in the past, but that was before the new, peppy Colleen to which the public had become accustomed. Therefore, the appropriate end for this Colleen Moore vehicle remained elusive.

The movie follows young Twinkletoes, whose mother—a dancer—died years earlier. Colleen's Twinkletoes grows up as a naturally graceful dancer herself. She is devoted to her father, Dad Minasi (Tully Marshall) and holds him in the highest esteem. While watching her father painting a sign early on (his public occupation is as a sign-painter), every "line of her expressive little face and expressive little body bespeaking her admiration of her dad. Big wondering eyes watch ... small mobile lips breathe an ecstatic sigh: 'Ain't my Dad wonderful! Ain't he the cleverest man in the world!'"[13]

One day a fight breaks out, and in the process of trying to calm things she meets Chuck Lightfoot (Kenneth Harlan), a prizefighter.[14] Chuck falls in love with her at first sight, but he is married to Cissie (Gladys Brockwell), a spiteful drunkard. After the fight they part, and Chuck "is stilled with the wonder that is Twinkletoes." Cissie, on the other hand "is aware of his abstraction and the reason for it. And that a child—she can't be over twelve, should strike him balmy, fills her with blind fury."[15]

"Twinks" dances as the head of the Quayside Kids, a dance group, in a local dance hall managed by Roseleaf, who "saunters past the dressing room ... to feast his eyes on the Quayside Kids' young loveliness." In their dressing room, Twinkletoes, swathed "in shining silk ... reaches for her powder—it ain't there. Aflame with wrath, she cries: 'Stinkin' Judas! Somebody's been and pinched me powder!' 'Ma' the matron tries to 'shhh' her—but she won't be 'shhhed'—thus proving that she has temperament—the stuff of which stars are made."[16]

Cissie decides that Twinks needs to be taught a lesson and, learning her father is a burglar, exposes him to the police. The arrest of her father shakes Twinks's faith in her father and the world. Distraught, she goes with Lilac to a party where she passes out. Roseleaf, who has his own designs on Twinks, takes her to his apartment. Discovering her whereabouts, Chuck attempts to rescue her.

That is where the major dilemma with the story as adapted arises: does she live or die? If she lives, how is it depicted? In Burke's story, Twinkletoes, distraught by the events that have whirled around her, walks into the Thames River and drowns. Would American audiences buy a tragic ending for one of Colleen's vehicles? The film *So Big*, while not a tragic story, still had to have its ending brightened.

Many people had been consulted for ideas on how to wrap up the story. Ben Tyrnin,[17] in an undated letter to John, suggested the she should love. From a photoplay standpoint, if she married, it would have to be to either Chuck or Roseleaf, which would require Chuck to be single, or Roseleaf to be rewritten from the beginning as a dreaming artist. If she did not marry, she "has the usual alternatives of entering a convent or devoting the rest of her life to good deeds in the East End." The scenes showing debauchery should not be dwelled upon, and only two were necessary: The one showing her aloof from the action, and the other showing her giving into temptation. If given a comic treatment, they might escape the censors. "The scene depicting Twinks in a tantrum, throwing shoes at the Kids can be made a classic!"

Tyrnin further suggested that the whole thing might be rewritten and set in New York's East Side. Markie Roseleaf from the book might be rewritten as the romantic interest, renamed Irving Roseleaf, a Jewish boy from the ghetto, and renamed Irving Roseleaf. With the Berlin-Mackey romance still in the headlines at the time it would have been a timely rewrite.

Two initial alternate endings were discussed and worked out. In one, Twinkletoes escapes Roseleaf and flees to the roof, running from chimney to chimney, warning the pursuing Roseleaf that she'll jump if he continues after her. He does, and she leaps off the roof into the river below. Chuck finds Roseleaf and demands to know where Twinks is. When Roseleaf confesses that she has jumped, Chuck sends him tumbling off the roof and dives into the water after Twinks. He pulls her from the water, and when she recovers she is wildly incoherent until she recognizes Chuck. She clings to him like a child.

In the other version, Chuck finds Roseleaf in his apartment and questions him there, leaving him alive when he rushes out to the streets. Twinkletoes has wandered to the end of a wharf where she stares into the water. She sees Cissie's spiteful face, followed by Lilac's mocking face, and finally Roseleaf's lustful face. She jumps into the water. Chuck sees her go in, follows her, and pulls her back to the dock. When she awakens, she sees him and feels a sense of security and contentment. In the first version, Twinks's father had been shot by the police; in this version he lived.

Neither version captured the spirit of the original story.

On August 2, John wrote to Charles Brabin to consult with Colleen regarding the casting of an actress in the part of Lilac. "Please check with Miss Moore if Julanne Johnston would be satisfactory.... This girl is satisfied to play the part and wants $500 a week. She knows it will only be about a week's worth of work."[18] While Colleen was exercising her rights to make decisions in casting, John's involvement in the production extended down to minute issues. This was evident once the memos started shooting from his desk.

In writing to Brabin, John commented: "Have now seen all your rushes and I think that from the directorial and dramatic standpoint they are splendid, but regret to say that I am disappointed in the photography in a great many spots." One main criticism was that many scenes were too dark, that the dramatic action Brabin is trying to record on film would not be visible because most theaters were small, and that it would not be good for business.[19] In a memo to Brabin two days later, he saw in an exterior shot of Dad Minasi's storefront that the "side walls are lighted, and the front of the store dark." An interior shot had shown a lamppost outside through the window, but it was missing in the exterior shot. "I can't reconcile myself as to why there should be a lamp post in one shot — and no lamp post in the exterior." In that same memo he had other comments: Colleen's bangs in scene 372 looked very "wiggy," Gladys Brockwell's hair looks like she had just come from a hairdresser, and Brockwell's makeup is an entirely different shade between shots, and Colleen's closeup in scene 374-A is "muddy and terrible."[20]

Colleen herself was not immune from John's torrent of memos:

> My understanding is that you're going to get a new waist for the sequence at the home where you have dinner with your father — which will be more tight fitting and will have a high collar.
> I also understand that in the little suit you wear to the theatre at the height of the performance — that either Van Trees will take steps to watch his light so that the bosom of the waist will not show up whiter than the neck of it or we will get a darker waist for that and do it over. It will probably be better to do it over because of the fact you changed the contour of your hair.
> Let's all hope we'll get everything right from now on so that there won't be any more retakes.[21]

In a memo to Roy Stone, John instructed him to tell Brabin that "it is absolutely necessary that he pick his takes as we go along. If he doesn't pick them tonight, let me know and I will have to pick them myself, because we cannot afford to get behind on this because it will only cost us money if we do, by having to call people back, whereas if we can see the stuff assembled now, we will know just where we are."[22] He wrote again to Brabin in nearly scolding terms:

> I wish, from now on, I could ask you to come in and talk with me on points on which there is any doubt in your mind because, otherwise, our cost is going to amount to huge proportions on account of retakes. I don't think I have to tell you that retakes cost money, and plenty of it, and I think a lot of them could be avoided if we will just work a little closer together on the rest of the picture.[23]

In an August 3 memo to Brabin, John began "I think you will agree that there is cause for alarm on my part." They had agreed on a tight script but after the first week Brabin had shot 51 scripted scenes and added an addition 27 unscripted scenes. At that ratio, the film would be a ten-reeler, and finished after 51 days. "Therefore, I must again say to you, Charlie, please step on it." He should only pick scenes to embellish that would propel the story forward. His August 4 memo to Brabin concluded "Please let's try to get going — because at the rate we are going now, we'll never get thru with this picture."[24]

John had reason to panic. On August 25, the *Los Angeles Times* had announced that Colleen's next film would be *Orchids and Ermine*, an original title by Carey Wilson. Filming was due to begin in two weeks, after the completion of *Twinkletoes*.[25] Colleen would have to move directly into the next production to keep up with the terms of her contract. As things were going, after *Orchids and Ermine* Colleen would need more than a few days of rest to recover.

Delicatessen premiered on August 22 under the new title of *It Must Be Love*.[26] "Should a girl put love of a sweetheart above the love of parents?" was the central question of the film as summed up in the *Reading Eagle*; Colleen's character being "one of the most interesting and appealing" in her repertoire to date. "The picture, however, is not all sentimental; it is full of laughter, as a Colleen Moore offering always is."[27] Helen Klumph, in the *Los Angeles Times*, however, suggested instead that there was some comedy, true, but "the romance and a drab note of realism overshadow it."[28] The *Meridian Daily Journal* called it a human story of a girl's struggle against mediocrity and her parents misunderstanding, another "of the heart appealing dramas, which Colleen knows so well how to deliver."[29] "The new Moore picture delighted Greater Movie Season crowds last night," it was reported in Sarasota; the consensus being that it was one of Colleen's best to date.[30] *It Must Be Love* was one of Colleen's brighter pictures.

Twinkletoes was a darker film, though the story did afford the opportunity for spectacle. "The Hollywood Bowl Ballet of 100 Ernest Belcher-trained dancers" were to be used in the film; the piece to be featured was from the dedicatory opening of the Bowl earlier in the year.[31] Colleen would be the featured star of the dance. She had learned to dance ballet for earlier roles, but she still spent an hour a day training with Ernest Belcher.[32] Ernest had managed to get her up on her toes in an "incredible" eight weeks.[33] In the background would be some faces (and legs) familiar to longtime moviegoers. "They are Frankie Bailey, whose $1,000,000 legs were widely exploited, Florence Lawrence, once more famed than Mary Pickford, and Polly Moran, formerly star of the Sheriff Nell comedies."[34]

On August 23, came news that Rudolph Valentino died. The next day, a riot broke out at the viewing of the body at the Frank E. Campbell Funeral Chapel. After a New York funeral mass, the body was sent to the West Coast for a funeral in Los Angeles. On the day of the funeral in early September, the whole West Coast motion picture industry came to a halt. John McCormick was an honorary pallbearer and Colleen was one of the many notables scheduled to attend.[35] Motion picture stars had become celebrities with almost unprecedented followings. Colleen had her share of devotees, though none as ardent as Valentino's. One devoted fan had been intercepted by the Traveler's Aid society in Los Angeles after she had crossed the country to find Colleen.

> Another young runaway began the long trail back to Brooklyn ... and another dream of filmland was dissipated. This time it was not to become a screen star, but to become the handmaid of no less a luminary than Colleen Moore. Not to shine as rival but to adore as a slave.

The young runaway was Mary Kolinsky, age 16, who had been deaf and mute since the age of seven. She had seen Colleen on the screen and read every story on her that she could. "She was suffering from a bad case of 'adoree,' so familiar to the social workers; it is a complex, they declare, with a large admixture of the inferiority variety." In late July, Mary had stolen enough money to travel west by train, after having found Colleen's home address in a film column. A Traveler's Aid worker spotted her in Chicago and asked after her plans. Mary said she was headed west to visit an aunt. A wire was dispatched ahead of Mary, and at the Central Station platform she was caught by another Traveler's Aid worker. Investigating the address of the "aunt," they found it was Colleen's. Mary's mother was contacted and informed of her daughter's whereabouts, and money was sent so that she could return home.[36] If she had waited a few weeks, she might have saved herself the expense, as Colleen was slated to travel to New York. Mary was an example of the devoted fan whose thinking was less rational than others. Some fans made the pilgrimage to Hollywood in an effort to see or meet their idols and might have come away disappointed, but not entirely empty-handed.

An acquaintance of Colleen's had been a resident of Alexandria, Louisiana: Mr. Walter Hill. He went to Hollywood, and one evening he and his wife attended a party at Colleen's house on Rossmore Street. His wife loved the house so much that when they returned home they carried photographs of Colleen's home, which they gave to a local architect who recreated the house as best as possible.[37]

Consuelo Romero was a tremendous fan of Colleen's. She kept an impressive (and neatly lettered) album of Colleen's clippings and photographs that appeared in newspapers and magazines. She had big Clara Bow eyes and wore her hair in a Colleen Moore Dutchboy. Her knowledge of Colleen's career paid off when she won first prize in a *Daily News* Contest by identifying nine photographs of films starring Colleen. She received a $50 prize for her accomplishment, and gave Colleen her clippings album, which Colleen kept.[38] One of the oddest accounts of Colleen's admirers — and therefore possibly an invented one — was of an individual Colleen met at a garden party. This individual, a young woman, carried on with great authority to anyone who would listen about the motion picture industry. Curious, Colleen asked the woman if she was in pictures. The woman said she was, and introduced herself as Colleen Moore. The original Colleen, without missing a beat, smiled, extended her hand and said: "Well, I am glad to meet me. And how am I to-day?"[39]

Twinkletoes still needed an ending. To get around it, several endings were shot, with the idea that the correct one would be selected after being shown to test audiences. There were three versions shot: One where Twinks dies; another in which she lives; and still another in which she lives and, some years later, is seen living a happy and healthy life with Chuck (whose wife had presumably died) on an idyllic farm. Everybody involved voiced an opinion, mostly in favor of the logical ending that mirrored the sad ending of the book. After viewing the happy ending an acquaintance of John's wrote him: "Just wanted to cast a vote for the logical ending.... I don't see how you can go half way." He was of the opinion that the movie lost its character in the last two reels. "An unhappy ending might make people indignant and the picture might be criticized but it certainly would create a whale of a lot of discussion.... The saccharine or puzzle finish would result in mild amusement and few have survived being laughed at ... only the comics thrive on laughter."[40]

John was leaning towards the happy ending. The idea that one of Colleen's characters might meet with a sad ending seemed to go against his sensibilities. After viewing the happy ending, LeRoy wrote John: "This finish is lovely, John, but it is too bad we cannot have the sad ending."[41] Alfred Santell, who was in New York and due to direct Colleen next in *Orchids and Ermine,* had his own ideas about how the ending should go, although thoroughly tongue-in-cheek: When Twinks is running towards the water, he wrote, the film should cut to Father Neptune, looking through a periscope. Twinks would trip on a cigar butt. Picking it up, she would read the cigar band: "Smoke while you live rather than hereafter." The inscription would give her the idea of ending things while a series of dissolves would show "what happens to bad girls who bump themselves off." This would allow for the use of some interesting depictions of Hell. In the meantime, Chuck starts after Twinks, but is stopped by the ghost of Nancy, who threatens to haunt him for the rest of his life. This would give them "some more weird stuff to do." Cut to a cuckoo clock tolling the hour of four or five or six.... "You judge the footage." The tolling awakens Twinks, who runs for the water, and Chuck, who damns the ghost and runs after Twinks. From a wharf, Twinks dives into the water. Chuck dives in after her. A moment later, Twinks wakes up to find herself in bed: "My God, it was only a dream." Walking on the street, Twinks and Chuck walk past each other, and they all live happily ever after.[42]

The issue of the ending had become public and Brabin aired his feelings about the possible reactions to a sad ending for a Colleen Moore film. He preferred the logical "sad" ending, the one most true to the book, and not just because "you just gotta have the unhappy ending now-a-days," as the *Los Angeles Times* summed up the public mood, but because, according to Brabin, "If you have a story that is big enough and deeply human enough, even though it has a sorrowful conclusion, provided that conclusion is logical, audiences will accept it." The audiences had agreed, it was reported, when the two endings[43] selected were show to a large test audience, and the vote was almost unanimously in favor of the logical ending.

On September 14, the production was delayed while Colleen posed for the requisite publicity photographs. A week earlier, photographer Henry Freulich had photographed Colleen, in costume for production stills on the sets. Seeing the results, John recorded his feelings in a letter: "Was surprised to note that you only took two shots of the exterior of the theatre and both of these where the large crowd was used, and none where the small crowd.... On the proofs where Colleen is dancing, I am more or less at a loss to know which poses to choose, and I wish you would see that Miss Moore gets a look at these so that she can pick them." He wanted Henry to personally supervise the retouching, especially of her legs. "Also, please, when you are taking portrait close-ups, don't take pouting or sad pictures, because people looking at them don't know that it is part of the action of the play ... they are all wrong in close-up portraits."[44]

John's obsessive supervision and careful choreography revealed his obsession with the Colleen Moore of his own creation. This was most dramatically demonstrated to her during one of their breaks between productions, when Colleen broached the subject of starting a family. John seemed horrified at the suggestion, not merely because it might disrupt the long string of hits they had made together, but because she was still "a little girl" herself.[45] Her public persona was that of youth; her roles were often childlike, when the characters were not children themselves, as in *Twinkletoes*, but she was in her 20s, by no means a child. She loved her work, but she wanted a family.

The next day, on the 15th, her work on *Twinkletoes* was completed.

Colleen had only a short break before she was on a train and headed back east for New York, where she was to begin shooting scenes for *Orchids and Ermine*. That same day, John was still sending off his memos, having moved from his careful watch over shooting to keeping a careful eye on editing. Roy Stone was instructed: "In the opening scene, let the tracking shot run all the way so as not to lose the value.... Move father's introductory title to where he's first seen on the ladder.... Stay with Twinks feet and legs before cutting to crowd, then back for further reveal of her full body, then title, then her close-up."[46]

The film was exhibited with two endings, a happy and sad one, and the exhibitors decided individually which they wanted to show.

Orchids and Ermine, *September 18–December 4, 1926*

Colleen Can Wear Own Tresses Again.
— *Los Angeles Times*, September 14, 1926, page A11.

The *Los Angeles Times*[47] pointed out that with the completion of *Twinkletoes*, audiences were to see a more familiar Colleen. Alfred Santell, who was on the East Coast, was to remain there as *Orchids and Ermine* was set in New York. Though the director had a new home awaiting him on the West Coast, he consoled himself with the fact that he would be able to watch the Jack Dempsey–Gene Tunney fight in Philadelphia. Jack Mulhall, the lead in *Even Stephen*, was to be the lead in *Orchids and Ermine*, and remained in New York as well.[48] "Colleen Moore left the west for New York ... to film the exterior scenes of her next picture for First National.... A New York hotel is the center of the action of *Orchids and Ermine*, in which Miss Moore will play the role of a switchboard operator. Many scenes will be filmed at famous landmarks of the metropolis."[49] John was with her on the ride.

Orchids and Ermine was another Cinderella story, with Colleen playing "Pink" Watson, a telephone operator at a cement factory who has big dreams of marrying rich and living a charmed life — of gold dust, not cement dust. She interviews at the Ritz Hotel for the job of hotel switchboard operator, and lands the position. She goes on a date with her friend Ermintrude (Gwen Lee), the flower girl at the hotel, who thinks she has hooked up a wealthy man on his way to a swanky resort. The resort is filled with rich old men who, when their wives turn 40 want to trade them in for "two twenties" (such as Colleen and Ermintrude) or men who are posing as rich when they are not. The latter is the case with their date. He is just a chauffeur on his way to pick up his boss.

Back at the Ritz, oil millionaire Richard Tabor arrives. He is disturbed by all the gold diggers after him for his money, so he trades places with his valet, Hank (Sam Hardy). Ermintrude chases after Hank, thinking he's the millionaire, and Pink has decided to date only rich men, which leaves Tabor in the rain. Her resolve begins to disintegrate when she falls in love. Tabor reveals his true identity to her and proposes, and she accepts. However, Hank, drunk and still living the identity of Tabor, marries Ermintrude, using that name. When the news hits the papers — and Hank's photograph is identified ad Tabor's — all is thrown into disarray. The men are thrown into jail but, in the end, everything works out for the best.

Just before Colleen's work began on *Orchids and Ermine*, she and John, with Alfred Santell and Jack Mulhall,[50] left for Philadelphia to watch the Jack Dempsey–Gene Tunney fight. The same day as the fight the press had begun to speculate on Colleen's next role, suggesting her film would be "Purple and Fine Linen," to be directed by either George Archainbaud or Millard Webb.[51]

In New York, on September 27, production began on the film. Exterior scenes were set up and prepared. The next day it rained, and it rained off-and-on for weeks. Colleen and the rest of the crew went to work in the rain on the 28th. There were delays that day waiting for the Fifth Avenue buses and for the traffic to clear. Some of the first scenes in the film were to be the ones in which Pink Watson climbs aboard a double-decker bus — taking the upper, open level in spite of the rain because the rest of the bus was full — to escape Mulhall's character, who was attempting to convince her of his love. Mulhall catches the next bus, pays the driver to catch up to Pinks bus, and manages to hop from one upper lever to the next.

The element of the bad weather (almost from the day of their arrival on the scene) would have been enough to depress anyone, but the crew was determined to work with it. However, add the weather to the fact that John's memo-writing barrage for *Twinkletoes* had lasted just over six weeks — six weeks of his usual energetic, frantic, rapid-fire genius — and Colleen would have been aware that John was due for another of his drinking episodes. It had been a stressful month and a half. Colleen was aware that, at any time, John might disappear. It happed after they shot the bus scenes on Fifth Avenue.

Exterior images, Plaza Hotel, New York, for *Orchids and Ermine*. Top: In the sun, September 27, 1927. Bottom: In the rain, September 28, 1926 (courtesy Joseph Yranski).

That night, Colleen and Mervyn returned to her suite at the Ambassador, on the 16th floor, where they planned to pick up John and head out for the Stork Club. When they got there, he was standing at the open window. He was glassy-eyed, and they both immediately recognized that he had been drinking. The fact was too much for Colleen. She rushed at him, raining fists on his back, berating him for his behavior and the fact that he was going to destroy both their careers with his drinking. "I can't save your job for you forever," she shouted.

Without a word, John grabbed her and tried to throw her out the window.[52] They were sixteen stories up. Mervyn kicked him and pulled her free, and the two of them ran out the door, leaving John behind. They spent the night walking the streets of New York. By dawn they returned to the hotel and John was gone.[53]

That morning Colleen arrived late to the set.[54] John had disappeared, and nobody said a thing about it. John's drinking and his near-monthly disappearing acts were becoming a joke around the studio. Though she had been unaware of it, the day before, the studio had let John know that the drinking had to stop.[55]

By September 30, both Colleen and the director were sick. Colleen returned to the set on October 2, though she was still feeling under the weather. John still had not turned up, and would not until the end of the day.[56] When he had shown up, he was unapologetic for his drinking and behavior. Colleen was infuriated. After all she had worked for, he still seemed intent on destroying her career through his drinking. She told him she wanted a divorce. She was Catholic, he told her, and she couldn't divorce him. "You're tied to me for life."[57] She was taken aback by the statement and his certainty of her commitment. She had given him little reason to think she would break with him. Once, caught by a police officer while on a bender, the officer had checked John into a bungalow at the Ambassador Hotel to dry out, then called Colleen. John had locked himself into the room and destroyed everything in it. It had taken two bellhops and Colleens chauffeur to wrestle him to the ground, and a doctor to sedate him before they could get him to the hospital. The next day she had resolved to leave him, when a Scottie dog, with a balloon attached, entered her room. "Please Let John Come Home," the writing on the balloon read. She acquiesced.[58]

She had not realized that she had been enabling his behavior throughout their marriage. What she thought of as protection was just the cover he needed to continue his path to self-destruction. Her concern for his pride and career was on a par with her concern for her own well-being. "For better or for worse," she would have thought.

Game Two of the 1926 World Series was played at Yankee Stadium on Sunday, October 3 and Colleen — "a rabid, dyed-in-the-wool baseball fan" — watched as the St. Louis Cardinals "trimmed" the New York Yankees. She called the weather "perfectly grand." She had a cold due to the change in weather from Hollywood, but even so, she wrote that she had been able to attend with John in the lightest of dresses. The summery weather had brought out the women to the game "which was in agreeable contrast with the practically unrelieved masculine attendance." When Billy Southworth hit a home run, she wrote that she hugged John so hard she almost "wilted his collar."[59] Only days after he tried to throw her out a window, she was still doing her best to protect her husband.

The fine weather for the World Series notwithstanding, much of the company's time in New York was spent working under poor weather conditions. The crew's strategy for dealing with the rain included shooting from behind store windows, so that street scenes showing the principals include plenty of New York natives caught unawares on film. It is one of the first times a city's daily life in the rain had been documented on film. This state of affairs lasted nearly straight through to October 16.[60] The publicists decided that when handed lemons, they would make lemonade. The story had been circulated to the press that the production of *Orchids and Ermine* had intended to shoot scenes in the rain, and the lengthy delays in New York were because there was too much sun in Los Angeles, preventing their return.[61]

"Good Lord, give us a rainy day!"

"Good Lord, give us a sunshiny day!"

"The above supplications were poured forth simultaneously recently at First National's New York studios. Colleen Moore was asking for rain and Ray Rockett, who was producing Ben Lyons's next feature, *The Perfect Sap*, was seeking sunshine.

Colleen won. It rained in vast gobs.

"Well, we both couldn't have our wish," said Ray as he watched the rain fall.

—*Daily Illini* (University of Illinois), January 30, 1927, page 10.

30

October 1926–April 1927

> Colleen Moore, First National star ... will step almost literally from the train into elaborate hotel sets at the Burbank studio, when she returns from New York. She plays a switchboard operator in a big New York hotel, in *Orchids and Ermine*, her new picture and some of the largest and finest interiors ever constructed are in readiness for her arrival.
> —*Evening Independent* (Massillon, OH), October 21, 1926, page 15.

When John and Colleen returned to Los Angeles it was announced that Colleen would go to Europe to make her pictures.[1] A dozen pictures were to be made abroad, by her and several other stars. The move was a reaction to the "internationalization" of motion picture production.

Colleen would depart after the expiration of her contract and make four pictures, one each in England, France, Germany and Italy. Each would have a native director and supporting cast. A production staff of locals in each country would be constituted, and a series of First National stars would be rotated to each. "A very great international benefit should arise from this procedure," John said. Will H. Hays, he pointed out, was delighted with the plan. European directors came to America, but few ever went back, and few American directors chose to relocate to Europe.

Following Colleen's European films, John declared, she would retire from motion pictures: "She is going to retire and raise little McCormicks." But before any of that could come to pass, *Orchids and Ermine* needed to be completed, and following that she would take time off. What film she would make next was still undecided. As to his recent trip to New York, John was clearly glad to be back. "If I never go back there again it will be soon enough!"[2]

Back on October 1, John had wired M.C. Levee[3] about this idea: "For your information and for publicity if you wish arrangements have been made whereby expiration of her present contract Colleen Moore will be initial First National star start invade Europe. First National has chosen Colleen Moore as their leading light ... so step on this as hard as you want to."[4]

How Colleen reacted upon seeing John's suggestion that she would soon be raising little McCormicks is unknown, but given her increasing understanding of John's feelings towards the importance of her career and image, she may well have seen it as a publicity move, the next act in a play for Colleen that John had scripted. Colleen wanted a family, but she also wanted a private life, not a life choreographed for her as a means of increasing her fame.

The rumors of John's drinking had become rampant around the studio, and they made their way to Colleen. The studio bosses had taken as much of his drinking as they could. He had even begun to drink at the studio, in his office. One day, John's secretary sent word

The various faces of Colleen. She often posed for portraits that had nothing to do with film roles so that the various magazines could have their own pictorial exclusives. These images all appear to have been taken in the same session (courtesy Judy Coleman).

to Colleen that John was blitzed. She went to his office with Mervyn LeRoy and photographer Henry Freulich and found him nearly passed out. They hustled him out of the office and into Freulich's car, and drove John home. Later that day, Colleens butler called to tell her that John had disappeared. He didn't show up for a week, and when he did, it was in a hospital, his memory of the previous few days a complete blank.

Realizing his job was in danger but wanting to spare him the kick to his pride if he were fired, Colleen placed a long-distance telephone call to New York, to Richard Rowland's office. When Richard answered, she announced herself as Mrs. John McCormick. She then said, "I just wanted to say hello."[5] It was a subtle warning to the head of the studio of her loyalty to her husband.

"She [Colleen] is now busy on interior scenes at the Burbank studio of First National. She is helping out on the big switchboard where she is learning to 'shoot plugs' with the skill of a professional."[6]

Production on *Orchids and Ermine* was finished on December 4, though there were additional shots made for during the ensuing week. In November, John had wired Richard Rowland[7] in New York that Colleen insisted on at least two months off after the completion of *Orchids and Ermine*, pushing the start of her next film back to February. Richard wired back the next day, saying that he could "appreciate how hard she works and know she would not request this unless she thought it vital ... only too happy to cooperate ... only want to point out fact as I understand it *Twinkletoes* and *Orchids* would only be two pictures for this year and have two more completed by May 20, which is practically the end of her second year." Perhaps during her layoff, Rowland suggested, her next two films could be prepared so that she could jump right back into production.[8] That same day John shot back that Colleen had jumped from *Twinkletoes* to *Orchids*, but that she might be able to start one film by the beginning of February and the second by end of March, allowing her to finish both by May. "However will get letter from Moore that each week she takes off in excess of four weeks before starting next picture is to be added on period of contract which will protect you from financial end."[9] The next day Rowland agreed to the arrangement.

Since *Twinkletoes* had been a "heavy" picture and *Orchids and Ermine* a "refined type of comedy," John wrote[10] the next picture ought to be a broad farce. Carey Wilson thought he could get a fast-moving film out of *Miss George Washington*, followed by a comedy characterization of a recently purchased story called "Bennie." Once the present year's program was completed, John wanted to be assured that Colleen would have at least one big production in the next year's program, maybe even two. He begged Richard and the sales department to remember that they were asking Colleen to keep pace with Norma Talmadge, Gloria Swanson, and others. Colleen felt she deserved the same chance. Instead of turning out four pictures, she would prefer to make three at a financial penalty to herself rather than to be rushed through productions to meet release dates.[11] The figure of three pictures in the year was one that would come up again.

On the 19th, Rowland wired Levee about John's request for a special for Colleen, stating that the studio was already prepared to sell one of Colleen's films for the next year's program as a special anyhow and perhaps a second. "Tell little Irishman not to worry."[12]

Twinkletoes was released at the end of November. "It reeks of the unsavory atmosphere of London's west end.... Through it all runs an undercurrent of sin, of starvation, of despair." The film, in an advanced screening, ran nine reels, but "Colleen is so sprightly, so winning, so utterly adorable" that the director, the reviewer guessed, could not decide where to trim the film. Colleen's blonde curls gave "depth to her black eyes and an appealing, whimsical touch to her small features."[13] The film was "freely sprinkled with sparkling comedy, but a powerful menace continually haunts the bright, lovable little heroine; the sinister powers of the Limehouse and its denizens gather to destroy her —-and keep the spectator tense with emotion." The combination of the star, the setting and the story made the film "one of the most promising entertainment offerings that has shown here in many years."[14] Some ads for the film listed it as having an ending that was "happy and satisfying."

Colleen got the two months off after *Orchids and Ermine*. Work on her next film moved forward. John wired Rowland that Santell had not played *Orchids and Ermine* as broadly as he had thought, and so *Miss George Washington,* by Lewis Allen Browne, would be next, as Carey Wilson felt he could pull a fast-moving comedy out of the premise.[15] The story had been made into a film in 1916, with Marguerite Clark playing the part of Bernice Somers ("Summers," in Colleen's version). The new version would get the newer, racier name *Naughty but Nice*. Naughty adventures, but nice at heart. In a production letter to Hugh McCollum, Wesley R. Jones stated that he film would start shooting January 31.[16]

This would be followed by *Bennie*, a human story "with a chance for a lot of gags." For her next season, John wanted to start Colleen off with *The Garden of Eden*, a serious film, followed by *Lilac Time*. "If demand continues for comedy can then do couple hokum stories finish out contract or do *It Could Have Happened Leghorn* or other story of serious nature."[17]

1927

On January 8 Richard Rowland came west for his yearly visit to the First National production facilities. With him were Ned Marin, western sales manager, and Mrs. Florence Strauss, the head of the story department in New York. Rowland was scheduled to spend several weeks in the West going over details of the upcoming production schedule.[18]

Colleen did research for her role in *Naughty but Nice*, which was to be the story of a girl in a finishing school, by visiting finishing schools in the Los Angeles area. Along with her went Carey Wilson and Mervyn LeRoy, who was "not at all protesting."[19] Because of his work with Colleen, LeRoy's real talents were being noticed: "Mervyn LeRoy, gag man for Colleen Moore's company, is so obviously promising as a director that no one need be particularly surprised in a few months hence when he gets his chance."[20]

Mervyn shared a rapport with Colleen: the two understood each other, not only because of their shared sense of humor but all the problems they had suffered though together. It was only natural that when Mervyn graduated to the ranks of director, he would direct Colleen, and directing a star of her magnitude would get his career off to the right start. They ate lunch together nearly every day at the First National commissary, Colleen letting Mervyn pick up the bill because that was the proper thing to do (and John bumping up

Naughty But Nice, *February 25–April 11, 1927*

The start date of *Naughty but Nice* was pushed back several times, finally to February 25, when the production started.[21] Millard Webb[22] had been selected to direct *Naughty but Nice*.[23] It would be a variation on the Cinderella story, with her character undergoing a transformation, there being a generous helping of mistaken identities and risky situations, and with the requisite happy ending. Whereas she had played orphans or waifs in her previous films, this time she was a member of the nouveau riche. Colleen's Berenice Summers starts off as a country girl who is freed from her uncle's Texas ranch when oil is discovered there, and is sent to a fancy Eastern school. At first she is taunted by her snooty schoolmates, publicly humiliated by local joker Paul Carroll (Donald Reed), leaving her mortified. With the passage of time however, she blossoms into a beauty and crosses paths with Paul again at a formal ball. He falls for her.

Berenice and her friend Alice (Kathryn McGuire) go to a hotel to meet Paul for a theater date, but in the lobby they run into the principal of their school and so and they invent a story — the first of a series of stories that build one upon the other — about visiting Alice's parents, Judge and Mrs. Altwold. The principal does not buy the story and calls their bluff, insisting on being taken to the parents' hotel room. They lead him to a room and enter it; the room belongs to Ralph Ames (Hallam Cooley) of the Secret Service. Berenice introduces the stranger as her husband and he goes along with the ruse. Berenice, however, is a chronic liar. Later, she and Ames meet at the judge's house, resulting in even more confusion. After a series of gags, Berenince is ultimately united in marriage with Paul Carroll after nearly losing him.

The film would be an economical production, requiring few location shots and most of the work being done in the studio. The role would still be hard on Colleen, who had already suffered her share of bumps and bruises for her art: "Rolling off the roof of a house gracefully is a feat that is taxing the skill of Colleen Moore. During the last few days she had made dozens of rolls down the shingled roof of a house, to provide one of the thrills and laughs of her new picture.... Wrapped in a quilt, Miss Moore supposedly is sleeping on the roof when, moving in her sleep, she begins a descent toward mother earth."[24] It had not been long since Colleen's neck had been injured, and after the cast had come off she was left sleeping in a neck brace for the rest of her life. Yet she was still doing stunts.

In filling roles with extras, the studio called on Polly Ann Young, but she was out. Her sister, Gretchen Young, answered the call and suggested she might be able to fill in for her sister. She got her sister's role, and after that she was given a contract.[25] "First National claims to have just signed the very youngest featured actress.... She is Gretchen Young[26]... who is just turned sixteen. Miss Young began her career at the age of 4.... During the past few years she has been studying dancing under Ruth St. Denis and Ernest Belcher. She recently played the part of a boarding-school girl in Colleen Moore's *Naughty but Nice*."[27]

The production slowed down in early March as Colleen was ill. She continued to show up for work, but ended the days early. A conference was held to determine how to continue. By the 11th, she was feeling sick enough to visit the doctor. She would recover and continue working on *Naughty but Nice*. In the meantime, it was necessary to announce the next five titles for Colleen. Grace Kingsley had already reported her next picture would be entitled *Something with a Kick*. It had nothing to do with alcohol; it was a film about football and was set in a coed college. About her break between pictures, Colleen was quoted as saying, "When I take my vacation I'm not going away from home. I find more happiness there than anywhere else."[28]

For the upcoming year John advised Gerald C. Duffy he wanted four different types of films for Colleen's next season: a "flapper" story, a brisk comedy-melodrama, another "Cinderella story" and a spectacular special. Her film to follow *Naughty but Nice* had not yet been decided upon. Duffy had been assigned on March 5 to look for suitable material for Colleen.[29]

"Colleen Moore is Peter Pan with a collegiate figure and a Wall-street brain," the *Los Angeles Times* reported. "This bright-eyed, vivacious lady ... goes on making comedies when down in her heart she longs for another *So Big*. Colleen as the eager young girl, the bitter wife, and the frail old little mother, contributed what many regard as the finest performance of that year in motion pictures.... 'But,' and here she shrugged expressively, 'the public wants to see me in comedy, and, after all, you know, this is a business.'"[30]

Duffy had two days to search for material before he was transferred to editing and titling Harry Langdon's *Long Pants*. He returned to reading on March 15. Between then and the end of the month he read 73 recommended stories. Potential material had been found for fitting the general guidelines John had suggested, but nothing for her next film. Around that time, after many meetings with John, the idea came up that it might be a good idea for Colleen's next film to be an Irish story.

Duffy liked the idea and pushed for it. He though the character would be "unusual and impressive." Both Colleen and John liked the suggestion, and Duffy was given all the available Irish material to review, about 25 stories in all. Nothing jumped out at him, but he had definite ideas about the sort of story and characters he wanted to see. He expanded the characters and themes, gave it the title *The Road to Dublin* and hoped to deliver the story to Richard Rowland, who had been in town at the time. Richard, however, had already departed for New York. Instead, he delivered the story to John at home that night. Within a few days McCormick called Duffy and Carey Wilson into conference regarding the various stories. They settled on Duffy's, and McCormick changed the title to *When Irish Eyes Are Smiling*.[31] McCormick began negotiating with M. Witmark & Sons for the title.[32]

Back on the set, photography went just over five weeks, three days over schedule.[33]

The problems concerning *When Irish Eyes Are Smiling* had to corrected. For nearly two weeks there were daily story conferences between McCormick, Wilson and Duffy; they worked on changes to the ending so that Colleen's character would have to travel from Ireland to New York. While the conferences continued, it had been decided that Mervyn LeRoy would be the director of the film, and so he was brought in on the conferences.[34] Both Colleen and Mervyn were elated.

Time was pressing, so on April 12 Colleen, John, Duffy and Mervyn LeRoy went to Arrowhead Hot Springs and worked on the story until the 18.[35] A few days later, Carey

30. October 1926–April 1927

Colleen, on the water. Left to right: Unknown woman, Carey Wilson, Virginia Valli, Colleen, unknown man.

Wilson joined the party. For the most part, Colleen did not attend the Arrowhead conferences. She had given her input, and now the work of fixing the problems was the job of the writers. Given a chance to enjoy a few days off, she chose to relax. John was enthused. He thought it could be Colleen's best story yet, and shared that opinion with everyone there.[36]

When they returned, Duffy went to work shaping the story into the continuity. John wired Rowland: "Happy to advise you we that had a very constructive period at Arrowhead and believe the boys have worked out best Colleen Moore story that have yet tackled stop Only thing worrying us now is that we are absolutely up against it for a leading man."[37] On May 5, John wired Rowland about an unexpected angle to exploit: "I wired you previously had commissioned Ernest Ball to write a new song for us to be used in this picture called "Killlarney Rose" and song was finished day before he died....[38] We can cash in on lot of valuable sympathetic publicity, because now that poor Ernie has gone he will be recognized more than ever as America's greatest balladist and the picture will serve to introduce his last ballad."[39]

May 18 was the official end of Colleen's contract. Her next contract had yet to be negotiated.

After several conferences on the story, it was decided the first two-thirds were too long and the end lacked "punch." Several sections were condensed and, working with LeRoy, more humor was injected. The end of the film was proving problematic. Conferences continued into May. Around the 13th, Duffy was "visited by an idea which seems to me to supply all that was desired and needed to make the finish just what we wanted." Duffy took his idea to LeRoy, who was enthusiastic. Together LeRoy and Duffy went to McCormick, and Duffy outlined the ending to him. McCormick approved of the idea and immediately put Duffy to work adding the new ending directly to the continuity. About five days later

Duffy brought the completed script back to McCormick. McCormick was to read the completed script, have Colleen read it, and then hold a joint conference at the earliest possible time to figure out what work was left to be completed before the story could finally be approved. However, the First National convention was in town, and this forced everything to wait.[40]

First National

The First National convention that year would be marked by uncertainty. The organization had been undergoing tremendous change. The threat represented by Paramount loomed larger than ever. The strong leadership needed by the organization was lacking.

Paramount had acquired interests in the theater chains of many original First National franchise holders. It was also in control of about a third of the stock interests of First National. A large portion of important outlets for First National films had fallen into the hands of their competitors, and so First National had lost the preferences they had previously enjoyed in playing times and extended runs.[41] In 1926, Sol Lesser had sold his interest in the West Coast Theatres chain of picture houses to Mike Gore, A.L. Gore and First National.[42] The year before they had fended off a takeover attempt by William Fox, leaving Fox with control of only one-third of the company. By 1927, however, Fox had gained control of West Coast, giving him control of about a third of First National's interests.[43]

While First National's fortunes sagged, those of the Stanley Corporation were soaring. Stanley, who were the original franchise holders, had expanded their theater chain. In 1926, they merged with several other First National Franchise holders.[44] They, in turn, had just merged with First National, a "$100,000,000 combine" that brought three organizations into a "motion-picture producing and distributing concern. The transaction is described as the largest development in the film world since the Famous Players-Lasky consolidation." With the consolidation, John J. McGuirk, president of Stanley, ascended to the position of President of First National Pictures, succeeding Robert Lieber. No changes in personnel were contemplated,[45] but with such a large combination it's doubtful that many believed the claim. Lieber had been a respected and trusted leader who had managed to keep First National's large cooperative organization working smoothly. With his resignation, First National began a stretch of acute managerial difficulties. John McGuirk would be succeeded in less than four months by Clifford B. Hawkley. In June of 1928, Hawkley would be succeeded, in turn, by Irving D. Rossheim. This period of rapid turnover left the organization without any form of aggressive leadership or a clear vision on where it should go.[46]

The intention of First National to hold its annual convention in Los Angeles was important as it gave First National men the opportunity to inspect the newly erected studio. The impressive studio would be a reassuring sight in uncertain times. The convention would bring Richard Rowland, heads of all the departments in New York, and all district managers, branch managers and salesmen from the company's 39 exchanges.[47] "Film Fans to be the Real Boss," the *Los Angeles Times* said,[48] an important observation for an organization that needed direction. On May 19, the First National delegates arrived at the Santa Fe station as 10:40 A.M. and were met by city officials and a large delegation of Hollywood actors.

Dressed alike in white trousers and blue coats and straw hats with blue First National bands, they lined up in parade formation, accompanied by a band, and led the delegation through the streets to Fifth Street and Grand Avenue, where they boarded buses that took them to the Ambassador Hotel. At the Ambassador, 375 delegates attending the First National sales convention would tell the men who make the films what they have found the public likes best.[49] An issue to be taken up on the 20th was how to spend $14,000,000 in the next year at the new studio. The big studio bosses would get ideas from their sales managers. John McCormick was the official host of the convention.[50]

In spite of the assurances that there would be no major changes in personnel with the Stanley merger, things did change. "W.R. Rothacker, president of Allen-Rothacker Film Laboratories," it was reported in the *Times*, was to "succeed M.C. Levee as General Manager of the First National Motion Pictures Corporation." He would work with John McCormick in the supervision of the First National Studios in Burbank.[51]

John had other ideas. He had been warned about his drinking, and he had been grumbling about his position. "He has been threatening to quit for more than a year."[52] He was displeased with the organization. He had a sharp mind and he knew something was afoot. John felt indispensable, but he knew the organization wanted Colleen without the complications of having him on the payroll. He had to do something dramatic to make sure they understood that, without him, there would be no Colleen.

And so, without warning, John resigned his position, and all hell broke loose.

31

Break with First National, May–June 1927

> Upon us is laid a great responsibility. We must accept the fact that our lives do not belong to ourselves. What hurts one, hurts all of us.
> — Mary Pickford, quote in "Film Industry Tired of Being Spanked," *New York Times*, May 13, 1927, page 29.

Back in January, three dozen big Hollywood names had convened on January 11 at the Ambassador Hotel in Los Angeles looking to create an organization that would speak for the industry as a whole. A proposal was made to create an International Academy of Motion Picture Arts and Sciences. Attendees included Louis B. Mayer, Mary Pickford, Sid Grauman, Jesse Lasky, George M. Cohan, Cecil B. DeMille, Douglas Fairbanks, Cedric Gibbons and Irving Thalberg. The idea was endorsed and work started on creating the organization.

Many people had been invited to that initial meeting including Colleen, through John, who did not pass the invitation along to her. When she heard about the meeting, she asked John why they had not been invited. John gave her no answer. She would only learn about the invitation some years later when shown a typed invitation. Colleen could only guess that John was feeling the pressure of his precarious situation at the studio. Everyone at the event would have been aware that it was Colleen who was the big shot of the pair. John did not want to face the most powerful Hollywood personalities under those circumstances.[1]

On May 11, an official organizational banquet was held at the Biltmore Hotel in Los Angeles. Of the 300 guests, 230 joined the Academy, paying $100 each.[2] Colleen and John — Colleen under the name "Colleen Moore" and not "Colleen Moore McCormick" — were in attendance, assigned to seats at Table Three.[3] Both joined the academy, Colleen as a member of the Actors Branch and John in the Producers Branch.[4]

Keeping the invitation to the initial meeting a secret was only a taste of what was to come for Colleen.

> She is "of special, unique and extraordinary attainments and has a large following among the public."
> — First National on Colleen, as quoted in *Chicago Tribune*, June 18, 1927.

When Irish Eyes Are Smiling was due to start shooting Tuesday, May 24. Monday morning, Mervyn LeRoy searched through the studio, looking for John. Stepping into John's office, he overheard John's side of a disturbing telephone conversation: John was yelling into the handset, red-faced. When he hung up he said: "That was Rowland I was talking to, and it's over."[5]

"What do you mean it's over? What's over?"

31. Break with First National, May–June 1927

John said that he and Colleen were through with First National. The bastards had tried to pull a fast one, and so he and Colleen were pulling up stakes and going to New York, he said, to make films with another studio. *When Irish Eyes Are Smiling* was canceled.

The film, in fact, was still clinging to life. It was John's association with First National that was dead. Everything had come to a head.

Colleen was bewildered by the news.[6] Hearing that John had resigned his position meant it would be impossible for the film to proceed. The studio was — as far as she was concerned — in breach of their contract. They could not reasonably expect the film to be completed, and so, under the terms of their contract, the studio had a financial obligation to her. Colleen was thinking to leverage her importance and the studio's obligations in John's favor.

The next morning, on May 24 Colleen sent a telegram to First National stating:

Under the terms of my contract you agreed to furnish facilities for production so that eight pictures should be produced prior to May 18, 1927 stop you have failed to do so and have thereby prevented me from completing eight pictures within that time stop if said pictures had been fully produced I would have been entitled to receive fifty-five thousand dollars in addition to that already paid stop I hereby demand immediate payment of said sum and am confirming this wire by letter[7]

On Wednesday, May 25, Gerald Duffy was called into a conference with Richard Rowland, Samuel Spring and Edwin Loeb. The story of John's departure had already made the papers. "M'Cormick Quits Studio. Production Manager for First National Resigns in Sudden Breech with Company."[8] John's departure complicated matter for the *When Irish Eyes Are Smiling* production. When Duffy arrived for the meeting, he was told that Miss Moore had rejected the continuity for *Irish Eyes*. Richard had her letter of rejection:

Gentlemen:
In connection with the continuity of *When Irish Eyes Are Smiling*, submitted to me for approval, I wish to advise you that I do not approve the continuity in its present form, and that I hereby disapprove the same as the basis of my next picture.

After reviewing the continuity carefully it is my opinion that the same as now prepared is entirely lacking in dramatic quality, is weak in many respects and gives me no opportunity for any characterization.

Very truly yours,
Colleen Moore McCormick[9]

Everybody had been enthusiastic about the project, and all had felt it would be one of Colleen's finest. Mervyn had come up with gags for the county fair sequence. Just a week earlier he had submitted the finished product to McCormick. If all had gone according to their usual routine, John would read it and then pass it along to Colleen to read. There had been, however, the recent First National convention.[10] In addition to the entertaining of the delegates, Colleen had hosted the First National sales chiefs at a beach barbecue at the Gables Club in Santa Monica.[11] Now, John had topped things off by making a break with the company. As a writer, Duffy worked most directly with John, who had always handled most of the story decisions when it came to materials for Colleen. John had not given any indication to him that the script was so bad it was worth breaking a contract over.

A major point of contention between John, Colleen and the studio heads (according to the McCormicks) was whether First National had prevented Colleen from completing her obligations as outlined by the contract. There had been delays. *Orchids and Ermine* had finished 11 days behind schedule. Colleen had requested and been granted two months' rest after the completion of *Orchids and Ermine*. R.W. Perkins pointed out in a telegram to Samuel Spring that "she did no work until February twenty fifth when she began next picture" and that "McCormick wired Rowland November sixteenth he would get the letter from her that each week she took off in excess four weeks would be added to period of contract to protect us" from acquiring the financial obligations should her time off delay her production schedule.[12]

Richard responded to Colleen with a two-page letter, asserting that the studio had made every effort to have a story ready for Colleen on time, and that the failure to meet with the studio and discuss problems with the story was not the fault of the studio:

> At the suggestion of your husband ... who was directly in charge of all productions starring you and produced by us, we submitted to you ... a complete continuity containing at least 123 scenes which had been previously approved by you and in addition many other scenes including a revised ending of the picture which we had endeavored to have prepared to meet Mr. McCormick's wishes, and presumably yours.
>
> Both Gerald C. Duffy ... as well as Mr. Mervyn LeRoy, who has been engaged, with your approval, to direct said photoplay have been ready, able and willing at all times since May 19th to meet with you, and with Mr. McCormick, for the purpose of discussing this continuity with you to ascertain whether the same met with your approval.[13]

He requested that Colleen meet with Duffy and LeRoy Thursday afternoon to discuss the continuity. Furthermore, Richard pointed out in the letter, McCormick, in his capacity as general production manager, issued instructions to start photographing *When Irish Eyes Are Smiling* on May 30. It indicated, he wrote, that at the time John had been reasonably certain that the continuity would be acceptable to Colleen. The gap between their positions, he seemed to suggest, might not be rectifiable.

The next day John McCormick sent a telegram to John C. Bullwinkle in New York:

> I regret to advise you that I have come to a parting of the ways with your company stop the reason for this move is that I cannot reconcile myself to certain steps that the executives of your company proposed to make in the studio stop I want to thank you and your boys for the splendid support you have given me personally and to tell you that as much as I would like to have remained on for the balance of the year and carried out the plans I outlined to you at the convention nevertheless under the present setup this was impossible.[14]

Reporters were clamoring for the story, calling Charles Einfeld in New York. Unsure of what to say about it, he telegrammed C.F. Chandler in Los Angeles for clarification. Chandler confirmed: "John McCormick has definitely resigned as production manager of First National Pictures Rothacker will probably take charge." Chandler told him to tell the press he knew nothing. "Just let them print their news and First National knows nothing about it until you hear from me."[15]

Richard Rowland sent Einfeld a telegram of his own, ordering him not to make any statements until he heard from him.[16]

It was decided that Duffy and LeRoy would get together with Colleen and confer over the continuity, hear her out and see if they could not overcome her objections. She had always deferred to John's judgment when it came to making story decisions, but with John officially out of the picture they might be able to prevail upon Colleen directly. Her contract gave her, not John final say over her material. A letter was composed and sent to Colleen.

The morning of the 26th Colleen sent her reply to Richard Rowland:

Gentlemen

I have your letters of May 25th, requesting me to meet with Mr. Duffy and Mr. LeRoy, at two o'clock this afternoon for the purposes of discussing the continuity of *When Irish Eyes Are Smiling.*

I wish to advise you that I will be present at the time and place indicated, but to also inform you that I am doing so solely for the purpose of facilitating the selection of a satisfactory story and the completion of a continuity based thereon, which will be satisfactory to me.

In no respect shall the fact that I am engaging in this appointment or discussing this feature of the matter, be deemed or considered as a waiver of my claim that I am now entitled to the sum of Fifty-five Thousand Dollars ($55,000.00) as compensation for the work completed by me during the past twenty-four months.

I am perfectly willing to have my representative discuss this matter with anyone that you may suggest and if they are unable to agree on the solution of the question to immediately submit it to arbitration in the manner required in my contract.

Very truly yours,
Colleen Moore McCormick[17]

Colleen sounded willing to let the whole matter be shifted to arbitration if they could not hash their problems out themselves. This buoyed the studio men, as they were certain they had done everything in their power to complete the terms of their contract. Perhaps if she saw this, it might cause her to split on the issue with John. She had an obligation, she could tell John.

For her part, Colleen felt that she had gone above and beyond for her company. Fresh out of a full-body cast after a fractured vertebra, she had gone straight to work before a grueling European tour. She slept at night with a leather neck brace because of her accident. Though John had been enthusiastic with the earlier material for *When Irish Eyes Are Smiling*, she was convinced that if he had found it lacking, then it was lacking. He would not let her star in a film composed of half-measures. His judgment had always been good. He was a prideful man. In a contest between loyalty to a company and loyalty to her husband, John would always win out.

Stories began to appear in the papers: "Colleen Moore Quits. Stops Work on Film After Husband, McCormick, Leaves First National." That story had appeared in the *New York Times* on May 26, and in the *Chicago Tribune* the next morning. It was naturally assumed that if Colleen's husband wished to leave, Colleen would leave with him.

Colleen arrived at her bungalow and telephoned Al Rockett, informing him that she was prepared for the meeting. Besides Mervyn and Gerald — director and writer — Richard Rowland had decided that he and his assistant, Ned Marin, would go along.

When she opened the door, Richard reported, she greeted them "rather coldly." This was a story matter, Colleen insisted. Was it appropriate for Richard and Ned to be in attendance? Richard pointed out that he was a vice-president, Ned was his assistant, and that if she did not want them there, then the meeting could be called off. Colleen let them stay.

Richard started the meeting by assuring Colleen that they wanted to achieve a continuity that would be agreeable to all. He asked what was wrong with the current one. First and foremost, she felt that the characterization of Kathleen was too generic. The part could be played "by several other and less individual stars." She also felt that the story unfolded mostly through the use of subtitles and not through action, and that it did not achieve a powerful enough climax to justify the picture.

She outlined a set of other minor objections, largely in the last part of the script.[18] Richard pointed out that John had approved the script a week earlier. Had he not quit, they would have ironed out the problems. Colleen shot back that John was not her manager. She was the artist and final judgment on stories rested with her.

Up until a few days ago, Richard told her, John acted as if he was her manager: "Practically all stories were negotiated by Mr. McCormick for her and accepted for her and that all stories she had were approved by Mr. McCormick." She had always deferred to his say. Therefore, he insisted, he was her manager. By precedent, through McCormick, she had already approved the story.

This was a story meeting, Colleen pointed out. They were not there to discuss legal matters. Richard asked if she would be willing to do *When Irish Eyes Are Smiling* if a reasonably acceptable continuity could be worked out. Yes, she said, she would accept a satisfactory continuity. Richard repeated "reasonably acceptable." He asked if she was satisfied with Mervyn LeRoy as director and Duffy as the writer. She was. She seemed inclined to make the film. That was good enough for Richard. He and Ned left Colleen and Mervyn and Gerald to work on their own.[19]

The first 124 scenes of the continuity were just fine. It was, Collen felt, at the point where her character of Kathleen arrives in America that things got derailed. She did not see the audience being sympathetic with Rory O'More (the male lead) since it did not appear he had ever made an attempt to send for Kathleen. Colleen felt it should be made clear that sending for Kathleen was something always on his mind. And the climax was too physical, not emotional enough. Upon discovering Rory a success, kissed on the stage by another woman, Kathleen announced her intention to leave Rory and return to Ireland. The following scenes showing Kathleen in steerage while Rory unknowingly enjoys first-class accommodations on the same ship was too abrupt. The subtitles for the film were excellent, but they did not afford her the opportunities of acting that she wanted. They worked on some ideas, left the meeting feeling hopeful.

It had been decided to "re-write and re-build the story from the point at which the character of Kathleen lands in America."[20] After their meeting, Gerald reported back to Richard that he had an idea for the story and would probably meet again with Colleen about it in a few days.[21]

> Al Rockett, formerly an independent producer for First National, yesterday was named production manager by Richard A. Rowland, first vice-president of the company. He takes the place of John McCormick, who resigned Tuesday.
> —*Los Angeles Times*, May 27, 1927, page A11.

With John's departure from First National, there was a sudden shift of personnel. Ned Marin from the New York office was to assume the business manager duties of M.C. Levee, who had resigned weeks earlier. W.R. Rothacker had been due to take Levee's position, but when John left it was believed he would instead be given the title of managing director. Colleen denied her intentions to sail for Europe, but it was believed the couple would soon

31. Break with First National, May–June 1927

take a vacation, therefore breaking her contract.[22] It was already known that Colleen wanted a break between films. The rumors to the effect that she would break her contract were persistent and continued to appear in the papers.

> Richard A. Rowland ... left here last night for New York. At the time of his departure the situation brought about a few days ago by the resignation of John McCormick, former general manager of the local studio, remained unchanged.
>
> Rumors to the effect that McCormick would be assigned with the company as an independent producer remained unverified yesterday.... His wife, Colleen Moore, has not as yet followed her husband's lead in withdrawing from the company, although it is expected she will do so within a short time.[23]

For a week an uneasy truce existed between the studio and Colleen and John. Friday's *Times* ran a photograph of Mervyn and his fiancée, Edna Murphy squeezed below a photograph of a decidedly exotic Myrna Loy ("An oriental charmer!") and above Mae Murray in Renaissance dress — that noted Mervyn had "been recently given the exalted position of 'director' and his first picture will be Colleen Moore's next starring vehicle."[24] Her next starring vehicle that is if disaster could be averted. Life went on in spite of the precariousness of the situation, though the pressure on all parties was increasing.

> Colleen Moore will be sued for damages if she continues in her refusal to go on with her next picture, *Baby Face*, First National officials hinted today. Meanwhile, John McCormick ... was reported to be negotiating with other companies for Colleen's services.
> —"Colleen Must Finish Film or Face Suit,"
> *Milwaukee Sentinel*, May 29, 1927, section 1, page 13.

On May 31, a Tuesday, Duffy finished work on the script and submitted it to Al Rockett, who had taken over John's duties. Al forwarded the script to Colleen. Colleen needed to read it and decide if they were close to a script that would be satisfactory, or reasonably acceptable, depending upon who was asked. If she liked it, the upcoming clash could be averted. If not: disaster. She did not mince words in her judgment. She wrote to Al Rockett:

> I have just read the new treatment of the ending for *When Irish Eyes Are Smiling* and I think it is very bad. I can see no improvement and think the changes to the boy's character only makes my part as the girl seem weak and insipid. The end is very long drawn out — in fact, the story as a whole is weak and I do not think it can be fixed. I think it would greatly injure my reputation to play in this picture.
> As a matter of fact, while I was quite receptive to Mr. Rowland's suggestion that I do an Irish story, I was not aware of the fact that this would entail my sitting around several weeks waiting for a story to be manufactured out of thin air. As many weeks had already gone by and nothing has so far been submitted that has any qualities that would make for a first class motion picture for me, I am compelled refuse story entirely.
> Very Truly Yours,
> Colleen Moore McCormick[25]

This was followed by a second letter. "I desire to advise you that my attorney, Mr. Alfred Wright, has today discussed with Mr. Edwin Loeb, representing you, the matter of the payment of Fifty-five Thousand Dollars ($55,000.00) now due me, under the terms of my contract.... Unless this payment is received on or before Friday, June 3rd, 1927, I will consider my contract of employment terminated and that I am released from any and all obligations there under."

If Colleen could make the argument that the studio was in breach of contract, she would be free to follow her husband. Colleen was worth her weight in gold. She was valuable enough that it would be almost worth the trouble of having John on the payroll if it meant getting Colleen in the bargain. Plans had already been suggested for Colleen going abroad to make four films,[26] and there might be nothing to prevent her from doing so under another studio's banner.

In New York, R.W. Perkins suggested they bring in an arbitration lawyer. Sam Spring thought it was a good idea and left it to him to look into it.[27] Edwin Loeb met with Colleen's attorney, Alfred Wright, that same day. They had a long conference.

"The first 24 months of the artist's employment expired on May 18," Wright told Edwin, to which Edwin replied that he was "definitely of the opinion that various acts and delays on the part of Miss Moore were responsible in part for the failure of the company to complete eight photoplays during the two-hear period." She had not shown due diligence in approving the form of the continuity, and that had contributed to the delay, Loeb argued. And it had not been until McCormick's troubles with the studio that Colleen had decided that she had been aggrieved. He would look into finding information on the various delays for which Colleen might have been responsible, but as John had been in complete charge of her productions, that might prove difficult. All this meant, in essence, that the case would have to go to arbitration, as required by the terms of her contract.

"Inasmuch as Miss Moore is receiving the claimed compensation at a rate of $10,000 a week," Loeb pointed out, "it seemed foolish to disturb the situation by her insistent demands at this time that she be paid the balance in full."

Wright did not want his client to waive any rights through the appearance of approving of the current arrangement of payment. Loeb assured Wright again that he would investigate the history of delays and report further to him. Afterwards, Loeb contacted Mr. Levee, who was of the opinion that documenting such a history would be difficult, given McCormick's control over the Colleen Moore unit. In his letter to Sam Spring at First National, Loeb stated it was of the utmost importance that a history of Colleen's productions since May 18, 1925, be assembled. Furthermore, he suggested a trusted employee be assigned the task of documenting difficulties in future difficulties of Colleen's productions.

Elsewhere, First National's counsel met with the McCormick's counsel. They stuck to their guns, as a letter to Samuel Spring from R.W. Perkins illustrates. "Colleen wires conference between her counsel and ours regarding fifty five thousand without results and since our failure [to] produce eight pictures [was] not caused by her she demands immediate payment balance due unless paid by Friday will consider her contract terminated."[28]

On June 3, John went to Colleen in her bungalow at the studio and told her: "We're leaving tonight for New York."[29]

It was disturbing news.

31. Break with First National, May–June 1927

"We're not making *Irish Eyes*," he told her "You're walking out on it."

Colleen asked: "But why?"

"I've done all right for you before picture-wise, haven't I? Trust me that what I'm doing is for your own good."[30]

That day they met with Sam Spring for two hours. Afterwards, Sam reported in a telegram to Richard Rowland that the couple had received him in a friendly manner and been pleasant, but the meeting had accomplished nothing. John had the idea that the whole matter could be settled if he left for New York and discussed it with the president of First National himself, as he felt they (the people back east, including the president) were the ones who had started the dispute.

Sam was convinced that John's goal was to get himself reinstated. The threat to leave, and the implied threat that Colleen would follow, was his leverage. John's decision to leave that day was doubtless prompted by the fact that, in just over a week, there would be a meeting of the Board of Directors[31] in New York.

Sam thought the idea was absurd, and that the entire industry would be behind them, but advised that the company should take a posture of "Stiff insistence upon our legal rights until she comes to see reason."

After his telegram to Rowland he fired one off on June 3rd to the President of First National, warning him that the couple was on their way to meet with him directly:

> Colleen and John are leaving for New York tonight with evident intent of seeing you and John McGuirk stop I spent last night and this morning with them and accomplished nothing stop I am leaving for New York tomorrow night stop looks like a battle Regards
>
> S. Spring

He left the next morning for New York.[32]

When Colleen was alone, she called Richard and told him she did not understand what was going on, but that she was firmly on her husband's side. It was important to her that Richard did not leave Mervyn LeRoy hanging. Regardless of their differences on this issue, it was no reason to ruin Mervyn's career.

Richard told her that he understood and was sure everything would be worked out once they got to New York.[33] In *Silent Star*, Colleen wrote, "I didn't know what to make of that remark," suggesting that she did not know what John had planned when they arrived, but that Richard did.[34] The telephone call ended with Richard's assurance that Mervyn would get his own.

Mervyn was crushed at the news that Colleen was departing. He walked to the stage where shooting was to have started. Suddenly a door opened and one of the studio police officers called to him, saying that he had a telephone call. It was Richard Rowland, who told him that Colleen had been so enthusiastic about him that Richard wanted to give him another film — not with Colleen unfortunately. Mervyn was told to look around for material, find something that interested him, and let Richard know.[35]

He'd have his directorial debut, but not with Colleen.

"Colleen Moore and McCormick Leave for Trip," the *Los Angeles Times* reported, avoiding reference to the disagreement. Unconfirmed by Colleen was the suggestion that, in leaving with her husband, she had broken her contract. She would only say that relations with her studio were "not entirely amicable" and that she was not starting her new picture because she did not like the script and because she needed a rest. "Reports that McCormick and Miss Moore would confer with officials of the company in New York could not be confirmed," the paper stated.[36]

On June 4 Edwin Loeb shot off a telegram to R.W. Perkins in New York: "Miss Moore left for New York last night on Santa Fe Chief stop on her arrival in New York please serve formal demand requiring her to return immediately to California studio for instructions and work under contract specifying demand is made without waiver of or prejudice to company's existing rights."

First National did not want to lose Colleen, but it was starting to look like that was John's plan if he could not manage to reinsert himself into the First National organization in a capacity that he felt suited him. He was using the threat to take Colleen elsewhere if he did not get what he wanted, and there would be plenty of bidders for Colleen's talents and image. "John McCormick will become an independent producer, featuring productions starring his wife Colleen Moore. This, at least, is his intention just now, although some of the many offers that have poured in since his resignation from First National may cause him to change his mind."[37]

It would be nearly two weeks before the million dollar lawsuit would move forward — on June 18, the news would appear in papers across the country — but her trip marked the beginning of a period of exile in New York while cooped up in her hotel room avoiding process servers. John was drinking again, trying to keep himself together. Fortunately Cleeve was there to keep her company.

32

New York and Arbitration, June–August 1927

Upon their arrival in New York, John and Colleen checked into a suite at the Ritz-Carlton Hotel on Madison Avenue where Cleeve met them. John was drinking heavily, Colleen wrote, but he was managing to keep his act together, given the seriousness of the situation. He had bought tickets aboard the Cunard Line's *Mauretania*, and he had told the press, and he and Colleen would sail for Europe and make their films there.[1] The *Mauretania* had arrived in New York on Friday, June 10,[2] and was due to depart for Europe on Wednesday, June 15,[3] just two days after the meeting of First National's board of directors.

"Will John and Mrs. John McCormick return to First National" the newspaper columnist pondered, "or will they not? Presumably, John and the Missus ... will sail for Europe tomorrow.... British National Pictures wants Colleen to make four in England and there are, of course, not a few other offers."[4]

> Motion arbitration under New York law served Thursday stop overtures from other side followed almost immediately and feel certain entire matter will be amicably adjusted next week[5]

First National had hired Nathan Burkan. To prevent Colleen from leaving the country, Burkan took action: "Colleen Moore ... is being sued by First National Pictures, Inc., for $1,000,000, it was learned today, when Nathan Burkan, counsel for the company, sought an order from Supreme Court Justice Mullan to compel her to arbitrate the terms of a contract."[6] While in New York, Colleen was a virtual prisoner in her suite at the hotel. Process servers were waiting for her to make an appearance so they could give her the order to appear in court. So long as she managed to avoid being served, she would not have to appear. Once served, she would either have to appear, or else Nathan Burkan could claim that Colleen was refusing to appear, and could ask for a default judgment against her. Once they had a judgment they could use it against any of Colleen's assets — bank accounts, real estate or even her clothes and dolls. The constant worry affected her appetite. She lost weight, dropping under 100 pounds. Cleeve had to send for a doctor.

During this time John tried to get into the board of directors meeting.[7] Everyone knew John's argument that Colleen's uniqueness was a result of his direction. He had been stating it for years to anyone who would listen. "Every star must fill some particular niche in the hearts of people to gain lasting fame," McCormick had said. "Miss Moore represents the girl we all know and love.... She is a live, warm-blooded, loyal little creature, joyous and earnest, modern to the last degree and always lovable." This is the summing up offered by John McCormick, whose keen knowledge of people's notions and emotions has given him a high place among the screen's most successful producers.[8] The article had essentially attributed Colleen's success to John.

Colleen had managed to avoid the process servers for a time, but everyone knew she was in town. One day there was a knock at the door. It was a little old lady, saying how much she adored her; could she get an autograph? Colleen was always happy to oblige a fan, but as soon as the lady handed Colleen something autograph, she turned her back and departed. Colleen looked at the paperwork in her hand and realized she had been served.

> "The differences between Miss Colleen Moore ... and First National Pictures, Inc., were taken into court yesterday, when Nathan Burkan, representing First National, asked Supreme Court Justice Mullan to compel Miss Moore to submit the dispute to arbitration under the New York law."
> —"Colleen Moore Must Arbitrate Movie Contract,"
> *Atlanta Constitution*, June 24, 1927, page 1.

In court, a week earlier, Nathan Burkan had contended that "Miss Moore's annoyance at delay and dissatisfaction with the continuity [for *Irish Eyes*] were not genuine. It was pointed out that her husband, John McCormick, was production manager of the First National studio at Burbank, Cal., until May 26, when he resigned and ... Miss Moore is merely attempting to leave the company with him."[9] Justice Mullan's decision came a few days later. "Her contract having contained an arbitration clause ... must arbitrate her differences with First National Pictures."[10]

With that, the issue went into negotiations. The studio's representatives wired Burbank for information to strengthen their hand. Perkins wired Ned Marin in Los Angeles: "We will need data soon stop Martineau report just received[11] stop also please forward registered airmail story treatment continuity and whatever there is on *Irish Eyes*."[12]

The report would show that, at best, delays in her various productions caused by Colleen were minimal. It did, however, show rejections of *Irish Eyes* that could easily look like foot dragging. In the end, the continuity was set aside and all parties came to an agreement as to how to proceed.

"Colleen Moore and Company Reconciled," read the page-one headline in the *Los Angeles Times*. The story was short but sweet: "The 'feud' between First National Studios and Colleen Moore seems to have been settled amicably. Richard A. Rowland ... has issued invitations for a tea-dance in Miss Moore's honor at the Plaza Hotel Thursday."[13]

The tea party was a success, with an enormous attendance that included "those representatives of the press who had been disgruntled by the reputed high hat tactics of Miss Moore in refusing to receive them during the recent crisis."[14] The press, used to easy access to Colleen, had not been pleased by her wish to pilot the rough waters as privately as possible.

Dear Colleen:

This letter will confirm our agreement with you to reimburse you for all counsel fees and legal expenses incurred in connection with the matter about which Arbitration Proceedings are now pending between us.[15]

In addition to picking up her fees and expenses, First National amended Colleen's.

Now instead of 12 photoplays, there were to be 11. Seven had already been completed; her term of employment was to be extended until the remaining four were done, one year from the time Colleen's work on the first of the remaining films began. Her work was to begin two weeks prior to the start of photography, and photography on the first of the remaining four was to be started on or before August 29, 1927. The studio remained obligated to provide facilities for the production of the films as before.

John had written in November 1926 that Colleen would prefer to make three films a year and take a penalty, rather than stick to the four-films a-year schedule. Whatever else John might have accomplished, he managed to get her out of one film with no penalty.

> Here comes Colleen Moore ... who does insist upon telling me of her exciting vacation in New York ... Colleen walked out on First National when her husband, John McCormick, quit ... and she returned at a salary $2,500 a week higher than her previous one.... Few actresses in Hollywood could get away with it, however."
> —*Piqua Daily Call* (OH), October 10, 1927, page 8.

The films to follow could be produced at whatever studio Colleen designated, and the first film would be adapted from *Synthetic Sin*, by Frederick and Fanny Hatton. The $70,000 already paid to Colleen would be credited to First National against her salary on the four films. The second film was to be *Lilac Time*, by Jane Cowl and Jane Murfin, to be directed by George Fitzmaurice, who would be kept available so that *Lilac Time* could begin by November 15. Every week he was not available to shoot, the studio was to pay Colleen $10,000. A continuity for *Lilac Time* was to be submitted by November 1, and should the continuity not be satisfactory, or if George Fitzmaurice was not be available and Colleen so elected, work could begin on another film instead, based upon materials that had yet to be selected.[16]

With this agreement, the arbitration proceedings were dismissed and the order of Justice Mullen was vacated without prejudice or cost to either side. The studio would reimburse Colleen and John for their expenses.[17]

John got $1,500 per week starting August 1, 1927. "This is in accordance with the terms of the new contract made by Messrs. Rowland and Spring," W.C. Boothby wrote to Rothacker on July 26. "His salary has been paid at this end from July 6th to July 30th inclusive, in the amount of $5500, which is to be charged to you by negative cost on the Colleen Moore pictures, as is all future payments of a like nature."[18] Payment for the upcoming films was not mentioned, but the details were to be ironed out later. John was to produce Colleen's films exclusively. He would no longer be running the studio.

And with that, the hatchet was buried.

Colleen was not overjoyed at the arrangement. She had been willing to walk out on the studio because she had the idea that after four really successful films—*Twinkletoes*, *Orchids and Ermine*, *Naughty but Nice*, and *When Irish Eyes Are Smiling*—she could retire while she was popular, following the example of Marguerite Clark,[19] who had retired from motion pictures in 1921 while still at the top of her game. If John had not made his move, she might have retired at the end of her contract.

While in New York John had purchased a yacht, the *Cojo*,[20] and she and John and Richard Rowland were to sail as far as New Orleans and return by rail the rest of the way while the yacht would be sailed home by the crew. While on the way, they were to begin working out the details for the first of Colleen's four films.[21] Grace Kingsley reported that they had decided to make a summer outing of their return trip, diverting from New Orleans to Havana to cruise the summer waters before returning to Louisiana and taking the train from there.[22] They were due back in Los Angeles on August 18.[23]

By the end of August an arrangement had been settled upon for John's employment; they agreed that he would continue to work at First National on a basis of $15,000 for the first picture, $20,000 for the next two pictures, and $25,000 for *Lilac Time*. John reserved the right to leave after the first film if Colleen was not happy.[24] At about that point it was decided that *Synthetic Sin* would be too big a production for the time they had, so it was set aside. New material was selected, a smaller film that could be done on location, with a minimum of sets. The story *I'll Tell the World* was picked, and it was speculated at first that Eddie Cline[25] would direct. Other reports pointed towards Mervyn LeRoy. "Mervyn LeRoy ... is now directing Miss Moore in *Oh, What a Life*."[26] That story was incorrect. LeRoy was already engaged with other projects.

Colleen knew that her friend Marshall Neilan was available. His studio had closed, and Colleen saw an opportunity to help him revive his reputation. She helped him secure a three-picture deal with First National and $50,000 to direct her. "The signing of Neilan ... is regarded as a masterstroke inasmuch as the story to be filmed is the type that has made both the director and the star famous."[27]

"Marshall Neilan is very enthusiastic about Colleen's new story," wrote Rothacker to Sam Spring. "John says that Colleen is very happy about the prospect, and John himself anticipates that the Colleen Moore picture which starts here next week, will be one of her best. It should be a corker!"[28] The title itself was reported differently: sometimes *Ain't She Sweet*, and sometimes *Tell the World*.

―⸻―

Tell the World (Her Wild Oat), *September 13–October 24, 1927*

As originally conceived by Howard Irving Young, the story was "mostly one of comedy, with some dramatic overtones, and a dash of melodrama towards the finish." Colleen's character, Mary Brown, lives with her domineering father, who chases off all potential suitors. When he dies Mary cashes out her inheritance and decides to find a husband at a popular resort. With the help of Tommy, a reporter, she reinvents herself as the adventuress Duchess de Granville, unaware that there is a real Duke de Granville whose estranged son lives on the beach near the spa.

The son, Philip Latour,[29] mistakenly believes Mary is his future stepmother, while Mary is unaware that he is the son of the duke. A stranger appears, Arthur Stanhall, and gives Philip's portrait of the duke—Philip's father—to Mary. Arthur Philip if he is the Duke's son, and he admits that he is. Mary returns to the hotel where she discovers she has been robbed. She is penniless, and, therefore, unable to settle her bill. Stanhall offers to cover the bill if Mary will let him have his way with her. She refuses. Elsewhere, the real duke has heard of the supposed duchess and leaves for the spa to confront her. Mary admits to being a fake. Unknown to her, the duke, moved by her story, pays her hotel bill for her.

Stanhall bribes the spa detective to deliver Mary to his yacht, and he sets sail with her, telling Mary that nobody would think twice about the adventurous duchess disappearing. The duke runs into his son, Philip, and Tommy at the hotel. They discover Mary is not at the police station and suspect Stanhill. They commandeer a motorboat and chase Stanhall's yacht, rescuing Mary. In the end, Mary becomes an actual duchess.[30]

The story of a press agent conjuring a character out of the air and creating a buzz around her must have appealed to John, who had seen himself in the same role. Mary and Tommy putting over a stunt on such a grand scale reflected the antics of the emir of Kurdistan, from 1925.

By the time Marshall Neilan was finished revising the story, it bore only a passing resemblance to Howard Irving Young's original version. There were secret identities, performances, action, adventure and a degree of drama. Neilan lightened the story, picked up the pace and dropped the undertones of danger. Mary's purity would not be threatened at the hands of the devious Arthur Sandhill. The story had to be shot fast and cheaply, while the rest of the unit went to work on Colleen's next productions.

Though the story was set on the East Coast, the Hotel Del Coronado in San Diego stood in for the coastal resort; stock aerial photography was used to introduce the sprawling structure. "The Hotel Del Coronado is one of those rambling old wooden structures where old ladies who have outlived two husbands and three poodles rock on verandahs."[31] was how the hotel was described. The film's Plymouth Beach Hotel was described in a similar vein in the intertitles: "It is such a rambling old maze that the guests down in the east wing are still voting for Bryan."

As the film was shot entirely in California, the streets of Los Angeles were used in place of New York's. Locations were used in and around the Hotel Del Coronado, palm trees visible in the background. Colleen's lunch wagon was an actual wagon. As entertainment and to set the mood while shooting, Marion Davies's quartet was hired to provide musical accompaniment.[32]

All possible details were worked out before shooting began. "Thorough preparation is the best means I've found for reducing the increase of gray hairs in a producer's head," McCormick was reported as saying. "If you go to the mat with your problems before you start the picture ... you can make better progress with less worry and expense." McCormick, Marshall Neilan and Gerald Duffy had spent most of their time together for two weeks to assure there would be no loose ends.

As revised by Neilan, Colleen's Mary Lou was an orphaned girl whose father had left her a lunch wagon. She saved her earnings from the wagon for the day she could retire. Philip Latour (Larry Kent) has been turned into a dissolute playboy robbed one night after an evening of revelry who, dressed in a borrowed workman's coveralls, meets Mary Lou at her lunch wagon. They strike up a friendship. Mary Lou has her mind set on a rich man, and she's convinced that Philip is just a worker.[33] Her best friend is Daisy (Gwen Lee), a dancehall floozy, upon whom Mary Lou relies for lessons in etiquette.

When Mary decides to spend her savings on a big weekend, she shows up at the resort dressed and acting like a dime-store tramp thanks to Daisy's fashion advice. She runs into Tommy Warren (Hallam Cooley) there, a reporter who frequents her wagon. As in the original, he decides to orchestrate a whole new persona for Mary Lou. Her grand entrance is by airplane, provided by Boeing, the landing filmed at the Brentwood Country Club course.[34] As in the original treatment, there are mistaken identities. Philip meets Mary Lou there, but does not recognize her (in her wig of curly blonde hair). The real duke arrives to meet Philip at the resort and introduce him to his new mother-in-law. Mary Lou has to avoid being discovered, and an extended chase scene ensues until Mary Lou flees the resort in shame.

During the final scenes, after Mary Lou has taken refuge in her wagon, it is hijacked by Philip, and taken to what will become their house when they are married. This effect was accomplished by the most direct means: towing the wagon through Los Angeles city streets. "Did you ever take a 35-minute ride in a lunch wagon? Colleen Moore tried it ... and reports it as being second only to parachute jumping in the matter of thrills.... Miss Moore behind the counter, startled citizens of Los Angeles as it zipped madly down the busy streets, careening dizzily."[35]

Early work on *Lilac Time* had begun in September. Adela Rogers St. Johns was contracted on the 1st to write the treatment, the deadline being September 29. On September 7, Mr. Cassell requested that a contract be drawn for Willis Goldbeck to write the continuity on *Lilac Time*. Cassell estimated that the Goldbeck continuity would take two months, which would make the date the continuity would be delivered as Sunday November 6. Ned decided on November 5 as the deadline.[36] From there it would be submitted to Colleen for approval.

Sound

The film industry had become a cutthroat industry in the years since its birth, a largely corporate industry interested in the bottom line. Among the bigger studios, Warner Bros. was moving up, and saw a new angle by which they could leverage a better position in the pantheon of big studios: sound. With this new sound technology, even the smallest Warner theaters could present to their patrons, the greatest vaudeville acts and musical accompaniment, which would have been prohibitively expensive to do live. In mid–1925 Warner and Western Electric agreed to joint forces to create a usable sound film technology. By the end of the year, the experiments had gone so well that a permanent sound picture corporation was proposed. The idea was delayed after some managerial mix-ups, but by mid–1926 the Vitaphone Corporation was formed by Warner Bros., Walter J. Rich and Western Electric.[37] For their fall premier, they began to screen "Warner overtures," which were sound shorts intended to replace the vaudeville and pre-film entertainment common in most first-run theaters.[38] The strategy was successful, and before the end of that year nearly a hundred sound systems had been installed in theaters, mostly in the East.

The arrangement between Warner Bros. and Western Electric did not last long however. John Otterson (in charge of exploitation of Western Electric's non-telephone inventions) made moves to appeal directly to the bigger studios. Only Fox was interested while the others sat on the fence to see what would happen with this new innovation.[39] Motion pictures, in the form they had taken since their inception years earlier, seemed firmly entrenched in the popular imagination in their present, silent, form. Even Warner Bros. had originally thought of sound films as shorts, not features.

The sound shorts had caught on. Sound features were starting to catch on, too. Warner Bros. had screened several Vitaphone features, including *Don Juan* in August of 1926 and *The Better 'Ole* in October 1926. On October 6, 1927, Warner Bros. premiered *The Jazz Singer* which, in addition to musical numbers like its predecessors, contained synchronized dialogue. It was fairly well received at the time and had a long run. Jolson's first spoken line in the film, after his first musical performance, was "Wait a minute, wait a minute, you ain't heard nothin' yet," a line that was one of his stage catchphrases. Following a rousing musical performance, the line, spoken to the audience in the film and to the audience *of* the film, seemed to promise great things were in the offing.

Very shortly, they would be.

33

October–November 1927

Lilac Time was due to start production soon, but a legal issue arose from the July 6 letter of modification to Colleen's contract, which stated that the company agreed to submit the continuity of *Lilac Time* to her by November 1. The letter had not been available when Willis Goldbeck signed his contract to produce the *Lilac Time* continuity, which would be late. The delay, however, was not a "violation of substantial obligation and no penalty is imposed."[1] It was not an insurmountable problem, though, and was worked out.

On November 3, a letter was sent to Colleen from R.G. Edwards, confirming the order of films planned as *Tell the World*, which has already been produced under the title *Her Wild Oat*, shall be deemed the first of said four photoplays; *Lilac Time* shall be the second ... *Synthetic Sin* shall be the third; and on condition that we are able to consummate the purchase of *Oh Kay.... Oh Kay* shall be the fourth."[2] *Lilac Time* would be the special production that John had wanted; this film, as well as the others, needed to be completed within the year.

Before the end of shooting *Her Wild Oat*, Colleen had received a visitor from Tampa. "Marie McKean, who lived across the street from Colleen Moore back in Tampa, Fla., admits she is enjoying the most gorgeous vacation of her life working as an extra in her girlhood friend's latest picture."[3] When work on the film had been completed, Colleen, her mother, and Marie left town for a few days, traveling around Arrowhead Springs.[4] While there, Colleen and her friend took in a western at a village movie house. Colleen spotted a handsome man in the picture whom she thought would exactly fit the bill as the pilot and romantic interest in *Lilac Time*. She made note of the name: Gary Cooper.[5]

Returning from Arrowhead, Colleen found a whirlpool of activity. In her absence, John started drinking again.[6] He had insisted on re-editing *Her Wild Oat* himself. All the carefully created gags and sight-jokes had been trimmed, and the resulting film made no sense. He might have wanted to strengthen the idea of a press man creating a sensation around an unknown woman. Fortunately, the original version had been duped before John started cutting. Between Alexander Hall, the film's editor, Colleen and Marshall Neilan, they were able to restore the film to its original state.

John went to a sanitarium to dry out.[7]

Lilac Time, *November 1927–February 1928*

On November 14, the continuity for *Lilac Time* was submitted to Colleen. Two weeks later, on November 28, she officially informed First National, "I do not approve, but expressly disapprove, the form of the continuity."[8] She followed up with a letter to First National on December 2: "This will confirm our understanding that the sum of TEN

THOUSAND DOLLARS ($10,000.00) per week to be paid me for every week or fraction thereof pending commencement of photography on *Lilac Time*."⁹

That same day, First National received a letter from Loeb, Walker and Loeb regarding that issue, suggesting the agreement was dangerous to the company, and that some limit might be placed on the agreement: for example, a "proviso that the payments should in no event extend for a period in excess of a certain number of weeks after November 15th, 1927." Furthermore, it was suggested that a paragraph be added to the letter of December 2 to the effect that on the conditions that First National had furnished all necessary facilities to complete her three photoplays in one year with a lay-off between the next succeeding two of no less than two weeks, First National shall be credited against Colleen's salary on the last photoplay "with any and all sums paid to me under this present agreement." To clear up any ambiguities, a paragraph was suggested where in Colleen could acknowledge the receipt of the sum paid, and how much remains. On December 6, Colleen returned a letter to First National with the modifications suggested by Loeb, Walker and Loeb.[10]

On November 29th, Rothacker had sent a telegram to Perkins explaining the situation stemming from Colleen's disapproval of the continuity.

> Supplementary contract July sixth nineteen twenty seven imposes weekly payment ten thousand dollars only in event conflicting engagements prevent Fitzmaurice from beginning photoplay by November fifteenth if any other reasons prevent Fitzmaurice from being available or if artist has not approved continuity by November fifteenth then there is no provision for this weekly payment and only right of artist is to reject *Lilac Time* altogether stop contract was drawn this way because artist when here in July feared conflicting engagement prevent Fitzmaurice from being available and desired special precautions to prevent this contingency have no copy here of letter referred Marins letter to Roland November tenth and if artist has agreed to this it may prevent her from rejecting *Lilac Time* stop our failure to submit continuity by November first is not violation of substantial obligation and no penalty is imposed but subject to provisions of employment contract we are obligated to furnish facilities for production of four photoplays within twelve months of beginning work on *Her Wild Oat*[11]

Colleen had rejected the continuity because Fitzmaurice was not yet available. Colleen had the right to elect that another photoplay be made in its place,[12] but there was no desire to stop production of *Lilac Time*.

Her Wild Oat was scheduled to be released on December 25, with a record number of bookings.[13] *Her Wild Oat* had been a quick production, made economically, and it was a draw even before its release. *Lilac Time* was going to be a massive production. Any problems with scheduling were dwarfed by the logistics of the shoot. Halting the film would have been impossible, as it had taken on a momentum of its own.

An army would be needed to make the film, and so the production outfitted itself like an army with a GMC three-ton truck; two three-ton Nash Quad trucks; a trailer constructed for carrying airplanes; a Nash Quad airplane machine shop (portable with lathe, tools and other equipment); and three experienced truck drivers. Eight "modern airplanes" were secured for the aerial scenes. The Anderson Boarding and Supply Company erected facilities for cast and crew on location for over two weeks, including sleeping accommodations; lavatories; a mess hall with a seating capacity of about 200 people supplying three meals a day or lunches; six deluxe tents with hot/cold showers and toilets; and 35 tents to house about four people each. Anderson also supplied kitchen and dining-room equipment and furniture, all beds and mattresses, and provided staff to police grounds and remove all garbage.

The battlefield was about 14 and-a-half miles east of El Toro, California, on 50 acres of the Louis Robinson Ranch.[14] On this site a working air field[15] was erected, along with a sacrificial French village. The eucalyptus trees along nearby Trabuco Road in the background looked, from a distance, like French yew trees.[16]

The press paid considerable attention to the selection of a leading man for Colleen: "John McCormick ... is devoting his efforts almost exclusively these days to the quest for a leading man to play the role of the British soldier-hero."[17] It was assumed by some that the role would go to someone not particularly well known in motion pictures.[18] "James Hall may be loaned to First National to play opposite Colleen Moore in *Lilac Time*; he's the chap Paramount was so enthusiastic about."[19] The enthusiasm came from the success of his film *Rolled Stockings*, a collegiate story that featured an increasingly visible actress, Louise Brooks. Hall's contract had been renewed by Paramount and it was "rumored that Hall will appear opposite Colleen Moore in a future release."[20]

By December, Gary Cooper was chosen for the part. On December 5, the core of the Colleen Moore unit (Colleen, John, Fitzmaurice and Carey Wilson) left Los Angeles for Palm Springs to discuss the film.[21] When they returned, filming commenced with interior work on sets built at the First National studio. Colleen was spotted on the studio grounds one day sporting a moustache painted on her upper lip, in preparation for a scene in which she was to try and entertain the demoralized troops in the family home.[22]

Her Wild Oat was released on Christmas as scheduled. The reviews were favorable but not enthusiastic. It was a programmer, and in spite of Colleen's enthusiasm and Neilan's direction, that was how the film was perceived. Edwin Schallert of the *Los Angeles Times* found it entertaining, but more on the strength of Colleen's comic performance than on the material: "[Colleen] does much to make the film blithely entertaining despite the ever-present scantiness of the plot material." Centering as it did on a lunch wagon owner, the film was signifying that this was a Cinderella theme, and so there was no surprise that Colleen ended up wedding the prince at the end. "There are spots that are very amusing and others that lapse into dullness." Mordaunt Hall of the *New York Times* saw the film as mostly a string of incidents, some "good, some unnecessary and others quite tedious." He thought it needed to be more sedate. "Miss Moore's antics are not altogether restrained," he observed, stating that Colleen should have acted more naturally, but "the manner in which Miss Moore struts around and rolls her eyes would ... create no little consternation and perhaps lead to apprehension." Still, the film had its bright spots and the closing was good enough to make up for everything that came before."[23] In Chicago, Mae Tinee saw the wisdom of releasing the film in time for the Christmas holidays, as it "goes well with the weary shopping crowds. Tired eyes can close and when they open again why — they will immediately grasp the meaning of what is going on — for it's just what they expected WOULD be going on." Even so, the film was described as a pleasant little attraction.[24]

The work on *Lilac Time* kept Colleen from dwelling on the reviews. From the studio, the company departed for El Toro. Hundreds of cast and crew members moved into the tent city erected for them. "Every one of the 300,[25] from the star down to the last extra, will remain in camp. Due to the uncertainty of February weather, George Fitzmaurice is pressing every advantage to complete the location work." It was among the better outdoor locations Colleen had experienced, with its tents with stoves and heat, and three squares a day. "George Fitzmaurice ... in mountain boots, sport shirt and riding breeches came along in a huge sedan. Gary Cooper looked splendid in his Royal Flying Corps captain's uniform and Colleen made a charming picture in her French farm girl's costume. Army trucks rumbled by the huge camouflaged canvas covered hangars."[26]

In the film, Cleeve (billed as "Cleve Moore") played the part of Captain Russell.[27] Playing the part of "The Infant" was Colleen cousin Jack Stone. "For a youngster ambitious to break into pictures what could be sweeter than to have Colleen Moore for a cousin?"[28] Also in the film's cast was Eugenie Besserer, with whom Colleen had appeared at the Selig studio.[29]

The army that First National raised was supplemented by an air force: "There are ten airplanes with practical hangars, machine shops, mechanics' quarters, supply sheds, hospital and other buildings."[30] Every air force needs pilots, and they were kept busy. "For more than two weeks, 20 of the finest pilots in the United States have arisen each morning to scan the sky for fields of billowy clouds necessary as background for the aerial 'dog' fight between combat planes." After a long stretch of cloudless skies, "The *Lilac Time* location is now 10,000 feet in the air."

Dick Grace was the stunt pilot in charge,[31] but his particular specialty was not to keep the airplanes up in the air — it was to bring them down to earth in spectacular fashion. He had worked just recently on the other big Great War romance film, *Wings*. The aerial acrobatics in *Lilac Time* were called astounding, and the "crack-ups" of the aircraft in the film were nerve-wracking. McCormick boasted that there were no injuries, but Dick Grace was put through the wringer.[32] He had been injured badly enough that he wanted to be examined by his own doctor. After an exam and X-rays, his doctor diagnosed him with a rib separated from its cartilage, a contusion of the chest wall, muscle and ligament strain on the left side of his neck and neuritis and partial paresis of the left arm and hand, and a general state of extreme nervousness.[33]

The cameras captured the aircraft as they taxied down the runway and took to the air. Colleen enjoyed the spectacle from a camp chair near the cameras, wrapped in a blanked against the chill. Fire and rescue crews sat ready. At one point, when filming the dogfight scenes, there were multiple aircraft in the air[34] executing close-quarter maneuvers as they would if they had been in actual combat. Most of the pilots had served in the war. John had spared no expense when it came to authenticity, and Fitzmaurice agreed with the philosophy in most aspects of casting — even the extras in the background. "'A real Frenchman is the only man who can be convincing in the uniform of a poilu.' And Fitzmaurice, having lived much of his life in France, knows whereof he speaks.... The First National casting office spent weeks enrolling Frenchmen to 'carry arms' in the military scenes.... In the 'army' thus gathered are many men who took part in the great conflict, including officers and enlisted men."[35] Colleen took the philosophy of authenticity seriously; she learned

Colleen at poolside, ca. 1928 (courtesy Judy Coleman).

most of her lines in French and delivered them phonetically so that her lips would look correct when speaking. The insults she delivered were taught to her untranslated, so that when Frenchmen who could read lips saw her, they were in for a shock.[36]

As always, when Colleen was at work on one production, the next production was taking shape. While *Synthetic Sin* had been intended to follow *Lilac Time*, it was once again pushed back. Instead, First National had bought an original story from Edmund Goulding for $10,000 called *Tomorrow*,[37] a temporary title for the property that would change its name many times. Goulding was tentatively slated to direct the film, the details and terms spelled out in a letter to him from First National: "The term of your employment shall commence within four (4) weeks of the completion of the photoplay entitled *Lilac Time*, now being produced by us ... and shall continue from and after the date of commencement for the period necessary to complete photographing of the photoplay." For his services, he would be paid $25,000; five thousand on the first day of work, 15,000 in six weekly installments of two 2,500, and the balance of 5,000 paid at completion of photography. Besides directing, he was to assist in editing, titling, and whatever other services were necessary.[38]

John, Goulding and Benjamin Glazer (the scenarist) left for Palm Springs in late January to go over the story and figure out all the details. They returned in early February, and John — the salesman in him coming out — was boasting that it would be a terrific film: "Next to *Lilac Time*, *Here Is My Heart* is the best story Miss Moore has ever had."[39]

The announcement that Goulding's story *Tomorrow* would be her next film was in the papers right away. "When Edmund Goulding's *Tomorrow* reaches the screen, it will be called ... *Here Is My Heart*."[40] The film would be a light romance on a small scale, making it a nice counter-balance to the weighty *Lilac Time*. After *Here Is My Heart* she would shoot *Oh, Kay!*, based on the popular musical. It would mark a return to the more rollicking entertainment that had done so well for Colleen in the past. *Sally* earned nearly as much gross income in the domestic market as *Flaming Youth* had. *Irene* had topped *Flaming Youth*.[41]

It was *Oh, Kay!* about which Colleen would be most excited, as it would finally team her with Mervyn LeRoy. "It is further understood that the clever young man has been given a very substantial increase in remuneration.... He will direct Colleen Moore next in *Oh, Kay*."[42]

That schedule would carry Colleen through much of the year: *Lilac Time*, *Here Is My Heart*, and *Oh, Kay!* In March, it was announced that Colleen had decided to stay with First National for another year, having signed a new contract on February 28 to star in four more motion pictures. There had been rumors that she might leave the studio for United Artists or Lasky, but they did not come to pass. John received a new contract himself,[43] as a producer engaged to produce four photoplays for Colleen.

The movie *Lilac Time* told the story of the romance between a French girl and British pilot, pulled apart by the war. A detachment of seven British pilots and their crew are billeted at the Berthelot farm, a plantation overgrown with lilac. They are cared for by the Berthelot family. Jeannine, daughter of Madam Berthelot (Eugenie Besserer), is the squadron's lucky charm. One of the flyers, Philip Blythe (Gary Cooper), gradually falls in love with Jeannine, even though he is annoyed at first by her comic antics. His father, a general, hopes he will marry the Lady Iris Rankin (Kathryn McGuire). On the morning before a dangerous mission Philip Blythe declares his love for her. He is shot down during the course of the mission, and Jeannine assists an ambulance crew pull his apparently lifeless body from the wrecked plane. The ambulance whisks Blythe away. Jeannine loses track of him but does not cease in her attempts to track him down. When she finds the hospital to which he had been admitted, she is mistakenly told Blythe has died. Jeannine delivers a bouquet of lilacs to the hospital and asks a guard to deliver them to his room. Philip, however, is alive. Seeing the flowers, he drags himself to the window and calls to her. The camera follows her as she hurries away from the hospital through a loud town square, where she encounters The Infant. While speaking to him, she hears Blythe's voice and they are united.

"More than seventeen hundred film players have been 'drafted' into service at the West Coast Studios," it was written about the scenes of war staged for *Lilac Time*.[44] Though they only occupied a small part of the film, they were massive and elaborate. "An atmosphere of world conflict is in the air.... Literally hundreds of tons of equipment have been imported to the studio[45] for these sequences." To capture the action from every angle, motion picture equipment was in abundance as well: "Seven cameras are trained upon a French village set during the evacuation of the town."[46]

The only thing that could have made the picture any more spectacular was sound. In April, Clifford Hawley announced that First National would adapt a sound system called Firnatone,[47] a sound-on-disc system, basically the same system as Vitaphone. The first Firnatone picture would be *Lilac Time*.[48] It was the perfect vehicle for a talking film. Colleen and John rejected the idea. The film had been conceived as a silent. Grafting dialog to the film using a new sound system was a bad idea. Synchronized sound effects were fine: films had been using canned sound effects since the beginning. Adding dialog could require reshoots, scenes rewritten for dialog, and because the system was sound on disk, the voice might go out of synch.

The other studios were rushing ahead with sound technology: whether adding sound and dialog to silents that had already been made but had yet to be released, or else ramping up to begin full-scale production of sound films. Because of the lack of direction, First National had yet to dip their toe in the waters. To prepare for the addition of sound to *Lilac Time*, music had been recorded for the film in the Victor studios in New Jersey and the sounds of airplanes, machine guns, and other noises that would be needed were recorded by crews in the field.[49] *Lilac Time* would not, however, be First National's first all-talking film.

Here Is My Heart (Happiness Ahead), *March 17, 1928*

Colleen's work on *Lilac Time* was completed before March, though work on the film would continue until its release, which would not be for several months. When *Here Is My Heart* began, Edmund Goulding was not at the helm: "Edmund Goulding will not direct

Colleen Moore's *Tomorrow* after all; he wrote the story and wouldn't accept on the screen treatment desired by John McCormick."[50] It is not difficult to see how the two might clash as they both had their ideas about Colleen's part. They were both intelligent and they both lived secret lives that were the polar opposites of their public images. John was a drinker and Goulding had a reputation for debauchery with wild parties that degenerated into orgies and strange sexual appetites.[51]

John, as the producer, had the final word on the matter.

In a letter dated March 1 between Goulding and First National, it was stated: "It is now the mutual desire of both parties ... to cancel and terminate your employment thereunder."[52] McCormick chose William A. Seiter as director, and Seiter went into consultation with Benjamin F. Glazer, who was writing the story.[53]

The film underwent another name change, at least in the press. "St. Patrick's Day saw the starting of *Heart to Heart*, Colleen Moore's forthcoming production for First National."[54] William Seiter had directed *Little Church Around the Corner*, one of Warners' first big successes. He was an easygoing man who loved golf and preferred to make smaller pictures rather than the big Hollywood productions that garnered so much attention. "He enjoyed making nice, medium pictures. Simply, easily, quietly."[55] Seiter's work focused primarily on the contemporary scene and his material had "taste and charm," presenting its material without exaggeration, but on a human scale.[56] His leveling influence would work to take some of the high drama off of Goulding's original story, so that it could be easier fit into the Colleen Moore formula of laughs mixed with tears.

The story started with cardsharp and gambler Babe Stewart (Edmund Lowe), hiding out from his former partner (Carlos Durnad) and his partner's mistress, Kay (Lilyan Tashman), after they threaten to turn him over to the police. While in hiding in rural uptown New York, he meets Mary (Colleen), daughter of the owner of a hardware store (Charles Sellon), and they get married. Marriage is good for Babe, and he struggles to reform himself so that he will be worthy of his wife. He finds gainful and respectable employment in the big city, until the police are tipped off by Kay. He's arrested, tried and sentenced to a six-month stay in jail. Rather than admit his crimes to Mary, he tells her he's off for a six-month trip to Buenos Aires and arranges for his letters to be relayed to her from South America. When he is released, he tries to confess to her, but she does not want to hear it for the sake of their unborn child.

It is a dramatic premise, nearly melodramatic, with Colleen suffering with the knowledge of her husband's secret for the sake of her family. It required changes to meet John's criteria for a Colleen Moore vehicle. The audience had to leave the theater with a laugh, and so complications were added. Mary discovers Babe's ruse to keep her in the dark about the nature of his "business trip," but she pretends she doesn't know. Babe discovers that she knows, but he pretends he doesn't know that she knows, and a good time was had by all. Posters for the film told the potential audience: "Keep Smiling."

Sets were built at the studio to represent New York streets, with imported autos and pedestrians of every variety to create the look of rush-hour Manhattan. It was just one of the many sets created for the film; included the interior of the hardware store, a banker's office, a state prison and a Park Avenue apartment.

The romantic title was changed once again to *Happiness Ahead*, something more in keeping with Colleen's optimistic persona.[57] When Mary was married to Babe, the ceremony was conducted by the Reverend Neal Dodd, well known for joining together some of Hollywood's best-known celebrities.[58]

33. October–November 1927

As the end of work on *Happiness Ahead* approached, John wrote to Obriger regarding Colleen's next project.

> I have taken up with Miss Moore contents of your note of April 2nd, and she reminds me ... [her new contract] provides that it is not necessary to definitely set the first of her new pictures under her new contract until immediately prior to the starting of production of the last one under her present contract.
>
> Miss Moore asked me to tell you that she is anxious to do *Synthetic Sin* next year, but she would much prefer to withhold any definite decision as to the order until the time provided for in the contract, because another story might come up in the intervening period that she might prefer to do first.
>
> If this is entirely agreeable to Mr. Rothacker and yourself, please do indicate to me and I will communicate this information to Miss Moore.[59]

So *Synthetic Sin* was on hold until the time seemed right.

34

Oh, Kay!, April–July 1928

> "Stay away from Hollywood if you have any tendencies toward regular eating."
> That's the advice of John McCormick, who is famous for three reasons —first, because he has given 'breaks' to more beginners than almost any other man in the picture industry; second, because he is one of filmland's leading executives, and third, because his wife is the more than charming Colleen Moore.
> —"Movie Chat," by Dan Thomas,
> *Olean Times* (NY), April 10, 1928, page 13.

Dan Thomas's profile of John depicted him as one of the people in Hollywood who were always looking for new faces. While everyone else was slow to hire beginners, John cultivated new talent. He counted Colleen among the greatest of "his" discoveries: "McCormick really discovered Colleen Moore. At least he gave her her first big chance—in *Flaming Youth* about five years ago."[1] That John was instrumental in furthering the careers of many at First National was beyond question, but he had blatantly claimed Colleen as his own discovery. That could not have been pleasing to Colleen, but she did not protest, and in June, she would give John credit for the success of most of her performances.

At the end of March, Colleen approved the story *Synthetic Sin* as the first photoplay to be produced under her February 28, 1928 contract. The *New York Times* reported that McCormick had purchased the film rights to *The Richest Girl in the World* as one of Colleen's potential next films.[2]

As the end of *Happiness Ahead* approached, John was distributing memos on Colleen's next production. He reminded Roy Obringer, "I anticipate that Colleen Moore will finish her services on *Heart to Heart* (#126) on Thursday, April 9th, therefore, please be prepared to pay her the balance due, namely; $35,000 on that date." In a second memo that same day he wrote: "We contemplate starting *Oh Kay* on May 21st, which means that according to contract Miss Moore would receive her fist salary check on this picture on April 23rd."[3] Payment would be $10,000, to be paid four weeks prior to the start of production.

Colleen at harbor, possibly at Catalina Island, circa 1928.

When Colleen finished *Happiness Ahead*, she departed for Hawaii with her parents: "Bound for a brief vacation in Hawaii, Colleen Moore is now aboard the S.S. *Malolo*, having sailed from San Francisco.... [Colleen] plans to be away from Hollywood three weeks, this trip being her first visit to the Islands." The story pointed out that she had gone almost straight from *Lilac Time* to work on *Happiness Ahead*, and that she was exhausted. "During her absence producer John McCormick is making preparations for her next starring vehicle, *Oh, Kay!* an adaptation of the stage success of the same name."[4]

While Colleen's fortunes continued to rise, the First National organization was in deteriorating condition. After the merger with Stanley, there had been a succession of presidents. Lieber had resigned and was replaced by McGuirk. McGuirk had, in turn, been replaced a short time later by Clifford Hawley. In June, Hawley would find himself out of the position, too. First National fell behind the rest of the studios in the race for sound pictures, though it was making slow lurches in that direction. First National Pictures, Electrical Research Products and the Victor Talking Machine Company were to develop "talking" motion pictures.[5]

Audiences wanted talking pictures. The new Warner Bros. Theater in Hollywood was being wired for sound, with shipped express from back east. Sound would play an increasing role in their productions, both features and specials. "Talking motion-picture devices are taking their place as the most important recent development in the amusement industry," it was written. "The picture company that has the foresight to acquire the rights to the most successful talking device should have a highly important edge over the competitors in the next few years."

First National was pointing to *Lilac Time* as their first Firnatone picture.[6] Ralph Poucher, the assistant production manager in charge of Firnatone, traveled west to consult with Clifford Hawley and Watterson Rothacker about current and projected productions, with the possibility that the First National studio in Burbank might add sound stages to the lot.[7]

In England, Jesse L. Lasky made the following prediction: "In five years there will be no silent motion pictures."[8]

One reason Colleen left for Hawaii was the hope that, if left alone, John might make some progress on his drinking problem. If her presence was a point of stress, he might keep sober if she was out of the picture for a time. And Colleen wanted time away from him. When not working, her second job had become covering for him during his benders.

While relaxing on the deck of the S.S. *Malolo*, her father suggested that they might build a new doll house to house her collection of miniature furniture. Her collection had outgrown the doll house she already had, a table-top house based on the design of their Rossmore house. Colleen had been present in March when Sir Nevile Wilkinson and Lady Beatrix attended a Children's Hospital ceremony featuring Titania's Palace, an elaborate doll house built by Nevile for his daughter to house "Queen Titania," the queen of the fairies. Nevile spent 18 years building the house and promptly took it on tour as a gift to all the crippled children of the world. Colleen had spent many weeks in a cast, crippled for a time herself. She faced the possibility that she might spend the rest of her life that way. Her father's suggestion sparked her imagination. Without John to worry about, the idea took firm root. Colleen would write that they hardly saw the Islands at all for all the time she and her father spent putting together ideas for the latest version of her dollhouse.[9]

> Colleen Moore is rapidly becoming a regular sea-going salt!
>
> For as soon as she returns from her ocean trip to Honolulu ... she will pack her dufflebag and go aboard a palatial sailing yacht which will be used as the background for several sequences of her next starring vehicle.
> —"Motion Picture Gossip," *Decatur Review* (IL) May 27, 1928, page 22.

Colleen returned from Hawaii on May 11 aboard the S.S. *City of Los Angeles*, flagship of the LASSCO[10] Line.[11] The papers reported that she had learned how to surf. She had been so enthusiastic about her swimming that she spent three days of her vacation in bed with sunburn. Jack Aylett, a Hawaiian member of the ship's crew, taught Colleen how to play the ukulele, "Hawaiian style."[12] She and John were to go to Balboa in two days, and Colleen said she hoped would be in good form as she showed off her newly acquired surfing skills.[13]

At the studio there was a shakeup in personnel: "Watterson R. Rothacker, vice-president and managing director of the First National studios, has decided to retire from the motion picture business.... Al Rockett, present production head, will assume full duties during his absence, with Ralph Poucher as executive assistant. Poucher will also be in charge of Firnatone operations."[14]

Between her return from Hawaii and the start of *Oh, Kay!*, Colleen went through the usual process of preparation for the role, with fittings and interviews and tests and conferences. *Oh, Kay!* was a return to the musical stage. The story rights had been bought in December 1927,[15] and Elsie Janis[16] adapted the story to film while Carey Wilson wrote the scenario. The story concerned the misadventures of the rum-running duke of Durham, forced into his occupation by circumstances beyond his control, and his sister, Lady Kay. They and their assistants — Shorty and Larry — have stashed their load of bootlegged hooch in the basement of the home of Jimmy Winters, a local playboy.

As usual, there are mistaken identities and confusion. Shorty presents himself to Jimmy as his new butler. Kay, chased by a revenue agent, takes refuge in Jimmy's bedroom and passes herself off, with Jimmy's help, as his new bride. Jimmy's actual wife has fled the house, awaiting the completion of Jimmy's annulment of his previous marriage. The couple had thought they were legitimately married, but, in fact, they were not. She returns the next morning to find Kay, who has dressed as a maid and introduces herself as Shorty's wife. Kay has fallen in love with Jimmy and vows to split up the marriage. Nobody is who they seem: there are twins; Kay passes herself off as bride and maid; Shorty passes himself off as butler and revenue agent; a famous pirate passes himself off as the revenue agent ready to truck away all the liquor in the basement of Jimmy's house; and the pirate's drivers working for Shorty and Larry.

The musical had been pure jazz-age comedy, as current a story as current could be, set during Prohibition, with characters on both sides of the law. This fact, however, presented a problem. The character of Kay, in the musical, was part of the bootlegging operation, part of a criminal enterprise. It was not the type of character that was associated with Colleen. To bring the character of Kay more in line with the types of characters Colleen played, the story was changed.

Instead of assisting her brother as a rumrunner, Colleen's character of Lady Kay Rutfield was fleeing an impending marriage to a man she could not stand. Kay first encounters the rumrunners when they rescue her from bad weather and take her prisoner. Anchored off Long Island Sound, she escapes and hides in Jimmy's mansion. From there, with Kay threatened by discovery by the bootleggers on the one hand and the revenue agent on the other, the comedy and confusion unfolds.

Alan Hale was borrowed from Pathé for the part of the revenue agent, named Jansen, a part that was described as suiting his comic talents admirably.[17] Lawrence Gray would play the leading part opposite Colleen.[18]

Shortly after the start of production, John and Colleen found themselves unwilling participants in a scene that might have been lifted from a Hollywood drama: "Two men were critically injured and six others suffered broken limbs and bruises in an explosion that wrecked the Russian Eagle Café,[19] a film colony rendezvous.... Feodor Lodijensky, former Russian general, who opened the roadhouse as representative of a syndicate of local czarists refugees, received a fractured skull and is expected to die. Irving Strother, insurance adjuster, was also reported critically hurt." The explosion followed the discovery of a fire at the establishment that broke up a party. "Among those who made a hasty exit when the blaze was discovered were Charles Chaplin, John McCormick and his wife, Colleen Moore; the marquis de la Falaise, Gloria Swanson's husband; Jack Dempsey and his wife, Estelle Taylor; Renee Adoree, Richard Dix and others." The blaze had been purposely set using a fuse delay arrangement: candles that had been lit hours before had burned down to a kerosene-soaked string that led to a pile of flammable material. In San Francisco, a Russian who spoke little English was arrested in connection with the explosion.[20]

Fires and explosions aside, the shoot was shaping into an enjoyable one for Colleen. One report gave the impression that the film was like a vacation: "Thanks to the scenarist of *Oh, Kay!*... Colleen is spending her days on the set quite comfortably in ... a bathing suit. It almost looks as though Colleen had an arrangement with the Weather Man to time the warm spell while she is thus garbed, for by the time she is more elaborately dressed ... she will be enjoying the cool breezes of the Pacific aboard a large sailing vessel off the Southern California coast."[21] Colleen had always enjoyed water sports, and in spite of the smell aboard the former fishing vessel used to film the rumrunner's scenes, she was learning to like yachting. Other scenes, shot on a less pungent yacht in the vicinity of Catalina Island, were very enjoyable.

First National

It was not smooth sailing for First National. Starting in June and continuing, changes in the organization came fast and furious. "Irving D. Rossheim was elected president to fill the unexpired term of Clifford B. Hawley, whose resignation, while not altogether surprising, was suddenly tendered the same day. Since January, Irving D. Rossheim ... has been president of the Stanley Company." This shifting of personnel was seen by many as proof that the long-expected combination of First National and Pathé was at hand.[22] It also severely demoralized First National. Long-time personalities at First National were taking their leave of the organization, some even leaving the state. "After serving as vice-president and general manager of the First National Studio, Watterson R. Rothacker and his family left Hollywood yesterday.... Since Rothacker resigned, Irving D. Rossheim has been elected president and Joseph Kennedy, head of F.B.O., named as special advisor."[23] The phrase "special advisor" had been an understatement. Kennedy demanded and, for a time, would have complete control to reshape the organization.

In June, the Stanley Company and Paramount's various affiliates — which between the two of them owned about two-thirds of First National's stock interests — deposited their stock under a voting trust agreement to ensure they would have management control of First National.[24]

Fox had entered into the exhibition business and had begun to rapidly expand its interests in theater chains so that it soon owned the final third interest in First National.[25] As a result, Fox and Paramount, both competitors, controlled most of First National's guaranteed outlets. Rossheim wanted to keep First National from whatever fate might befall the organization at the hands of Zukor and Fox. First National board members wanted someone tougher than Richard Rowland as general manager. That was when he had brought in Kennedy, who was given total control, $3,000 a week for five years and an option to buy a quarter of the company's stock if he so chose.[26] Kennedy was already running several film companies: FBO, Pathé, and the Keith-Albee-Orpheum theater chain. Eddie Rossheim was officially in charge, but it was Kennedy who was running the show.[27]

Happiness Ahead was released in late June to good reviews: "[Colleen] proves herself as adept in moments of emotional drama as in comedy and lends such realism to her characterization that *Happiness Ahead* is one of the most believable screen stories to be seen in months."[28] This was a serious role for Colleen, with enough comedy that had been "interpolated with sufficient skill to keep Miss Moore within her forte."[29] It was that ability to incorporate the comic elements into the overall dramatic story that made it a "Colleen Moore Film," and the star was willing to give credit for the ability to modulate the comedy to John: "Found — a film star who frankly admits that her husband's advice is the most valuable external aid in the making of her pictures." So Edmond Behr reported of Colleen's reliance on her husband in guiding her career. In praising John she gave him credit for her performances, while simply doing the best she could. "I have learned that John knows more about how a scene should be acted, how a character should be portrayed for the screen than I do. So I just follow his advice and do my share with the best acting of which I am capable." John felt the audiences wanted to see in her characters that same underlying innocence, that same little girl which John perceived.

Talking while on the set of *Oh, Kay!*, Colleen admitted that the successful combination of actress and manager as husband and wife was unusual, but she insisted that over time, listening to John's advice on how to give her portrayals "punch" was usually correct. "He picks the stories I'm to play and I do my best to play them as he thinks they should be."[30] It was the sort of statement that had helped her maintain her image as Hollywood's Good Girl. No matter how wild her characters might behave, she was still the obedient wife. John was in charge; he chose the stories that suited her image.

There were those who disapproved of such arrangements, those who did not like the idea that one's persona should dictate the stories in which they appeared. "They [studio executives] figure your name and personality will sell the pictures," said one actress. As a featured player, she pointed out, one might appear in a good story to good reviews, but if the story was a dud, the blame did not fall on her.[31] The young actress was Louise Brooks. Her star was on the rise, but it would be a short ascent, and an ironic one given her professed distaste for stories being tied to character. Louise was the latest incarnation of freewheeling, urbane youth, and her roles largely reflected that. She made no claim to possessing great acting ability, and she was better known for her flashy lifestyle than her impact on the films: "She hides her true self beneath a mask of indifference."[32] Louise was simply happy to be recorded on film, so long as it did not keep her from the next party. She could not be more different from Colleen, who was a performer and in control of the character she presented to the audience.

Colleen was still known primarily as a flapper, but she seldom made flapper films. Times were changing. The type of films Colleen was known for were strongly tied to their times. When those times changed, Colleen would have to change to suit them. The question now was whether Colleen would want to start from scratch.

In July, Joseph Kennedy arrived at the First National lot and began the process of firing writers and producers and directors. He reduced the number of actors on long-term contract to the studio by nearly half.[33] "Many Heads Fall before Kennedy; Seventeen Departments of First National minus Directors after Long-Distance Shake-Up," summed up Edward Mitchell of the *Baltimore Sun*.[34] The studio had been operating with multiple separate units working with their own budgets and schedules. Discovering that, Kennedy reorganized the studio to bring it more in line with the practices of other Hollywood studios. Rowland resigned suddenly, and many First National people followed,[35] including the assistant production manager, the head of the operating department, the chief of the accounting department, the chief of the research department, and the newly appointed head of Firnatone. Al Rockett was named head of production at the Burbank plant.[36]

Kennedy brought the Photophone sound film process with him, a sound-on-film system, a direct competitor for the Vitaphone sound-on-disk system and Fox's Movietone sound-on-film process. David Sarnoff of RCA had been responsible for developing the system and had joined forces with Kennedy as a means of securing film outlets for the process. RCA brought financing and labs to the table while Kennedy brought the companies he controlled and his assurance that the companies he controlled would only use the Photophone system. With the purchase by FBO of the Keith-Albee-Orpheum theater chain, Photophone was assured the venues needed to exhibit films produced with the process. They would only need to be wired for sound.

"*Lilac Time* will be the first production offered with the new sound device Photophone (said to have been adopted by First National in place of Firnatone) and McCormick, Miller,[37] and their associates promise some new and startling innovations."[38] Nathaniel Shilkret had been directing the Victor Symphony Orchestra at its studies in Camden, New Jersey, while a crew had been in the field gathering sound effects for the airplanes and guns and various other war machines.[39] All that work would have to be scrapped and the process started over, and whatever theater would premiere the film would have to be wired for the Photophone system. The premiere was scheduled at the Carthay Circle Theater in Los Angeles in mid-July.

Oh, Kay! was finished on July 11, which gave Colleen less than a week to prepare for the gala opening of *Lilac Time*. On the tenth, the Carthay Circle announced they had "just obtained the consent of Mayor 'Jimmy' Walker of New York ... to act as master of ceremonies for the gala world premiere of *Lilac Time*."[40] The mayor had extended his stay in Los Angeles so that he could be there. In addition to the feature attraction, *Lilac Time* would be shown with several Movietone features and novelties as well as a "wonderful concert program by Carli Elinor's world famous concert orchestra." A packed bill.[41]

The Carthay Circle Theatre had been built at 6316 San Vicente Boulevard in 1926. Designed by Dwight Gibbs, it drew its name from its circular interior. Spanish Revival in style, the theater sported a 140 foot-tall steeple in front, like an exclamation point.[42] The Carthay Circle was the crowning glory of an upscale residential neighborhood along the San Vicente Boulevard line of the Pacific Electric Railway. The theater had been imagined as a museum as well as a movie theater: "It is planned to make the Carthay Circle Theater a museum of early California material. An invitation is therefore extended to all lovers of the Golden State who have relics worthy of presentation, to communicate with the Historical Committee at Carthay Center."[43] The streets surrounding the theater were strewn with monuments, including the Jedediah Strong Smith Boulder, brought from El Cajon pass; the Forty-niner Statue; and a bust of San Juan Bautista de Anza. The theater housed the paintings "California's First Theater," by Frank Tenny Johnson, depicting the Eagle Theater in Sacramento, "Jedediah Smith at San Gabriel," by Alson Clark; and "An Emigrant Train at Donner Lake," by Frank Tenny Johnson, the image painted on the drop curtain.[44]

While visiting the First National studios in Burbank, Mayor Walker was persuaded to act in a short film with Colleen. Colleen played the part of the vamp to Walker's straight man. The film was entitled *Burning Daylight* and would be shown before the premiere of *Lilac Time*.[45]

The morning of the premiere, the completed *Lilac Time* and its separate sound strip of film had arrived, and during the first practice run of the system in the Carthay, the sound strip broke three times. Panicked, John arranged for Carli Elinor, the conductor, to keep the orchestra at the ready during the actual showing.[46] The orchestra had already been scheduled for the evening, but John wanted them to step in and provide the music if the sound strip broke again.

There were several parties thrown in advance of the film in honor of Colleen and John. One, on the evening of July 16 was hosted by Mervyn LeRoy and his wife, Edna Murphy. Among the guest were Jack Dempsey, Estelle Taylor, Al Green, Olive Borden and Darryl F. Zanuck. At their home, John and Colleen hosted their own party. Among those who had come to town for the premiere was her uncle Howey. "Although he is largely responsible for Colleen Moore's entrance into motion pictures, Walter Howey, uncle of the star, saw her work before the camera for the first time a few days ago, when he visited the First National Studios in Burbank during the production of *Oh, Kay!*" The article went on to recap the standard story of her discovery by D.W. Griffith while she was supposedly visiting Howey, and mentioned that his visit to California was for the premiere of *Lilac Time*.[47]

Colleen's gown had been designed by Sylvia Wacher, and was "a billowing cloud of peach chiffon." James Walker was scheduled to be a guest, along with George Fitzmaurice and Diana Kane, Dorothy Mackaill, Lupe Velez, Julanne Johnston, Al Jolson, Charles Chaplin and Joseph P. Kennedy. After the film, Colleen would leave for the Montmartre,[48] where there would be several dinner parties.

From Colleen's house, all of her guests were to drive to the theater. The route was marked by searchlights and fans. The arriving party was nearly mobbed at the theater, a scene that recalled Colleen's European premieres in 1925. "So dense was the crowd that it was long after nine before the program began."[49] When Colleen and John stepped out of their car, a tremendous cheer went up. Before they headed to the audience, Colleen noticed that John was having a better time than she was, waving to the crowd as if the cheers were for him. At the sight of John waving, Colleen was embarrassed for him.[50]

The lobby of the theater was crowded with floral arrangements and the wrecked carcasses of some of the airplanes used in the film. Congratulatory wires sent to Colleen were tacked to a billboard, and a telegraph stand had been set up in the lobby where patrons could wire their friends about the film.[51] Conrad Nagel, as the master of ceremonies, introduced Colleen and several others in the cast. *Burning Daylight* was shown before the feature presentation: "It was 'rich, rare and racy,' and the hit of the evening."[52] Carli Elinor's Concert Orchestra played its Symphonic Prelude, which included music from the movie, including: 'A Few Songs of Home' ... 'Enemy Plane Drops Bomb' ... 'Taps' ... and 'Jeannine I Dream of Lilac Time,' the primary musical theme of the picture." Stanley Bently was at the Wurlitzer. The sheet music was on sale at the Log Cabin, opposite the theater entrance.[53]

And then *Lilac Time* itself was shown.

The Photophone presentation went off flawlessly, though the sound quality was not perfect. The roar of airplane engines produced too deafening a roar, even "taking it for granted that seven aeroplanes combined can stir up quite a lot of racket."[54] Nevertheless, the sound thrilled, and the story captivated audiences. The film was widely released in silent form and with sound disks. In Cleveland, *Lilac Time* proved a great audience picture that "broke all previous records.... Extra morning matinees were introduced during the second week of engagement and were kept up until the close."[55] It was reported that both Colleen and John returned to the Carthay Circle Theatre for the occasional showing to enjoy the crowd's reactions.[56] In fact life hadn't slowed down for either John or Colleen. There was always another film for which to prepare.

On July 23, Colleen approved William A. Seiter as the director for *Synthetic Sin*.[57] After directing *Happiness Ahead*, Seiter had been signed to a four-picture deal with First National.[58] Colleen also approved Sid Hickox as cameraman.[59] On August 1, in a letter written on her own stationery, Colleen indicated that she accepted the continuity of *Synthetic Sin* that had been prepared for her by Tom J. Geraghty. The photography on the film would start on September 10, 1928. After many delays, *Synthetic Sin* would finally be made into a motion picture.

After *Synthetic Sin* Colleen would move on to "The Richest Girl on Earth." Al Rockett wrote a memo to McCormick on July 25 stating that he wanted Tom Geraghty to start writing the story.[60] Geraghty was eager, and Colleen "expects you to allow him to work on it." On the 28th, Rockett sent John a house telegram that Colleen wanted to start right away with her next story, "The Richest Girl on Earth" and would like to start shooting November 5, with Seiter as director. Rockett duly added Seiter to his production schedule.[61]

While the details of her productions were ironed out, a little over a week after the

Top: Colleen and John aboard the yacht *Aimee*, off the coast of Southern California. Bottom: Colleen in a gag photo, with the stuffed sea turtle she received during her visit to Mexico, August 1928 (courtesy Judy Coleman).

premiere of *Lilac Time*, Colleen left on vacation, the long break she had wanted between contracts so that she could rest and catch her breath. In fact, Colleen had lost weight and needed to relax. She and her family chartered the yacht *Aimee*, a "bald-headed schooner," according to Colleen.[62] "Colleen Moore ... arrived in Santa Barbara harbor yesterday aboard her schooner-yacht, the *Aimee*, with a party of friends and close relatives, and will sail this morning after being joined by her husband, John McCormick, for a cruise about the Santa Barbara Channel Islands."[63] She had been seized by "yachting fever" while making *Oh, Kay!* with Mervyn. She amused herself by popping balloons floating on the water with a rifle, displaying uncanny good marksmanship at hitting the targets up to 60 feet away. Her cousin Jack Stone was the second-best shot, followed by brother Cleeve. They had spent a day in Los Angeles Harbor between jaunts to the Santa Cruz and the Channel Islands. They fished by day and played bridge by night. While visiting Mexico, Colleen was presented with a stuffed sea turtle. They also visited Catalina Island.[64]

While *Lilac Time* had been a sound film, it had not been a "talkie." There had been no synchronized, recorded dialog between characters. Aside from the gestures and expressions, all communication between characters on the screen unfolded through title cards. John had seen a demonstration of the Vitaphone process, watching a George Jessel[65] short, and had decided that, while it was interesting, the process would only be good for short subjects, the sort of thing that could be shown before the feature presentation.

While John and Colleen had not been sure of the future of sound, at least insofar as it applied to *Lilac Time*, others were jumping on the bandwagon. George Jessel's *Lucky Boy*, could not be released as a silent, so the Tiffany Stahl Picture Company paid him to add songs where possible.[66] Unreleased silent films had additional scenes shot so they could be released with sound. Existing silents were re-released with dialog added. When Colleen returned from vacation, she found the motion picture landscape rapidly changing. "Far-seeing actors and actresses in the California film colonies are already rushing to voice culture schools. The voices of some stars are hopeless for talking movies, but others, particularly those will stage experience, are well suited to the new systems. The First National studio has instituted compulsory voice classes for its players and Fox and other producers plan similar training classes."[67]

35

Colleen and Sound, August–October 1928

James O. Spearing wrote: "Just as it [the motion picture industry] was becoming settled in style, just as it seemed to grow up with its own people, its own technique, sound, the element characteristically lacking, has been added.... The absence of the human voice and other sounds has played a vital part in the development of screen acting technique. Many of the devices used in the treatment of a motion-picture story, the developed pantomime of the players themselves came into being because of this missing element of sound. They were evolved to make up for the deficiency. Now that the deficiency has been supplied."[1] The very definition of motion picture acting was in the process of being redefined. Nobody knew how sound would impact the entrenched industry. The advent of sound threatened the long-standing nature of things in Hollywood and nobody knew where they would be when the dust settled: "When the screen actors began to speak their lines, the silent drama was attacked. Voices invaded its particular domain."[2]

More had changed then just the movie industry. Society had changed. It was reported that in Hollywood short hair on women had become the norm. "Long hair is a fad. The girls who are letting their hair grow ... were children when bobbed hair became popular." That was the opinion of hairdresser Perc Westmore: "They get a thrill out of letting it grow; but after the novelty wears off they will go back to conservative styles such as the widely copied Colleen Moore bob.'"[3] The fifth annual convention of the National progressive Chiropractic Association called bobbed hair as the "greatest boon" for women in the last century. Dr. W. Gano Compere said, "Hair cut short, together with knee-lengthed skirts, is giving to women a new freedom of movement, which will shortly cause them to eclipse the men in speed of thought and action." He insisted, "There is nothing vulgar nor imperious in the short cuts to freedom which have been adopted."[4]

Short hair and short skirts, once thought dangerous and damaging, had become commonplace. Everyone wore their hair short, and nobody gave it a second thought. Seven years earlier, when Adela Rogers St. Johns had seen actress Mary Thurman with bobbed hair, it stopped her:

> It is Paris. It is Egypt. It is Hollywood. It is the Italian Lakes.
> Whether or not it is beautiful, I do not know.
> To me it suggests Cleopatra barbered on Hollywood Boulevard.
> It is the last word in chic, in fashion. It is so startling it annoys, so gorgeous it allures.[5]
> I don't like it a bit and I adore it.

The young women with short hair in 1928 had been children when St. Johns wrote her observations. They had been graduating high school when the Colleen Moore Dutch-Boy Bob made its debut. Nearly a generation had passed. They had grown up with the wild flappers and jazz parties and all the threats to civil society that Colleen had represented.

35. Colleen and Sound, August–October 1928

In 1928, *Our Dancing Daughters* was released; it is the film that put Joan Crawford on the map. Crawford played Diana, one of three daughters from three families. One daughter had strict parents and appeared to be a prude; the other was a gold digger. "Dangerous" Diana had parents in the Frentiss family mode of leniency. She seemed the wildest of the bunch, shown dancing before a mirror while dressing, pulling unmentionables up over frenetically dancing ankles, and later at a party in the process of undressing, and yet she is the most well-adjusted daughter. It was a sign of acceptance of the younger generation that the daughter most like Patricia Frentiss would be the heroine. The movie had secured Crawford her position in the top tier of motion picture flappers. The easy categories that had served motion pictures in the past were becoming inadequate. Audiences were looking for realism and to characters with whom they could relate.

It had taken Colleen as Pat Frentiss to open the door for characters like Dangerous Diana, but now that the door had been opened, the room was becoming crowded.

Oh, Kay! was released in late August to decent reviews, but not the sort of stellar reviews Colleen's other stage musical adaptations had received. She received good marks for her performance, but there were hints that the formerly bullet-proof Colleen Moore formula was showing cracks. Mordaunt Hall admitted the film was a farce, true, but "it might have been infinitely funnier if the players portrayed some scant idea of submerging their own identities into those of the characters. It is surprise, anxiety and obliviousness on the part of a character that make an incident mirthful, not the idea of somebody throwing food around a room." If Colleen had acted in a more natural style, he thought, she might have earned gales of laughter.[6] The *New York Times* was not especially fond of motion pictures as a whole, but had still managed in the past to give Colleen credit for saving films they felt were otherwise thin.

Mordaunt Hall was not the only reviewer with this opinion. "In applying her flapper tomboy methods to the interpretation of the role ... [Colleen] turns much of the comedy into something very near akin to slapstick." The reviewer thought that this might have been the fault of the two authors, P.G. Wodehouse and Elsie Janis. "The story is rapid and full of thrills coming from unexpected situations.... There is a woeful lack of logical sequence, of interpreting the possible, of kinship to the elements of real life."[7] Marquis Busby enjoyed the film: "It comes very near being a laugh-a-minute picture ... It has been a very long time since Miss Moore has had as sprightly a comedy as *Oh, Kay!*, or one tailored so perfectly to her comic gifts." The film elaborated pleasantly on the original musical, filling in the story. The cast was nearly all-star, and "George Marion, Jr., has seldom written better titles. Mervyn LeRoy's direction is excellent."[8]

William Seiter had done such a good job directing Colleen in *Happiness Ahead*, it was reported, that he was signed up to direct her again. "No one could direct the star quite so well in *Synthetic Sin*, her next picture, and *The Richest Girl on Earth*, which will follow.... Tom Geraghty is working on the scenarios of both stories."[9]

On September 1, 1928,[10] Al Rockett submitted to John a list of potential future stories to follow *Synthetic Sin* and *The Richest Girl on Earth*. His suggestions included *Pygmalion, Coquette, Brook Evans, The Children, Military Mary, Sunny, The Constant Nymph, Susi,* and *Funny Face*.[11]

Five days later John wrote Roy Obringer: "It begins to look as if it would be impossible to choose *The Richest Girl on Earth* for the picture to succeed *Synthetic Sin*, because all we have is an idea and we have not had sufficient time to develop it."[12] That same day Rockett suggested they revive *When Irish Eyes Are Smiling*. "If you want to reconsider this story I will be very happy to change my production plans and turn it over to you. It is the type of story I feel Colleen is best in and even though there is a weak ending I am quite sure this could be built up."[13]

That *When Irish Eyes Are Smiling* was an excellent starting point for a Colleen Moore vehicle was not in doubt. Revised as an all-singing, all-talking production, it would have even more bang for the buck. Just over a week later on the 14th, First National put forward its three suggestions: *When Irish Eyes Are Smiling*, *Funny Face* by George Gershwin, and *The Children* by Edith Wharton, but withdrew them on the 20th when Colleen officially designated a two-week break between *Synthetic Sin* and her next film.[14] On the 24th, First National submitted three new film suggestions: *Where There's a Will* by Reita Lambert (published as "Clipped Wings"), *Roundabout* by Nancy Hoyt, and *Dangerous Nan McGrew* by Garrett Fort and Charles Beahan.[15]

While the studio worried about what was to follow *Synthetic Sin*, the movie itself went into production in mid–September when Colleen returned from her vacation aboard the *Aimee*. The production suffered a setback, however, when it was decided to drop the male lead.

―⁂―

Warner Bros.–First National, August–October 1928

Joseph Kennedy had been juggling companies and making deals while trying to work his budget-cutting magic on First National. His style and juggling and unfulfilled promises had rubbed many in Hollywood the wrong way. He and the rest of the world had been convinced a merger of his companies and First National was in the offing, but the deal fell through and many in the First National organization were happy to see him leave.

"Kennedy's Departure Astonishes; Hollywood Believes He Swung Ax So Vigorously That He Decapitated Himself. First National Employees Breathe Sigh of Relief."[16] With his departure, the presumed combination of Pathé, FBO and First National was dead. The gossip was that the directors of First National did not like his suggestion of consolidation between his companies and First National.[17] Instead, it looked like First National and Warner Bros. would work out a deal.

First National by that point, was in a very shaky state. The Stanley Company, which owned a third of the interest in First National, was also suffering managerial difficulties. A few years earlier the company had lost Jules Mastbaum, the driving force behind the Stanley Company. He and his brother Stanley had founded their company together in Philadelphia and built an empire of ornate movie palaces. They had bought out Sigmund "Pop" Lubin when he decided to cash out of the business. After Stanley's death in 1918, Jules had reorganized the company and named it in honor of his brother and concentrated on acquiring theaters in the mid–Atlantic area of the country. When Jules died, it left the Stanley Company without strong leadership.[18] It was after a two-year stretch of managerial problems Warner Bros. moved on the company.

After the success of *The Jazz Singer* and *The Singing Fool*, Warner Bros. was newly flush with cash. They were negotiating with First National, some suggested, because they needed the studio as storage space for the surplus cash they were raking in with talking films.[19] As the pioneers of sound film, they were on the cutting edge of the new technology, but their vaunted position would only last until the other studios started turning out sound films of their own. If that happened, the Warners films would be lost in the wash. To capitalize on their new success and momentum, they purchased Stanley. On October 2, 1928, Stanley Corporation entered into an agreement with the Warner Bros., whereby Warners acquired a majority of the stock of the Stanly Company. Stanley's third of the stock interest was tied in with voting trust with Paramount affiliates. Under the agreement, if the Stanley stock was acquired by a buyer, the buyer was required to buy the other third of First National stock controlled by Paramount. Warners did and, as a result, they owned two-thirds of First National stock.[20]

> Warner Brothers Pictures, Inc., has acquired an additional block of 19,000 shares of First National Pictures Corporation common stock ... increasing the holdings in the corporation to 42,000 of the 75,000 shares outstanding.... Fox Film Company still holds 21,000 shares, and the remaining 12,000 are scattered.

The newly acquired shares represented the trustee holdings of Balaban and Katz, Skouras Brothers, A.H. Blank, Finkelstein and Ruben and Robert Lieber.[21]

"The transaction is regarded as very important, in that it will give First National an early outlet for their production with sound sequences. In fact, certain pictures ... will have synchronized portions ordered within the course of a few weeks, which will mean that the voices of such stars as Milton Sills, Corinne Griffith, and a little later, probably Colleen Moore will be heard.[22]

Between the terms of Colleen's and John's contracts with First National, Colleen had almost complete control over the making of her films, from story to director to editing. If she did not want to make talking films, she was under no contractual obligations to do so. At least not until her present contract ended. If she wanted more pay to talk in films, she was in a position to ask for practically any figure she wanted. She had been the biggest box-office money-maker for two years running and her films were still tremendously popular. The only question was, as she put it herself, "Could she talk?"[23]

Synthetic Sin, *September–October 1928*

Synthetic Sin was a return to the stage for inspiration. Frederic Hatton and Fanny Hatton, the writers of the play *Synthetic Sin*, had been writing movie scripts and, according to reviews, they had "bobbed up again" at the Forty-ninth Street Theater with the play. For the character Betty Fairfax, they pulled a background character from an earlier production, *Lombardi Ltd.*, and made her the subject of the whole story. "She is required, as the story advances, to be almost unbelievably dumb." She had to invent a past, and "then stamps her pretty feet in annoyance when the hero, instead of offering illicit love, persists in protecting her." When others make their passes at her, she recoils. The final act, when it arrived, turned into "fairly believable melodrama."[24] The play was poorly received, running for just 24 performances.

In the play, Betty Fairfax is star of a play that flops in Aston, Pennsylvania. The playwright says she cannot be a great star unless she experiences life first. He has suggestions, but she rejects them in favor of moving to New York's West Side. It is an unsavory neighborhood, rife with criminal types, and just when she doubts she will gain the experience she needs, she meets a handsome gangster. The criminal, however, is revealed to be another playwright looking for atmosphere and experiences to add to his work.[25]

The story has all the ingredients of a Colleen Moore film, with mistaken identities or disguises, a good girl in bad circumstances but managing to stay pure, and a handsome prince to sweep her off her feet. There is comedy mixed with drama, and an opportunity for a big production number or two.

As in *Lilac Time*, the leading male role opposite Colleen was at first given to a relative unknown. The decision to cast James Ford did not work out. Discovered by Corinne Griffith in *The Divine Lady*, William Seiter picked him for *The Outcast* using the "camera-test method."[26] "James Ford, formerly an extra, picked to play the male lead opposite Colleen Moore in *Synthetic Sin*, was discovered after four days to be not suited for the role and was replaced by Antonio Moreno."[27]

Besides Antonio Moreno, with whom Colleen had worked in *Look Your Best*, and Edythe Chapman, who appeared in *Naughty but Nice*, they picked up Julanne Johnston, a regular of Colleen's films, and Jay Eaton, known as "one of the best-dressed film players in Hollywood."[28] Like Loretta Young, who had started off in small parts, Kathryn McGuire was graduated to a bigger role. "Kathryn McGuire probably is the next one you'll read about 'becoming a star overnight.' Her work in the leading feminine role opposite Colleen Moore in *Lilac Time* was well-liked and she has been cast for an important part with Colleen again, in *Synthetic Sin*."[29] In an unusual bit of casting, another "Colleen Moore" was given a small part in the film:

> The name of Colleen Moore is winning honors in new fields.
> At a recent dahlia show at the Biltmore Hotel in Los Angeles, a particularly beautiful bloom named after the popular star won two awards in competition with the finest flowers in Southern California, which is noted for its gorgeous dahlias.
> The Colleen Moore blossom was the entry of Peter Parabino of Santa Monica, an amateur horticulturist, who secured Miss Moore's permission to use her name before the flower show opened....
> Because a flower possessing the name of Colleen Moore should certainly be in the movies, William A. Seiter, who is directing Miss Moore in *Synthetic Sin*, has given a conspicuous position to a bouquet of Miss Moore's namesakes in this production.[30]

When multiple units were at work in limited studio space, they sometimes found themselves working at cross purposes. When two productions were diametrical opposites — drama and comedy — the units were often incompatible. Drama and comedy at the same time did not always mix: "A First National director[31] found that out when Billie Dove seriously was engaged in trying to shed tears while under the same roof Colleen Moore and her company noisily were trying to make laughs." It was not an ideal situation for productions beginning to utilize sound technology. Dove's director, Frank Lloyd, while "directing the motor," decided that it was best not to shoot during the same hours as Colleen's productions. Instead, they shot in the evening. "That was done and his company worked all night in entire peace."[32]

In the film version of *Synthetic Sin*, Donald Anthony, a famous playwright, returns to his home town of Magnolia Gap, Virginia. He proposes to Betty Fairfax, an aspiring actress, who only agrees to marry him if he gives her the lead part in his next play. Betty gets the part but the production turns out to be a tremendous flop. Deciding she hasn't really lived and experienced enough of life and its many hard knocks to be a good actress, Betty travels to the city, hoping to experience a little of life's darker side. She ends up in a rough neighborhood with four gangsters as neighbors. When Frank comes for her, the gangsters attempt to kick him out. There is a gunfight and confusion, and after both Betty and Donald are arrested and finally released, Betty decides she's had enough excitement and settles down with Donald.

To assure the success of her films, Colleen had always been willing to go along with whatever gags might bring an honest laugh. Knowing audiences liked actresses who were self-deprecating, Colleen was one of the few glamorous actress willing to be filmed in unflattering ways; she was happy to allow her face to be marred for the sake of a laugh. In *Ella Cinders*, she received a face full of soot; in *Lilac Time*, she painted herself with a moustache and had grease wiped on her face: for *Synthetic Sin*, she appeared in blackface. The latter made for so unusual a sight, that pictures of her in the makeup appeared in the papers. In one such photo spread, the caption asks the rhetorical question as to whether Colleen is attempting to rival Al Jolson (who wore blackface in *The Jazz Singer*). No, the story reported, it's what one does when "one isn't given a role in an ultra society musical — and when one sees one's cousin making passes at one's boyfriend." The result was Colleen "metamorphosing a reign on infinite quietude to riotous uproar."[33]

With Mervyn LeRoy now busy with his own productions, John McCormick looked to the Colleen Moore unit for his new comedy constructor: "Al Hall, film editor, has been promoted to comedy constructor on the unit."[34] With the popularity of the theme song from *Lilac Time*, John looked to duplicate that success as well. "Nathaniel Shilkret, famous composer, has written a new theme song for *Synthetic Sin* called 'Betty,' which promises to be as popular as 'Jeannine, I Dream of Lilac Time.'"[35]

Between scenes, Colleen and Seiter were reported to be engaged in an industrial contest over who had more feature productions under their belt since the start of their careers. Colleen had 42; to Seiter 39. "But of course a player appears in more pictures than one director directs. Accordingly, they can each put in a claim to the industrial picture championship."[36]

Warner Bros.–First National

The Warner brothers not only inherited the sprawling Burbank studio from First National, but many productions as well. First National had been producing pictures with extravagant budgets, and paying stars high figures, while the Warner brothers had a shoestring budget. A First National production could run a budget of $300,000, while the average Warner Bros. production came in at about a third that figure. Jack Warner had toured the First National Burbank studio and had been stunned, and he knew Harry Warner would not believe it.[37]

Harry didn't much like the idea of big salaries for stars. He felt they were being paid for what the cameramen did for them. Sound would be a leveling agent, and would bring all the over-priced and overinflated stars back down to earth.[38] Since the merger the studio had been letting Colleen know in subtle ways that she would not be treated with kid gloves.[39] John's drinking was an open secret and he was only of value to a studio as long as Colleen was of value. Colleen had already been aware, without needing her studio to remind her, that John had the potential to drag her down with him.

If Colleen remained popular, she could ask to do anything she wanted in talking films. Two things could prevent that: enough bad press, or a speaking voice that was unsuitable for talking films. Either one had the potential to make her demands during the next round to contract negations more reasonable, assuming the Warner brothers would even keep her.

With sound, it was her voice that mattered. Nobody was special, nobody was exempt, and it was the microphone that would decide her future.

October 1928

The test for Colleen, as well as many other big names in the industry, came in early October. The science of sound film was still poorly understood in the industry as a whole, but especially by the performers who had honed their skills in silence. Even those with stage experience did not understand which odd quirks of acoustics might render their voices inadequate. It was the same as with Colleen's mismatched eyes over a decade earlier; she had known they photographed well in still images, but they still had to be tested in Chicago to see how they registered in moving pictures.

The man who would pass judgment on Colleen was Roy J. Pomeroy, a quiet and somewhat unassuming technical man who, because of his knowledge of the technology of sound films, had become one of the most powerful men in Hollywood. He was in his late 40s, small and balding, with an arrogant attitude and a habit of spitting when he talked. An all-around technical wizard, he had always been given wide latitude for his imperfections.[40] Pomeroy had been sent for training on the new sound technology at Western Electric and RCA. It was because he returned with a head full of indispensable information that he gained such importance.[41] When it came time to test actors for speaking parts in films, he was given complete power. His pronouncement could make or break an actor's career.[42]

"Roy J. Pomeroy, director of sound at the Lasky studio, has just made a talkie test of Colleen Moore." In addition to Colleen, tests were made of Mary Pickford, Harold Lloyd, Norma Shearer and Lupe Velez.[43,44]

Colleen later described having been accompanied to the sound studio by John and several of the big First National franchise holders.[45] They all crowded into the sound booth while Colleen was alone in the studio. She was told by the sound engineer to speak into the microphone, to say anything, to recite a nursery rhyme. She recited: "Little Bo Peep has lost her sheep and can't tell where to find them. Leave them alone and they'll come home wagging their tails behind them."

There was a long pause while the engineer consulted is instruments. When he finally looked up, he indicated to Colleen that her voice had recorded just fine. She could speak. She could make talking films.

35. Colleen and Sound, August–October 1928

Before her sound test, on October 2, in a letter to First National, Colleen wrote to expressly disapprove of the three stories they had submitted to her as candidates for the photoplay to follow *Synthetic Sin*: *Where There's a Will, Roundabout,* and *Dangerous Nan McGrew*.

In Colleen's opinion, *Where There's a Will* did not have enough material to make a feature-length picture. It was the story of a flapper who stands to inherit a fortune if she could only conduct herself as a lady for six months. Colleen felt that such a slim premise would not offer enough audience appeal. *Roundabout* was a story which Colleen also felt couldn't hold the audience's interest. "The author took four chapters in the book to paint the girl's character." It would require too much film time to make the audience understand the character. "The story rambles from country to country and proves nothing, except that the girl comes to the conclusion that the free and easy life with her father in the Montmarte of Paris is preferable to the customs and habits of America." And *Dangerous Nan McGrew*, Colleen declared, has "not a single sincere quality and, in my opinion, is totally unbelievable and is not even good burlesque." Colleen then put forward her own three suggestions for stories that she would desire to do: *Balkan Love*, a story by Erich von Stroheim, based on George Barr McCutcheon's *East of the Setting Sun*; *Sunny*, the famous musical, and "Rogue's Moon," a series of pirate stories by Robert W. Chambers, published in *Liberty Magazine*.[46] First National considered the suggestions and went to work looking for its own alternatives.

Because the terms of Colleen's contract gave her control of the finished product, she needed to be finicky when it came to the choice of stories, cameramen, directors and editors. Blame for a failure would be placed directly on her and John. As Louise Brooks said of the advantage of being only a featured player: "If the picture doesn't turn out good, all the blame doesn't fall on you."[47]

Some described Colleen's need for control over her product as being akin to moody temperament. In the First National organization, Jerome Beatty[48] composed and circulated a letter that cast Colleen in an unflattering light and leaked it to magazine editors and editors of syndicated publications, intending to make Colleen look spoiled.

Beatty had been confronted by John in writing in the past on the lack of adequate magazine representation for Colleen.[49] Perhaps Beatty knew of the Warners wish to bring down the public popularity of some of their newly inherited stars in advance of contract negotiations. Whatever the reason, Beatty's responses to John's concerns, so far as Colleen was concerned, were antagonistic and irrelevant. It was from one of the letters John had written that Beatty culled the quotes for his own letter.

Colleen had been having concerns about her coverage in the magazines since the split from First National. The press had groused about Colleen's "high-hatted" aloofness towards them during her exile. When Colleen found out about the letter being circulated by the publicity department of her own studio she was not only hurt, but she nearly blew her top.

In a long telegram to Ned Depinet, First National general sales manager in New York — hardly composed in the carefully cost-conscious manner in which most people composed telegrams at the time, but in a telegraphic letter giving vent to a great reserve of frustration — Colleen described her anger at the incident:

[Beatty] very obviously intended that the letter would shock and completely upset me as it would anyone because Al (Rockett) agrees completely with me that to have sent this letter to editors would only have antagonized every editor against me and completely shut out all possibility of my getting any sympathetic treatment in future stop your statement that all fan magazines are reacting favorably only goes to prove that the contents of Beatty's letter were not based on facts because if editors are willing to now give me publicity which has been denied me for a year then it goes to prove I have not been properly represented stop

Colleen continued to say that she had shown her willingness to work with the publicity department, and while it was sad that it took a "situation like this to convince Beatty that it was time I was getting some fan magazine representation," she nevertheless felt she at least deserved decent representation "and not the aggressive and arbitrary reactions that we continually get from Beatty stop I will not be satisfied until a competent person is appointed to handle my publicity contacts in New York."[50]

Beatty's letter had been written to antagonize the editors of the various fan magazines. It was an approach that might have worked if the numbers for *Lilac Time* had not started to come in. Cash always speaks louder than words, and *Lilac Time* was an unabashed success. It had cost more than twice the amount of Collens previous two productions, but before the end of the year, *Lilac Time* had not only earned back every cent the studio had spent, but had made more than a million dollars in the domestic market alone.

"Colleen Moore's picture *Lilac Time* ... has cracked more records than any picture ever ... and is still thrilling thousands at every performance, the management [of the Carthay Circle Theater] declares."[51] At a time when a film might only have an expected shelf life of a few weeks before the next one in the studio's program replaced it, *Lilac Time* was still playing in October when Colleen's problems with Beatty came to a head. In November, the film opened at the Criterion, where the management expected "heavy patronage."[52] At the Carthay Circle in Los Angeles, the premiere pulled in $19,000, those attending paying $5 a head. Between July 28 and September 22 the film brought in an average of $13,533 per week. At the Central Theater in New York, which was charging between $1-$2 per showing, between August 11 and December 1 the film averaged $13,870 per week. At the Grand Central Theater in St. Louis the film outperformed *The Jazz Singer*.[53] *Lilac Time* was a good performer, trumping any effort to harm Colleen's stellar reputation.

The day after the star's lengthy long telegram, Ned Depinet wrote back that he was sure everything would work out for the best. There would only be "constructive results" to Beatty's letter, and the organization did "appreciate your standpoint and the most important thing to us is to keep you happy and giving us your very best stop we have always cooperated to the utmost in the past and will continue doing so." Ned wired Al to that effect and assured Colleen that if she and John were to take the matter up with him, some arrangement could be worked out.[54] Based on the strength of *Lilac Time*'s performance, Warners approached John McCormick with an offer of a new contract for Colleen at $15,000 a week. John never told Colleen about the offer because there was a catch. The offer was for Colleen only; they did not want John.[55]

By the end of October, Colleen and First National settled on the story *Why Be Good?*—which was being referred to by the press as *That's a Bad Girl*—as the film to follow *Synthetic Sin*. On October 27th the continuity for *Why Be Good* was submitted to Colleen, which she approved in November. "Neil Hamilton, the capable young leading man ... in Paramount's *Beau Geste*, has been signed by John McCormick for the male lead opposite Colleen Moore in her next First National picture, *That's a Bad Girl*, by Carey Wilson." Camerawork was still underway for *Synthetic Sin*, but production on *Why Be Good?* was "scheduled to start ... within a few days after *Synthetic Sin* is disposed of. William A. Seiter will direct."[56]

With a brand new year approaching, Al Rockett announced First National's upcoming program for 1929. Though First National was controlled by Warner Bros., the two studios were operating separately as two different brands and cooperating on sound films. This was reflected in Rockett's announcement that 26 "dialogue pictures" and 11 more with sound synchronization — costing some $7,000,000 — were to be included in the program. Eight of the films in the program would be special productions, three of which would be Colleen's films, including *Synthetic Sin*, *That's a Bad Girl*, and an untitled third.[57] In addition to the films themselves, the sound stage building program at the Burbank studio would cost an additional $500,000.

On the 16, First National submitted *Clipped Wings*, *When Irish Eyes Are Smiling*, and *A Garret in Paris*, by Sir Philip Gibbs for consideration to follow *Why Be Good?* When work on *Synthetic Sin* was finished, Colleen left town for a working vacation, taking the submitted story suggestions with her. "Taking advantage of the opportunity for a brief vacation.... Colleen Moore has gone to Palm Springs.... Accompanying Miss Moore is her husband, John McCormick." William Seiter, who would direct *Why Be Good?*, was going to visit them and go over the script and production details of the coming picture. "The double task of supervising the editing and cutting of *Synthetic Sin* and selecting the players to support Miss Moore in *Why Be Good?* faces McCormick when he returns.... *Why Be Good?*... is scheduled to start within two weeks."[58]

36

Why Be Good?, November 1928–January 1929

On November 16 it was settled that the film to follow *Why Be Good?* would be *When Irish Eyes Are Smiling*.[1] With Colleen's approval, First National went to work on a continuity.

Why Be Good? had many of the requisite elements: a bad girl who is actually good deep down; poor girl imported into a rich environment; mistaken identities; and the fairy-tale ending. Pert Kelly (Colleen), a counter girl in a New York department store, has a reputation for promiscuity, but is secretly a virtuous woman. She meets Peabody, Jr. (Neil Hamilton), at a roadhouse one night, and they make a date to meet again the following evening. The next morning, Pert is late for work and is called on the carpet by the personnel manager, who turns out to be Peabody, Jr. His father, who owns the store, fires Pert, but Peabody, Jr. is (predictably) smitten with her. He invites her to one of his parent's fancy soirées. His father doubts Pert's virtue, so Junior decides to evaluate her by bringing her to a disreputable roadhouse where he has staged an elaborate test. She protests and, convinced, Junior marries her right away.

Bodil Rosing was brought into the production "portraying the mother of Colleen Moore…. It will be remembered that Miss Rosing once before gave a very convincing portrayal of Colleen's mother in *It Must Be Love*."[2] In one of her first appearances on film, Jean Harlow had a small part as an extra, and William Seiter is supposed to have commented on her to Colleen: "Look, you've never seen anything like it."[3] While the cameras were rolling on *Why Be Good?*, work proceeded on *When Irish Eyes Are Smiling*. John wrote to Obringer on December 4 to "please ascertain whether or not the following songs are in the public domain: 'Come Back to Erin,' 'Kathleen Mavourneen.'" He was hoping to use the songs in a talking picture.[4] The next day Colleen approved her photo for use on the cover of the sheet music for the song "Betty," which was to be marketed to the public as the "theme to *Synthetic Sin*." Everything was sliding into place for *When Irish Eyes Are Smiling*, on December 12 a continuity was submitted to Colleen for her approval.

Three days later Colleen rejected it.

The rejection put the schedule for the next film on pause, but *Why Be Good?* rolled along. Colleen did her usual interviews, posed for publicity photographs, and did her part. First National might not be terribly happy with her contract, but she knew what a successful film meant to John.

In lieu of *When Irish Eyes Are Smiling*, Colleen expressed a willingness to substitute *Early to Bed* as her next film. First National was willing, and agreed on the following conditions: that submission for a continuity be postponed for long enough to reasonably prepare a continuity; That the obligation to begin photography on the next film two weeks after the completion of *Why Be Good?* be waived; that photography begin one week after approval of a continuity, provided that a director and cameraman have already been agreed upon; that any extra time between the productions beyond the original two weeks is an excusable delay; and that First National agreed to submit, for Colleen's approval, a director and cameraman by January 7, 1929.[5]

At the end of the year, the upcoming program of movies for 1929 included Colleen in *Early to Bed*, referred to as "a college story by Lynn and Lois Seyster Montross."[6]

In December, Colleen's attorney submitted to First National a draft for a proposed new contract. Her 1928 contract had been a subject of some agitation at First National because of the generous terms, but at the time there was nothing to do. Colleen had shown herself too valuable to let go. The new proposed contract was even more agitating.[7]

1929

> It's almost a temptation to puzzle over the reason why Colleen Moore keeps theater ticket-takers so busy. But such heresy would almost be as great as not believing in Santa, the efficacy of the Eighteenth Amendment and Calvin Coolidge's prowess as a big game hunter.
> —"Colleen Moore Makes 'Sin' Household Mot,"
> *Dallas Morning News*, January 12, 1929, page unknown.

With the passing of the old year, the new one brought with it news of a disappointing reversal of fortune for Colleen: after two years as the biggest money-making actress (according to motion picture exhibitors), Colleen lost her top slot on the list to Clara Bow.[8]

Clara was propelled past Colleen partly because of her sexy roles. In the last year she had appeared in films like *The Fleet's In*, as a taxi dancer with a heart of gold; *Ladies of the Mob*, as a crook; *Red Hair*, as a gold-digger; and *Three Week-Ends*, as a chorus girl. None of the roles were necessarily any racier than those written for Colleen, but it was Clara's depiction that differentiated them. Colleen's stories suggested racy characters and situations, but Clara injected her roles with a degree of sexuality that was absent from Colleen's.

Colleen might have pulled off playing Hawaiian-born "Hula" Calhoun, but she would not have done the drunken suggestive shimmy or the skinny-dipping scenes. While Colleen teased the audience with the promise of racy highjinks, Clara Bow delivered. Colleen's popularity had been eclipsed by the flashier, explosive Clara.

Work on *Why Be Good?* was wrapped by early January[9] and the film went into editing. *Synthetic Sin* was released the first month of January to good reviews for its peppy, fast-paced humor. Some saw it as a return to Colleen's earlier mode of light-hearted flapper humor. Some welcomed the return to her earlier forte, others bemoaned it: "*Synthetic Sin* was but a so-so stage comedy," one reviewer wrote, acknowledging the film's less-than-stellar roots, but "as a screen farce it has become unusually amusing, and as lively as a flapper at a college prom. Colleen Moore has seldom given a more sprightly performance, nor has she had better opportunity to make the most of her highly individual style of acting."[10] In St. Petersburg, the film drew large crowds to the Florida Theater in spite of a fireworks display scheduled at the time of the opening.[11]

Mordaunt Hall was one of the reviewers who did not appreciate the return to Colleen's flapper-type stories. He called the film an absurdity: "Of all the insane stories in which

Colleen Moore has appeared, *Synthetic Sin* is perhaps the worst. It is ridiculous, it is true, but it hasn't even the plausibility of a custard pie comedy." He called it meaningless as well as witless, a vehicle saddled upon "a really clever actress." The director was not to blame, he decided, as it had some of the same "infantile" strains that coursed through *Lilac Time*. Nor was the writer, so the selection of the story rested upon Colleen and John.[12]

Mae Tinee was less harsh in judgment: "Little Colleen's latest vehicle is, more or less, a farcical affair and doesn't do a great deal for her, to my way of thinking. May the new year be kind to this small lady and bring her more yarns like *Happiness Ahead*.... Miss Moore does the best she can with her improbable role." She also called it well staged and photographed, and that the direction was adequate to the role.

Things were looking good for Colleen's next film. While *Synthetic Sin* was still in release, a test audience screened *Why Be Good?*,[13] at the Westlake Theater. Whitney Williams was impressed: "Remember *Flaming Youth*? With Colleen Moore flaming all over the place, setting cushions on fire at the slightest touch, and what not? *People*, as the ancients were wont to chatter, 'You hadn't seen *nothin'* then!'" *Why Be Good?*, it was declared, was livelier than *Flaming Youth*, and if *Why Be Good?* had been around then it would have created an even greater uproar. "*Why Be Good?* is strictly comedy, of the most delectable sort, up to the last reel or so. Even then, for all its dramatic treatment, a sense of comedy pervades the action." The rough cut was not perfect. It suffered from "sketchiness, a slackening of tempo at times somewhat disconcerting." This was the fault of the film's length, in its attempt to cover too much territory. Overall, the reviewer felt this would be corrected by the final cut. Colleen's acting was excellent and Neil Hamilton, in "a role requiring little more than ordinary acting, will be well received."[14]

There were promising developments on the domestic front for Colleen at the start of 1929. After years of renting their house on Rossmore, Colleen and John bought a house in Bel Air.[15] "Colleen Moore [through the purchase] became one of the first motion-picture stars to have a residence including equipment for projection of talking motion pictures." They signed papers that gave them the title to the Bel-Air estate, including a half-completed mansion. Originally being built for C.F. Stewart of Chicago, the home "so exactly suited Miss Moore and McCormick that they persuaded Stewart to sell." The home was designed by Theodore J. Scott and was being constructed by Clarence Cox.[16]

When the house was half finished, Colleen was contemplating where to find an interior decorator. She bumped into Carmelita Wilson, who was with a young man she introduced as Harold Grieve, a former art director at the Marshall Neilan studio. Grieve had gone into business for himself, and when Colleen asked him to design her bathroom for her, he told her he would either do the whole house, or nothing at all. She agreed on the spot, and, before long, she had fired the architect they had brought in to finish the house and let Harold go to work. The completion of the house would be an event that Colleen would anticipate much of the year.

First National had submitted to Colleen the name of William Seiter to direct *Early to Bed* and Sid Hickox as cameraman, both approved by Colleen on January 7.[17] As usual, before the production began, John and Colleen and the writers left for a short working vacation. They traveled to Yosemite and ended up snowbound. They were only expecting to stay a few days, but the weather had other ideas. They wired First National to inform the organization of their predicament at the first opportunity they had, and then waited. Colleen spent the time tobogganing and enjoyed the wait thoroughly.[18]

Back in Los Angeles, *Lilac Time* was still playing, having been booked for a four-day run at the Figueroa Theater, Fred Miller's million-dollar theater.[19] The theater boasted of the film's realistic sound effects, calling the film one of Colleen's "most gripping" to date.[20] It had been nearly six months since *Lilac Time* had been released; for it to still be booked by a prestigious, first-run theater spoke to the film's staying power.

John was thinking ahead to the next vehicle to follow *Early to Bed*. Carey Wilson had come across a story in *College Humor* magazine that he felt contained the kernel of a good Colleen More story. John wrote Al Rockett: "I believe I can sell to Colleen the Carey Wilson adaptation of the Katherine Brush story *Footlights and Fools*.... Wilson recommended the story, but it was without a beginning or an end. I told him that if he would write a short, sketchy treatment filling in the holes, I would be interested." He asked Al to look it over and give his impressions, and if Al liked it, John would have Carey Wilson write the script and he would try and interest Colleen in the project. The story would lend itself, John felt, to musical and singing numbers.[21]

In mid-February, First National's attorneys, Loeb, Walker and Loeb, gave their opinion of the proposed contract Colleen's attorney had submitted back in December.

> Enclosed copies of agreements prepared by Colleen Moore's attorney, including supplemental agreement to Colleen Moore's present contract, draft of proposed new contract with Colleen Moore and draft of proposed new contract with John McCormick. In our opinion, the present contract dated February 28, 1928 between yourselves and Miss Moore is extremely cumbersome and in some respects dangerous to the company. It was, however, the best that could have been worked out at the time.
>
> The enclosed contracts, however, contain additional changes, including changes which were not set forth in the draft which was submitted in December 1928, and which in my opinion make the contract very materially more objectionable even than the present contract. The changes have been pointed out in the enclosed comments.
>
> I would very strongly recommend that the company refuse to exercise the proposed contracts unless a very decided change is made in the entire setup.[22]

Sound films gave First National the excuse needed to start the process of making changes. They took a firmer hand with Colleen than in the past; pushing back against the generous terms Colleen had operated under before, they went about attempting to delineate more narrow interpretations of terms.

On February 27, First National wrote a long letter to Colleen regarding the next few films, confirming the understanding between them that while, in December 1928, Colleen approved *Early to Bed*, she had since reversed her decision and opted instead for *When Irish Eyes Are Smiling*, which would be the third film under her February 1928 contract. First National was willing to go along with the choice, but with a long list of conditions including that she accept William Seiter and Sid Hickox as director and cameraman; that she accept the continuity for *When Irish Eyes Are Smiling*, written under the supervision of John McCormick; and the excusable delay initiated two weeks after the completion of *That's a Bad Girl* (*Why Be Good*) would end with the start of the new production.

First National agreed in the letter that it would begin production a week after confirmation of the terms, but if there was a delay on Colleen's part and the production did not start on or before March 11, it would constitute an excusable delay. *Footlights and Fools* would have to be agreed upon as the next production, and Colleen would have to agree that wherever the phrases "motion picture" or "motion picture production" or "photoplay" or the like appeared in any of her legal documents, they would be construed to include talking picture projects. Along these lines, Colleen would have to agree that the third and forth productions under her February 1928 contract would be "all-talking" motion pictures. She would have to give First National rights to record, reproduce and transmit her voice in conjunction with her productions, and would film and record promotional materials for her films.

The conditions were not one-sided. Colleen would be getting $175,000 for each photoplay, a boost in compensation of $25,000 per film.[23] Colleen agreed to the terms; *Early to Bed* was dropped in lieu of *When Irish Eyes Are Smiling*, the continuity of which had already been supervised by John McCormick and was ready for immediate production.[24]

Changes were made in the draft of Colleen's supplemental agreement at the request of Colleen's attorney, and were set forth in a redraft. In the opinion of Loeb, Walker and Loeb, the conditions were not objectionable, and a request made at the suggestion of First National was one that gave the organization the option of using a voice double for Colleen in her songs, if necessary. For John's contract: "Concurrent with the amendment and modification of the Colleen Moore contract, Mr. McCormick's contract is likewise affected. Mr. McCormick's compensation, however, shall be changed so that in lieu of the $32,500.00 each for the third and fourth photoplay, he shall be paid $35,000.00 each, payable in installments of $3500.00 per week."[25]

At the end of February, Colleen had accepted *Footlights and Fools*, to be the fourth photoplay under the contract of February 28, 1929. For director and cameraman she approved William A. Seiter and Sid Hickox.[26] By March 1, John was writing Al Rockett to authorize Roy Obringer to draw a contract for Carey Wilson to write a continuity for the story "Love is Like That." Colleen was interested in the story, and they had ideas for lyrics for a theme song of the same name.

When March 5 came around, *When Irish Eyes Are Smiling* was not ready to begin. John wrote Al that more time was needed for Vitagraph tests. In the meantime, Colleen and James Hall were out taking singing lessons, and James was learning the violin. Unfortunately, he was making slow progress in getting rid of his Cockney accent. Unofficially, Colleen was requesting three weeks off after *When Irish Eyes Are Smiling*.

When Irish Eyes Are Smiling (Smiling Irish Eyes), *March 17–April 28, 1929*

> Loose talk: Colleen Moore is going to make a talkie and then retire from the screen. Anyway, that's the story.
> —*Photoplay*, February 1929, page 48, (Joseph Yranski Collection).

The start of *When Irish Eyes Are Smiling* fell, by fortunate happenstance, on St. Patrick's Day. The studio made the most of that in their publicity: "Selecting the anniversary of St. Patrick's as an auspicious time to start the production off an Irish romance, director William A. Seiter launched Colleen Moore's first dialogue picture ... with the appropriate

36. Why Be Good?, *November 1928–January 1929*

accompaniment of Erin's tunes, jigs and brogues. In fact, brogues are among the first requisites on Colleen's sets these days."[27]

Brogues, accents and voices were among the chief concerns of the motion picture industry at that particular moment. First National had selected Constance Collier as voice coach for Colleen. Collier had gotten her start in acting, and had starred as Cleopatra to Herbert Beerbohm Tree's Antony in a 1906 revival of the play *Antony and Cleopatra*.[28] She had not been impressed by Colleen's accent: Michigan via Florida with a hint of English from the influence of her cousins Jack and Maran Stone.[29] The voice lessons were long and tedious and, in the end, given that most of Colleen's roles were those of working-class girls, largely useless. Colleen always managed to acquire whatever accent was needed as part of her total immersion into the role. She delivered lines in a Cockney accent in *Twinkletoes*, and spoke lines in French in *Lilac Time*. If she ever needed a proper English accent,

Colleen in a publicity photograph from *Smiling Irish Eyes*, First National, 1929 (courtesy Judy Coleman).

she would have been able to acquire that as well. Still, the bosses insisted on a voice coach.

Why Be Good? was released in mid–March. Mae Tinee liked this one considerably more than *Synthetic Sin*: "You'll like *Why Be Good*. It's bright, lively, and well acted, and gives the cunning and (I think) clever child, Colleen Moore, considerable opportunity to show what she can do, emotionally, dramatically, and comically." A light story, it was still intriguing and well handled. "A few more mothers like Mrs. Kelly, as portrayed by Bodil Rosing, and a few more fathers such as Edward Martindale's Peabody Sr., would be acceptable in this old world of ours."[30] Marquis Busby was less impressed: "In spite of high production value, excellent acting performances and direction, *Why Be Good* doesn't quite make the grade on account of a weak, silly story. The subject of the flapper, and whether or not she is a good girl, is just a bit nauseous after so much pounding from the pulpit, press and screen." As the story was at time risqué, the reviewer had doubts that Colleen's fans would want to see her "careening about on thin ice." The production was excellent with good direction and titles that brightened the story.[31] Still the flapper-style stories were becoming passé. With luck, *When Irish Eyes Are Smiling* would be better received.

> The larger purpose of our economic thought should be to establish more firmly stability and security of business and employment and thereby remove poverty still further from our borders.
>
> — Herbert Hoover inaugural address, Monday, March 4, 1929.

The economy was booming in early 1929, and Hoover came into the White House with a plan to loosen regulation over the economic system. Stocks had been on the rise for years and some saw the stock market as a safe investment for the future. Many people even acted upon their dreams of making fortunes in the stock market by jumping into it largely on credit and buying on the margin: the investor putting down 10 percent of the cost of a given stock while borrowing the remaining 90 percent from the mortgage broker. With the economy chugging along and the stock market on a seemingly endless rise, few people worried that there would ever be an end to the prosperous times.

The promise of easy money fed the hedonistic mood of the public consciousness. Everyone wanted to be rich, or else look rich. It was an evolution of the mood of American youth. The newly affluent, made weary by industrialized war, simply wanted escape. The party atmosphere had not, by any means, permeated through all strata of society, but it had saturated those who where spending money on motion pictures, and the motion picture industry fed the fantasy. Sound pictures added to the allure of motion pictures as an escape, and as long as escapism to a world of lavish fantasy was the point, Colleen's films retained their audience.

Irish accents and music were important elements of *When Irish Eyes Are Smiling*. William Seiter referred to Tom J. Geraghty, the writer, as a "Gaelic linguist," and commented that *When Irish Eyes Are Smiling* positively "sparkles with Irish humor, and is admirably suited to Colleen Moore...."[32] When the film had gone into production, the only major parts that had been cast were James Hall[33] and Claude Gillingwater.[34]

In preparation for the more old-fashioned role, reminiscent of earlier parts, Colleen reportedly let her hair grow out, which caught the eyes of Hollywood observers: "Colleen Moore appeared at luncheon yesterday looking like the second smuggler in *Carmen*. She is letting her famous square bob grow out so she may impress the public at large as an ingenuous Irish colleen. Ingenuousness, in movieland, is found in the cylinder of a lady's curl."[35] Colleen continued her voice lessons, and took singing lessons as well.

The story of *When Irish Eyes Are Smiling* was similar to Colleen's earlier picture with Rupert Hughes, *Come on Over*, with Colleen playing the part of the Irish lass left behind in the old country while her sweetheart crossed the ocean to make his fortune in America before sending for her. In *When Irish Eyes Are Smiling*, Rory O'More (James Hall), the sweetheart, was a songwriter working in a peat bog. He writes a song with Kathleen O'Connor (Colleen) and it becomes their special song. He goes to America, leaving Kathleen behind. He writes her letters daily, but without good news to relate he refuses to mail them. Unlike *Come on Over*'s Shane O'Mealia, who bounced from job to job until good old-fashioned Irish patronage finds him steady work, Rory was talented and found a gig playing his violin in a theatrical production on Broadway. With success he seems to forget Kathleen and finds himself drawn to more sophisticated ladies like Frankie West (Betty Francisco) and Goldie DeVeer (Julanne Johnston). Meanwhile, back in Ireland, Kathleen becomes impatient, and borrows the money necessary to travel to America. When she finds Rory, he's on stage singing the song he wrote with Kathleen to one of his more cosmopolitan lady friends while she kisses him (as part of the production). Heartbroken — and moved to song — Kathleen leaves angrily and returns to Ireland. Rory shows up and explains himself. She forgives him, and the whole family immigrates to America in the end.

George "Gabby" Hayes had a small part as a New York taxi driver in the film. Over 160 Irish men and women, "big and little, fat and thin," were reported as serving as extras in a county fair scene. "Colleen has learned all the intricate steps and words to several Irish jigs, but that tall, spare veteran, [Claude] Gillingwater, proved to her that she hadn't learned them all by getting out and flinging his long legs through nimble evolutions."[36] In keeping with the grand size of the production and musical and theatrical themes, the production cast a group of performers in one large lot. "The first complete screen chorus to be organized and signed under individual contracts, has just been mobilized at First National-Vitaphone studios in Burbank.... Included in the chorus are two dozen pretty and talented girls, and 12 male singers and dancers." New York stage producer Larry Ceballos assisted in the selections and choreography. They would appear in the theatre scenes of the film. "The chorus will be used both as a unit and for various tap and toe dancing and singing specialties to be performed by various members of this trained group."[37]

The technology of talking motion pictures was still in its infancy at the time. The main limiting factor was the fact that the camera was required to be immobile, encased in a sound-proofed booth so that the sound of the rolling camera would not be recorded along with the voices of the actors. The result was an unintentionally stilted look to the staging of the scenes. In *Lilac Time*, there were several scenes in which the camera swept up to the actors, or tracked along with them during the action. Not so in the new sound films. There was no overdubbing with the Vitaphone system, no chance to correct mistakes. As Colleen wrote, "Since the film was matched to the record, and there was no known way to cut the record, we couldn't cut the film." As a result, the film had to follow the script exactly. There was no rough cut to the film; material that did not work could not be cut before the final product was screened.

Furthermore, the method of acting for sound films had not been perfected. During the production they delivered their lines as they might deliver them for a silent film, pantomiming gestures that would have been visual cues for silent film audiences. Much of the gesturing was unneeded and looked out of place. In the end, Colleen described the film as "the longest, slowest, dullest picture ever made."[38]

In spite of Colleen's singing lessons, she would insist she was a terrible singer. She sang several songs, including "Old Killarney Fair," "Then I'll Ride Home with You," "A Wee Bit o' Love," and "Smiling Irish Eyes." During one scene she was to sing "Come Back to Erin." At the end of the song when she was supposed to hit her high note, she instead broke down and cried for her Rory. She still was not satisfied. The hundred-piece orchestra that accompanied her tried to play over her, but her voice carried right through to the microphone.[39]

All in all, Colleen found it to be a disappointing experience.

At the end of March, Colleen approved William Seiter as director and Sid Hickox as cameraman for the upcoming production of *Footlights and Fools*. It would be the fourth film under her contract as agreed upon under the February 28, 1929, contract.[40] Production on *When Irish Eyes Are Smiling* was set to wrap up on April 25. *Footlights and Fools* had been settled on for Colleen's next vehicle, the last film under her contract. *Irish Eyes* had fallen behind about a week, and in early April, Al Rockett wrote Roy Obringer: "According to Director's Reports, *When Irish Eyes Are Smiling* should finish in 16 more days or by April 25, 1929. I believe it is safe to say that Mr. Seiter will make up a couple of the 7 days they are behind schedule."[41] One possible reason for going over schedule was sickness: "Colleen Moore caught herself a couple of germs and the cold lowered her voice a notch or two. Or is the word pitch? At all events, the 'mikes' know a cold larynx when they hear one, so Colleen enjoyed a few days off. Pitch on the up and up now, if you please."[42]

Al Rockett wanted someone to check on the status of the continuity of *Footlights and*

Fools.[43] The continuity had proven difficult for the reasons outlined earlier — no beginning or end — and in anticipation of delays the studio had gotten an extension on the deadline for the continuity signed by Colleen on April 13. However, the extension was not to exceed 30 days from April 13.[44] On the 15th John wrote Rockett that he had a revised draft, and that some more conferences with Seiter and Colleen were needed to go over the dialog. They had had to write a whole new story and lines, and all this had fallen during a time when they had been having problems with *Irish Eyes* such as "weather, wind, pig trouble, actor trouble, recording trouble, etc. etc."

That month Colleen was on the cover of *Motion Picture Magazine*, an Irish-themed cover of Colleen wearing an Irish Donegal Walker over her bobbed hair. There was a feature inside that edition on *When Irish Eyes Are Smiling*, now titled *Smiling Irish Eyes*. The photographs, however, were of Colleen from the earlier version that would have been directed by Mervyn LeRoy. A name from the scuttled production of 1927 resurfaced posthumously: Gerald Duffy, the First National writer who had come up with the original story after reviewing other materials being considered for Colleen. After John and Colleen split with First National and the project was abandoned, Duffy moved on to other projects. In October of that year, Duffy's wife sued for divorce, accusing him of being a drunkard and an all-around unpleasant man: "A property settlement has been effected, the complaint recited, whereby Duffy has undertaken to pay his wife $20,000 in monthly installments."[45] Duffy had died in 1928, but in May, when the film was released, his former wife would turn up again to sue First National: "Mrs. Marjorie Duffy, widow of Gerald Duffy, screen writer, launched a suit against First National Studios and indirectly against Colleen Moore, based on allegations that First National paid neither her nor her dead husband for the screen story 'Irish Eyes Are Smiling.'"[46]

Footlights and Fools, *May–July 1929*

Colleen had designated three weeks' break between *Irish Eyes* and *Footlights and Fools*. Unfortunately, the process of adapting the story for *Footlights and Fools* was taking longer than anticipated.

Roy Obringer reminded Al Rockett that he had the extension whereby the obligation to submit a continuity on *Footlights and Fools* has been extended to May 13: "I believe and hope by this time McCormick and Wilson will thrash out the difficulties on this continuity, but believe it advisable to check about May 9, 1929, as to the status in order that we will not be in default by not making the submittal on the 13th."[47] By the ninth it was completed and Colleen approved the continuity of *Footlights and Fools* by Carey Wilson.

William Seiter had gone back east for his vacation as he had not expected approval of the continuity so soon, which was a premature move: "William A. Seiter has arrived from New York. He had to cut his first vacation in two years to a brief ten days to accept the assignment." It would mark the fifth time he had directed Colleen. Production was to start immediately.[48] Cleeve would put in an appearance as a press agent, as would another familiar face: "Jack Stone, who played the infant aviator in *Lilac Time*, will have a role in Colleen Moore's *Footlights and Fools* at First National-Vitaphone Studios."[49]

"After speaking an Irish brogue for two months during the filming of her first talking picture, *Smiling Irish Eyes*, Colleen Moore is now acquiring a French accent for her next First National–Vitaphone picture, *Footlights and Fools*."[50] Colleen would work mostly at the old Vitagraph lot at Prospect Boulevard in Hollywood, which had been bought by Warner Bros. in 1925 and had been refurbished for sound film production.[51] Color segments were shot back in Burbank, but there were problems; it had been a hot summer, with record high temperatures in the interior of the state,[52] and high temperatures in Los Angeles sending throngs to the beach in hopes of escaping the heat.[53] Shooting color sequences during the summer heat proved problematic: "The number of lights required on a set sends the temperature soaring to anywhere between 120 and 145 degrees." In an enclosed studio with no air circulating, it would have been extremely uncomfortable, even dangerous to the electrical crews who had to stand by their lights for extended periods. "The shooting schedules have been rearranged so that the electrical crews double up, each crew working a short shift during the day and another short shift at night."[54]

This was to be a production with a heavy emphasis on musical productions. There were multiple identities in the film, as Colleen played Fifi D'Auray, a seemingly exotic French actress who was the talk of the town in the Follies-like production, *The Sins of 1930*. The fancy name belied the fact that Fifi was actually Betty Murphy, an American girl who traveled to France at the behest of her producer and returned with a more sophisticated, international persona. She had been in love with Jimmy Willet (Raymond Hackett) since her chorus-girl days. Unfortunately, Jimmy was a gambler and crook, though she didn't realize it. He wants to marry her but she refuses to marry him until he finds himself a respectable job, a demand he resists. Along comes rich playboy, Gregory Pyne (Fredric March), who becomes infatuated with the Fifi persona. He bribes his friend Claire to allow him to bring her to supper. Once he is in her dressing room they fight and she storms out, pretending to be upset and insisting that the only way he can make it up to her is to give Jimmy a good job. Gregory agrees, and appoints him treasurer of the theater. With a good job under his belt, Jimmy and Betty secretly marry. Later, there is a robbery of the theater and an arrest warrant is issued for Jimmy. Fifi insists Pyne has framed Jimmy for the crime. Jimmy reveals his marriage to Betty, leaving Gregory disillusioned with Betty/Fifi. In a dramatic and unexpected twist, Betty discovers that Jimmy has used her all along and that he is guilty of the theft. She sends him away and realizes she must divorce him. It was an oddly prescient ending for a Colleen Moore film, given her thoughts on marriage at the time.

As with the chorus hired for *Smiling Irish Eyes*, musicians were hired for this production to augment the musical skills of the actors and actresses. "Earl Burtnett's Biltmore Trio,[55] whose harmony entertains the elite of Southern California's pleasure-loving population nightly, has been engaged by John McCormick to sing a number specifically written for Colleen Moore's present talking picture, *Footlights and Fools*." The trio consisted of a high baritone, tenor and falsetto accompanied by steel guitar, ukulele, and standard guitar. The trio broadcast nightly over radio station KHJ from the Biltmore Hotel. They were to record "If I Can't Have You" by Al Bryan and George W. Meyer.[56] Songs for the film included "If I Can't Have You" "(If You Can't Have Me)," "You Can't Believe My Eyes," "Ophelia Will Fool You," and "Pilly Pom Pom Plee."[57] Colleen not only needed to sing her own songs again, but she had to sing in a French accent.[58]

Lessons had been learned with *Smiling Irish Eyes* and applied to *Footlights and Fools*; Seiter had been emphatic about this point months later: "I want to tell you I think *Footlights and Fools* is 1000 percent better than our first talkie. First we had a story superior to the

Cinderella stuff so often used for her. She dances, sings and speaks well, and we have learned how to crisp up the dialog and maintain the fast tempo of a silent as well. Colleen's performance is marvelous ... three distinct characterizations, as her Irish self, sweet and natural, as the French dancer, and as the tough girl. It is the last picture under Colleen's contract and she deserves a long holiday."[59]

"When the cameras stopped grinding on *Footlights and Fools* a few days ago First National lost its most popular star. That film completed Colleen Moore's contract. Colleen will vacation for a couple of months and will then move to another studio, although she doesn't know yet which one it will be. According to John McCormick ... negotiations are now being carried on with several major studios. He expects to announce their new affiliation within a few weeks."[60] Grace Kingsley made the announcement as well, noting that Colleen had been working continuously since the middle of March, and she was planning to take a vacation until September, when she would consider the next step in her career. John boasted that negations were already going on, and that he would announce her future affiliations.[61]

Filming and editing of *Footlights and Fools* was completed on July 12 and on that day a letter was sent to R.W. Perkins that the cutting was completed, thus "obligations under contract dated February 28, 1928 are fulfilled."[62]

37

The Belair House and a Fairy Castle

> Colleen Moore has disbanded her entire staff of technicians, publicity writers and others, who have been with her for many years.
>   Miss Moore, we understand, will take a trip around the world, accompanied by her husband, John McCormick.
>   The star has long wished to make this tour. On this occasion she expects to be gone several months.
>   Many professional offers have come to Miss Moore, naturally, since she is one of the most successful of the present day stars, but so far as she has signed no contracts.
>   —"Irish Star Plans Trip Around World," by Grace Kingsley,
>   *Los Angeles Times*, July 30, 1929, page A12.

Smiling Irish Eyes had been released about the same time the Colleen Moore unit at First National was dissolved. Colleen "out-Irishes the Irish" with the "sort of Mick conversation that was so popular in the musical comedy days of Chauncey Olcott, when an Irishman was not an Irishman unless he said 'whist' every fifteen minutes or so." There were spirited scenes, such as chasing a greased pig at the fair and a "spirited Irish argument" between Sir Timothy and Grandmother O'More that was "almost worth the price of admission." The second half of the picture was "dragged out boringly" while Rory goes to America. "The producers arrange a stupid misunderstanding between the lovers at this point and another reel of film is wasted." James Hall exhibited a Times Square Irish dialect and the ability to play every note on his violin without moving his hand, both of which were forgivable, but the reviewer was irked by his sideburns. "To Miss Moore's credit it must be said that she speaks remarkably well with her dialect. The talkies will not detract from her popularity if proper judgment is used in choosing her future stories."[1]

Colleen was well received. "Chiefly as a novelty, and as a demonstration of a popular star's ability to act and speak naturally in a new medium — as well as sing, begorra!— will *Smiling Irish Eyes* invoke attention." The potential for future progress in her future performances was great, and her performance in numbers like "Return to Erin," which "Miss Moore invests with much pathos" was enjoyable. The reviewer did not realize that the pathos was Colleen's strategy to avoid the unreachable notes.

Overall, the film was panned, while Colleen was seen as a bright spot: "The picture is an utterly juvenile interpretation of Ireland as it used to flourish on the stage thirty years ago, but it is devoid of the drama which enabled Chauncey Olcott, Andrew Mack, Fisk O'Hara and others to hold their audiences.... Yet at the outset it must be said that Colleen scored a pronounced personal success in her first venture into audible pictures. Her voice ... is charming."[2] Even the *New York Times* gave tepid approval of the quality of Colleen's voice: "In speaking, Miss Moore seems to have a good voice."[3]

However, going into August, Colleen's thoughts were elsewhere.

The Bel Air house was elaborate and fancy. Lee Shippey expected, when he arrived on the doorstep, to be met at the door by footmen. John and Colleen were still in the process of moving into the house,[4] with books spread out all over.[5]

There were two separate suites upstairs for Colleen and John, both with their own sitting room and restroom, with a guest room in-between. Colleen had made that decision out of necessity: John's drinking had only gotten worse, his episodes coming every few weeks. Colleen needed her own room where she could sleep and rehearse when John was drinking. The guestroom between their suites suggests the distance that had grown between them. Colleen's suite had been painted yellow and turquoise with silk-pile turquoise rugs. Her mirrored restroom was yellow and onyx. John had insisted his suite be painted dark blue, perhaps a reflection of inner turmoil. His restroom had a steam room attached. John said it would keep him from getting fat; Colleen had other ideas for potential uses, such as sobering him up. The drinking had taken a toll on John. Once a tall, slim man, later photographs of him show a man who had put on weight, with bags under his eyes and a double chin. Sometimes looking glassy-eyed, it's easy to imagine him hungover in any number of those images. With his drinking only getting worse, John's position at First National had become untenable. When their contracts with First National ended, they walked away from the organization, John promising he'd arrange a contract somewhere else.

The doctors would tell Colleen that John's liver was nearly gone, that the drinking had ruined it, and that he was living on borrowed time.[6]

The house was completed during the making of *Footlights and Fools*, and in anticipation of the completion John had gone on the wagon. This time it seemed to be working. John and Colleen drove past the house from time to time when it was being worked on. One time, stopping at the house one night after a party, John gave Colleen a bracelet. In the last few years jewelry had been his way of apologizing. "Peace offerings," Colleen called them. The bracelet he gave her that night had been the one piece she treasured.[7]

The day before they were to move in, John had fallen off the wagon and disappeared again. He turned up a few days later in the Hollywood Hospital. This time Colleen did not rush to his side. She moved into their house alone and telephoned John's parents. She told them where he was and asked them for their help.

John's parents retrieved him from the hospital and brought him home to Colleen, along with his doctor, who told her there were options to cure his drinking. A cure could be administered to him at home, under the supervision of a male nurse, so that he could avoid the public humiliation of being checked into a hospital.[8] John's mother told Colleen that he would not live much longer as his liver was shot. She begged Colleen to stay with John, and she agreed reluctantly. If the cure worked and he managed to stay on the wagon, it might be possible for them to reconcile. They all agreed John would try a cure at home.

A "gold cure" was suggested, Colleen wrote, though the process Colleen described sounds more akin to an aversion therapy. In any case, at the time there were a number of home cures available. The cure John took was three weeks of hell. Having dried out, the male nurse gave him drinks on a regular basis which, immediately after drinking made John violently ill. While being sick, the nurse would repeat: "This is what will happen to you if you ever take another drink." Colleen feared the cure would kill him.

At the end of it all, she wrote that he was weak, but managed to return to his duties as producer. He and Colleen toured their completed house. She went out of her way to accommodate John for fear of creating pressure that might bring on a relapse. He had treated her like his "little girl" in the past. He had insisted on it again, told Colleen to call him "daddy." Once again, she was his little girl. She was mortified, but she did as he asked.

Two weeks later he returned to the bottle. He had hidden liquor all over the house, so when he snapped, there was no keeping him from drinking. He became paranoid, convinced she had hired someone to chase off his bootlegger. By September, John had become threatening enough that Colleen feared he might become violent toward her. With the exception of the time in New York when he had tried to throw her over the balcony, his drunken spells had been largely characterized by impotent boasts and bragging. On the evening of September 18, 1929, when Colleen told John how difficult he was making life for her, he displayed a wild look and told her that he had made her a star, and without him she was nothing. He could break her as easily as he made her.[9]

It was frightening, but when she retired to her suite, she was beyond crying. The next day when she went to his suite, he was glassy-eyed drunk, and in his shorts. There was no chance that he was going to put in an appearance at the Churchill lunch. Enraged, she pulled off her shoe and pounded his chest with the heel, leaving "D"-shaped indentations. John told her "D" stood for dummy.

She went to the lunch alone. Afterwards, she found Harold Grieve, who knew about John's drinking. The two had dinner. When she returned home that evening, John was gone. She packed up her own clothes and moved in with her parents.[10]

While they were living in separate homes, they still kept up the pretense of marriage, though rumors of the separation had started to circulate.[11] John continued on in his capacity as her business manager and tried to negotiate a deal for them. He had told her that he was attempting to set up a Colleen Moore unit at United Artists, but nothing came of it. Colleen returned to the Bel Air house nightly for the sake of appearances before going on back to her parents. Sometimes they entertained at the house, sometimes Colleen had friends over. This continued for weeks.[12] In October, they went east to New York for contract negotiations, but the negotiations broke off around October 20, when Colleen suffered an attack of appendicitis. Colleen's parents flew east when they got word of her condition, making the trip by air in a fraction of the time it had taken her to travel west by train more than a decade earlier. Colleen returned to California, and on October 30, she was to be examined by physicians to see if an appendectomy was necessary.[13] It was, and it was scheduled for a week later.

On November 8, she was operated on at the Hollywood Hospital, her condition afterward was reported as satisfactory.[14]

In November *Footlights and Fools* was released. Cleeve got good reviews in the *Hamilton Daily News* for his part of the press agent. He was "rapidly achieving success in the same field that carried Colleen to international fame." Colleen was barely mentioned in the review. "When talking pictures became popular he [Cleeve] went on the stage for several months to equip himself for dialog." *Footlights and Fools* was his first appearance in a talking film.[15] In Chicago, Colleen was a revelation, hinting towards her future film persona: "She is French, she is red headed. She is luscious lipped and naughty eyed. She wears clothes ravishingly. She dances and sings — oo-la-la! She is the star of a revue and, as she steps forth, you exclaim: 'Why that CAN'T be Colleen Moore!'" However, as the film goes on, she was less convincing. "Hard to say just why." Overall, the film was acceptable. "It has some humor, some horseplay, some tenderness and a soupçon of surprise. It is clean, nicely acted and not too long."[16] In New York, they came to the same conclusion: "There are moments during *Footlights and Fools* ... when one feels that Colleen Moore is a very talented performer, when she does not resort to cloying cuteness or indulge in the lavish exaggeration in the part of Mlle. Fifi." The film came off as a string of irrelevancies, the characters in the color sequences looked "as red as Indians," and at least one sequence was thrown in for no purpose other than to add another musical number. Still, in some scenes, Colleen's voice "is nicely interpretive of her feelings." Overall, in her "serious moods Miss Moore is quite acceptable."[17]

When Colleen had recovered from her operation, she and John continued with the pretense of marriage, though John's episodes were occasionally loud and nasty. When she had returned with the nurse from the hospital, John ordered them from the house.[18] He ordered Colleen out of their house in December in front of guests. In January, he disappeared again.[19] They went to social functions together, put in appearances,[20] but the marriage had disintegrated. In February, Julanne Johnston paid Colleen a visit at the house, when John "came out and told, 'Why in hell don't you get out of here? I want to go to bed.'" The final separation came in March. Colleen recalled, "I had no choice and simply left. He became worse and worse and I couldn't stand it any more."[21]

On a Thursday night she ventured back to the Bel Air house, resigned to the fact that the marriage was over. She asked her chauffeur to wait for her in the hall while she went to talk to John.

John was alone in his room, in a chair, bloated and red and drunk. What they had was no longer a marriage. She spent her time tip-toeing around him, avoiding him. She sat on his bed, looked at him, and told him she wanted a divorce.

It took a moment to sink in. He stood, walked over to her, grabbed her by the throat and shouted, "You'll never divorce me!" Hands around her neck, choking her, he pushed her on the bed. The chauffeur in the hall had heard the shout and came into the room, managing to pull him off of Colleen. They fled the house. That night her mother told her never to go back to the Bel Air house. Then she picked up the telephone to call a lawyer. When they met again at the Bel Air house, Colleen's parents and lawyers were at her side. John had his own lawyers with him. Afterwards, when they were alone, John said he could not believe he had tried to choke her. She told him he nearly killed her and that he had to face the fact that he needed help. He asked her to keep any mention of the drinking out of the papers. She agreed.[22]

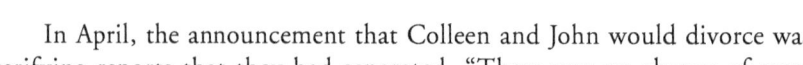

In April, the announcement that Colleen and John would divorce was made public, verifying reports that they had separated. "There was no chance of reconciliation, she [Colleen] asserted. A property agreement has been drawn. They are to dispose of their home in Bel Air."[23] Colleen charged John with abuse and cruel treatment, outlined a number of incidents wherein he was abusive, without mention of alcohol.[24]

In May, the case went to court. "Superior Judge Thomas Gould granted her [Colleen] an interlocutory decree after the actress testified briefly on many humiliations she suffered from John E. McCormick."[25]

At a party on Christmas eve, she said, McCormick drove his automobile across the lawn of her home.

"Was he intoxicated?" Judge Gould asked.

"Yes, he was," Miss Moore answered.[26]

After her testimony in court, Colleen turned camera shy outside the courthouse. "Oh you bums!" they reported her exclaiming before friends and attorneys rushed her to an elevator that took her to the street. The photographer followed her into the street: "On Spring Street the sprightly comedienne dashed across the sidewalk and jumped into a small rattletrap car of ancient vintage. The car gave several quick coughs and gasps, got underway and rattled up Spring Street, leaving the army of photographers greatly disconcerted."[27]

If Hollywood had written Colleen's story, the above article would have been the final scene of the film — Colleen driving off in an old tin lizzy as the camera irised out. In Hollywood's version, Colleen's stratospheric rise to fame would have been followed by a meteoric fall to obscurity. Over a period of months, the world had changed under Colleen's nose. The film industry had changed. John, who had managed her career for years, was gone. The country as a whole had changed. In October, the stock market crashed and took thousands with it. The country was plunged into the early stages of what would be called the Great Depression. Once upon a time audiences had flocked to motion picture palaces to enjoy lavish productions of escapist fantasy; now they were looking simply to escape. Nobody wanted fairy tales any more. It might have been assumed that with Colleen's "type" of character vanished from the screen, Colleen would vanish as well. However, Colleen had largely written her own story, and her stories were modeled on fairy tales, regardless of what was happening around her. There was always a happy ending.

Before the end of the year John had announced his engagement to marry actress Mae Clark, though it would not be until the divorce from Colleen was final, on May 14, 1931. Then it was said he was engaged to Dorothy Mackaill.[28] Instead, he married Janet Gattis, but the marriage was over within months. It was another case of mental cruelty, Gattis explained, only this time because McCormick cried whenever he saw a photograph of Colleen.[29]

Colleen turned to the stage for a time in *A Church Mouse*, a rag-to-riches story like many of her most successful films. Many of her friends and former directors were in the audience when it opened at the El Capitan Theater: George Fitzmaurice, Mervyn LeRoy, Alfred Green, Irving Cummings, Millard Webb, and Marshall Neilan. Other directors in the audience included Ernst Lubitsch, Raoul Walsh, and Josef von Sternberg. Stars included Lionel Barrymore, Norma Shearer, Estelle Taylor and William Haines.[30] "Miss Moore has assurance and poise. She romps right into her role. She met the challenge of the first-night audience, star-bedecked as it was, in a way that surprised, and as if she had been doing this routine of the stage for years."[31]

She married stockbroker Albert Scott, from whom she picked up many tips about handling her money. She had always been a wise investor; at parties, when other actresses were talking about the industry, she was talking about investments.

Two years after leaving Hollywood, she returned to the industry: "Whether it's the stage success or the new romance or both, happiness is very becoming to the new Colleen who has grown up charmingly and looks oh, so Parisienne in her clothes these days." The bob was "gone forever," replaced by a "very Frenchy curled bob and believe me, there's a dash to the lady."[32]

Colleen, as far as the press was concerned, had grown up, and become a sophisticate. Though removed from the Hollywood scene for two years, she was still in demand. Colleen signed with MGM in May 1932, with plans to give her roles that suited her new adult persona. "Indeed, we find that she had been definitely urged by Metro-Goldwyn-Mayer to play the name role in *Red-Headed Woman*, with Colleen hesitant because of its nature, and with Anita Loos arguing with Colleen that it is just all in fun, anyway, because she has written the character to be played in broadly humorous fashion, emphasizing the ex-working girl's social errors rather than her hard-heartedness. The jury was out last night."[33]

Test were made of Colleen in costume for the part of the red-headed woman, Lil "Red" Andrews, in which she is nearly unrecognizable without her bangs, with some more weight, looking every bit as slinky as was demanded. There is a tantalizing air of possibility in those photographs: it was a completely new Colleen, with no trace of the girlish, wholesome charm on which her films had previously banked. If she had chosen to take the role, there is no doubt she could have summoned the "hard-heartedness" necessary to lead men on and to work her way up the ladder using her feminine wiles. It would have been, after all, a refinement and more fully fleshed-out variation on her first role opposite Robert Harron 15 years earlier.

In the end, she defaulted to the opinion of her grandmother, who told her that "Red" never got her comeuppance in the story. Grandmother Kelly didn't want Colleen playing women who didn't get their comeuppance, and it was an opinion that resonated with her. Her favorite stories had been the fairy tales where the girl ends up with the man she was supposed to be with at the end.

Her next project was slated to be *Flesh*, with Wallace Beery, with whom she starred with in *So Big*. "It will be an entirely new Colleen that is presented to the public. Miss Moore has said that the day of the screen Cinderella is past."[34] That role fell through as well, the part of Laura going to Karen Morley. "Metro-Goldwyn-Mayer heads after "spending six months ordering stories to be written for Miss Moore, and then tearing the stories up and throwing them on the floor, loaned her to Fox for *The Power and the Glory*." She was set to appear in *Turn Back the Clock*, but was hit with a bad case of flu that had her in bed with a high fever that caused her to miss the opening of *The Power and the Glory*.[35] Her role went to Mae Clark. Colleen was "still being spoken of for the outstanding feminine role" in *Beauty Parlor*,[36] but it fell through.

Her time at MGM was short and her contract was torn up amicably.

Without a studio, Colleen teamed up once again with Marshall Neilan for *Social Register*, a romantic story that

Colleen in a costume test for her unfulfilled role in *Red-Headed Woman*, Metro-Goldwyn-Mayer, 1932.

37. The Bel Air House and a Fairy Castle

crossed social lines, more like Colleen's preferred stories in that the girl gets her man in the end. With RKO she made *Success at Any Price* as the girlfriend of Douglas Fairbanks, Jr., who was ten years younger than she. Colleen was still able to pull it off. Her last film was *The Scarlet Letter* in 1934.

The Scarlet Letter was the only film she made strictly for the paycheck. The film was not very good, especially when compared to Lillian Gish's version made seven years earlier, which was a masterpiece of silent cinema, but it gave her an opportunity to gather many people she had worked with in the past. It allowed her to kick off the tour of her doll house, and when the tour began Colleen considered herself retired from motion pictures.

All throughout this time, Colleen's attention had been focused on her Fairy Castle, the elaborate dollhouse she and her father had originally conceived while on vacation in Hawaii. She enlisted the aid of industry friends in its design and construction and furnishing. As was done with Queen Titania's castle, Colleen knew she wanted to take the castle on tour. When she had been laid up in bed in a cast after *The Desert Flower*, she had seen the suffering of children and knew she wanted to bring them a little joy with the house. She would take the castle on tour and raise funds. Dolls had always provided her with entertainment; now her dolls could entertain other children.

Filmography

Many of Colleen's early films are in the public domain and so DVD copies are often available; some of Colleen's films are included in larger collections. Kino's *Reel Baseball*, for example, contains *The Busher*. Colleen's First National films from 1923–1929 are owned by Warner Bros., and no official DVDs of these have been released. *Ella Cinders*, however, is an exception, and is in the public domain. This list includes Colleen's credited films only. It does not include *Life in Hollywood*–type films, newsreels, *Burning Daylight*, *Ben-Hur* (in which she was one of several hundred faces in the stands), or the novelty film produced during the first Wampas Frolic.

In the last two decades many of Colleen's films thought to be lost have been rediscovered and are awaiting preservation and restoration. (*Her Wild Oat* is a good example.) By the same token, some films previously known to have existed have since disintegrated. It is entirely possible that some films listed here as surviving could be lost in the coming decade. This fact underscores the importance of preserving our cinematic heritage.

Films listed as surviving are those that retain a substantial amount of their original content. *Her Wild Oat*, for one, is mostly intact. Some exist with substantial portions missing; in those cases, I list what is known to remain. *Flaming Youth* survives in the Library of Congress as a single reel only, and so it is listed as lost. Some films exist but nevertheless are considered lost until preservation is completed. Some films are entirely lost. Trailers remain for some films. These are noted at the end of the filmography.

The genres listed are only the broadest description. Many of Colleen's films were a mix of drama and comedy, and so the genre reflects the basic premise of the story. Though several of her films could be categorized as "Flapper" films, it is a subjective classification that is not used here; flapper films could be either serious or comedies. "Musical" is used to describe silent features adapted from musical stage productions wherein music in the score was often an important aspect of these films

While still working in the film industry, Colleen's voice was occasionally heard on radio, though these appearances were infrequent. Following her film career, Colleen hosted the Mutual Network's *Safety Legion* radio program in the mid–1940s, a 15-minute feature that played daily at 5 P.M. As a Chicago socialite, she was often mentioned in the *Chicago Tribune*'s "Tower Ticker" column. She made occasional television and motion picture appearances, such as in 1972's *75 Years of Cinema Museum*; she was interviewed by Kevin Brownlow for the 1980 documentary series *Hollywood*; and appeared in *The American Film Institute Salute to Lillian Gish*, in 1984. The key:

> ***Title***; director; production company; release date(s); number of reels; current status (availability or special note). Genre, and "Colleen's character name."
> Synopsis of Colleen's part in brief.

Affinities; Ward Lascelle; Ward Lascelle Productions; 24 September (or 15 October) 1922; 6 reels; lost. Drama, "Fanny Illington." Dissatisfied with her marriage, Fanny attends an "affinity" party with the husband of a friend and suffers through a series of problems in attempting to return home.

April Showers; Tom Forman; Preferred Pictures, Inc.; 21 October 1923; 6 reels; lost. Drama, "Maggie Muldoon." The daughter of a police lieutenant, and sweetheart of Danny, Maggie is jealous of pretty Miriam, whom does social work in her neighborhood and who Maggie fears will distract Danny. Danny thinks he has failed a police exam and takes up boxing; the mistake is later discovered and he learns he can marry Maggie.

The Bad Boy; Chester Withey; Triangle Film Corp.; 18 February 1917; 5 reels; lost. Drama, "Ruth." Ruth is a sophisticated city girl who distracts hero Jimmie.

Broken Chains; Allen Holubar; Goldwyn Pictures; 24 December 1922; 7 reels; survives. Drama, "Mercy Boone." Married to Boyan Boone, Mercy has just lost her child and is kept chained in her cabin home by Boyan, leader of a group of local petty criminals. She is eventually freed by her new sweetheart, Peter Wyndham.

Broken Hearts of Broadway; Irving Cummings; Irving Cummings Productions; July 1923; 7 reels; survives (available on DVD). Drama, "Mary Ellis." The story of how small-town girl Mary Ellis finds success and romance in show business while narrowly avoiding the pitfalls of fame.

The Busher; Jerome Storm; Paramount Pictures; 18 May 1919; 5 reels; survives (available on DVD). Drama, "Mazie Palmer." The sister of Billy Palmer and sweetheart of Ben Harding, Mazie is left behind by Billy when he finds brief fame in the big city, playing baseball. With fame, Billy forgets his roots and sweetheart until he is fired and returns home where he eventually wins back the respect and girl he has lost.

Come On Over; Alfred E. Green; Goldwyn Pictures Corp.; 11 March 1922; 6 reels; survives. Drama, "Moyna Killiea." The sweetheart of Shane O'Mealia, Moyna is left behind by Shane while he travels to America to find work. He is unsuccessful until Moyna is brought over to America by family friends; when she runs off and becomes lost, the search results in such a feeling of community that Shane ends up with a good job and a bright future.

Common Property; Paul Powell; Universal Film Mfg. Co.; 18 October 1919; 6 reels; lost. Drama, "Tatyone Pavlovitch." The daughter of Anna and Paval Pavlovitch, her virtue is threatened when all the young women in her Russian village of Saratov are declared common property of the community. The arrival of the American cavalry saves her from mobs and the edict is rescinded.

The Cyclone; Cliff Smith; Fox Film Corp.; January–February 1920; 5 reels; lost. Western/Adventure, "Sylvia Sturgis." The fiancée of Sergeant Tim Ryerson of the North West Mounted Police, Sylvia is kidnapped by the boss of a human smuggling ring and taken to Vancouver's Chinatown, where she is rescued by Ryerson in dramatic fashion.

The Desert Flower; Irving Cummings; First National Pictures; 21 June 1925; 7 reels; lost. Comedy, "Maggie Fortune." As the stepdaughter of abusive Mike Dyer, Maggie has run away to the town of Bullfrog. Attempting to reform Rance Conway, a drunk, she realizes she is in love with him. Her stepfather arrives in town and there is a fight, leaving three people (including Maggie) accused of the same murder.

The Devil's Claim; Charles Swickard; Haworth Pictures Corp.; 2 May 1920; 5 reels; survives. Drama, "Indora." The inspiration for many stories by the writer Akbar Kahn, Indora ceases to be his muse until a social worker manages to begin a new tale for him, wherein he realizes he is in love with Indora.

Dinty; Marshall Neilan; Marshall Neilan Productions; 29 November 1920; 7 reels; survives. Drama/adventure, "Doreen O'Sullivan." The mother of the title character Dinty O'Sullivan, Doreen arrives in America, only to find her husband has been killed. She works as a charwoman until Dinty is old enough to become the breadwinner as a paperboy with a complicated knowledge of the San Francisco underworld. After Doreen dies of tuberculosis, Dinty is adopted by a respected judge.

The Egg Crate Wallop; Jerome Storm; Thomas H. Ince Productions; 28 September 1919; 5 reels; survives. Action/drama, "Kitty Haskell." Kitty is the daughter of Dave Haskell and sweetheart of Jim Kelly. Her father is believed by Jim to be a thief, so Jim leaves town to deflect suspicion from his sweetheart's father. Eventually, he is reunited with Kitty and the truth is revealed.

Ella Cinders; Alfred E. Green; First National Pictures; 6 June 1926; survives (available on DVD). Comedy, "Ella Cinders." As the put-upon stepdaughter of the Pill family, Ella dreams of escaping to Hollywood and finding fame and fortune. When she arrives in Hollywood, she makes the best of her situation and becomes famous until she is retrieved by her sweetie, Waite Lifter.

Flaming Youth; John Francis Dillon, First National Pictures; 12 November 1923; 9 reels; lost (portions of 1 reel survive). Drama, "Patricia (Pat) Frentiss." The youngest daughter of the free-wheeling Frentiss family, Pat is adventurous and anxious to experience the grownup word, in spite of the dangers of her actions. She falls for an older man — her deceased mother's former lover — and settles into semi-respectability when she agrees to an experimental marriage. Often thought of as a comedy or farce, it was, in fact, a drama.

Flirting with Love; John Francis Dillon; First National Pictures; 17 August 1924; 7 reels; lost. Comedy, "Gilda Lamont." An aspiring actress whose first successful play closes, she feigns mental illness in order to gain the trust of the doctor responsible and later disgrace him. In an unexpected turn of events, she learns that she has fallen in love with him.

Footlights and Fools; William A. Seiter; First National Pictures; 4 November 1929; lost (some Vitaphone sound discs survive). Drama, "Fifi D'Auray/Betty Murphy." Fifi D'Auray is actually Betty Murphy, a chorus girl who was sent to Paris to acquire a French veneer. She has returned to America and becomes a hit, but romantic complications ensue.

Forsaking All Others; Emile Chautard; 10 December 1922, 5 reels; lost. Drama, "Penelope Mason." Oliver Newell's mother concocts an excuse to remove her son from Penelope, only to learn that Oliver is involved with a married woman. Mrs. Newell must prevail upon Penelope to capture Oliver's heart again.

Hands Up!; Tod Browning; Fine Arts Film Co.; 29 April 1917; 5 reels; lost. Western/Drama, "Marjorie Houston." Daughter of John Houston, railroad president, Marjorie falls for outlaw Dan Tracy when his gang robs her railroad car. She secretly meets Dan in town and plans to elope, leaving for the mountains. Marjorie faces the realities of outlaw life and is eventually rescued by her father after Tracy is killed by a jilted lover.

Happiness Ahead; William A. Seiter; First National Pictures, Inc.; 24 June 1928; 8 reels; lost. Drama, "Mary Randall." Daughter of a hardware-store owner, Mary meets and marries a former cardsharp on the run. Her new husband turns over a new leaf until his past is revealed and he is sentenced to a jail term. He tells Mary he is going on a business trip, but she knows the truth and hides it from him and their expected child, for the sake of their marriage.

Her Bridal Night-Mare; Al Christie; Christie Film Company; 30 January 1920; 2 reels; survives. Comedy; Mary; On her wedding day, Mary faces the complications that arise from sabotage by a rejected suitor, a hired pickpocket, a falsely imprisoned groom, and her own wish to commit suicide after she believes she has been rejected by her beloved. After a series of misunderstandings and double-takes, everything works out in the end.

Her Wild Oat; Marshall Neilan; First National Pictures; 25 December 1927, 7 reels; survives. Comedy, "Mary Lou Brown." Owner of a lunch wagon she has inherited, orphaned Mary Lou resolves to spend her savings at a plush resort and find herself a husband. Mary's lack of social skills encourages a friend to create a new persona for her; posing as royalty, she must maintain the pretense as it begins to crumble around her.

His Nibs; Gregory La Cava; Exceptional Pictures; October 1921; 5 reels; survives. Comedy, "The Girl." As the nameless girl in *He Fooled 'Em All*, the film within the film, she is the sweetheart of "The Boy" and smiles, has fun and looks pretty while the action is given a sarcastic narration by the projectionist exhibiting it.

A Hoosier Romance; Colin Campbell; Selig Polyscope Co.;18 August 1918; 5 reels; lost. Drama, "Patience Thompson." The sunny daughter of a greedy father, Patience Thompson is betrothed to a man she does not love to increase her father's fortunes. With the help of neighbors, she manages to escape the unwanted marriage and wed her sweetheart.

The Huntress; Lynn Reynolds; First National

Pictures; 20 August 1923; 6 reels; lost. Comedy; "Bela." A white girl raised by Indians, Bela decides to find herself a white husband when her true heritage is revealed to her. When she finds a suitable groom, she proceeds to hunt him as she might hunt prey.

Irene; Alfred E. Green; First National Pictures, Inc.; 21 February 1926; 9 reels; survives (available on DVD). Musical/comedy, "Irene O'Dare." An Irish girl looking for work in New York, Irene is discovered by rich playboy Donald Marshall, who finds her work as a model. Dressed as a socialite to bring attention to a fashion designer friend of Marshall, she is mistaken as a high-society type, until Marshall's mother reveals her background. Marshall still proclaims his love for her.

It Must Be Love; Alfred E. Green; John McCormick Productions; 22 August 1926; 7 reels; lost. Comedy, "Fernie Schmidt." Living with her parents over a delicatessen, Fernie Schmidt longs to escape the smells of the gastronomic world in which she lives. Rejecting her parents' choice for a husband, she finds work in an upscale department store and falls for the manager, but is distraught to learn the store manager wishes to buy a delicatessen while her family's choice of husband is about to buy a new house away from the deli.

Lilac Time; George Fitzmaurice; First National Pictures, Inc.; 18 October 1928; 11 reels; survives (available on DVD). Drama, "Jeannine Berthelot." A French farm girl serving WWI British aviators stationed at her family farm, Jeannine falls for a new pilot and is separated from him when German forces shoot his airplane down and overrun her village. She finds her beloved at the very end only by chance.

Little Orphant Annie; Colin Campbell; William N. Selig; December 1918; 8 reels; survives (available on DVD). Drama, "Little Orphant Annie." The trials and tragic life of Annie, an orphan who delights children with her stories. Brought into a loving home, she falls for Big Dave, and is heart-stricken when leaves for war.

Look Your Best; Rupert Hughes; Goldwyn Pictures Corp.; 18 February 1923; 6 reels; lost. Drama, "Perla Quaranta." An Italian dancer given a spot in a chorus line, Perla rejects the advances of Krug and the act's manager, Bruni, beats him. Once Bruni is released from jail, he produces a new act with Perla as the star, and the two marry.

The Lotus Eater; Marshall Neilan; Marshall Neilan Productions; 27 November 1921; 7 reels; lost. Drama, "Mavis." When wealthy Jacques Lenoi is stranded on an island inhabited by shipwreck survivors, he meets and falls for Mavis, a native of the island. Jacques leaves the island, but eventually returns to Mavis and happiness.

The Man in the Moonlight; Paul Powell; Universal Film Mfg. Co.; 28 July 1919; 6 reels; lost. Drama, "Rosine Delorme." On her wedding night, Rosine receives word that her wayward brother is in the company of a notorious outlaw nearby. She postpones the wedding and leaves with a stranger to find her brother, only to discover the stranger is actually the outlaw. She is kidnapped and later rescued by her brother.

Naughty but Nice; Millard Webb; John McCormick Productions; 26 June 1927; 7 reels; lost. Comedy, "Berenice Summers." Fish out of water Berenice Summers is caught in a lie and continues to try and bluff her way out, to comic effect.

The Ninety and Nine; David Smith; Vitagraph Co. of America; 17 December 1922; 7 reels; survives. Drama, "Ruth Blake." As the lone villager who believes in the good nature of drunkard Tom Silverton, Ruth stands by him when a forest fire threatens their town and Tom is left as the only man who can rescue the villagers.

The Nth Commandment; Frank Borzage; Cosmopolitan Productions; 18 March 1923; 8 reels; survives. Drama, "Sarah Juke." The wife of sickly Harry Smith, Sarah Juke struggles to keep her family together although she is embarrassed by her lot in life. Tempted by the riches around her, she nearly succumbs, until she makes a turn and saves her family.

Oh, Kay!; Mervyn LeRoy; First National Pictures; 26 August 1928, 6 reels; lost. Comedy, "Lady Kay Rutfield." Fleeing before her marriage Lady Kay Rutfield falls in with a group of bootleggers, but manages to escape them and hide in the mansion of wealthy Jimmy Winter. There are numerous disguises and mistaken identities before Kay ends up with Jimmy.

An Old Fashioned Young Man; Lloyd Ingraham; Fine Arts Film Co.; 15 April 1917; 5 reels; lost. Drama, "Margaret." The adopted daughter of Mrs. James D. Burke, Frank Trent wins her love when he defends Mrs. Burke's reputation.

Orchids and Ermine; Alfred Santell; John McCormick Productions; 6 March 1927; 7 reels; survives. Comedy, "Pink Watson." With dreams of landing a rich husband, Pink finds a job as a hotel switchboard operator and meets an oil baron who has switched places with his butler. She falls for him without realizing his true identity, and he must convince her he is wealthy after his butler marries under his identity.

Painted People; Clarence Badger; Associated First National Pictures; January 1924; 7 reels; lost. Comedy, "Ellie Byrne." Childhood friends Don and Ellie take separate paths in life and become engaged to different people, but when they are working on a play together they discover they are made for each other.

The Perfect Flapper; John Francis Dillon; Associated First National Pictures; 25 May 1924; 7 reels; survives (first three-quarters only). Comedy, "Tommie Lou Pember." Unpopular Tommie Lou's jazzy antics to increase her popularity during her coming-out party lead to misunderstandings that threaten marriages and lead her to fall for a divorce lawyer.

The Power and the Glory; William K. Howard; Fox Film Corp. 6 October 1933; 8 reels; survives. Drama, "Sally Garner." A schoolteacher who marries Tom Garner, Sally is the force that drives him to climb to the position of president of the railroad. When Tom leaves her for a younger woman, she jumps under a speeding streetcar.

A Roman Scandal; Al Christie; Christie Film Company; 30 November 1919; 2 reels; survives (available on DVD). Comedy, "Mary." Stage-struck, Mary insists she will not marry Jack because she has decided to dedicate herself to acting. Her debut is unplanned and hectic as the local troupe of unionized actors walk out on their production, leaving Mary to draft Jack into helping her stage the play. Humorous disasters ensue.

Sally; Alfred E. Green; First National Pictures; 29 March 1925; 9 reels; lost. Musical/comedy; "Sally." An orphan, Sally works at the Alley, until her dance skills are discovered. She poses as a famous Russian dancer at the estate of a wealthy man, but her dishwasher origins are revealed. Florenz Ziegfeld is in the audience; he makes Sally a star and she marries the man she loves.

The Savage; Rupert Julian; Bluebird Photoplays, Inc. (Universl); 19 November 1917; 5 reels; lost. Drama, "Lizette." A half-breed girl, Lizette is in love with Julio Sandoval and follows him everywhere, but Julio falls for another woman. Jealous, Lizette conspires to avenge herself.

The Scarlet Letter; Robert G. Vignola; Larry Darmour Productions/Majestic Producing Corp.; 22 September 1934; survives (available on DVD). Drama, "Hester Prynne." Refusing to reveal the identity of the father of her child, Hester is condemned to wear a red latter "A" for the rest of her life, marking her as an adulterer. Her husband, thought dead, appears on the scene and forces her to keep his identity a secret.

The Sky Pilot; King Vidor; Cathrine Curtis Corp.; May 1921; 7 reels; survives (available on DVD). Western/Drama, "Gwen." A rough-riding daughter who was raised in the West, Gwen is injured in a stampede and left crippled until her love is endangered. The strength of her love allows her to overcome her physical limitations, and she regains the use of her legs so that she might save her him from a fire.

Slippy McGee; Wesley Ruggles; Oliver Morosco Productions; 11 June 1923; 7 reels; lost. Drama, "Mary Virginia." Mary Virginia is blackmailed by George Inglesby to marry him instead of the man she loves. She is saved by former safecracker "Slippy" McGee, who uses his skills to save her reputation so that she can marry the man she wants.

Smiling Irish Eyes; William A. Seiter; First National Pictures, Inc.; 28 July 1929, 8 reels; lost (sound exists). Musical/Comedy, "Kathleen O'Connor." Left behind in Ireland by her love, Rory (who leaves for America to find fame), she follows him to America and finds him onstage, performing their song and kissing another woman. She returns to Ireland; Rory follows her. They reconcile and return, for good, to America.

So Big; Charles Brabin; First National Pictures, Inc.; 28 December 1924; 9 reels; lost. Drama, "Selina Peake." Born to a gambling father who teaches her to appreciate the better things in life, Selina marries, raises a child on the harsh prairies and watches him nearly destroy his life through greed.

So Long Letty; Al Christie; Christie Film Co.; 17 October 1920; 6 reels; survives. Comedy, "Grace Miller." A natural homebody, Grace discovers her husband and his neighbor have conspired to divorce their wives and marry each other's spouse. She, in turn, conspires with her neighbor's wife to teach their husbands a thing or two during an experimental (and platonic) wife-swap.

Social Register; Marshall Neilan; Associated Film Productions/Columbia Pictures Corp.; 10 March 1934; 8 reels; survives (available on DVD). Drama, "Patsy Shaw." Wealthy Charlie Breene has fallen for Patsy, a hard-working girl, but his mother tries every trick in the book unsuccessfully to break up their engagement.

Success at Any Price; J. Walter Ruben; RKO Radio Pictures, Inc.; 16 March 1934; 8 reels; survives. Drama, "Sarah Griswold." Girlfriend of Joe Martin, Sarah intervenes with Joe's boss after he is fired to give him a second chance. Joe meets the boss's mistress, Agnes, and determines to win her over, beginning a drive for money that leaves Sarah behind in the dust. Joe works his way to the top, marries Agnes, but is still dissatisfied, especially after discovering that Agnes is having an affair. He tries to end his life, but is saved by Sarah, who takes him back.

Synthetic Sin; William A. Seiter; First National Pictures, Inc.; 6 January 1929; 7 reels; survives. Comedy, "Betty." An aspiring actress, Betty goes to the big city to gain some experience and become a better actress. She moves into a rough neighborhood, where she encounters danger. She is rescued by Donald, the playwright, who proposes to her.

Through the Dark; George Hill; Goldwyn-Cosmopolitan Distributing Corp.; 6 January 1924; 8 reels; lost (two reels survive). Drama, "Mary McGinn." The daughter of Mother McGinn, Mary rescues escaped convict "Boston" Blackie. Mary falls for him and joins his gang in an effort to help him reform, and he eventually turns himself in for her.

Twinkletoes; Charles Brabin; John McCormick Productions; 28 November 1926; 8 reels; survives (available on DVD). Drama, "Monica 'Twinkletoes' Minasi." A talented dancer, "Twinkletoes" worships her father and has a sunny disposition. Chuck, a married man, is in love with her, and his jealous wife decides to take revenge on Twinkletoes. She gives the police information about Twinkletoes's father's criminal activities. This leaves her feeling distraught — even suicidal.

The Wall Flower; Rupert Hughes; Goldwyn Pictures; May 1922; 6 reels; lost. Drama, "Idalene Nobbin." With the help of friends plain Idalene transforms herself from a wall flower to a beauty. Idalene falls for the man whom Pamela, her friend, secretly loves, and Pamela steps aside to allow Idalene to find happiness.

We Moderns; John Francis Dillon; John McCormick Productions; 15 November 1925; 7 reels; lost. Drama, "Mary Sundale." A young, modern English girl and member of the "we moderns" set, Mary flaunts her modern sensibilities and rejects those of her parents', especially their preference for a potential husband. Her reckless actions lead to near disaster, and the respectable favorite of Mary's parents comes to her rescue, changing her mind.

When Dawn Came; Colin Campbell; Hugh E. Dierker Photo Drama Productions; April 1920; 7 reels; survives. Drama, "Mary Harrison." A blind girl, Mary, lives in a mission town and prays to regain her sight. Dr. John Brandon has taken to drinking and has lost his faith. His faith is slowly restored by Mary, with whom he falls in love. With his newfound faith, he operates on Mary giving her back her sight.

Why Be Good?; William A. Seiter; First National Pictures, Inc.; 12 March 1929, 8 reels; lost. Drama, "Pert Kelly." Though Pert has a wild reputation, she's really a good girl at heart. One night she meets Peabody, Jr., who turns out to be her new boss at the department store where she works. Peabody Sr. cautions his son against Pert because of her reputation, and Peabody, Jr. devises tests of her faithfulness, which she passes.

The Wilderness Trail; Edward J. Le Saint; Fox Film Corp.; 6 July 1919; 5 reels; lost. Western/Adventure, "Jeanne Fitzpatrick." Jeanne's father falsely accuses Donald's son of being leader of a band of outlaws. Jeanne is kidnapped by the real leader. There is an employee revolt, but Donald manages to stop it and lead them in battle against the outlaws and to free Jeanne.

KNOWN TRAILERS: *The Desert Flower*; *Lilac Time*; *The Perfect Flapper*; *So Big*; *Synthetic Sin*; *Why Be Good?*

Chapter Notes

Chapter 1

1. "Chinamen Bound for Atlanta," *New York Times*, September 5, 1895, page 9.
2. "205 Chinese Arrive; They Attract Great Attention at the Station and on the Streets. Thirty-six are Beauties," *Atlanta Constitution*, September 15, 1895, page 14.
3. Walter G. Cooper, *The Cotton States and International Exposition and South, Illustrated ...* (Atlanta: Illustrator Co., 1896). "Here's the Midway Shows," *Atlanta Constitution*, September 1, 1895, page 2.
4. "A High Compliment. The Exposition Board of Directors Pass upon the Cotton Picker," *Atlanta Constitution*, November 27, 1895, page 9.
5. On the Library of Congress website, *History of Edison Motion Pictures: Origins of Motion Pictures — the Kinetoscope* states: "A prototype for the Kinetoscope was finally shown to a convention of the National Federation of Women's Clubs on May 20, 1891.... A patent for the Kinetograph (the camera) and the Kinetoscope (the viewer) was filed on August 24, 1891."
6. "Here's the Midway Shows," *Atlanta Constitution*, September 1, 1895, page 2.
7. *Fred Ott's Sneeze* may be one of the most viewed films in history; certainly it is the most-viewed sneeze. The film is in the public domain, which allows future generations to enjoy his suffering. Library of Congress Motion Picture, Broadcasting and Recorded Sound Division Washington, D.C. 20540 USA. CALL NUMBER: FEC 8091 (viewing print), LC 26A (paper positive).
8. This information from *Port Huron Daily Times*, September 11, 1895, page 7. Two items mention Charles: "Norman D. Plues, of Saginaw, has visited C. R. Morrison the past week" and "Charles R. Morrison, of Saginaw, who has for the past month visited his parents in the city, left last evening for Atlanta, Ga., to attend the exposition, after which he will spend the winter in Florida." Thanks to Steve Moore for his research. Much of the Port Huron material is the product of his research.
9. Edmond K. Hogan, *The Work of the Railway Carman*, by Edmond K. Hogan, Brotherhood Railway Carmen of America (Kansas City: Brotherhood Railway Carmen of America, 1921), page 171.
10. If Charles leaves Tuesday night (September 10), and we assume a day to a day and a half's travel by train south, then he ends up arriving on or about Friday, September 12.

Chapter 2

1. Daniel Colt Gilman, Harry Thurston Peck, and Frank Moore Colby, *The New International Encyclopædia*, Vol. 14 (New York: Dodd, Mead, 1903), page 386.
2. Mike Connell, "Part 5: Bright ideas gave city status; Inventors and attitude made Port Huron an early industrial leader," http://www.thetimesherald.com (October 4, 2007).
3. Frank Lewis Dyer and Thomas Commerford Martin, *Edison: His Life and Inventions* (New York: Harper & Brothers, 1910), page 23.
4. In alphabetical order: Agnes, Beatrice, Elizabeth (or Liberty), Josephine, Kathleen, May, and Nan.
5. *St. Clair Count Directory* of 1887–1887 gives the address as "w s Ontario 2s of Stanton" while later editions give the address as 817 Ontario. This would be the same house, as 817 is on the west (w) south (s) side of the street, and at the time may have been the second home south of Stanton (earlier directories list it as "1s"). It should be noted that, in 1885, May J. and Josephine M. Kelly lived at 21 Ontario and that May J., and Josie M. Kelly were dressmakers at 17 Huron Ave.
6. "North Middle part of the City of Port Huron," in *Standard Atlas of St. Clair County, Michigan* (Chicago: Geo. A. Ogle, 1897).
7. Newspaper clipping, *Port Huron Daily Times*, courtesy Steve Moore of Port Huron.
8. The images of her mother in the book show a woman who is indeed an oval-faced beauty with dark hair and light-colored eyes. Her mother was often pictured with the latest hairstyle, though her poses and outfits suggest a Victorian stiffness that is not visible in casual snapshots of her. Photographs of Colleen's aunts can be found in family albums. Her aunts were: Beatrice Stone, later Beatrice Warren, mother of Lisbeth and Jack Stone (Jack would later appear in Colleen Moore's films); Josephine Grieg; Kathleen Johnstone, mother of Maran; May Spencer, mother of Leroy, William and Earl; Nan Krakow and Elizabeth Board. In *Silent Star* Colleen wrote in a caption: "I came of a tradition of beautiful women — my mother was lovely.... I don't know what happened to me." Colleen Moore, *Silent Star* (Garden City, NY: Doubleday, 1968), p. 13.
9. Ibid., page 18.
10. Much of the information on the Kelly and Morrison families comes from Judy Coleman's family albums.
11. The observation of the crowded house comes from an image of the house itself, as well as snapshots of large groups of people, in the Judy Coleman Collection. There was an age range of almost a decade between youngest and oldest daughter, so as the younger siblings were coming of age, the older ones might be marrying.
12. In alphabetical order: Charles, Elizabeth (Lizzie), Mary, Robert, Jr., and William. (1870 Port Huron Census, page 35, lines 2–7).
13. *Port Huron Commercial*, November 4, 1885, page 4.
14. From *St. Clair County, Michigan Marriages 1887–1898*. Book 4, Volume 3, (October 23, 1897). Name: Charles R. Morrison, age: 26, race: W, residence/born: Port Huron, occupation: Clerk, parents: Robert Morrison & Jean Henderson.
15. *The Companion Series. Our Country: East* (Boston: Perry Mason, 1898), page 9.
16. For example, a small silver spoon in Colleen's family's possession appears to be a teething spoon engraved with the name "Kathleen Morrison" and the date

August 19, 1902. Silver spoons were a common gift for newborns on the event of their christening.
  17. As much of what was written about Colleen presumes a birth year of 1902, this chapter proceeds with that same assumption.
  18. Port Huron City, St. Clair County, 1900 census, sheet 9, lines 10–14.
  19. The obituary for Robert Morrison, Sr., mentions he died of paralysis, though it does not note if there had been any other long-term health problems.
  20. Notation to photograph of Kathleen Kelly Johnstone in the Judy Coleman Collection.
  21. Moore, *Silent Star*, page 14.
  22. LeRoy, William and Earl, from the Judy Coleman Collection.
  23. Maran.
  24. William, Charles, Robert and George, from the Judy Coleman Collection. Charles would later grow up to become mayor of Port Huron.
  25. Unknown title, *Port Huron Times Herald*, November 24, 1930, no page number. Colleen is quoted thus: "'I looked for those old marks today [November 1930],' she said, '"but they have been papered over. I was disappointed."' A photocopy of this disintegrating clipping and several others were provided by Mike Connell, senior reporter and columnist. He kindly raided the paper's morgue for Colleen-related article for this researcher.
  26. Robert, Hiram, William and David, from the Judy Coleman Collection.
  27. Morrison, Charles, collector, Commercial Bank res 817 Ontario, page 251 *Port Huron Directory*, 1899–1900.
  28. Morrison, Chas, sec and mngr Crosby C, res 1027 Ontario, page 265, *Port Huron 1902 Directory*.
  29. "See Hanging," *Port Huron Times-Herald*, April 19, 1904, page unknown, from Judy Coleman Collection.
  30. Mike Connell, *Port Huron Times Herald*: "Moore's family lived across Lincoln Street from the stone arch at the entrance of Pine Grove Park in a house later owned by Judge Harvey Tappan."
  31. Going by records, in the middle of 1901, Agnes had given birth to a son, recorded by the county just over a year later as a healthy white boy named Cleeve T. Morrison. Again, this is an example of sloppy recordkeeping: Cleeve's middle name was Palmer. Cleeve was named after Sir Thomas Cleeve (from a notation in album in the Judy Coleman Collection).

Chapter 3

  1. Gerhard K. Lang and Oskar Gareis, *Ophthalmology: A Pocket Textbook Atlas* (Stuttgart, NY: Thieme, 2007), page 211. "Impaired development of the pigmentation of the iris can lead to a congenital difference in coloration between the left and right iris (heterochromatic). One iris containing varying pigmentation is referred to as iris bicolor. Isolated heterochromia is not necessarily clinically significant (simple heterochromia)." Newspapers and magazines often incorrectly identified both eyes as brown.
  2. Colleen Moore, *The Story of My Life*, an authorized autobiography released to the press around 1926.
  3. The city is mentioned as one of her home towns in various sources: Jack Spears, *Hollywood: The Golden Era* (South Brunswick, NJ: A. S. Barnes, 1971), page 198; *Films in Review*, Volume 14, National Board of Review of Motion Pictures, 1963. Both likely took this information from Colleen's *The Story of My Life*. Newspapers around that time started mentioning the town's name in stories on her life, including the *Luddington Daily News* (Michigan) of February 5, 1926, page 3, and "Colleen Moore in *Happiness Ahead* Strand Offering," *Hartford Courant* (CT) June 17, 1928, page D4.
  4. *Hillsdale Democrat*, June 30, 1905, page 1.
  5. In at least one instance, Colleen mentioned just such an arrangement. When a rumor started in the city of Rome, New York, that Colleen had lived in the city as a child, she wrote back that it was her parents and brother who lived there while she remained in school in Chicago.
  6. *Polk's Hillsdale City and County Directory 1905–1906*: "Morrison, Charles, trav agt Alamo Mnfg Co. bds 89 S. Howell," page 108. This is doubtless Charles R. Morrison of Port Huron, as he is listed in the Tampa directories as having a similar job.
  7. Robert P. Hudson, *Michigan: A Summer and Health Resort State* (Michigan: State Board of Health, 1878), page 118.
  8. This is based on an online search, and comparing the results to the map *Birds Eye View of the City of Hillsdale, Hillsdale Co., Mich. 1866* (Michigan: A. Ruger, 1866). MEDIUM: col. map 50 x 72 cm.; CALL NUMBER: G4114.H65A3 1866 .R8 Rug 85; REPOSITORY: Library of Congress Geography and Map Division Washington, D.C. 20540-4650 USA; DIGITAL ID: g4114h pm003510 http://hdl.loc.gov/loc.gmd/g4114h.pm003510. The map shows the area to be near the outskirts of town, though in the 40 years to follow there was, doubtless, much growth.
  9. "24-Hour Wait for Maude Adams," *New York Times*, November 2, 1905, page 9.
  10. "A Joyous Night with 'Peter Pan'; Maude Adams Triumphs as 'The Boy Who Wouldn't Grow Up.' An Exquisite Dream Play. The Fanciful Barrie, at His Best, Sympathetically Acted — New York's Second Childhood," *New York Times*, November 7, 1905, page 9.
  11. Dorothy, "The Play's the Thing," *The Young Woman's Journal* Vol. 18, No. 4 (Church of Jesus Christ of Latter-Day Saints, Young Women's Mutual Improvement Association, Juvenile Instructor Office, April 1907), page 153.
  12. In *Silent Star*, Colleen does not specifically state where she saw *Peter Pan*. In *The Story of My Life*, she wrote that the play that had changed her life was *Uncle Tom's Cabin*. At that time there was any number of traveling productions of the play, in addition to short film versions.
  13. Moore, *Silent Star*, page 11.
  14. "News of the Theaters," by W.L. Hubbard, *Chicago Daily Tribune*, March 27, 1907, page 6. This episode, or one like it, is also noted by Armond Fields in *Maude Adams: Idol of American Theater*, 1872–1953 (Jefferson, NC: McFarland, 2004), page 202, though, in this instance, the voice is identified as coming from the balcony.
  15. "King Jones Made a Fortune; It Came Nickel by Nickel," by Charles Edwards, *Chicago Daily Tribune*, October 11, 1908, page C3.
  16. *New York Times*, October 23, 1907, page 4.
  17. Charles Musser, *Before the Nickelodeon: Edwin S. Porter and the Edison Manufacturing Company* (Berkeley: University of California Press, 1991), pp. 372–374.

Chapter 4

  1. Moore, *Silent Star*, page 15.
  2. *Atlanta City Directory, 1908*, Vol. 32 (Atlanta: Foote and Davies, 1908), page 1027: "Charles R (Agnes), manager, r 301 Capitol av"; and *Atlanta City Directory, 1909*, Foote and Davies Company, vol. 33, page 1208: "Charles R (Agnes), manager, r 41 Linden."
  3. "Kelley, Mary, widow Patrick, r 301 Capitol av" *Atlanta City Directory*, Foote and Davies Company, vol. 32, 1908, page 877.
  4. *Sanborn Fire Insurance Maps, Atlanta, Ga. 1911*, vol. 4, sheet 495. That plot now lies near a knot of freeways, a short distance from Turner Field.
  5. *Shrine of the Immaculate Conception (Atlanta, Georgia) Collection, 1846–1992*. Office of Archives and Records, Roman Catholic Archdiocese of Atlanta, Atlanta, Georgia and Sacred Heart Church (Atlanta, Ga.) Collection, 1935–1998. Office of Archives and Records, Roman Catholic Archdiocese of Atlanta, Atlanta, Georgia. Thanks to Brittany Bennett Parris, MLIS, Assistant

Notes — Chapter 4

Archivist, Archdiocese of Atlanta, Office of Archives and Records.

6. *The Story of My Life*. In addition to reading the *Swiss Family Robinson*, Colleen described her reading as including "cops and robbers" stories which she enacted with the neighborhood kids. The anecdotes she repeats in *The Story of My Life* may have been partly inventions for the press, or may have happened earlier or later than described — at different Atlanta residences or even in other towns — but certainly these were the sorts of activities with which children of the time would have been engaged.

7. *Sanborn Fire Insurance Maps, Atlanta, 1911*, vol. 1, sheet 50. Linden Ave. is now Linden Ave; NW and Linden Way is simply Linden Ave. Kathleen's block is now gone, incorporated into the Linden Avenue exit off Interstate 75/85. Her house would have been on the inside curve of the onramp to the 85, on a plot of grass between the onramp and a parking lot.

8. "Society," *Atlanta Constitution*, August 13, 1909, page 8.

9. "Society," *Atlanta Constitution*, September 5, 1909, page A5.

10. First name Earl. This would be the child of Agnes's sister May Kelly Spencer. There were three children: LeRoy, William, and Earl. From family album, the Judy Coleman Collection.

11. "Society," *Atlanta Constitution*, September 5, 1909, page A5.

12. "Society," *Atlanta Constitution*, November 2, 1909, page 8.

13. *Sanborn Fire Insurance Maps, Atlanta, Ga. 1911*, vol. 2, sheet 185. It is now Parkway Drive NE. The house was located near the end of East Street, which is now the Atlanta Medical Center, at what is the exit to 336 Parkway Drive NE, the Atlanta Medical Center Health Pavilion. Their front yard is now the exit from an asphalt loop in front of the pavilion.

14. The 1919 map of Atlanta shows the area as being heavily wooded to the point that the several homes that front Jackson look lost along the trees. In *The Story of My Life*, Colleen wrote, "My parents rented a very spacious old southern mansion surrounded by extensive grounds." While none of the homes she lived in could be classified as a mansion, she might have been recalling the extensively wooded area in the vicinity of Jackson Street. *Atlanta*, Foote and Davies Company (Atlanta, GA), [n.p.] c1919. CALL NUMBER: G3924.A8A3 1919 .F6; REPOSITORY: Library of Congress Geography and Map Division Washington, D.C. 20540–4650 USA; DIGITAL ID: g3924a pm001230 http://hdl.loc.gov/loc.gmd/g3924a.pm001230.

15. "Barnum & Bailey in Atlanta Today," *Atlanta Constitution*, November 9, 1909, page A3.

16. Several different versions of this story have been told over the years. Sometimes the American Stock Company was supposed to be created in Atlanta, sometimes in Tampa. *The Story of My Life* gives it as having been created while in Atlanta. In *Silent Star*, it seems to be created in Tampa, with the visit of Barnum & Bailey afterwards. This was described as being the impetus for Kathleen and Cleeve to stage a backyard circus.

17. "Motion Picture Star Here for Visit on Honeymoon," *Atlanta Constitution*, November 28, 1923, page 25. The Jackson Street property did have a rear car barn, unlike the two earlier homes. The November 28 story claims that Colleen visited the site of the old home, but it had been destroyed in the fire of 1917.

18. Moore, *Silent Star*, page 17.

19. "Social Items," *Atlanta Constitution*, January 20, 1910, page 8

20. "Social Items," *Atlanta Constitution*, February 18, 1910, page 8.

21. "Social Items," *Atlanta Constitution*, March 9, 1910, page 10.

22. The Lucille Love series did not begin until 1914, too late for her to have seen in Atlanta; so, regardless of the names of the theaters, she would have seen these films in Tampa.

23. "On New Bijou Theater Work Starts This Week," *Atlanta Constitution*, March 8, 1908, page A5.

24. There was a Strand Theater in Tampa, but built too late for Kathleen to have been a patron: "Built in the Spanish Colonial style in 1917, it opened in 1918 and was hailed as 'the most beautiful theatre in the South.'" Cinema Treasure website, http://cinematreasures.org/theater/8513 (July 25, 2010).

25. The 1910 Federal Census confirms that the family was living in Atlanta: Charles, Agnes, Kathleen, Cleeve, but no mention of Grandmother Kelly at the time of the enumeration. She had either gone ahead to the next destination, or was waiting for the move with family elsewhere, perhaps in Chicago, with Kathleen.

26. *Atlanta City Directory, 1910*, vol. 34, page 1232: "Charles R (Agnes), traveling salesman, r 240 N Jackson."

27. "Social Items," *Atlanta Constitution*, June 2, 1910, page 10.

28. *Kerwin's Warren Borough & Warren County Directory, 1910*, page 165: "Morrison, CR, trav salesman 107 S. Irvine." On page 54, the directory also places the Jacobson Manufacturing Company as being at 107-115 Irvine Street (S).

29. Colleen's Fairy Castle, on display in Chicago, sports a full library of miniature editions.

30. "The Nearest Port to Panama," *National Waterways*, vol. 1 no. 2, National Rivers and Harbors Congress, 1912, page 160.

31. *Insurance Maps of Tampa, Florida*, Tampa, Hillsborough County, Florida, 1915, page 87, supplement.

32. School records for Cleeve, before his arrival with the rest of the family in Los Angeles, have not yet been found. In several articles Colleen was quoted as saying that Cleeve was sent to school in Toronto. Certainly, for an upper-middle-class family, sending the son to boarding school while keeping the daughter nearby would not have been unusual.

33. In a letter to Sophia S. Earle, dated August 9, 1977, Colleen mentioned swimming in a hot springs. From the Hampton Dunn Collection, University of South Florida Special Collections, USF Library, Tampa, FL. In the letter, she could not recall the name of the springs. Sulphur Springs is the closest springs, but still some miles away from her neighborhood. The TECO streetcar, however, ran out to the springs, which was a popular tourist destination at the time. This would seem to be the springs to which she was referring.

34. Slide, Anthony, *Inside the Hollywood Fan Magazine: A History of Star Makers, Fabricators, and Gossip Mongers* (Jackson: University Press of Mississippi, 2010), pp. 14, 18.

35. Ibid., page 47.

36. *Insurance Maps of Tampa, Florida*, Tampa, Hillsborough County, Florida, 1915, page 87 supplement.

37. The piano-box stage was a story retold about Colleen from the very earliest days of her career.

38. *St. Petersburg Times* (FL), February 6, 1982, page unknown. From the Hampton Dunn Collection, University of South Florida Special Collections, USF Library, Tampa, FL.

39. *Evening News*, August 13, 1938, page unknown. From the Hampton Dunn Collection, University of South Florida Special Collections, USF Library, Tampa, FL.

40. "Colleen Moore Recalls Fun of Her Childhood in Tampa," (Tampa) *Times*, January 26, 1963, page unknown. From the Hampton Dunn Collection, University of South Florida Special Collections, USF Library, Tampa, FL.

41. The Greeson Theater is cited as one of the theaters where Colleen had watched movies, in a 1938 *Evening News* clipping, but the 1914 *Tampa City Directory* does not list it among the city's movie theaters (they are: Alcazar, Bonita, Colon, Dreamland, The Gasparilla, The Kinodrome, Maceo [on 1610 and 1310 Central Avenue], Majestic, Montgomery, Prince, Sans Souci, Vaudette and Venus Theatres). The Greeson Theater building is mentioned in volume 17 of the *Automobile Trade Journal*, 1912 ("Everitt Motor Car Company ... has leased quarters in the

Greeson Theatre Building"). Perhaps it was converted to a motion-picture venue at a later date.

42. *Evening News*, August 13, 1938, page unknown. From the Hampton Dunn Collection, University of South Florida Special Collections, USF Library, Tampa, FL.

43. Ibid.

44. Lorin Blodget, *Climatology of the United States* (New York: Lippincott, 1857), page 250.

45. Edwin James Houston, *The Wonder Book of the Atmosphere* (New York: F. A. Stokes, 1907), page 280. "The United States Weather Bureau has made a careful study of the thunderstorms of the United States. It would appear from this study that there are three regions where thunderstorms are especially common. One of these is situated in the southwest with its crest over Florida."

46. Moore, *Silent Star*, page 19.

47. Ibid., page 21. Charles to Agnes: "I always told you Walter was crazy."

48. Harry Allen Smith, *The Life and Legend of Gene Fowler* (New York: Smith, Morrow, 1977), pages 180–182.

49. Moore, *Silent Star*, page 19.

50. "Moving-picture Business Enjoys a Frenzied Boom," *Baltimore Sun*, September 1, 1907, page 14.

Chapter 5

1. Based on the descriptions of John McCormick's behavior in adulthood — characterized by episodes of talkativeness, charm, and ecstatic outbursts of creativity and mania, divided by deep depressions — it is possible that he suffered from bipolar disorder, and that his drinking was a form of self-medication. He was already drinking when Colleen met him, and the behavior worsened during their marriage. This would seem to point to an adolescent onset, the behavior probably misunderstood as episodes of adolescent moodiness interrupting an otherwise brilliant and charming personality. Adolescent bipolar disorder often presents in much the same manner as adult bipolar disorder: "Generally speaking, adolescent-onset bipolar disorder is similar to adult-onset bipolar disorder.... [In adolescents] the first presentation of bipolar disorder often is depression ... which may obscure the true diagnosis." David A. Wolfe and Eric J. Mash, *Behavioral and Emotional Disorders in Adolescents: Nature, Assessment, and Treatment* (New York: Guilford Press, 2008), page 328.

2. 1910 Census, State of Illinois, Cook County, 25th ward, sheet 10, lines 20 and 21; "Walter Howey 27 editor/ newspaper, Elizabeth, 25."

3. Stops based on map published in *This Week in Chicago*, September 4– September 10, 1921, pages 16–17.

4. *The Chicago Blue Book of Selected Names of Chicago and Suburban Towns*, (Chicago: Chicago Directory Company, 1914), page 669. "Howey W. C., 4942 Sheridan rd."

5. Mordaunt Hall, "How She Started Screen Career," *New York Times*, May 17, 1925, page X2.

6. Viewing the film at the George Eastman House, film historian David Kiehn of the Niles Essanay Silent Film Museum spotted the actress and wrote about it in an email, dated Thursday, February 22, 2007: "After stopping the film on the flatbed machine I studied the frames very closely, and came to the conclusion I was right [the actress was Colleen Moore]."

7. Production date based on David Kiehn's list of still code numbers giving the order that Essanay films made before and after *The Prince of Graustark* were shot, and the observation that, while it generally took about two months for a film to go from completion to the screen, *The Prince of Graustark* was evidentially delayed:

4367: *The Higher Destiny*, 2 September 1916
4368: *A Million for a Baby* ,9 September 1916
4372: *Twin Fates*, 30 September 1916
4381: *The Pacifist*, 5 September 1916
4383: *The Prince of Graustark*, 6 November 1916
4384: *When Justice Won*, 19 September 1916
4426: *A Failure at Fifty*, 9 December 1916

8. Stories mentioning a start at Essanay began to appear in the latter half of Colleen's career. A few quote Colleen stating this as fact, though at least once the quote was given while in Chicago, perhaps intended to please a home-town audience. One mention of an Essanay connection was: "It takes some people half a lifetime to learn that in the entertainment world there is one prime requisite for success. Colleen Moore learned it at the mature age of 12 when during a school vacation she went to work as an extra at the old Essanay studio in Chicago." Helen Klumph, "Tenacity and Versatility Bring Colleen Success," *Los Angeles Times*, September 12, 1926, page C17. The stories continued into the final years of her career, including: "E. H. Calvert, as an actor-director with Essanay, is credited with having discovered the talents of numerous celebrities of the day. Among them were Gloria Swanson, Virginia Valli, [and] Colleen Moore." Philip K. Scheuer, "Stepping-stones Show Slipperiness," *Los Angeles Times*, March 29, 1931, page B13.

9. Moore, *Silent Star*, pages 20–24.

10. Helen Ferguson's film credits do not begin until 1917, but Kevin Brownlow states that her earliest role was in *The Raven*, 1915, as part of a triple exposure. In her 1970 interview, when referring to Colleen Moore, she is vague enough that she may be referring either to pre–Hollywood film appearances or to the film test itself.

11. Transcript of Kevin Brownlow interview with Helen Ferguson, Palm Springs, California, January 1970.

12. Ibid.

Chapter 6

1. In *Silent Star*, Colleen says they took the Santa Fe Chief from Chicago to Los Angeles, but that train would not begin service until a decade later. The California Ltd. ran roughly the same route in about the same time; Colleen said it lasted "three days and three nights."

2. Date conjecture, based on three days' travel time, and mention in a newspaper clipping ("Just Can't Vacation," *Los Angeles Times*, August, 1919) that Colleen arrived on a Saturday and by the following Monday she was at work on her first film. In *Silent Star*, she writes that she arrived in Los Angeles two days after Thanksgiving, so this timing seems about right. In either case, her first film was released a few short months after her arrival, so she had little time to prepare before she was at work.

3. Moore, *Silent Star*, page 25.

4. The article was never identified.

5. *New York Times*, July 21, 1915, page 11.

6. The routes I describe — "southward out of Barstow" and so forth — are based on the 1903 map, "Route of the California Limited — Santa Fe all the way." Atchison, Topeka, and Santa Fe Railroad Company, from the Rumsey Map Collection.

7. These are my assumptions here; there were more than one station in Los Angeles, but the La Grande handled all AT&SF traffic in Los Angeles.

8. "Mrs. Brown, a sort of studio chaperone, met us at the station," Colleen wrote in *Silent Star*. Karl Brown's *Adventures with D.W. Griffith* (New York: Farrar, Straus and Giroux, 1973) stated that his mother Rose was employed at the studio as "Frank Wood's assistant in charge of women," a position that came with a badge that designated her as "City Mother No. 1" and bestowed upon her the power to make sure there was no hanky-panky on studio property.

9. The walls were finally torn down in 1919, though the elephant statues remained.

10. A brief history and detailed description of the studio can be found in G. P. von Harlenman, "Motion Picture Studios of California," *Moving Picture World*, March 10, 1917, including such

details as: "What is now known as the Fine Arts Studio at 4500 Sunset Boulevard, Los Angeles, was a residence property five years ago, and was converted into a studio.... Originally there were only three acres, part of which was covered by an orchard. There was a residence building which was used for offices, dressing rooms and laboratory; one stage 50 by 60 feet; and a small building used for a property room and projection. The payroll then approximated $2,000 a week for the one company in Los Angeles.... The studio has grown until seven acres are now fully occupied.... There are now two open-air stages, one 50 by 100 and the other 70 by 200; also two enclosed electric light studios, one with a stage 60 by 70 feet and the other 60 by 120 feet, each equipped with enormous generating units and the stages lighted with the latest type of Cooper-Hewitt, Aristo, Winfield and Majestic lamps."

11. Kalton C. Lahue, *Dreams for Sale: The Rise and Fall of the Triangle Film Corporation* (South Brunswick and New York: A.S. Barnes, 1971), page 77.

12. Anthony Slide, *The Kindergarten of the Movies: A History of the Fine Arts Company* (Metuchen, NJ: Scarecrow Press, 1980), page 21. Bessie Love recalled, "You might even go through Mr. Griffith to get to Mr. Woods."

13. Moore, *Silent Star*, page 27.

14. This is conjecture on my part: Woods co-wrote the scenario for *The Bad Boy* himself and might have known if there were still parts to fill with the production about to start.

15. Grace Kingsley, "Rialto, behind the Curtain," *Los Angeles Times*, March 7, 1916, page III4.

16. Colleen gives a full description of the conversations and the gossip she heard, on pages 28 and 29 of *Silent Star*. Accurate or not, it does get across the point that many in the stock company were remarkably young for the roles they would be playing.

17. Colleen listed a few of the rumors of the time: some were not studio secrets, as Mae Tinee (in the February 5, 1917 edition of the *Chicago Tribune*) responded to a letter from "C.D.F." thus: "I have not heard that Dorothy Gish and Robert Harron are engaged, so live a little longer, C.D.F. It may not be true."

18. Regarding some of the personal antics going on at the Triangle lot at the time, Colleen is quoted by Stuart Oderman in *Lillian Gish: A Life on Stage and Screen* (Jefferson, NC: McFarland, 2000), pages 78–79, as saying: "It must have been hard for Lillian to watch old man Griffith making an ass out of himself for this absolute no-talent airhead Dempster, but she was very stoic about it. For the first time in Lillian's life, something had happened which she couldn't control. None of us could say anything to her, because she never discussed her social life. I never knew if Lillian had a social life of any kind. I knew, everybody knew, what Dorothy did. Dorothy always talked about Bobby [Robert Harron] and where they went.... Lillian, on the set, was very professional. Whenever she was with Griffith, her mother was always there, acting as chaperone." Colleen and Lillian would meet on the Triangle lot, and would remain friends for the rest of their lives.

Chapter 7

1. Moore, *Silent Star*, page 36: "If I was told to be on the set at nine, I was there at seven-thirty." Not referring to that day specifically, but to her work ethic in general.

2. Inez Klumph, Helen Klumph, "The Question of Make-up," *Screen Acting, Its Requirements and Rewards* (New York: Falk, 1922), pages 142–144.

3. Frances Taylor Patterson, *Cinema Craftsmanship: A Book for Photoplaywrights* (New York: Harcourt, Brace and Howe, 1920), pages 96–100.

4. "The Weather," *Los Angeles Times*, November 27, 1916.

5. Slide, *The Kindergarten of the Movies*, page 92.

6. See Ben Turpin's comments in David Kiehn, *Broncho Billy and the Essanay Film Company* (Berkeley, CA: Farwell Books, 2003).

7. It is unknown if her actual first shot was on location, but this is what she described in *Silent Star*.

8. The cemetery was transferred from the Veterans Administration Medical Center to the National Cemetery System in 1973 (United States Department of Veterans Affairs).

9. Much of the information on this day and the amalgamation of days that would follow are speculation, as Colleen gave no details. In *Silent Star* (page 36), Colleen only wrote that she got through her first role by "simply doing what the director told me to do."

10. My description of Mildred's youthful flirtatiousness is based on Chaplin's *My Autobiography* and more specifically on David Robinson's description in *Chaplin, His Life and Art* (New York: Da Capo Press, 1994), pages 245–246.

11. Moore, *Silent Star*, page 34.

12. Advertisement, *Moving Picture World*, September 9, 1916, pages 1636–1637.

13. "The Camera Detects Thought," by Chet Withey, *Photoplay*, October 1920, page 29.

14. The photo is on page 39 of *Silent Star*, and shows the characteristic curl of Colleen's fingers as she rests her cheek on Robert's shoulder, her hand just brushing his arm.

15. Moore, *Silent Star*, page 38.

16. Grace Kingsley, "Reported in 'Rialto,'" *Los Angeles Times*, January 7, 1917, page III21. The actual scene was probably shot mid-month.

17. *Los Angeles City Directory, 1917*. Address listed as 1326 N. Virgil Ave. According to the story, "City Population Nears Six Hundred Thousand," in the June 27 *Los Angeles Times*, compilation of the 1917 directory began in January, and the directory was in the last stages of printing by the publication of the article. So Colleen's mother was still in town, listed as a resident, as late as January.

18. Colleen wrote that she and Carmel would walk to work, but Carmel (or at least her father) lived at 4525 Prospect Ave. Prospect was north of her studio, while Colleen's home on Virgil was south.

19. Moore, *The Story of My Life*.

20. Ibid. (The baths themselves no longer exist; the hot springs still flow beneath the street in the old location.)

21. "The 'Bimini Baths' New Local Wonder," *Los Angeles Daily Times*, December 28, 1902.

22. *Moving Picture World*, February 17, 1917, page 952.

23. Moore, *Silent Star*, page 38. Colleen writes that she watched the film at "Talley's Theater in Los Angeles," though by the beginning of March, *The Girl Philippa* was in the second week of its run at Tally's Broadway Theater. I find no evidence that this theater ever played the film; in all likelihood, she meant Clune's Broadway Theater.

24. Moore, *The Story of My Life*.

25. The film, at least in the article, was unnamed, but the director and cast listed are that of *A Gentleman of the Old School*.

26. *Moving Picture World*, February 3, 1917, page 693.

27. Grace Kingsley, "Studio," *Los Angeles Times*, January 21, 1917, page III16.

28. Slide, *The Kindergarten of the Movies*, page 116.

29. Moore, *Silent Star*, page 47.

30. Ibid., page 33. Colleen writes that *Hands Up!* was shot about three or four weeks after her work in *The Bad Boy*. *An Old Fashioned Young Man* would not have required much of her time, and it was released within weeks of *Hands Up!* She made no mention of a cross-country excursion in *Silent Star* (or anywhere else), so it's safe to assume that she was busy at work on her third film while the rest of the cast and crew of *Gentleman* were riding the rails.

31. "Ex-Bandit's Home Fried," *Los Angeles Times*, January 4, 1917, page III.

32. Moore, *Silent Star*, page 50.

33. Ibid.

34. Grace Kingsley, "Frivols," *Los Angeles Times*, March 12, 1917, page II8.

35. Moore, *Silent Star*, page 45.

Chapter 8

1. Moore, *Silent Star*, page 47.
2. Grace Kingsley, "Studio," *Los Angeles Times*, March 25, 1917, page III1.
3. Colleen wrote in *Silent Star* that Frank recommended a theatrical agent to help her, but that she pounded the pavement herself. In all likelihood, she did her own job hunting, saving herself the cost of an agent's commission.
4. Oderman, *Lillian Gish: a Life on Stage and Screen*, page 72.
5. John A. Barry, secretary of DWG Incorporated.
6. "Huck" was Frank "Huck" Wortman, Griffith's set designer who would be put to work before too long on *Hearts of the World*.
7. Telegram to: E.C. Bidwell, from: J.A. Barry, August 7, 1917, D.W. Griffith and the Museum of Modern Art, *The Papers of D.W. Griffith, 1897–1954* (Sanford, NC: Microfilming Corporation of America, 1982).
8. "Colleen Moore, Bluebirder," *Moving Picture World*, September 8, 1917, page 1512.
9. "Over six feet tall and weighing two hundred pounds, he was ideal for the rugged mountain men he portrayed." W. Lee Cozad, *Those Magnificent Mountain Movies: The Golden Years 1911–1939* (Lake Arrowhead, CA: Rim of the World Historical Society, 2002), page 42.
10. *The Papers of D.W. Griffith, 1897–1954*, Letter to: Albert H.T. Banzhaf, from: EC Bidwell, September 3, 1917.
11. Ibid. Telegram to: Albert H.T. Banzhaf, from: EC Bidwell, September 9, 1917.
12. Ibid. Telegram from: to: EC Bidwell, Albert H.T. Banzhaf, September 18, 1917.
13. Ibid. Telegram from: Colleen Moore, to: Albert H.T. Banzhaf, September 22, 1917.
14. Ibid. Telegram to: EC Bidwell, from: Albert H.T. Banzhaf, September 24, 1917.
15. Ibid. Telegram to: Albert H.T. Banzhaf, from: EC Bidwell, October 6, 1917.
16. "Griffith Soon to Stage Short Picture Dramas," *Los Angeles Times*, April 8, 1917, page III1.
17. Grace Kingsley, "Studio," *Los Angeles Times*, April 15, 1917, page III1.
18. Ibid., May 5, 1917, page II3.
19. Assuming a six-month term, starting in November.
20. Interview with Joe Yranski, June 18, 2010.
21. Moore, *Silent Star*, pages 63–65.
22. *The Papers of D.W. Griffith, 1897–1954*, Ledger sheet, 1917.

Chapter 9

1. In *Silent Star*, Colleen wrote she went to Selig Polyscope, specifically for *Little Orphant Annie*. However, of the two films adapted from the work of James Whitcomb Riley that she appeared in, *A Hoosier Romance* was the first to be made and released. She likely went to Selig looking for any work at all, or for a part in *A Hoosier Romance*. It is possible, however, she asked about *Little Orphant Annie* and was offered the part in *A Hoosier Romance* first.
2. *Indianapolis Star*, May 10, 1918, page 12.
3. Grace Kingsley, "Frivols," *Los Angeles Times*, October 6, 1917, page II3.
4. There were about 20 of the farcical comedies, including *A Trip to Chinatown*, which played more than 600 times at Hoyt's own Madison Square Theater. It was 1926 before *A Trip to Chinatown* made it to the screen, with Anna May Wong—who would appear in *Dinty*—in the cast.
5. Mae Tinee, "Right off the Reel," *Chicago Daily Tribune*, February 3, 1918, page C3.
6. Ibid.
7. Interview with Kevin Brownlow, *Hollywood* series, transcript, page 1.
8. William Selig Collection, folder 63, Margaret Herrick Library, Academy of Motion Picture Arts and Sciences.
9. Eugenie Besserer would appear with Colleen again in *Little Orphant Annie*.
10. A note in a film synopsis on *A Hoosier Romance* (page 4) reads: "This is not an argument for communism. The story will be found unique inasmuch as it subtly represents propaganda for the big interests as against communism, yet the word communism is at no time mentioned. Withal, it is a powerful red-blooded story, of love, of romance, and adventure, that should make a strong pull at the box-office of our theaters on purely entertainment values." William Selig Collection, folder 64, Margaret Herrick Library, Academy of Motion Picture Arts and Sciences.
11. Interview with Kevin Brownlow, page 2.
12. "MaGee" was Colleen's spelling. James McGee had been appointed business manager of the California Selig Company. He joined Selig, in 1909, as an actor and was later promoted to business manager of the Edendale property. *Paste Pot and Shears* (Selig house publication), May 8, 1916, page unknown. A native of Brownsville, Nebraska, he died in his home, at 1333 Edgecliff Drive, at the age of 62. *Los Angeles Times*, February 19, 1936, page A18.
13. Moore, *Silent Star*, page 78. Colleen lists the order of films as *Little Orphant Annie* first, and then *A Hoosier Romance*. Selig's office she places in New York instead of Chicago.
14. Grace Kingsley, "Flashes," *Los Angeles Times*, June 4, 1918, page II3.
15. Now Lincoln Park.
16. William Selig Collection, folder 65, Margaret Herrick Library, Academy of Motion Picture Arts and Sciences.
17. Ibid., folder 96, page 4.
18. "Another Movie Made in Pleasanton," *Livermore Herald* (CA), November 29, 1917, page unknown. (Thanks to David Kiehn for calling this article to my attention.)
19. "Movie Folks Like Pleasanton Hotels," *Livermore Echo* (CA), December 13, 1917, page unknown. (Again, thanks to David Kiehn for calling this article to my attention.)
20. Harlow Lindley, *The Indiana Centennial, 1916: A Record of the Celebration of the One Hundredth Anniversary of Indiana's Admission to Statehood, Indiana Historical Collections*, Volume 5 (Indiana Historical Bureau, 1919), page 31.
21. William Selig Collection, folder 453, Clark scrapbook 3. Letter to: William Selig from: Colleen Moore, October 17, 1918, 22.
23. Mae Tinee, "Right off the Reel," *Chicago Daily Tribune*, January 12, 1919, page C3.

Chapter 10

1. "Movie News Notes," *Lima Daily News* (OH), January 13, 1919, page 6.
2. "The Screen," *New York Times*, September 29, 1919, page 13.
3. Mae Tinee, "Right Off the Reel," *Chicago Daily Tribune*, January 5, 1919, page C3.
4. Letter as quoted in "Tom Mix Will Mix Picture Here," *Coconino Sun* (Flagstaff, AZ), February 7, 1919, page 10.
5. Ibid.
6. Moore, *Silent Star*, page 54. In 1910, Flagstaff precinct and Flagstaff town, Coconino County, had a combined population of 2,176 people, or 543 and 1633, respectively. In terms of population, it was the largest population in Coconino County, not including the various Indian reservations (including the Hopi, Navajo and Walapai). *Thirteenth Census of the United States, 1910: Population by Counties and Minor Civil Divisions, 1910, 1900, 1890* (Washington, D.C.: Government Printing Office, 1912), page 18.
7. Moore, *Silent Star*, page 52.
8. *Coconino Sun* (Flagstaff, AZ), February 7, 1919, page 10.
9. "Flagstaff Wins Tom Mix from Prescott," *Arizona Daily Journal-Miner*, February 13, 1919, page 2.
10. "Tom Mix and Company and Bara Bear Here," *Coconino Sun*, February 14, 1919, page 10.

11. Mrs. Frank Harrison, "Interesting Events in the Local Social World," *Coconino Sun*, February 14, 1919, page 5. In addition to Colleen and her mother, the Fox people were reported to be staying at the Commercial Hotel. The company included Ed Rosenbaum, Jr., business manager; Edward De Saint, director of the company, and his wife; Walter de Courtesy; Mr. F. Baker; Mr. A. E. Weller, cameramen; Walter Williams, Mix's trainer; and Bob Pattee, property master. In addition to these individuals were "a number of Mexicans and Indians" who were members of the company.
12. "Lively for Mix," *Los Angeles Times*, March 16, 1919, page III9; incorrectly reports the whole hotel being renamed; only the dining room was.
13. Mrs. Frank Harrison, "Interesting Events in the Local Social World," *Coconino Sun*, February 14th, 1919.
14. "He Likes Tom, but He'll Be No Target," *Oakland Tribune*, April 6, 1919, page 2.
15. "Lively for Mix," *Los Angeles Times*, March 16, 1919, page III9.
16. "Tom Mix Company Leaves for Coast," *Coconino Sun*, February 28, 1919, page 1.
17. Lillian Wurtzel Semenov and Carla Winter, eds., *William Fox, Sol M. Wurtzel and the Early Fox Film, Letters 1917—1923*, (Jefferson, NC: McFarland, 2001), page 68.
18. *The Works of Gilbert Parker, Volume 1* (New York: Scribner's, 1912), page 125. The title comes from a line by the character of Pierre in "She of the Triple Chevron"—"You spoke true. But devils have their friends—and their whims."
19. "At the Savoy," *Atlanta Constitution*, June 15, 1919, page D9. "Colleen Moore, who played in support of Monroe Salisbury in *The Savage*, is his leading woman in *Devils Have Their Friends*, Salisbury's newest Universal special attraction, which Paul Powell is directing."
20. *Fort Wayne Journal-Gazette*, June 29, 1919, page 6, section 4.
21. Elspeth Cameron, *Canadian Culture: An Introductory Reader* (Toronto, Ontario: Canadian Scholars' Press, 1997), page 56; points to Salisbury depiction as the sole exception to Hollywood's depiction of French-Canadians villains in early Hollywood films as having simple names, being fiendish, lecherous, and irredeemably evil.
22. "Studio," *Los Angeles Times*, June 1, 1919, page III13.
23. *Decatur Review* (IL), July 13, 1919, page 18.
24. Mae Tinee, "Right Off the Reel," *Chicago Daily Tribune* April 27, 1919, page E4.
25. *Billings Gazette* (MT), July 20, 1919, page 2.
26. Ibid.
27. Unidentified newspaper clipping, Joseph Yranski Collection.
28. *Washington Post*, November 21, 1919, page 3.
29. "Bolshevism Bared by R.E. Simmons," *New York Times*, February 18, 1919, page 4.
30. J. C. Jessen, "In and Out of West Coast Studios," *Motion Picture News*, vol. 20 no. 5, July 26, 1919, page 911–912.
31. Ibid., vol. 2, no. 6, August 2, 1919, page 1139.
32. This is an early example of what has come to be called "viral marketing," wherein an advertisement referring obliquely back to a film and giving minimal information is sprung on the public, leading to curiosity and word-of-mouth advertising. The practice is defined by Jeffery Rayport in "The Virus of Marketing," *Fast Company Magazine*, December 31, 1996, http://www.fastcompany.com/magazine/06/virus.html (September 3, 2010).
33. "Press Agent Stirs Storm," *Los Angeles Times*, December 12, 1919, page I11.
34. "Just Takes Vacation," *Los Angeles Times*, August 10, 1919, page III 13.

Chapter 11

1. "Just Can't Vacation," *Los Angeles Times*, August 17, 1919, page III35.
2. Grace Kingsley, "The Story of a Miracle Maid," *Los Angeles Times*, September 7, 1919, page III1.
3. Ibid., "Flashes," October 30, 1919, page III4.
4. His autobiography (written with Cameron Shipp), in fact, was entitled *The King of Comedy* (Garden City, NY: Doubleday, 1954).
5. In *Silent Star*, there is passage which describes Colleen as posing before a mirror in a swimsuit, attempting to evaluate her potential as a bathing beauty. Her grandmother walks in on her and declares that no granddaughter of hers will prance around on film dressed like that. A similar scene appears in Adele Rogers St. Johns's book *Love, Laughter, and Tears* (Garden City, NY: Doubleday, 1978), released ten years after *Silent Star*. The major difference between the two versions is that Adela puts herself in the bedroom with Colleen. Given her role in helping write *Silent Star*, it begs the question of its authenticity.
6. Brownlow Interview, page 5.
7. Ibid.
8. *Out West Magazine* (Vol.16, no.1), Los Angeles: Archaeological Institute of America, Southwest Society, 1902, page 101.
9. William Henry Robinson, "Prescott," *The Story of Arizona*, The Berryhill Co., 1919, page 395.
10. Richard D. Jensen, *The Amazing Tom Mix: The Most Famous Cowboy of the Movies* (Bloomington, IN: iUniverse, 2005), page 83.
11. Brownlow Interview, page 1. Also *Silent Star*, page 57, in which she states that it was Buck Jones who taught her one-handed cigarette rolling.
12. John Schwartz, "Movie Great Tom Mix filmed Many Movies in Prescott," *Sunday Prescott Courier*, November 19, 1995, page 4A.
13. *The Santa Fe Magazine* (Vol. 14, No. 1), Atchison, Topeka, and Santa Fe Railway Company, 1919, page 98.
14. "For Bigger Mix Productions," *Fort Wayne Journal-Gazette*, July 6, 1919, page 6, section 4.
15. "Special Scenic Construction for *The Cyclone*," *Motion Picture News*, vol. 21 no. 8, February 14, 1920, page 1718.
16. In *Silent Star*, Colleen points out that, in an episode of life reflecting art, she was kidnapped off a wagon buckboard while on the way to a location by a local Indian who had been stalking her and sending her presents every day. Pulled off the wagon onto his horse, the Indian had gotten a few blocks away before Colleen managed to kick the horse, causing it to rear, and knocking her off in the process. The Indian was never seen again.
17. Jimmy Starr, *Barefoot on Barbed Wire: An Autobiography of a Forty-year Hollywood Balancing Act* (Lanham, MD: Rowman & Littlefield, 2001), page 109.
18. "Celluloid Chatter," *Atlanta Constitution*, October 26, 1919, page D2.
19. *Indianapolis Star* (IN), May 2, 1919, page 9.
20. "Comedy for Training," *Los Angeles Times*, September 21, 1919, page III10.
21. "Christie Advancement," *Motion Picture News*, vol. 20 no. 20, November 8, 1919, page 3484.
22. Gregory Paul Williams, *The Story of Hollywood: An Illustrated History*, 2006, page 62, www.storyofhollywood.com.
23. Kevin Brownlow, *The Parade's Gone By ...* (Berkeley, CA: University of California Press, 1968), page 32.
24. "Christie Advancement," *Motion Picture News*, vol. 20 no. 20, November 8, 1919, page 3484.
25. "Good cast in the prospective Christie Special Comedy," *Motion Picture News*, vol. 20 no. 20, November 8, 1919, page 3469.
26. Al Christie, *The Elements of Situation Comedy* (Los Angeles, CA: Palmer Photoplay Corp., Dept. of Education, 1920), page 4.
27. "Here and There," *Motion Picture News*, vol. 20 no. 21, November 15, 1919, page 3626.
28. "Hollywood Hokum," *Motion Picture News*, vol. 20 no. 24, December 6, 1919, page 4123.

29. "Christmas on Sands in Bathing Suits," *Oakland Tribune*, January 4, 1920, page 6.
30. In *Silent Star*, Colleen writes that her arrangement with Christie was strictly verbal. However, *Motion Picture News* reported a contract had been signed in early 1920: "Colleen has signed a long-term contract and will return to Christie to resume work once done on her work with Sessue Hayakawa." ("Colleen Moore Contracts with Christie Film," *Motion Picture News*, vol. 21 no 9, February 21, 1920, page 1937.) If Colleen was starting a long-term arrangement with a new studio she would have gotten details in writing.
31. "Colleen Moore to Be Featured in Another Christie Comedy Soon," *Motion Picture News*, vol. 20 no. 24, December 6, 1919, page 4115.
32. Ibid., pages 4002–4003.
33. Daisuke Miyao, *Sessue Hayakawa: Silent Cinema and Transnational Stardom* (Durham: Duke University Press, 2007), page 153.
34. "Colleen Moore in 'Her Bridal Night-Mare,'" *Motion Picture News*, vol. 21 no 9, February 21, 1920, page 1916.
35. *History of First National*, page 26, Warner Bros. Archives, School of Cinema-Television, University of Southern California.
36. In May 1919, her film *Daddy Long Legs* was released, directed by Marshall Neilan with Al Green assisting; both would be among Colleen's best-known directors.
37. "The Film War," *Los Angeles Times*, January 17, 1919, page II2. The story predates the actual official establishment of United Artists, and so the organization is not named.

Chapter 12

1. "Colleen Denies Engagement," *Los Angeles Times*, November 23, 1919, page III15. The Angelino is not identified.
2. "Vaudeville," *New York Tribune*, June 27, 1920, page B2.
3. "Monte Cristo, Jr., the New Winter Garden Spectacle," *New York Tribune*, March 30, 1919, page D6.
4. Chatterbox, "Reel Chatter," *Pittsburgh Press* (PA), December 27, 1919, page 7.
5. "Christie Buys Rights to *So Long Letty*," *Motion Picture News*, vol. 21 no. 13, March 20, 1920, page 2733.
6. Hugh Dierker Productions would make *Cause for Divorce* some years later, with Colleen's brother acting under his professional name, Cleve Moore.
7. "Young Atlanta Girl Making Big Success as Screen Star," *Atlanta Constitution*, January 16, 1920, page 1.
8. *Motion Picture Classic*, vol. 10 no. 1, March 20, page 100.

9. "Camarillo Lady Visits Famous Laboratories," *Oxnard Daily Courier* (CA), October 15, 1920, page 1.
10. Mrs. A. S. C. Forbes, *California Missions and Landmarks: El Camino Real* (Los Angeles: self-published, 1915), pages 83–84.
11. And it produced a song as well: "When Dawn Came to Me," words by E. O. Van Pelt, music by Hampton Durand [of U. S.] [13452 © Apr. 23, 1920; 2 c. Apr. 24, 1920; E 475776; Hugh E. Dierker, Los Angeles. *Musical Compositions: Part 3*, by Library of Congress, Copyright Office, Library of Congress, 1920, page 814.
12. The film was released in October by the Producer's Security Corporation, which had only recently come into being and was announced in the December 6, 1919 issue of *Motion Picture News*, vol. 20 no. 24, page 3992: "To the Motion Picture Producers of the World, Mr. Richard Gradwell, formerly President of the World Film Corporation, announces the formation of The Producers Security Corporation," its purpose was "to adequately safeguard and protect the interests of the Motion Picture Producer by rendering him Guaranteed Service."
13. "Christie Film Extends Hollywood Property," *Motion Picture News*, vol. 21 no. 14, March 27, 1920, page 2945.
14. "Work started on First 'Chic' Sales Comedy," *Motion Picture News*, vol. 21 no. 16, April 10, 1920, page 3326.
15. Richard Koszarski's notes on the film for the 29th Pordenone Silent Film Festival would prove to be of invaluable insight into the odd history of this film, which extends from this chapter into the next.
16. "To Clean Up Picnic Roads," *Los Angeles Times*, May 23, 1920, page VII.
17. "A Dandy Place to Get Hit," *Los Angeles Times*, June 27, 1920, page VI1.
18. Daisy Dean, "News and Notes from Movieland," *St. Petersburg Daily Times* (FL), May 27, 1920, page 3.
19. Carolyn Lowrey, *The First One Hundred Noted Men and Women of the Screen* (New York: Moffat, Yard, 1920), page 134.
20. "In and Out of West Coast Studios," by J. C. Jessen, *Motion Picture News*, vol. 21 no. 7, February 7, 1920, page 1542.
21. His love of a good party and snappy comeback are well-known and documented, but his habits also managed to land him in trouble with regularity: "A stock of high-grade liquors valued by the authorities at more than $100,000 was placed under government seals in the basement of the Los Angeles Athletic Club late yesterday afternoon after a raid on the place officers of Capt. Plummer's vice division ... absinthe was found along with other liquors marked 'Marshall Neilan.'" ("Find Liquor at Athletic Club," *Los Angeles Times*, February 9, 1924, page A1.) Seizure of the cache of liquor did not slow him down, as seen a year later: "Marshall Neilan ... was on the set at his studio yesterday morning after he spent the night in the Santa Monica Jail with a charge of driving an automobile while intoxicated." Earlier that evening he had crashed his car into the traffic signal at the intersection of Fourth Street and Pico Boulevard. "A beautiful woman, whose identity was not learned, fled from the machine after the accident and hastily left in a taxicab, motorists said," the reporter added. "Marshall Neilan Jailed," *Los Angeles Times*, July 14, 1925, page 20.
22. Lowrey, *The First One Hundred Noted Men and Women of the Screen*, page 134.
23. She was "sent for out." As it happens, the idea of a character back in the old country (Ireland), waiting to be called for by her sweetheart, would be the basis of several of Colleen's films.
24. In *Silent Star*, on pages 77 and 109, she puts the figure at $750. On page 5 of Kevin Brownlow's interview with Colleen for *Hollywood*, she put the figure at $700.
25. Moore, *Silent Star*, page 109.
26. J. C. Jessen, "News Notes from the West," *Motion Picture News*, vol. 21 no. 24, June 5, 1920, page 4658.
27. C. Nario, "Film and Screen," *Oakland Tribune*, July 4, 1920, page 3.
28. "Moore, Miss Colleen, 1119 Grand View," Louis S. Lyons and Josephine Wilson *Who's Who Among the Women of California: An Annual Devoted to the Representative Women of California*, Volume 1 (San Francisco, Los Angeles: Security, 1922), page 331.
29. 4RS, Student Records, 1910–1940, Carton 36, Mendeiros to Mulholland; University Archives, Santa Clara University. The records indicate that the Gardner School for Boys and Girls had formerly been the "Westlake School for Boys." It was, in fact, the "Westlake School for Girls," and as of 1920, still was. John Steven McGroarty, *Los Angeles from the Mountains to the Sea: with Selected Biography of Actors and Witnesses to the Period of Growth and Achievement*, Volume 2 (Los Angeles: American Historical Society, 1921), page 199.
30. "Finishing 'Dinty' Role," *Los Angeles Times*, June 6, 1920, page III13.
31. Edwin Schallert, "Radios," *Los Angeles Times*, June 3, 1920, page III4.
32. "'Dinty' Waits," *Los Angeles Times*, June 13, 1920, page III35.
33. J. C. Jessen, "News Notes from the West," *Motion Picture News*, vol. 22 no. 1, June 26, 1920, page 111.
34. Grace Kingsley, "Flashes," *Los Angeles Times*, July 8, 1920, page III4.
35. J. C. Jessen, "News Notes from the West," *Motion Picture News*, vol. 22 no. 4, July 17, 1920, page 640.

36. "Neilan Shows Film on Newspaper Life," *San Francisco Chronicle*, July 2, 1920, page 19.
37. Photo and caption, "News and Gossip of the Rialto," *New York Times*, July 25, 1920, page 66.
38. "Open House to Be Kept for Stars of Film," *San Francisco Chronicle*, July 25, 1920, page 2.
39. *Oakland Tribune*, July 24, 1920, page 3.
40. Grace Kingsley, "'Flashes' New Neilan Star," *Los Angeles Times*, August 31, 1920, page III4.

Chapter 13

1. J. C. Jessen, "News Notes from the West," *Motion Picture News*, vol. 22 no. 10, August 28, 1920, page 1719.
2. "Titling Letty," *Los Angeles Times*, August 8, 1920, page III11. This would be her brother Cleeve, and very likely her cousin Jack Stone, who would appear with her in *Lilac Time* as well.
3. This theory was initially suggested by Richard Koszarski in his notes on the film for the 29th Pordenone Silent Film Festival. There is no specific mention in any paper or trade publication at the time of the original film being abandoned in favor of a new structure, and it is possible that the completed film, *His Nibs*, was released as intended. But, given the long delay from the initial announcement of completion of shooting to the final announcement that the film had been completed under its new title, it's not unreasonable to assume that something happened on its way to the theater screen. The different look and feel of *He Got 'Em All* and *His Nibs* also suggests two separate productions.
4. "Comedy Shows Good Cast," *Motion Picture News*, vol. 22 no. 12, September 11, 1920, page 2075.
5. For *Lilac Time*, Colleen would say that she had learned her lines in French and delivered them phonetically, without knowing what they meant.
6. Grace Kingsley, "Flashes," *Los Angeles Times*, September 24, 1920, page III4.
7. Raymond Durgnat and Scott Simmon, *King Vidor, American* (Berkeley: University of California Press, 1988), page 25.
8. Ibid.
9. "King Vidor Believes in Clean Production," *Atlanta Constitution*, October 10, 1920, page A6A.
10. King Vidor, *A Tree Is a Tree* (Hollywood: Samuel French, 1981), page 88.
11. Little is known about the personal life of this activist. In Glen Jeansonne's *Women of the Far Right: The Mothers' Movement and World War II* (Chicago: University of Chicago Press, 1997), page 57, the chapter "Cathrine Curtis and the Women's National Committee to Keep the U.S. Out of War," describes her (in later years) as an "isolationist who fused propaganda with maternalism, feminism, and rabid nationalism ... distinguished by her shrewdness, energy, charisma, combativeness, and talent for organizing."
12. "The Only Woman Producer of Motion Pictures in the United States," *Oneonta Daily Star* (NY), November 8, 1920, page 4.
13. Grace Kingsley, "Flashes," *Los Angeles Times*, September 24, 1920, page III4.
14. "To Be Show Place," *Oakland Tribune*, November 14, 1920, page D-3.
15. Hazel Shelley, "The Young Veteran," *Motion Picture Classic*, January 1921, pages 34–35. Joseph Yranski Collection, *So Long Letty* Clippings Folder.
16. Grace Kingsley, "Flashes; Colleen with Vidor," *Los Angeles Times*, September 24, 1920, page III4.
17. "'Moving the Movies'— The S.P. and Filmland," *Southern Pacific Bulletin*, Southern Pacific Company, vol. 9 no. 6, June 1920, page 8.
18. In *Silent Star*, Colleen only refers to location work in the Truckee area of California. This is also backed up in David Butler and Irene Kahn Atkins, *David Butler* (Issue 5 of Directors Guild of America Oral History Series) (Metuchen, NJ: Scarecrow Press, 1993), page 24, which only mentioned Truckee and Folsom. Newspaper reports of the time also mostly refer to location work in California having been done in Truckee. There were several reports of work done in Canada, with two specific locations — Banff and Wainwright, both in Alberta — being given. Later printed recollections of the experiences of David Butler, Colleen Moore, and King Vidor make no mention of Canada. It is possible that the planned trip to Canada never happened, but the anticipated location still showed up in reportage (either that or a second unit was sent to Canada to shoot scenes). Weather-related difficulties reported in newspapers have the same events occurring in both the Truckee and Canadian locations. To add to the confusion, the same difficulties are described as occurring during both trips to Truckee, depending on when the story is reported. For this chapter, I defer to Colleen's description of the problems arising in Truckee. I split the events between the two trips to Truckee, based on the report in Edwin Schallert's "Radios; Holiday's Theirs" (*Los Angeles Times*, November 25, 1920, page III4), that they were returning north to their original locale because the original conditions were not "sufficiently severe."
19. Grace Kingsley, "Flashes; Vidor Understudies Cook," *Los Angeles Times*, October 1, 1920, page III4.
20. "Easy Costuming," *Los Angeles Times*, October 17, 1920, page III14.
21. "Secures *The Sky Pilot*," *Winnipeg Free Press* (Canada), October 23, 1920, page 45.
22. Butler and Atkins, *David Butler*, page 24.
23. "Auto Parties Are Snowbound," *Los Angeles Times*, October 20, 1920, page I1.
24. Vidor, *A Tree Is a Tree*, page 88.
25. Grace Kingsley, "Flashes," *Los Angeles Times*, October 23, 1920, page I17.
26. "Canadian Snowstorm Cause of Change in Sky Pilot Script," *Atlanta Constitution*, December 12, 1920, page 6F. It should be noted that this story places the events in Canada, in December.
27. Vidor, *A Tree Is a Tree*, page 88.
28. Butler and Atkins, *David Butler*, page 24.
29. Durgnat and Simmon, *King Vidor, American*, page 40.
30. *Hutchinson News* (KS), August 13, 1921, page 9.
31. Butler and Atkins, *David Butler*, page 24.
32. Edwin Schallert, "Radios; Holiday's Theirs," page III4.
33. The suggestion that Colleen and Vidor acted like schoolchildren with a crush comes from Sidney Kirkpatrick's *Cast of Killers* (New York: E. P. Dutton, 1986), pages 36–37. The book, when released, was a source of aggravation to Colleen, who was displeased with the characterization of her relationship with King. Colleen was interviewed by the author on several occasions, in 1984 and 1985, at her home in California, and the manuscript was reportedly submitted to Colleen for review prior to publication. The details mentioned by the author still made it into print. Primarily focusing on King Vidor's search for the killer of director William Desmond Taylor, the book also depicts a relationship between Colleen and King dating back to the filming of *The Sky Pilot*. Their relationship has been called an "infatuation" by Raymond Durgnat and Scott Simmon in *King Vidor, American* (page 25). Several factors would argue against a romance between the two at the time, not the least of which would be a) Colleen's religious convictions; b) her concern for her career and public image; and c) the fact that her mother was present as chaperone (either her mother or grandmother accompanied her to all location work during the early stages of her career, a fact confirmed by Colleen's stepdaughter). People might have whispered about Colleen and King's behavior at the time and speculated on the nature of their relationship, but while their relationship may have been flirtatious it was otherwise chaste.
34. Edwin Schallert, "Not from the

County Mayo," *Los Angeles Times*, November 21, 1920, page II11.
35. "Canadian Snowstorm Cause of Change in Sky Pilot Script," *Atlanta Constitution*, December 12, 1920, page 6F. The second location was reported as Banff in the *Atlanta Constitution*, December 19, 1920, Page 4F.
36. "River Scenes along the San Joaquin Delta Are Exact Duplicates of Those of the Orient," *Oakland Tribune*, November 28, 1920, page 8.

Chapter 14

1. "Finishing Touches on *So Long Letty*," *Motion Picture News*, vol. 22 no. 15, October 2, 1920, page 2667.
2. "Neilan Ties Up on *Dinty*," *Motion Picture News*, vol. 22 no. 6, November 6, 1920, page 3566.
3. *The Little Movie Mirror Books; Colleen Moore* (New York: Ross, 1920).
4. Lillian R. Gale, "Live Notes from the Studios," *Motion Picture News*, vol. 22 no. 26, December 18, 1920, page 4643.
5. "Colleen Moore Recovers," *Los Angeles Times*, January 7, 1921, page II14.
6. The Internet Movie Database (IMDb) lists a Bessie Waters in the cast of the 1916 film *The Female Swindler* in the role of Mary. A November 16, 1923 article in the *Hamilton Daily News* (Ohio) lists her as appearing in a supporting role in *Kindred of the Dust*.
7. Miriam Cooper and Bonnie Herndon, *Dark Lady of the Silents; My Life in Early Hollywood* (Indianapolis, IN: Bobbs-Merrill, 1973), pages 165–166.
8. "Hollywood Hokum," *Motion Picture News*, vol. 22 no. 26, December 18, 1920, page 4648.
9. "First Neilan Release for 1921," *Motion Picture News*, vol. 23 no. 5, January 22, 1921, page 873.
10. "Colleen Moore Cancels Her Trip," *Los Angeles Times*, January 16, 1921, page III43.
11. "Hollywood Hokum," *Motion Picture News*, vol. 23 no. 7, February 5, 1921, page 1207.
12. "'Other Woman' in Neilan Case," *Los Angeles Times*, March 17, 1921, page II10.
13. "Film Maker Neilan Sued for Divorce," *Los Angeles Times*, February 10, 1921, page II1.
14. "Jessen's Studio News by Wire," *Motion Picture News*, vol. 23 no.10, February 26, 1921, page 1710.
15. Moore, *Silent Star*, page 111.
16. James Kotsilibas-Davis, *The Barrymores, The Royal Family in Hollywood* (New York: Crown, 1981), page 34.
17. Jessen's Studio News by Wire," *Motion Picture News*, vol. 23 no. 8, February 12, 1921, page 1353.
18. "*The Sky Pilot* Pleases," *Winnipeg Free Press* (Canada) February 19, 1921, page 26.
19. Jessen's Studio News by Wire," *Motion Picture News*, vol. 23 no. 8, February 12, 1921, page 1353.
20. Frederick James Smith, "The Unsophisticated Colleen," *Motion Picture*, June 1921, pages 54–55, 95.
21. Moore, *Silent Star*, page 113.
22. Mention of the rental of one of Mr. Jones's yachts is in "John Barrymore Visits Everglades Club," *Palm Beach Post* (Florida), March 16, 1921, page 4.
23. Lillian R. Gale, "Live Notes from the Studios," *Motion Picture News*, vol. 23 no. 14, March 26, 1921, page 2249.
24. "John Barrymore Visits Everglades Club," *Palm Beach Post* (Florida), March 16, 1921, page 4.
25. Moore, *Silent Star*, page 111.
26. Jack Kofoed, *Moon Over Miami* (New York: Random House, 1955), page 68.
27. "Miami Is a Wonder Place for Pictures, Mr. Barrymore Says," *Miami News*, March 26, 1921, page 20.
28. Garson Kanin, *Hollywood: Stars and Starlets, Tycoons and Flesh-Peddlers, Moviemakers and Moneymakers, Frauds and Geniuses, Hopefuls and Has-Beens, Great Lovers and Sex Symbols* (New York: Viking Press, 1974), page 47.
29. Ibid.
30. *Miami News*, March 26, 1921, page 8.
31. Michael A. Morrison, *John Barrymore, Shakespearean Actor* (Cambridge [England]: Cambridge University Press, 1999), page 124. No mention of the film is made here, just the opening date; Barrymore would have needed those two weeks for rehearsal. In note number 9 for "Chapter 3. Hamlet, 1922–1924," Morrison states, "During the days in May 1921, while appearing in *Clair de Lune*, Barrymore filmed interior scenes for *The Lotus Eater*."
32. Moore, *Silent Star*, page 113.
33. "Colleen Moore Tells New York Gossip," *Los Angeles Times*, March 14, 1921, page II9.
34. "Colleen in New York," *Oakland Tribune* (CA), March 20, 1921, Entertainment Section page 1.
35. "Miss Moore says New York Stifles Romance," *Pittsburgh Press* (PA), June 19, 1921, page 1.

Chapter 15

1. *Los Angeles Times*, April 17, 1921, page III16.
2. At 851 S. Grand. The Trinity Auditorium, by architects Fitzhugh Krucker & Deckbar, still stands.
3. *Los Angeles Times*, April 17, 1921, page III15.
4. Ibid.
5. Edwin Schallert, "Radios," *Los Angeles Times*, April 29, 1921, page II4.
6. Ibid.
7. Grace Kingsley, "Flashes," *Los Angeles Times*, May 27, 1921, page III4.
8. "Jessen's Studio News by Wire," *Motion Picture News*, vol. 23 no. 24, June 4, 1921, page 3452.
9. *Los Angeles Times*, March 30, 1916, page III4.
10. http://www.actorsfund.org (April 5, 2010).
11. The location is the Hippodrome in the *Picture-Play Magazine* article of September; newspapers gave the location as the Beverly Hills Speedway.
12. "Actors' Benefit Fest to Thrill," *Los Angeles Times*, June 4, 1921, page II9.
13. Herbert Howe, "The Wildest Day in Hollywood," *Picture-Play Magazine*, September 1921, page 24.
14. "News Notes from Movieland," *Olean Evening Herald* (NY), June 24, 1921, page 10.
15. "Hollywood Hokum," *Motion Picture News*, vol. 23 no. 24, June 4, 1921, page 3454.
16. "Jessen's Studio News by Wire," *Motion Picture News*, vol. 23 no. 24, June 4, 1921, page 3452.
17. "Honors John McCormick," *Atlanta Constitution*, June 26, 1921, page D2.
18. "Jessen's Studio News by Wire," *Motion Picture News*, vol. 23 no. 25, June 11, 1921, page 3576.
19. Agnes Morrison, when hearing about Colleen's engagement to John, seems to have known about John's drinking; either word had reached her, or she had discerned the signs. Based on the likelihood that she had heard stories, it therefore seems probable that McCormick had already begun drinking.
20. Mary Virginia, or Virgin Mary?
21. *Natchez Democrat*, July 12, 1921, page 4.
22. *Proceedings of the American Society of Civil Engineers* (volume 46), The Society, 1920, page 623.
23. Thomas Dionysius Clark and John D. W. Guice, *The Old Southwest, 1795–1830: Frontiers in Conflict* (Norman: University of Oklahoma Press, 1996), page 93.
24. *Proceedings of the American Society of Civil Engineers*, page 623.
25. Sylvia Higginbotham, *Marvelous Old Mansions: And Other Southern Treasures* (Winston-Salem, NC: John F. Blair, 2000), page 93.
26. George W. Healy, Jr., *A Lifetime on Deadline* (Gretna, LA: Pelican, 1976), page 12.
27. *Woodville Republican* (MS), July 3, 1920, page 1.
28. Joan W. Gandy and Thomas H. Gandy, *Natchez: City Streets Revisited* (Charleston, SC: Arcadia Publishing, 1999), page 108.
29. Ibid.
30. Mrs. Marie Conway Oemler, *Slippy McGee: Sometimes Known as the

Butterfly Man (New York: Century, 1920), page 6.
31. Gandy and Gandy, *Natchez: City Streets Revisited*, page 99.
32. *Natchez Democrat*, June 19, 1921, page 4.
33. "*Slippy Magee* is Story that Could Have Happened Here," *Natchez Democrat*, June 19, 1921, page 4.
34. "Morosco Company Will Start Shooting Scenes Here Today," *Natchez Democrat*, June 16, 1921, page 3.
35. *Natchez Democrat*, June 19, 1921, page 4.
36. Grace Kingsley, "Natchez Is on the Map," *Los Angeles Times*, August 14, 1921, pages III1, III16.
37. Ibid.
38. "Colleen Moore," *Hamilton Evening Journal* (OH), August 27, 1921, page 6.
39. "Colleen Moore Charmed with Natchez — Says Girls Pretty and Well Dressed," *Natchez Democrat*, June 18, 1921, page 2.
40. "The Colleen Curl," *Atlanta Constitution*, October 2, 1921, page D8.
41. *Natchez Democrat*, June 22, 1921, page 5.
42. *Natchez Democrat*, June 19, 1921, page 4.
43. Ibid.
44. 115 S. Pearl Street, Natchez, MS 39120, Cinema Treasures, http://cinematreasures.org/theater/31644/ (March 6th, 2010).
45. Owned by Eddie Peerson, as reported in the *Democrat*. Prior to *Slippy McGee*, Queenie was in *Peck's Bad Boy*, again with Wheeler Oakman.
46. The third position was considered "top billing," as the first act was staged while the audience was still filing into the venue and the second was performed before a closed stage curtain to warm up the audience and allow the stage hands to erect the sets behind the curtain.
47. "Opportunity Is Given by Motion Pictures," *Natchez Democrat*, June 22, 1921, page 2.
48. Kingsley, "Natchez Is on the Map."
49. Ibid.
50. *Natchez Democrat*, June 19, 1921, page 4.
51. *Natchez Democrat*, June 24, 1921, page 3, et al.
52. *Natchez Democrat*, June 30, 1921, page 2.
53. George W. Healy, Jr., *A Lifetime on Deadline* (Gretna, LA: Pelican, 1976), page 18. The first few chapters give a good description of Natchez, from the point of view of a young man.
54. At a time before the Rural Electrification Administration, even areas near the center of town could still be without either electricity or telephone service.
55. "About *Slippy McGee*," *Indianapolis Star*, January 1, 1922, page 40.
56. "Stormy Weather Not Suited for Motion Picture Robbery," *Natchez Democrat*, July 8, 1921, page 3.
57. *Natchez Democrat*, July 19, 1921, page 4.
58. *Natchez Democrat*, July 22, 1921, page 8.
59. *Natchez Democrat*, July 12, 1921, page 4.
60. *Natchez Democrat*, July 24, 1921, page 1.
61. *Los Angeles Times*, July 10, 1921, page III15.

Chapter 16

1. *Los Angeles Times*, March 31, 1920, page II1.
2. "Movie Censor Law Passed by Miller," *New York Times*, May 15, 1921, page 1; Richard Andress, *Film Censorship in New York State*, New York State Archives, http://www.archives.nysed.gov/a/research/res_topics_film_censor.shtml (March 19, 2010).
3. "Philadelphia to Censor Theaters," *New York Times*, February 1, 1921, page unknown.
4. "Work of Criminals Barred from Moving Pictures in Chicago," *Lima News* (OH), January 1, 1921, page 1.
5. "Hits Picture Censorship," *Los Angeles Times*, February 4, 1921, page II1.
6. "Motion Pictures and Crime," by A. T. Poffenberger, *Scientific Monthly*, American Association for the Advancement of Science, vol. 12 no. 4, April, 1921, page 336–337.
7. This is an argument that continues to the present day, and has expanded beyond motion pictures to television, video games, the internet, and will no doubt carry over into whatever the next big medium is.
8. At least, it would appear to be a string of men. Sightings of Colleen and a gentleman were seldom accompanied by names, and the descriptions were vague. In all likelihood, the men were co-stars, but the idea of a mysterious handsome stranger makes for the most titillating reading.
9. *Ogden Standard-Examiner* (UT), July 3, 1921, page 5, et al.
10. "West Is East, a Few Impressions by Delight Evans," *Photoplay* (vol. 20, no. 2), July 1921, page 51.
11. "When Mickey Neilan lost his studio and went to Goldwyn, he was still so convinced that I was a budding Bernhardt that he sold Rupert Hughes ... on casting me in *The Wall Flower*." Moore, *Silent Star*, page 117.
12. *News-Sentinel* (Fort Wayne, IN), September 18, 1921, Theatrical Section, part 3, page 1.
13. *Los Angeles Times*, July 31, 1921, page III15.
14. *Atlanta Constitution*, July 17, 1921, page 34.
15. Kingsley, "Natchez Is on the Map."
16. "Natchez Resents Opinion of Motion-Picture Star," by A.N. Ryan, *Los Angeles Times*, September 4, 1921, page III28.
17. "Colleen Moore Selected for Difficult Part," *Motion Picture News*, vol. 24 no. 9, August 20, 1921, page 960.
18. Eve Golden, *Golden Images: 41 Essays on Silent Film Stars* (Jefferson, NC: McFarland, 2001), page 99.
19. Colleen — a true aficionado of stories — would have been aware that such narratives are the basis for most fairy tales.
20. "Motion Picture Notes," *New York Times*, January 2, 1921, page X4.
21. "Radios," *Los Angeles Times*, July 21, 1921, page III4.
22. "Film Censors Coming Here," *Los Angeles Times*, August 10, 1921, page II14.
23. *Capital Times* (Madison, WI) August 19, 1921, page 8.
24. Agnes had already allowed Colleen to remain in New York and travel to Florida in Mickey's care, unescorted. Colleen had enough of a social life at that time to be a minor fixture in local social columns. It's doubtful she would have needed permission to go out with Neilan on a simple group date, but this time Neilan did have a man for Colleen to meet.
25. The description of the Sunset Inn, in the opening epigraph in *Laughter Limited*, concludes: "I don't believe I ever really hated jazz except at that moment. Jazz has no business butting in on a person's private troubles." Nina Wilcox Putnam, *Laughter Limited* (New York: A.L. Burt, 1922), page 121.
26. Gulian Lansing Morrill, *On the Warpath* (self-published, 1918), page 195.
27. E. J. Fleming, *Wallace Reid: The Life and Death of a Hollywood Idol* (Jefferson, NC: McFarland, 2007), page 147.
28. *Atlantic City Gazette*, November 20, 1921, Colleen Moore Scrapbook 1 of 36, Margaret Herrick Library, Academy of Motion Picture Arts and Sciences.
29. Grace Kingsley, "Flashes," *Los Angeles Times*, August 12, 1921, page III4.
30. John Kobal, *People Will Talk* (New York: Knopf, 1985), page 29. The other woman is not named.
31. Moore, *Silent Star*, page 114.
32. Kobal, *People Will Talk*, page 29.
33. Ibid.
34. At this time, Colleen was working on *The Wall Flower* with Rupert Hughes. Shooting had not yet begun and would not begin for some weeks. While it was Colleen's habit to be at the studio whenever possible, there would have been little for her to learn or contribute until sets and costumes existed, and rehearsals had begun.

35. "Girl Dead After Wild Party in Hotel," *San Francisco Chronicle*, September 10, 1921, page 1.
36. "Arbuckle Dragged Rappe Girl to Room, Woman Testifies," *New York Times*, September 13, 1921, page 1.

Chapter 17

1. "Movie Facts and Fancies," *Boston Evening Globe*, September 24, 1921, page 10. Also in Colleen Moore Scrapbook 1 of 36, Margaret Herrick Library, Academy of Motion Picture Arts and Sciences.
2. "Jessen's Studio News by Wire," *Motion Picture News*, vol. 24 no. 12, September 10, 1921, page 1376. If this report and the following week's column are correct, the total duration of shooting would have been one week.
3. Kevin Lewis and Arnold Lewis, "Include Me Out: Samuel Goldwyn and Joe Godsol," *Film History*, vol. 2 no. 2, (Bloomington: Indiana University Press, 1988), page 146.
4. An aficionado of stories such as Colleen would have been aware that such narratives are the basis for most fairy tales.
5. Kingsley, "Natchez is on the Map."
6. *Oakland Tribune*, August 28, 1921, page 25.
7. *Oakland Tribune*, September 11, 1921, page W3.
8. "Colleen Moore Reel Accident Victim," *Los Angeles Times*, September 14, 1921, page III4. This was likely the same trick was used in John Ford's *Stagecoach* by stuntman Yakima Canutt; a trench was dug in the center of the road to give the actor the additional clearance needed for safety. The trick has been repeated many times since.
9. Ibid.
10. "Jessen's Studio News by Wire," *Motion Picture News*, vol. 24 no. 13, September 17, 1921, page 1549.
11. Ibid., no. 15, October 1, 1921, page 1770.
12. Ibid., no. 19, October 29, 1921, page 2352.
13. Ibid., no. 20, November 5, 1921, page 2452.
14. Ibid., no. 21, November 12, 1921, page 2576.
15. "Goldwyn Studio Active," *Motion Picture News*, vol. 24 no. 16, October 8, 1921, page 1879.
16. "To Present *His Nibs* Oct. 6," *Motion Picture News*, vol. 24 no 16, October 8, 1921, page 1.
17. *Oakland Tribune*, October 9, 1921, page W3.
18. Grace Kingsley, "Flashes; Goldwyn Gets Ralph Graves," *Los Angeles Times*, October 20, 1921, page III4.
19. *Reading Eagle* (PA), March 13, 1922, page 18.
20. *Atlantic City Gazette*, November 20, 1921, page unknown, Colleen Moore Scrapbook 1 of 36, Margaret Herrick Library, Academy of Motion Picture Arts and Sciences.
21. "Learns the Irish Brogue to Play Part for Screen," *Miami News*, April 22, 1922, page 5.
22. "Shadows on the Screen," *New York Tribune*, December 4, 1921, page C4.
23. "Jessen's Studio News by Wire," *Motion Picture News*, vol. 24 no. 24, December 3, 1921, page 2960.
24. The clipping reads as follows: "Colleen Moore's father, born in Port Huron in 1875, gave up business interests to join daughter last year except for as treasurer of the James E. Morrison Co. of Detroit, production engineers." Saginaw *News-Courier*, December 22, 1921, Colleen Moore Scrapbook 1 of 36, Margaret Herrick Library, Academy of Motion Picture Arts and Sciences. The founder of this Morrison Company does not appear to be directly related to Charles.
25. *Oakland Tribune*, December 25, 1921, Amusement Section, page 1.
26. "Closeups," *Chicago Daily Tribune*, January 11, 1922, page 14.
27. "Another Rupert Hughes Story for Goldwyn," *Motion Picture News*, vol. 25 no. 3, January 7, 1922, page 419. The January 21, 1922 column on page 628b would report that the story had been purchased and that Hughes would direct.
28. Carey Wilson would become a fixture in the Colleen Moore unit at First National.
29. "Jessen's Studio News by Wire," *Motion Picture News*, vol. 25 no. 1, December 24, 1921, page 136.
30. Ibid., no. 8, February 11, 1922, page 1016.
31. Edwin Schallert, "Radios; Hughes as Director," *Los Angeles Times*, February 22, 1922, page III4.
32. Ibid.
33. "Movie Facts and Fancies," *Boston Globe*, February 19, 1922, page 44.
34. Grace Kingsley, "Flashes; Wedding Chimes?" *Los Angeles Times* February 9, 1922.
35. *Los Angeles Times*, March 5, 1922, page II2.
36. Roy Lieberman, *The Wampas Baby Stars, A Biographical Dictionary, 1922–1934* (Jefferson, NC: McFarland, 2000), pages 2–5.
37. "Wampas' Film Revue," *Los Angeles Times*, February 26, 1922, page III9.
38. "Colleen Moore Is Picked for Honors," *Los Angeles Times*, March 12, 1922, page III27.
39. "Attractive *Come On Over* Lobby at Salt Lake City," *Motion Picture News*, vol. 25 no. 18, April 22, 1922, page 2311.
40. Advertisement, *New York Tribune*, March 12, 1922, page C2.
41. Mae Tinee, "Well! Well! Now Here's a Broth of a Picture!" *Chicago Daily Tribune*, March 16, 1922, page 18.
42. Advertisement for Ascher's Merrill Theater, *Milwaukee Journal*, March 12, 1922, page 21.

Chapter 18

1. "Jessen's Studio News by Wire," *Motion Picture News*, vol. 25 no. 14, March 25, 1922, page 1847.
2. "Hard Luck," *Olean Evening Herald* (NY), March 31, 1922, page 6.
3. Grace Kingsley, "Flashes; Colleen Russian Dancer," *Los Angeles Times*, March 23, 1922, page III1.
4. "Novel Act in Hughes Film," *Oakland Tribune* (CA), April 23, 1922, page 4-W.
5. "Here's a Cast," *Atlanta Constitution*, May 14, 1922, page D5.
6. "Makes Her Debut," *Los Angeles Times*, April 13, 1922, page II3.
7. Grace Kingsley, "Flashes," *Los Angeles Times*, May 5, 1922, page III1.
8. "Rupert Hughes is editing *Bitterness of Sweets*," from "Jessen's Studio News by Wire," *Motion Picture News*, vol. 25 no. 19, April 29, 1922, page 2440.
9. "Rupert Hughes Aiming at Titleless Film," *Motion Picture News*, vol. 25 no. 23, May 27, 1922, page 2958.
10. In spite of the novelty of the article's format and the doubtful nature of the quotes, the article offers some interesting insights into the writer's perception of Colleen and gives some useful information regarding her various productions.
11. "Choice Films on the Menu," *Los Angeles Times*, June 11, 1922 page III32.
12. "Colleen Moore Is Bright Wallflower," *Los Angeles Times*, June 12, 1922, page I7.
13. *Picture-Play Magazine*, April 1922, page 57.
14. Gordon Gassaway, "With a Dash of Green," *Motion Picture Magazine*, June 1922, pages 40–41.
15. Ibid.
16. "Goldwyn Names Winners of Scenario Contest," *Motion Picture News*, vol. 25 no. 17, April 15, 1922.
17. "Goldwyn Subjects Finished," *Motion Picture News*, vol. 25 no. 20, May 6, 1922, page 2576.
18. "Holubar to Film Prize Story for Goldwyn, *Motion Picture News*, vol. 25 no. 21, May 13, 1922, page 2688.
19. "Colleen Moore to Lead Prize Picture Cast," *Motion Picture News*, vol. 25 no. 22, May 20, 1922, page 2853.
20. Ibid.

21. Grace Kingsley, "Flashes," *Los Angeles Times*, May 17, 1922, page III1.
22. Mary Roberts Rinehart, *Affinities: and Other Stories* (New York: George H. Doran, 1920), page 11.
23. In the film, an "affinity party" is represented as being like a swingers' party. The short story describes it in a dialog between characters: "Every picnic we've ever had has been a failure — because why? Because they were husband-and-wife picnics. There's no trouble about a picnic where nobody's married, is there?"
"Humph! What's the peach of an idea? To get divorces?"
"Certainly not! Have husbands and wives, only somebody else's husband or somebody else's wife...."
Rinehart, *Affinities: and Other Stories*, page 11.
24. *Deseret News* (UT), July 8, 1922, page V.
25. Grace Kingsley, "Flashes," *Los Angeles Times*, November 18, 1922, page III3.
26. Edwin Schallert, "'Affinities' Is Farce Plus Satire," *Los Angeles Times*, November 20, 1922, page III3.
27. Grace Kingsley, "Flashes," *Los Angeles Times*, July 28, 1922, page I7.
28. Hallet Abend, "An Interview in Verse," *Los Angeles Times*, June 11, 1922, page III15.
29. "Reel Chatter," *News-Sentinel* (Fort Wayne, IN), August 23, 1922, page 16.
30. "Well Known Author Writes Continuity for Prize Scenario," *Deseret News* (UT), May 22, 1922, Section 3, page 5.
31. "Jessen's Studio News by Wire," *Motion Picture News*, vol. 25 no. 26, June 17, 1922, page 3244.
32. "*Broken Chains* Is Laid Among Santa Cruz Trees," *Oakland Tribune*, June 11, 1922, page W-3.
33. *Santa Cruz Daily Surf*, February 16, 1915, page unknown, as quoted in Ann Young's "Early Film Studios in Santa Cruz County," Santa Cruz Public Libraries, http://www.santacruzpl.org/history/articles/295/ (October 13, 2010).
34. Josephine Clifford McCrackin, "Brett Harte in 'The Movies,'" *Overland Monthly*, vol. 65 no. 6, 1915, page 491.
35. "Jessen's Studio News by Wire," *Motion Picture News*, vol. 25 no. 27, June 24, 1922, page 3332.
36. *Oakland Tribune*, June 11, 1922, page W-3.
37. E. J. Fleming, *Paul Bern: The Life and Famous Death of the MGM Director and Husband of Harlow* (Jefferson, NC: McFarland, 2009), page 71.
38. *Los Angeles Times*, Dec 10, 1922, page III33.
39. "Jessen's Studio News by Wire," *Motion Picture News*, vol. 26 no. 7, August 12, 1922, page 714.

Chapter 19

1. May 26, 1917; illustrated by James Montgomery Flagg.
2. "Jessen's Studio News by Wire," *Motion Picture News*, vol. 26 no. 12, September 16, 1922, page 1382.
3. Richard Abel, *Encyclopedia of Early Cinema* (London: Taylor & Francis, 2005), pages 161, 285, 286.
4. "Jessen's Studio News by Wire," *Motion Picture News*, vol. 26 no. 13, September 23, 1922, page 1522.
5. *Oakland Tribune*, October 8, 1922, page W3. Among her "vamp" roles were *The Lure of Woman* (1915) and *The Poison Pen* (1919).
6. "Unusual Picture," *Atlanta Constitution*, October 22, 1922, page D2.
7. "Camera Chatter," *Oakland Tribune*, October 10, 1922, page W-3.
8. "Studio and Player Brevities," *Motion Picture News*, vol. 26 no. 16, October 18, 1922, page 1883.
9. "Colleen Moore Keeps Busy," *St. Petersburg Times* (FL), October 18, 1922, page 9.
10. John would have Colleen follow this same pattern at First National after her ascent to fame with *Flaming Youth*; he knew the novelty of the flapper story would fade if it was not rationed between other types of roles.
11. Gladys Hall, "Flappers Here to Stay, Says Colleen Moore," *Chicago Daily News*, reprinted in *The Flapper* (Flapper Publishing Company, October 1922), page 38.
12. "First National Names Rowland for High Place," *Los Angeles Times*, June 18, 1922, page III33.
13. Certainly these jealousies weren't helped by stories like the following in the *San Antonio Express*, on December 3, 1922, page B15: "Richard Rowland, general manager of Associated First National Pictures, Inc., told a good one on Louis B. Mayer, the producer, at a luncheon gathering of film men in New York the other day. Mr. Mayer, according to Mr. Rowland's narrative, at one time had a theater in Lynn, Mass., that was losing money. He called in his press agent and said: 'Write an advertisement offering the theater for sale.' The p.a., an artist in his line wrote a beautiful 'ad' calling attention to the marvelous bargain, a 2,000-seat house, magnificently equipped, doing a fine business, going for a song. Mr. Mayer, after reading his advertisement, sent for the p.a. and said: 'Take that ad out of the paper at once. After reading it I have decided to keep the theater myself. I had no idea it was so good.'"
14. *First National*, box 15494A, February 23, 1940, Warner Bros. Archives, School of Cinema-Television, University of Southern California.
15. Grace Kingsley, "Flashes," *Los Angeles Times*, May 27, 1922, page II3.
16. "Rowland Is Now Head of Film Circuit," *Los Angeles Times*, October 28, 1922, page III1.
17. "Vitagraph Ill," *Los Angeles Times*, February 28, 1922, page III4.
18. "Vitagraph Builds Semon New Studio," *Los Angeles Times*, January 10, 1922, page III4.
19. "Vitagraph Plans Many Large Films," *Los Angeles Times*, December 9, 1922, page III1.
20. Elizabeth C. Clephane, "The Ninety and Nine," *The Children's Hour*, 1868.
21. Adolph Klauber, "Stray Bits from Stageland," *New York Times*, June 8, 1902, page SM7.
22. "Smith Cast Complete," *Oakland Tribune*, October 15, 1922, page W-3.
23. "Shadows on the Screen," *New York Tribune*, October 15, 1922, page D4.
24. "Press Agents Say," *Miami News-Metropolis*, November 13, 1923, page 11.
25. "Beauty and Grace to Flash across the Silver Screen Here This Week," *Reading Eagle* (PA), February 23, 1923, page 21.
26. "Ninety and Nine Is Thriller," *Motion Picture News*, vol. 26 no. 21, November 18, 1922, page 2567.
27. "Real Forest Fire Filmed for 'The Ninety and Nine,'" *Boston Daily Globe*, January 21, 1923, page 38.
28. "Colleen Moore Is Busy," *Capital Times* (Madison, WI), December 2, 1922, page 14.
29. "'Ninety and Nine' Vintage Picture," *Los Angeles Times*, February 20, 1923, page III1.

Chapter 20

1. *Lima News* (OH), November 28, 1922, page 17.
2. *Indianapolis Star*, January 3, 1923, page 9.
3. Ibid.
4. *Evening Tribune-Times* (Hornell, NY), March 7, 1923.
5. "Studio and Player Brevities," *Motion Picture News*, vol. 26 no. 24, December 9, 1922, page 2917.
6. Ibid., no. 25, December 16, 1922, page 3093.
7. Louis Pizzitola, *Hearst over Hollywood: Power, Passion, and Propaganda in the Movies* (New York: Columbia University Press, 2002), page 212.
8. "Studio and Player Brevities," *Motion Picture News*, vol. 26 no. 23, December 2, 1922, page 2834.
9. *Salt Lake Tribune* (UT), December 3, 1922, page 4.
10. *Deseret News* (UT), December 2, 1922, section III, page 3.
11. "Topics of the Times," *New York Times*, March 20, 1923, page 20.
12. Samuel V. Kennedy, *Samuel Hopkins Adams and the Business of Writing*

(Syracuse: Syracuse University Press, 1999), page 131.
 13. *Flaming Youth* folder 12727, Warner Bros. Archives, School of Cinema-Television, University of Southern California.
 14. "First Nat'l Buys Rights to Flaming Youth," *Motion Picture News*, vol. 27 no. 14, April 17, 1923, page 1669.
 15. *Indianapolis Star*, January 7, 1923, part 6, page 1.
 16. Tom Forman was a cousin of actress Madge Bellamy, who was a friend of Colleen's. Because the two were about the same size, had similar builds and profiles, Madge is often mistaken in still photographs for Colleen.
 17. "Preferred's Technical Staff of Experts," *Motion Picture News*, vol. 27, no. 3, January 20, 1923, page 323.
 18. Grace Kingsley, "Flashes; No More Stars," *Los Angeles Times*, January 11, 1923, page III3.
 19. "Studio and Player Brevities," *Motion Picture News*, vol. 27 no. 6, February 10, 1923, page 747.
 20. "Picture Plays and People," *New York Times*, February 4, 1923, page X3.
 21. "Priscilla Bonner Featured on Return to Screen," *Oakland Tribune*, March 4, 1923, page 48.
 22. *Iola Daily Register* (KS), March 23, 1923, page 2.
 23. Harlan had recently shot *The Beautiful and the Damned*, adapted from F. Scott Fitzgerald's recently published second novel.
 24. Born: Johnny Wilson, alias: Giovanni Francisco Panica, http://boxrec.com/ (October 20, 2010).
 25. Born: Norman Selby, alias: Kid McCoy. His reference at the end of the paragraph to "domestic battling" seems to have been apt, as on August 14, 1924, he shot and killed the married woman with whom he was living, and then went to the husband's store to kill him as well. Finding only employees, he robbed them and shot up the place. He ended up doing a stretch in San Quentin. He was eventually paroled and released. On August 3, 1937, he married Miss Sue Cowley, a distant cousin of Irvin S. Cobb, of *The Smart Aleck* fame. She was his ninth wife.
 26. Born: Louis C. Wallach, alias: The Fighting Dentist.
 27. "Johnny Wilson to Fight in Pictures Before Comeback," *Wisconsin State Journal*, January 21, 1923, page 13.
 28. *San Antonio Express*, February 25, 1923, page B-11.
 29. "'April Showers' to Be Finished Soon," *Los Angeles Times*, March 2, 1923, page III1.
 30. "Colleen Moore Wins Her Wager," *Los Angeles Times*, March 18, 1923, page III27. The pier in Santa Monica, at the end of Hollister Avenue, had once been home to the Café Nat Goodwin — the most beautiful café in the world over the ocean — an elegant eatery frequented by many stars, until it closed, sometime before 1920.
 31. "Studio and Player Brevities," *Motion Picture News*, vol. 27 no. 9, March 3, 1923, page 1090.
 32. "Closeups," *Chicago Daily Tribune*, April 8, 923, page D1.
 33. "MacCurdy in City to Approve of Picture," *Los Angeles Times*, June 7, 1923, page II22.
 34. Colleen only described John pasting her photograph to the mirrors of members of the board of directors, each with a clever saying, but without a doubt John would have made personal efforts, face-to-face, to convince the board members as well.
 35. *Flaming Youth* folder, Memo to: Mr. Spring, from: Mr. Rowland, April 5, 1923,
 36. *First National Franchise*, May–June, 1923.
 37. "Actress is Signed for New Roles," *Los Angeles Times*, May 3, 1923, page II21. Though the story was released on May 3, the contract wasn't signed until May 18.
 38. *Flaming Youth* folder, Story Digest.
 39. "Colleen Moore Starts on Cosmopolitan Vehicle," *Motion Picture News*, vol. 27 no. 19, May 12, 1923, page 2272.
 40. The AFI Silent Catalog lists the director as George Hill, though with the mention of reshoots and completion of the film, the director is reported as Paul Powell, Colleen's director from *Little Orphant Annie*.
 41. *Davenport Democrat and Leader*, August 26, 1923, page 13.
 42. "Picture Plays and People," *New York Times*, October 14, 1923, page X5. Paul Powell is listed as the director.
 43. "Picture Plays and People," *New York Times*, November 18, 1923, page X5. A month earlier, in "*Mother McGinn* Finished," in the *Norwalk Hour* (CT), October 19, 1923, page 20, it was reported that the film had just arrived in New York for editing and that it "is now being prepared for release."
 44. "Activities at United Studios in High Speed," *Los Angeles Times*, June 26, 1923, page II19.
 45. In *Silent Star*, Colleen puts the date of this first disappearance towards the end of 1922, mentioning it as being autumn. However, she also writes that his first disappearance came after she was signed by First National and after John was promoted, which would have been early to mid–1923. Either his first disappearance came earlier than she remembered — before her signing with First National when the weather was still cold enough to have a fire — or the episode with the hot poker came at a later point in time and she associated it with that first disappearance. During the second half of May 1923, the temperatures in Los Angeles averaged between 50 and 70 degrees, based on local weather reports in the *Los Angeles Times* — there were no recorded cold snaps during that period. The episode happened in the evening, so it's possible that Colleen's family had a fire going. A third possibility was that the incident came later, in autumn 1923, immediately before or after John's disappearance on their wedding night. I place the incident after Colleen's signing with First National and John's promotion, and I assume it was late enough in the evening that a fire may have been going. The signing and promotion were important markers and Colleen would have remembered if John's disappearance was before or after.
 46. George Landy was the head of publicity at First National at the time.
 47. Moore, *Silent Star*, page 119.
 48. Ibid., page 120.

Chapter 21

 1. "Production of *Huntress* to Be Started Soon," *Motion Picture News*, vol. 27 no. 21, May 26, 1923, page 2518.
 2. "Studio and Player Brevities," *Motion Picture News*, vol. 27 no. 20, May 19, 1923, page 2418.
 3. Ruth Wing, ed., *The Blue Book of the Screen* (Hollywood, CA: Pacific Gravure Company, 1923), page unknown.
 4. "Film People Active," *Inyo County Register*, June 14, 1923, page 1.
 5. James Van Trees, A. S. C., was reported to have left Los Angeles to work on location for *The Huntress* in the June 1922 issue of *The American Cinematographer*; the July issue had him returning. *The American Cinematographer*, 1922 vol. 3 no. 3, June 1923, page 19; and vol. 3 no. 4, July 1922, page 14. In addition, the "What's Going on at West Coast Studios" column in the *Los Angeles Times* (July 25, 1923, page WF15) listed a release date for *The Huntress* as August 13, roughly three months after Colleen first signed with First National.
 6. "Studio and Player Brevities," *Motion Picture News*, vol. 27 no. 22, June 2, 1923, page 2698.
 7. Clarence A. Hall, *Natural History of the White-Inyo Range, Eastern California* (Berkeley: University of California Press, 1991), page 16.
 8. Moore, *Silent Star*, page 121. Colleen wrote, "It was the middle of winter and cold." However, shooting on *The Huntress* happened in the summer. Given the extremes of the region, however, it is understandable that she would recall it as winter-like.
 9. "Film People Active," *Inyo County Register*, June 14, 1923, page 1.

10. The specific location is not given, so I assume it to be in the general Bishop area. The production moved from location to location, and Bishop seems to be centrally located.
11. "New State Highway Opens Scenic Owens Valley to Motorist," *Los Angeles Times*, July 2, 1925, page A11.
12. Brownlow, *The Parade's Gone By ...*, pages 331, 334.
13. "Film People Active," *Inyo County Register*, June 14th, 1923, page 1.
14. "Money-Mad Indians Give Peaceful Town a Thrill," *Camera* (vol. 6 no. 1), page 11. From Clippings from *CAMERA*, June 30, 1923. Compiled by Joe Moore, with assistance from the special collections staff of Arizona State University, Tempe, Arizona, http://www.slapsticon.org/mugshots/CameraJun3023.htm (February 22, 2010). Also mentioned in "Film People Active," page 1.
15. Unidentified clipping, Colleen Moore Scrapbook 4 of 36, Margaret Herrick Library, Academy of Motion Picture Arts and Sciences.
16. *Boston Traveler*, July 5, 1923, page unknown. Colleen Moore Scrapbook 4 of 36, Margaret Herrick Library, Academy of Motion Picture Arts and Sciences.
17. "What's Going on at West Coast Studios," *Los Angeles Times*, July 18, 1923, page WF15.
18. *Los Angeles Times*, July 25, 1923, page WF14.
19. Her son, Lincoln Stedman, was cast in the part of Donny in *Black Oxen*. "Notes of the Film," *New York Times*, September 16, 1923, page X4.
20. *New York Times*, November 21, 1923, page 22.
21. "Pittsburgh Heiress Who Says Society Is Headed for a Smash Passes Up Its Frivolities to Work as 'Movie' Extra,'" *Pittsburgh Press* (PA), September 4, 1923, page 24.
22. "Contest Winner in *Flaming Youth*," *Oakland Tribune*, September 16, 1923, page W-3.
23. "Logansport Beauty Gets Job in Film," *Indianapolis Star*, September 2, 1923, page 37.
24. "Prize Beauty Arrives," *Oakland Tribune*, September 9, 1923, page W-4.
25. "Scores of Beauties in *Flaming Youth*," *Washington Post*, August 12, 1923, page 42.
26. Identified in *Silent Star* as Malibu Beach. For many years there were very few roads into this isolated beach in western Los Angeles.
27. Derived from the Gaelic *a leanbh* (O child). Teresa Norman, *A World of Baby Names* (New York: Perigee, 2003), page 299.
28. Moore, *Silent Star*, page 130.
29. "Film Idyll Culminates," *Los Angeles Times*, August 18, 1923, page II8.
30. "Colleen Moore Weds Film Man," *Los Angeles Times*, August 19, 1923, page II5.
31. "Film Idyll Culminates," page II8.
32. *Los Angeles City Directory*, 1923, v.1923, page 2213. Also, Santa Clara University records list his address from 1921–1922 as 1231 Gramercy Pl., Los Angeles, California.
33. Moore, *Silent Star*, pages 131–132.
34. *Love Never Dies* was the title of King Vidor's first film after *The Sky Pilot*. It was the working title for Colleen's film *Lilac Time*.
35. Oliver Reginald Taviner, "*The Huntress* Goes Far to Bag a Husband," *Los Angeles Times*, August 15, 1923, page WF5.
36. Jack Jungmeyer, "Latest Film Adds Little to Colleen Moore's Fame," *Evening Independent* (St. Petersburg, FL), August 18, 1923, page 3.
37. "Ban on Studio Visitors Complete," *Laredo Times* (TX), November 2, 1923, page 2.
38. *New York Telegraph*, September 30, 1923, page unknown. Colleen Moore Scrapbook 2 of 36.
39. Grace Kingsley, "Flashes; Colleen Moore Honeymoons," *Los Angeles Times*, October 5, 1923, page II11. Also mention of their late honeymoon spent at the Grand Canyon in "Movie Facts and Fancies," *Boston Daily Globe*, October 20, 1923, page 6.
40. *Los Angeles Examiner*, October 21, 1923, page unknown. Colleen Moore Scrapbook 2 of 36.
41. "Colleen Is Given Part as Hoyden," *Oakland Tribune*, October 14, 1923, Amusement section, page 1.
42. *Los Angeles Times*, October 24, 1923, page WF15.
43. *First National*, page 35, box 15494A, February 23, 1940, Warner Bros. Archives in the University of Southern California's School of Cinematic Arts.

Chapter 22

1. *Lodi News*, March 5, 1923, page unknown, Colleen Moore Scrapbook 4 of 36.
2. "Clara Bow Due Today to Work for 'Maytime,'" *Los Angeles Times*, July 20, 1923, page II8.
3. The timing here is based on the assumption that Clara's work on *Black Oxen* was finished in mid– to late–October, and that she had moved on to *The Swamp Angel*. The *St. Petersburg Evening Independent* (FL), on October 12, 1923, page 10, reported: "Clara Bow, a brunette high school athlete, 17, has been selected by Frank Lloyd, screen producer, to play the role of Janet Oglethorpe, in his production, 'Black Oxen.'" The date Charlotte Merriam was scheduled to join the production (presumably to replace Clara) was November, as reported in "She made the Grade at One Jump," *Los Angeles Times*, November 23, 1923, page II10: "Charlotte Merriam, who was this week added to the cast of 'The Swamp Angel,' being directed by Clarence Badger and featuring Colleen Moore."
4. Joe Morella and Edward Z. Epstein, *The "It" Girl: The Incredible Story of Clara Bow* (New York: Delacorte Press, 1976), page 59.
5. Given that Colleen was aware of how much help she had received on the way up through the ranks in the movie industry, and how loyal she had been to people she had worked with, it is doubtful she would have acted so vindictively towards an actress in what was, essentially, a bit part.
6. Moore, *Silent Star*, page 147. It is unlikely that Colleen would have barred Clara from a close-up, knowing it might help another actress. She had been helped by other actors in her early years, and would help others herself.
7. Joshua Zeitz, *Flapper: A Madcap Story of Sex, Style, Celebrity, and the Women who Made America Modern* (New York: Crown, 2007), page 238.
8. Unknown clipping, November 11, 1923, page unknown, Colleen Moore Scrapbook, 4 of 36.
9. Program from Joseph Yranski Collection.
10. "Threaten Writ to Stop Film *Flaming Youth*," *Capital Times* (Madison, WI), November 21, 1923, page 1.
11. "Seattle Censors File in *Flaming Youth* Act," *New York Telegraph*, March 2, 1923, page unknown, Colleen Moore Scrapbook 3 of 36.
12. "Hackensack Women Oppose Film," *New Brunswick, New Jersey Home News*, January 17, 1924, page unknown, Colleen Moore Scrapbook 3 of 36.
13. Helen Klumph, "Colleen's Flapper Queen," *Los Angeles Times*, December 12, 1923, page II3.
14. The trip had initially been announced in the papers after their wedding, planned after the finish of *The Swamp Angel*: "The couple will go East to New York and other Atlantic Coast cities for a protracted stay." Their home, after September 1, was at 389 South Bronson Avenue. "Colleen Moore Weds Film Man," *Los Angeles Times*, August 19, 1923, page II5.
15. No such movie was ever made, at least not bearing that title.
16. *New York Film Weekly*, November 29, 1923, page unknown, Colleen Moore Scrapbook 2 of 36.
17. Colleen Moore Scrapbook 4 of 36.
18. "'The Demi-Virgin' Ban Is Upheld in Court," *New York Times*, January 4, 1922, page 9.
19. Helen Klumph, "Colleen's Flap-

per Queen," *Los Angeles Times*, December 12, 1923, page I13.

20. Presumably, this is all invention: there was no mention of John McCormick in the *Atlanta Constitution* between 1905 and 1915, at least none that would seem to apply to John Emmett McCormick. Nor was there any mention of a James or Jane (or Jean) McCormick as a resident of the city during that period. Nor does this information seem to correspond with the movements of the McCormick family, as documented elsewhere.

21. "Motion Picture Star Here for Visit on Honeymoon, *Atlanta Constitution*, November 28, 1923, page 25.

22. *New York Motion Picture News*, December 22, 1923, page unknown, Colleen Moore Scrapbook 2 of 36.

23. "Picture Plays and People," *New York Times*, December 16, 1923, page X5.

24. *New York Motion Picture News*, December 19, 1923, Colleen Moore Scrapbook 2 of 36.

25. "Picture Plays and People," *New York Times*, December 16, 1923, page X5.

26. *New York Motion Picture News*, December 22, 1923, Colleen Moore Scrapbook 2 of 36.

27. "Colleen Happily Married," *Los Angeles Times*, December 18, 1923, page I4.

28. *Chicago Herald-Examiner*, December 19, 1923, page unknown, Colleen Moore Scrapbook 2 of 36. Presumably a reference to a Chicago and Northwestern Railroad named passenger car, there are no other references to it; it could have been a one-time run.

29. Moses Finkelstein and Isaac Ruben.

30. *Minneapolis Tribune*, December 21, 1923, page unknown, Colleen Moore Scrapbook 2 of 36.

31. Eleanor Very, "Right Off the Reel," undated clipping in the Colleen Moore Scrapbook 2 of 36.

32. *Sailors' Wives* was made in 1928 by First National, directed by Joseph E. Henabery, and starring Mary Astor, based on the Samuel Hopkins Adams book, which had been serialized in *Telling Tales*. Set in the same fictional town as *Flaming Youth*, Dorrisdale, it used characters from *Flaming Youth*.

33. "Honeymooners Come Home," *Los Angeles Times*, December 27, 1923, page II10.

Chapter 23

1. *Times*, March 3, 1924, city and page unknown. Colleen Moore Scrapbooks, 4 of 36.

2. This was a visit to a sanitarium, for her physical health, and not a sanatorium for mental health. Milk cures were a common rejuvenating treatment, using raw milk, rich in butterfat (the only milk commonly available in its day). The diet is a detoxifier and provided nutrient-dense feeding at the same time. Elizabeth A. Monaghan, *What to Eat and How to Prepare It* (New York: George H. Doran Company, 1922), pages 165–166.

3. Inez Klumph, "The Film Flapper Says," *Washington Post*, February 26, 1924, page 11.

4. *Sioux City Journal*, March 13, 1924, page 20.

5. Alma Whitaker, "Modern Girl Craves More Attention," *Los Angeles Times*, March 23, 1924, page B22.

6. Karl Vollmoeller, "Notes of the Cinema," *New York Times*, April 6, 1924, page X4.

7. Jack Jungmeyer, "Colleen Moore Depicts Flapper Type Again," *Steubenville Herald Star* (OH), May 23, 1924, page 18.

8. Alma Whitaker, "Modern Girl Craves More Attention," *Los Angeles Times*, March 23, 1924, page B22.

9. Santa Clara College records, 4RS, Student Records, 1910–1940, Carton 36, Mendeiros to Mulholland.

10. Braven Dyer, "Off to a Flying Start," *Los Angeles Times*, April 20, 1924, page 13.

11. Grace Kingsley, "Flashes; Picture Athletes Compete," *Los Angeles Times*, May 3, 1924, page 13.

12. "Stage Olympic Swim Trials in Pasadena Tank," *Los Angeles Times*, May 11, 1924, page 13.

13. Frank B. Howe, "Kegeris Easy Victor," *Los Angeles Times*, May 18, 1924, page 11.

14. "Hollywood Stars to Swimming Meet," *Los Angeles Times*, May 24, 1924, page 12.

15. *Oakland Tribune*, June 15, 1924, page W-3.

16. Also directed by John Francis Dillon, this is a story of divorce and temptation, with Corinne losing custody of her child, Rose, when her husband leaves her. A model, she refuses temptation when it is presented in the form of a wealthy suitor, who is, in fact, testing her. When he helps her regain custody of her daughter, love flourishes.

17. A complicated story of love and loss, Claire Windsor is pulled between the wishes of her father and her own desire to marry her true love. Embezzlement, financial hardships, social disgrace, and accidental death all play into this story which culminates with Claire taking poison, only to be saved by her true love.

18. "Producers Will Again Specialize in Society Plays," *Oakland Tribune*, April 27, 1924, Amusement section, page 1.

19. This based on a First National document outlining highlights of Colleen's contracts (Excerpt of Colleen Moore's Old Contracts, folder #2727, Warner Bros. Archives, School of Cinema-Television, University of Southern California), which makes mention of a November 1924 amendment increasing Colleen's salary by $800 to a total of $2,000 per week, making her base salary at the time $1,200 per week.

20. Mae Tinee, "Why a Flapper Flaps Herein Is Explained," *Chicago Daily Tribune*, June 10, 1924, page 21.

21. "The Screen," *New York Times*, June 23, 1924, page 22.

22. "Stars Depict 'Flapper' at Metropolitan," *Washington Post*, July 6, 1924, page AA2.

23. An accounting of the earnings of Colleen's pictures, dated December 31, 1928, lists to total earnings, domestic and foreign, for *Flaming Youth* as $798,777. *Painted People* earned $426,330.76, just over half of *Flaming Youth*, while *Perfect Flapper* earned $531,008.56. Colleen Moore Legal File 13100A, Warner Bros. Archives, School of Cinema-Television, University of Southern California.

24. "From the Studio's Paint and Powder to the Theatre's Shadow," *New York Times*, June 22, 1924, page X2.

25. Grace Kingsley, "Flashes; Many New Ones," *Los Angeles Times*, May 10, 1924, page 13.

26. Mae Tinee, "Alienist Falls for Vamping in This Movie," *Chicago Daily Tribune*, August 19, 1924, page 15. Description of story comes from this article and other sources.

27. "Two at United," *Los Angeles Times*, May 8, 1924, page A11.

28. "Flapper Ball," *Los Angeles Times*, June 24, 1924, page A11.

29. "Will Welcome Some New Ways to Wear Hair," *Los Angeles Times*, May 19, 1924, page A7.

30. Unknown clipping, Colleen Moore Scrapbook 4 of 36.

31. *Cumberland Times*, July 12, 1924, page unknown. Colleen Moore Scrapbook 4 of 36.

32. *Davenport Democrat and Leader* (IA), September 14, 1924, page 17.

33. Moore, *The Story of My Life*, page 22.

34. In 1924, *So Big* would win the Pulitzer Prize.

35. J. E. Smyth and Thomas Schatz, *Edna Ferber's Hollywood: American Fictions of Gender, Race, and History* (Austin: University of Texas Press, 2009), pages 31–32.

36. Ibid. Smyth and Schatz identify the studio as Warner Bros. However, there were several versions of the film made over the years, and Warner Bros. was the successor to First National.

37. "Voice of the Fan; Blaming the Director," *Chicago Daily Tribune*, October 19, 1924, page E4.

38. Myrtle Gebhart, "Colleen For-

swears New Role, *Los Angeles Times*, May 18, 1924, page 19.
  39. "Odd Facts," *Oakland Tribune*, June 15, 1924, page W-3.
  40. Grace Kingsley, "Flashes; Charles Brabin to Direct Colleen Moore," *Los Angeles Times*, July 16, 1924, page A9.
  41. Brownlow, *The Parade's Gone By* ..., pages 391–395.
  42. "Closeups," *Chicago Daily Tribune*, July 16, 1924, page 21.
  43. "Colleen Moore Started New Film," *Davenport Democrat and Leader*, August 24, 1924, page 28.
  44. Smyth and Schatz, *Edna Ferber's Hollywood*, pages 52–53.
  45. Ibid., pages 50–52.
  46. "Milla Davenport to Support Moore," *San Antonio Light*, October 19, 1924, part 3, page 9.
  47. Moore, *The Story of My Life*, page 23.

Chapter 24

  1. Grace Kingsley, "Flashes; Colleen Moore Another Flapper," *Los Angeles Times*, September 17, 1924, page A11.
  2. "Huge Film Pact Planned," *Los Angeles Times*, October 14, 1924, page A1.
  3. "Film Corporation Moves," *New York Times*, October 18, 1924, page 18.
  4. Helen Klumph, "Hudson Settles in East," *Los Angeles Times*, October 26, 1924, page C19.
  5. "Eastern Film Boom Is Over," *Los Angeles Times*, October 13, 1924, page A16.
  6. "Studio Exodus Rumor Killed," *Los Angeles Times*, October 20, 1924, page A5.
  7. Excerpt of Colleen Moore's Old Contracts, file #2727, Warner Bros. Archives, School of Cinema-Television, University of Southern California.
  8. Bernard L. Peterson, "Sally in our Alley," *A Century of Musicals in Black and White: An Encyclopedia of Musical Stage Works By, About, or Involving African Americans* (Westport, CT: Greenwood, 1993), page 303.
  9. Ethan Mordden, *Ziegfeld: The Man Who Invented Show Business* (New York: St. Martin's Press, 2008), page 194.
  10. Alexander Woollcott, "The Play," *New York Times*, December 22, 1920, page 19.
  11. "Leon Errol in 'Sally,'" *Los Angeles Times*, October 30, 1924, page A9.
  12. Grace Kingsley, "Flashes; Leon Errol Among Us," *Los Angeles Times*, November 1, 1924, page A9.
  13. "Film Actor Was on Roman Stage," *Los Angeles Times*, November 23, 1924, page C34.
  14. Grace Kingsley, "Flashes; Al Green Gets Atmosphere," *Los Angeles Times*, November 21, 1924, page A9.
  15. "Star's New Garb Gives Extras Joy," *Los Angeles Times*, November 30, 1924, page C27.
  16. Moore, *Silent Star*, page 174.

Chapter 25

  1. Mae Tinee, "'So Big' Isn't So Big in Film as in Story," *Chicago Daily Tribune*, January 7, 1925, page 17.
  2. Mordaunt Hall, "The Screen," *New York Times*, January 5, 1925, page 19.
  3. "Colleen Moore on Location in Mojave Desert," *Oakland Tribune*, February 15, 1925, page 2W.
  4. "*The Desert Flower* Blooms at Longacre," *New York Times*, November 19, 1924, page 18.
  5. "Colleen Moore on Location in Mojave Desert," *Oakland Tribune*, February 15, 1925, page 2W.
  6. "Cup for Ex-Baby Stars," *Los Angeles Times*, February 3, 1925, page A9.
  7. Kenneth Taylor, "Stage Set for Wampas Frolic," *Los Angeles Times*, February 1, 1925, page 17.
  8. There is no mention of being in a cast at that point, and given that the cast she wore severely restricted her movement, it's doubtful she had been to the doctor yet.
  9. *Oelwein Daily Register* (IA), March 10, 1925, page 3.
  10. Moore, *Silent Star*, pages 251–252.
  11. Grace Kingsley, "Flashes; Colleen Moore Improves," *Los Angeles Times*, February 6, 1925, page A9.
  12. Colleen Moore, "Speaking of Hospitals—Well!" journal and page numbers unknown, 1925, Colleen Moore Scrapbook 6 of 36.
  13. "Receives Film Award in Bed," *Los Angeles Times*, February 10, 1925, page 22.
  14. Grace Kingsley, "Tea-cup Tête-à-tête with Stella, the Star-Gazer," *Los Angeles Times*, February 11, 1925, page C10.
  15. "Queen Has Nothing on Colleen Moore," *Kingsport Times* (TN), May 25, 1925, page 4.
  16. Grace Kingsley, "Tea-cup Tête-a-tête with Stella, the Star-Gazer."
  17. Moore, *Silent Star*, page 139.
  18. "'We Moderns' Purchased for Colleen Moore," *Milwaukee Sentinel*, May 18, 1925, page 8.
  19. Meri-Jane Rochelson, *A Jew in the Public Arena: The Career of Israel Zangwill* (Detroit: Wayne State University Press, 2008), page 130.
  20. Colleen Moore Controversy, *Irene*, page 4, Warner Bros. Archives, School of Cinema-Television, University of Southern California.
  21. Produced by Carle Carlton and Joseph McCarthy with book by James Montgomery; music by Harry Tierney; lyrics by Joseph McCarthy; based on a play by James Montgomery; the musical director was Gus Salzer; it was staged by Edward Royce. http://www.ibdb.com/production.php?id=6724 (December 2, 2010).
  22. Colleen Moore Controversy, *Irene*, page 4.
  23. Appeared in *The Saturday Evening Post* on July 14, 1923. It was filmed as *Man Crazy* in 1927, starring Dorothy Mackaill and Jack Mulhall.
  24. Grace Kingsley, "Flashes; Big Doings," *Los Angeles Times*, April 15, 1925, page A9.
  25. Grace Kingsley, "Flashes; Colleen Moore Better," *Los Angeles Times*, March 20, 1925, page A9.
  26. She would wear a neck brace at night for the rest of her life.
  27. "McCormick and Colleen Moore to Tour Europe," *Oakland Tribune*, April 19, 1925, page 3W.
  28. Helen Klumph, "Manhattan Likes Colleen in *Sally*," *Los Angeles Times*, March 22, 1925, page 22.
  29. "Colleen Moore at Capitol," *Reading Eagle* (PA), November 28, 1925, page 12.

Chapter 26

  1. "Colleen Moore, Husband Start European Trip," *Los Angeles Times*, April 23, 1925, page A1.
  2. *San Francisco Bulletin*, April 24, 1925, page unknown, Colleen Moore Scrapbook Travelogue Clippings, Scrapbook 5 of 36.
  3. *Omaha News* (NE), June 27, 1925, page unknown, Colleen Moore Scrapbook Travelogue Clippings, Scrapbook 5 of 36, Margaret Herrick Library.
  4. "Colleen Moore Visits City," *Chicago News*, April 27, 1925, page unknown, Colleen Moore Scrapbook Travelogue Clippings, Scrapbook 5 of 36.
  5. Of course, if Colleen had worked as an extra in mob scenes, as she was reported as saying in the previous quote, it is unlikely that she would have been invited to view rushes, and even less likely that her mother would have been included in the invitation. And while the family supported Colleen's career once she had established herself, they had been initially wary of acting as a career for her.
  6. Paul T. Gilbert, "Colleen Moore, Flapper of Films, Returns to City," *Chicago Post*, April 26, 1925, page unknown, Colleen Moore Scrapbook Travelogue Clippings, Scrapbook 5 of 36.
  7. *Washington Herald* (D.C.) April 26, 1925, page unknown, Colleen Moore Scrapbook Travelogue Clippings, Scrapbook 5 of 36.
  8. *Variety* (NY), April 29, 1925,

page unknown, Colleen Moore Scrapbook Travelogue Clippings, Scrapbook 5 of 36.
9. John J. Daly, "Up and Down the Aisle," *Washington Post*, April 29, 1925, page 8.
10. *Baltimore News*, April 30, 1925, page unknown, Colleen Moore Scrapbook Travelogue Clippings, Scrapbook 5 of 36.
11. Helen Klumph, "Broadway's Lure Draws Film Stars," *Los Angeles Times*, May 3, 1925, page 21.
12. *New York American*, April 30, 1925, page unknown, Colleen Moore Scrapbook Travelogue Clippings, Scrapbook 5 of 36.
13. *Baltimore News*, April 30, 1925, page unknown, Colleen Moore Scrapbook Travelogue Clippings, Scrapbook 5 of 36, Margaret Herrick Library, Academy of Motion Picture Arts and Sciences.
14. *New York American*, May 1, 1925, page unknown, Colleen Moore Scrapbook Travelogue Clippings, Scrapbook 5 of 36.
15. Passengers Bet as Big Liners Sail, *New York Times*, May 3, 1925, page E2.
16. Mohammed Said Zerdechino. The "Emir" was known in the fancier hotels and restaurants of both New York and London as an impostor who passed himself off as royalty, checking himself into expensive hotels, eating and drinking lavishly, and making expensive purchases from high-end shops. He was seldom asked for payment up front — he was, after all, considered to be quite an important personage — and tended to disappear when management began to lean on him for a down payment towards services rendered. "Born in Morocco, he had immigrated to the New World at an early age, and got a job in a valeting-service shop as a 'pants presser'.... [In New York] ... he first announced himself as the 'Emir'.... The charlatan preyed upon hotel-keepers as he had done in London, until the managers found his particular form of Royalty was singularly minus a chequebook." Harold Brust, *I Guarded Kings: The Memoirs of a Political Police Officer* (New York: Hillman-Curl, 1936), pages 137–139. The scam was not unlike the one Colleen's character would pull in *Her Wild Oat*.
17. "6,000 to Sail Today on 12 Steamships," *New York Times*, May 2, 1925, page 24.
18. "'Woe to America!' Says 'Emir' Leaving," *New York Times*, May 3, 1925, page 22.
19. "Colleen Moore Well, Thanks," *Los Angeles Times*, May 6, 1925, Page A9.
20. *Schenectady Union Star*, May 23, 1925, page unknown, Travelogue Clippings, Scrapbook 5 of 36.
21. *Newcastle Chronicle and North Mail*, May 9, 1925, page unknown, Colleen Moore Scrapbook Travelogue Clippings, Scrapbook 5 of 36.
22. *Motion Picture News*, June 13, 1925, page unknown, Colleen Moore Scrapbook Travelogue Clippings, Scrapbook 5 of 36.
23. *Manchester Guardian*, November 7, 1924, page 1.
24. *Staffordshire Sentinel*, January 24, 1925, page 1.
25. *Times of India*, February 24, 1925, page 12.
26. The news accounts of the visit often vary, making it difficult to determine the exact itinerary from news sources alone.
27. "Colleen Moore Is Back from Europe," *Davenport Democrat and Leader* (IA), July 19, 1925, page 16.
28. Menu, "Dinner of Welcome," Savoy Hotel, from the Joseph Yranski copllection.
29. Moore, *Silent Star*, page 136.
30. *Glasgow Weekly Record*, May 23, 1925, page unknown, Colleen Moore Scrapbook Travelogue Clippings, Scrapbook 5 of 36.
31. *Sketch*, June 3, 1925, page unknown, Colleen Moore Scrapbook Travelogue Clippings, Scrapbook 5 of 36.
32. Menu from Travelogue Clippings, Scrapbook 5 of 36.
33. In *Silent Star*, Colleen says that while they were going to relax in Lucerne, Switzerland, after the filming of the scenes for *We Moderns*, but instead they went to Zurich. It is doubtful that they were making decisions as to which destination they should visit during the trip; it was all choreographed ahead of time, and only an emergency would have caused a change in the schedule. In *The Story of My Life*, she says they did indeed visit Lucerne, calling the time (on page 24) "two ideal weeks." The exact order of cities given in some articles indicate the visit to Switzerland came later in the tour, but an examination of dates shows several weeks between their arrival in England, and their arrival in Paris, of approximately the duration Colleen described.
34. From translation of article in film paper *Estrade*, 1925, page unknown, Margaret Herrick Library, Academy of Motion Picture Arts and Sciences.
35. Moore, *Silent Star*, pages 138–139.
36. Ibid., page 137.
37. In *Silent Star*, Colleen has blurred together two separate events: her cross-country tour of the United States to promote *Flaming Youth*, and the European tour to promote *So Big*. In *Silent Star*, she describes the events of her European tour as being a promotion for *Flaming Youth*. However, *Flaming Youth* had already opened and was playing in Europe.
38. *Cinema*, June 4, 1925.
39. In *Silent Star*, she says she gave a speech, but in *The Story of My Life* she says she did *not* give a speech — she only bowed from the box.
40. The plucking of the feathers was a story confirmed by Colleen's daughter Judy in an interview in November 2010.
41. *Boston Post*, June 24, 1925, page unknown, Colleen Moore Scrapbook Travelogue Clippings, Scrapbook 5 of 36.
42. *Boston Post*, June 24, 1925, page unknown, Travelogue Clippings, Scrapbook 5 of 36.
43. "Film in Trafalgar Square," *Daily Express*, June 29, 1925, page unknown, Colleen Moore Scrapbook 7 of 36.
44. "First National Now Shooting at Full Speed," *Los Angeles Times*, July 8, 1925, page A9.
45. "Mammoth Set Built for Use in 'We Moderns,'" *Los Angeles Times*, August 15, 1925, page 7.
46. Grace Kingsley, "Flashes," *Los Angeles Times*, July 2, 1925, page A9.
47. "Studio and Stage," *Los Angeles Times*, August 5, 1925, page A9.
48. Grace Kingsley, "Flashes; United Works Hard," *Los Angeles Times*, July 23, 1925, page A7.
49. "Fox Buys Interest in 120 Playhouses," *New York Times*, July 9, 1925, page 3.
50. "History of First National," Warner Bros. Archives, School of Cinema-Television, University of Southern California.
51. "Colleen Moore Forms Own Production Unit; John McCormick Will Direct Star in Twelve Big Features," unidentified newspaper clipping, August 1925, page unknown, Colleen Moore Scrapbook 7 of 36.
52. "Excerpt of Colleen Moore's Old Contracts," Colleen Moore legal files #2727.
53. Letters of July 9 and 10, 1925, Colleen Moore Legal File #2727, folder 6 of 7.
54. Colleen Moore contract, Colleen Moore Legal File #2727.
55. Letters of July 9 and 10, 1925, Colleen Moore Legal File #2727, folder 6 of 7.
56. Codenames are used in the report for various individuals here: "Verse" is June Mathis; "Model" is Colleen Moore; "Lumber" is John McCormick; and "Cups" is Richard Rowland.
57. Production letter to: Ray Rockett, from: unknown, Colleen Moore Controversy, *Irene* page 4.
58. Grace Kingsley, "Flashes," *Los Angeles Times*, July 17, 1925, page A11.
59. "McCormick Promoted at Studio," *Los Angeles Times*, July 17, 1925, page A9.

Chapter 27

1. History of First National, Box 15494a, pages 36–40, Warner Bros. Archives, School of Cinema-Television, University of Southern California.
2. Ibid., p. 46.
3. "Three New Stocks Listed by Exchange," *New York Times*, June 11, 1925, page 28.
4. History of First National, Box 15494a, page 36.
5. *Movie Magazine*, October 1925, page 68, Joseph Yranski Collection, *Irene* Clippings Folder.
6. In her writing, Colleen gives the impression that from the time of her wedding John was responsible for the direction of Colleen's career and that events during their marriage took her by surprise. However, this message implies that the idea to use *Twinkletoes* as a vehicle had its roots with Colleen. At a minimum, it shows that Colleen had a hand in the decision-making in her career, and later archival material will show she was very active in the decisions affecting her career.
7. Wire to: Rowland, from: McCormick, August 26, 1925, Colleen Moore Controversy, page 12.
8. Distributed by United Artists and premiered on May 13, 1919, it starred Lillian Gish, Richard Barthelmess and Donald Crisp. Unlike Griffith's earlier grand-scale productions, *Broken Blossoms* was small and intimate.
9. Colleen Moore Controversy, Folder #16079B.
10. "New Picture by Colleen Moore to Be in Color," *Los Angeles Times*, November 15, 1925, page C39.
11. Production letter to: Ray Rockett, from: unknown, Colleen Moore Controversy, *Irene* page 4.
12. *San Francisco Examiner*, September 27, 1925, page unknown, Colleen Moore Scrapbooks 9 of 36.
13. *Los Angeles Record*, October 12 (and 14), 1925, pages unknowns, Colleen Moore Scrapbooks 9 of 36.
14. P.J. Schulte; Designer/Contractor/Builder, 3516 W. Washington St., Los Angeles, Cal., EMpire 4960, Colleen Moore Bungalow #2727A.
15. Description from notice of completion, September 4, 1925, Colleen Moore Bungalow #2727A.
16. Letter to: M.C. Leevee, from: C.P Butler, September 11th, 1925, Warner Bros. Archives, School of Cinema-Television, University of Southern California.
17. *Photoplay*, May 1926, page unknown. Joseph Yranski Collection.
18. Moore, *Silent Star*, pages 149–151.
19. *Hollywood Citizen*, August 14, 1926, page unknown, Colleen Moore Scrapbook 10 of 36.
20. Frank Cullen, *Vaudeville, Old & New: An Encyclopedia of Variety Performers in America*, Volume 1 (New York: Routledge, 2007), page 652.
21. "Colleen Starts Work on *Irene*," *Charleston Gazette* (WV), October 25, 1925, page 6.
22. "None but Beauties to Support Colleen," *Sioux City Journal* (IA), October 18, 1925, page 24.
23. Colleen Moore Controversy, page 8.
24. Ibid., pages 5–7.
25. *Los Angeles Herald*, January 20, 1926, page unknown, Colleen Moore Scrapbooks 9 of 36.
26. "'Shebo' Is Colleen's Next Opus," *Los Angeles Times*, December 13, 1925, page C29.
27. As told to Joseph Yranksi by Charles Plumb, repeated to author January 31, 2011.
28. *Ella Cinders* folder 12726A, Title: *Ella Cinders*, Author: William Conselman, and Charles Plum. Warner Bros. Archives, School of Cinema-Television, University of Southern California.
29. Colleen Moore Controversy, page 9.

Chapter 28

1. "Gigantic Film Merger Planned," *Harrison Times* (AR), January 15, 1926, page 3.
2. "Schulberg Joins Lasky," *Los Angeles Times*, October 25, 1925, page 6.
3. "Famous Players Buy Big Studio in Hollywood," *Oakland Tribune*, January 5, 1926, page 4.
4. Scott Eyman, *Empire of Dreams: The Epic Life of Cecil B. DeMille* (New York: Simon & Schuster, 2010), page 481. This was the first of several moves the nomadic barn would make. It was dedicated Landmark Number 554 in 1956, and in October 1975 it was moved to Vine Street. In the early 1980s it was moved again, this time to 2100 North Highland Avenue, where it currently serves as the Hollywood Heritage Museum in the Lasky-DeMille Barn. Marc Wanamaker, *Hollywood 1940–2008* (Charleston, SC: Arcadia, 2009), page 54.
5. "Hamilton to Have No Part in Theatre Combination," author's name illegible, Managing Director, Palace Theater, *Hamilton Evening Journal* (OH) January 9, 1926, page 2.
6. *Miss Nobody* was made by First National, with Anna Q. Nilsson in the lead; it was directed by Lambert Hillyer. The synopsis — an heiress whose father dies leaving her penniless and her subsequent decision to take to the rails as a hobo, discovering love on the way — would have been ideal as a Colleen Moore vehicle, as it contains many of the familiar elements, including mistaken identity, hidden romance, and reversals of fortune. It would have made an interesting comparison to the later Louise Brooks film *Beggars of Life*, wherein she also disguised herself as a man and went on the run.
7. "In the Twirly-Whirl of Playdom," *Los Angeles Times*, January 1, 1926, page B3.
8. "Studies Chinatown in San Francisco," *Los Angeles Times*, January 10, 1926, page C14.
9. "Adaptation of 'Twinkletoes' Given Approval," *Los Angeles Times*, January 24, 1926, page B13.
10. "Burbank Gets Costly Studio," *Los Angeles Times*, January 28, 1926, page A1.
11. Founded in 1771, the San Gabriel Mission is less than 20 miles southeast of the studio. When Warner Bros. opened its new post production facility at the site of the First National studio, they made a point of maintaining the Mission style evident throughout the rest of the studio's buildings. Press release, "World's Most Advanced Post Production Sound Facility to Open at Warner Bros. Studios in Winter 2005," http://wbpostproduction.warnerbros.com/news/pps_fac_pr.pdf. (July 10, 2010).
12. "Old Mission Style for New Studios," *Los Angeles Times*, February 21, 1926, page B7.
13. Letter to: Rowland, from: McCormick, January 25, 1926, Colleen Moore Controversy, *Ella Cinders*, page 9.
14. Grace Kingsley, "Flashes," *Los Angeles Times*, February 3, 1926, page A9.
15. "Ma" Cinders (Vera Lewis), and sisters Lotta Pill (Doris Baker) and Prissy Pill (Emily Gerdes).
16. Harry Langdon's cameo appearance in *Ella Cinders* was to be part of a reciprocal deal, with Colleen slated to make a cameo in one of Langdon's films. However, Colleen's scenes ended up getting cut, according to Joseph Yranski (interview conducted March 12, 2011). It should be noted that, at the time, Harry Langdon was a very popular comedian, easily as popular as Harold Lloyd or Buster Keaton. His character was that of a babyish innocent. He had developed it during his vaudeville years, and it adapted well to film. When well directed, his films were great successes and he commanded a respectable following.
17. Richard Scheinin, *Field of Screams: The Dark Underside of America's National Pastime* (New York: W. W. Norton, 1994), page 123.
18. "'Ella Cinders' Filming Rushed," *Los Angeles Times*, March 7, 1926, page B5.
19. According to the *Hamilton Evening Journal* of Ohio, the location was Encino, which is just over 50 miles west

Chapter 29

1. Monica "Twinkletoes" Minasi was a blonde, described thusly: "Her peach-soft face; her nineteen golden curls; her eyes like flowers that made a resting place for a thousand expressive butterflies." Thomas Burke, *Twinkletoes: A Tale of Limehouse* (New York: McBride, 1918), page 9.
2. *Post Standard* (Syracuse, NY), August 15, 1926, page 4.
3. "Limehouse Romance for Colleen Moore," *Los Angeles Times*, July 16, 1926, page A9.
4. Grace Kingsley, "Flashes; Brabin Starts *Twinkletoes*," *Los Angeles Times*, July 26, 1926, page A9.
5. Burke, *Twinkletoes: A Tale of Limehouse*. ("'Ullo, 'ere's a norse. What a nice norse! Poor old norsey-porsey. 'Ave a banana? I ain't got one, but you could 'ave one if I 'ad.")
6. Ibid., page 106.
7. Ibid., page 123.
8. Ibid., page 22. (On pages 23–24 he amends her age to 15, nearly 16.)
9. Ibid., page 27.
10. Ibid., page 28.
11. Ibid., page 176.
12. Brabin's treatment of the film used Burke-like phrases, with an emphasis on Twinkletoe's physicality, such as Twinkletoe's "lovely slim body," and "Twinks poised light as a humming bird; her body vibrant with the joy of life and eager to express it in dancing. And clean and beautiful as a white flame, she is unaware of Roseleaf's glances."
13. Sequence 1, *Twinkletoes*—Treatment, Charles J. Brabin papers collection, Academy of Motion Picture Arts and Sciences, Margaret Herrick Library.
14. The last time Harlan and Colleen had appeared together in a film was *April Showers*, in which Harlan also played a prizefighter.
15. Sequence 1, *Twinkletoes*—Treatment, Charles J. Brabin papers collection.
16. Sequence 2, *Twinkletoes*—Treatment, Charles J. Brabin papers collection.
17. Presumably an acquaintance of John's; his work experience suggests he had some expertise in publicity, as did John. "Trynin is a Harvard man. He gained his early experience on the *Brooklyn Daily Eagle* editorial staff, and was advertising assistant for the *Encyclopedia Britannica* Corporation and R. H. Macy and Company and later assistant advertising manager of the Chevrolet Motor Company." (*The Associated Grower*, California Associated Raisin Company and the California Peach and Fig Growers at Fresno, California, vol. 2, no. 11, November 1921, page 43.)
18. *Twinkletoes* Production Box #2294, Warner Bros. Archives, School of Cinema-Television, University of Southern California.
19. Letter to: Brabin, from: John McCormick, August 2, 1926, *Twinkletoes* Production Box #2294, Warner Bros. Archives.
20. Letter to: Brabin, from: John McCormick, August 4, 1926, *Twinkletoes* Production Box #2294, Warner Bros. Archives.
21. Letter to: Miss Moore, from: John McCormick, August 5, 1926, *Twinkletoes* Production Box #2294, Warner Bros. Archives.
22. Letter to: Roy Stone, from: John McCormick, August 18, 1926, *Twinkletoes* Production Box #2294, Warner Bros. Archives.
23. Letter to: Brabin, from: John McCormick, August 18, 1926, *Twinkletoes* Production Box #2294, Warner Bros. Archives.
24. Letter to: Brabin, from: John McCormick, August 4, 1926, *Twinkletoes* Production Box #2294, Warner Bros. Archives.
25. Herbert Moulton, "Colleen's Nex [sic] Announced," *Los Angeles Times*, August 25, 1926, page A8.
26. *Reno Evening Gazette* (NV), July 3, 1926, page 12.
27. "Colleen Moore at Capitol," *Reading Eagle* (PA), September 15, 1926, page 20.
28. Helen Klumph, "Tenacity and Versatility Bring Colleen Success," *Los Angeles Times*, September 12, 1926, page C17.
29. *Meriden Daily Journal* (CT), August 21, 1926, page 2.
30. *Sarasota Herald-Tribune* (FL), August 31, 1926, page 5.
31. "In 1926, a cooperative society of 33 local Los Angeles architects, known as Allied Architects, built the Bowl's first arched proscenium. The curved wooden frame consisted of two different shapes: a low elliptical arch in the background with a circular arch inside, framing the musicians. The acoustic problems found in the design caused the shell to be torn down at the end of the season." From "History of the Hollywood Bowl Shell," http://www.hollywoodbowl.com/about/bowl-shell.cfm (January 7, 2011).
32. Rosiland Shaffer, "Colleen Learns Toe Dancing," *Chicago Daily Tribune*, August 22, 1926, page D3.
33. "Ernest Belcher, Dance Master, Turns from Stage to Screen," *Los Angeles Times*, October 31, 1926, page C23.
34. Gilbert Pickard, "Behind the Screen," *Billings Gazette* (MT), August 22, 1926, page 3.
35. "Players Ready for Valentino," *Los Angeles Times*, September 5, 1926, page 7.
36. "Filmland Dream Dissipated," *Los Angeles Times*, August 18, 1926, page A3.

37. Story told to Paul Smith of Alexandria, Louisiana, by Betty Blaine, daughter of Walter Hill, in January 2011. The house survives and is being preserved by Mr. and Mrs. Paul Smith.
38. Album and unidentified clipping about the contest from Judy Coleman Collection.
39. "How Am I To-day?" *Morning Leader* (Regina, Saskatchewan, Canada), October 9, 1926, page 42.
40. Letter from "Perrett," possibly Frank Perrett. Later in the same letter, the author writes, "Perrett staggered to a three set tennis victory over Santell the younger," indicating that Perrett was at least familiar with the First National director. *Twinkletoes* Production Box #2294, Warner Bros. Archives.
41. Ibid.
42. Letter to: John McCormick, from: Al Santell, November 18, 1926, *Twinkletoes* Production Box #2294, Warner Bros. Archives.
43. This article mentions only two endings, one happy and one sad. Many internal First National memos refer to *three* endings. Perhaps because two were relatively happy (Colleen lived), reports were simplified. Or else to eliminate ambiguity, the ending which depicted Twinks some years later as a happy farmer's housewife was selected over the one where she merely lives.
44. Letter to: Henry Freulich, from: John McCormick, September 8, 1926, *Twinkletoes* Production Box #2294, Warner Bros. Archives.
45. Moore, *Silent Star*, page 171.
46. Letter to: Roy Stone, from: John McCormick, August 18, 1926, *Twinkletoes* Production Box #2294, Warner Bros. Archives.
47. *Los Angeles Times*, September 14, 1926, page A11.
48. Grace Kingsley, "Al Santell Remains East," *Los Angeles Times*, September 8, 1926, page A10.
49. "Colleen Moore in *Orchids and Ermine*," *Sioux City Journal*, September 19, 1926, page 38.
50. Grace Kingsley, "Alfred Santell Begins," *Los Angeles Times*, September 25, 1926, page 12.
51. Grace Kingsley, "Which Shall It Be?" *Los Angeles Times*, September 23, 1926, page A8.
52. In *Silent Star*, Colleen identifies the film being worked on as *Naughty but Nice*. However, it was *Orchids and Ermine* that was shot on location in New York. *Naughty but Nice* was shot entirely on the West Coast.
53. Moore, *Silent Star*, page 176.
54. Colleen Moore Controversy, *Orchids and Ermine*, page 18.
55. Moore, *Silent Star*, page 175.
56. Ibid., page 176. Colleen wrote that John stayed away for three days. Assuming three days from Wednesday September 29th, his return would be on Saturday, October 2. He was back, in any case, before the 3rd, given his attendance at the Word Series.
57. Moore, *Silent Star*, page 176.
58. Ibid., page 174–175.
59. *Border Cities Star* (Windsor, Ontario) October 4, 1926, page 8.
60. Colleen Moore Controversy, page 19, Warner Bros. Archives.
61. "Scarcity of Rain Delays New Film," *Emporia Gazette* (KS), November 2, 1926, page 9.

Chapter 30

1. Grace Kingsley, "John and Colleen Home," *Los Angeles Times*, October 12, 1926, page A10.
2. "Twelve pictures were to be made...." Grace Kingsley, "Will Make Twelve Abroad," *Los Angeles Times*, October 13, 1926, page A8.
3. If the dates of John's bender following his September attempt to throw Colleen out the hotel window are correct, then an October 1 wire from McCormick to Levee would fall near the end of the three days that Colleen mentioned he was missing. Though he had not shown up on the set, he had apparently managed to drag himself to a telegraph office and send a message regarding Colleen's next big career move.
4. Colleen Moore Controversy, page 26, Warner Bros. Archives.
5. Moore, *Silent Star*, page 177.
6. *Post Standard* (Syracuse, NY), October 31, 1926, section 4, page 5.
7. November 15, Colleen Moore Controversy, page 26, Warner Bros. Archives.
8. Ibid., November 16.
9. Ibid, pages 26–27.
10. Ibid., page 27: writer and recipient not strictly identified, but the information follows a wire quoted from John to Richard Rowland.
11. Ibid.
12. Ibid.
13. "A Blonde Colleen Plays Cockney Role," by Roberta Nangle, *Chicago Daily Tribune*, January 9, 1927, page D1.
14. "Metropolitan Films Thomas Burke Story," *Atlanta Constitution*, January 30, 1927, page C4.
15. The *American Film Institute Catalog of Motion Pictures* (Berkeley: University of California Press, 1997), identifies the source material for the film as *The Bigamists*, by Lewis Allen Browne, on page 537. The listing is unclear if it was a story or a play, though at least one newspaper identified it as a stage play. The plot summary for the movie *Miss George Washington* sounds strikingly like the final *Naughty but Nice*, so it is reasonable to assume *The Bigamist* underwent a title change to *Miss George Washington* in the earlier screen version, just as *Miss George Washington* was renamed *Naughty but Nice*. Name changes were evidently a theme with this movie, as afterwards Gretchen Young would change her first name to Loretta.
16. Colleen Moore Controversy, *Naughty but Nice*, page 21.
17. Wire from: McCormick to: Rowland, Colleen Moore Controversy, page 28, Warner Bros. Archives.
18. "Film Chief Arrives Here," *Los Angeles Times*, January 9, 1927, page 10.
19. Grace Kingsley, "Colleen Moore Investigates," *Los Angeles Times*, January 13, 1927, page A8.
20. Helen Klumph, "Far Fields Look Greener," *Los Angeles Times*, June 20, 1926, page D24.
21. Colleen Moore Controversy, *Naughty but Nice*, page 21, Warner Bros. Archives.
22. Millard Webb had directed the 1926 John Barrymore adventure *The Sea Beast*, co-starring Dolores Costello. Born in 1893 and raised in Kentucky, according to his biography in a program of *The Sea Beast*, Webb had started off as a civil engineer, but after an injury moved to Los Angeles to recuperate. Motion pictures captured his fancy, and he moved swiftly up the ranks from extra to writer to director. Carol Stein, *The Barrymores: Hollywood's First Family*, (Lexington: University Press of Kentucky, 2001), page 74.
23. Grace Kingsley, "Webb to Direct Colleen," *Los Angeles Times*, February 5, 1927, page 6.
24. *Los Angeles Times*, April 3, 1927, page 28.
25. E. J. Fleming, *The Fixers: Eddie Mannix, Howard Strickling, and the MGM Publicity Machine* (Jefferson, NC: McFarland, 2005), page 147.
26. She would go on to great fame under the name Loretta Young. The name Loretta was given to her by Colleen; it was the name, Loretta would find out some years later to her chagrin, of one of Colleen's favorite dolls.
27. Grace Kingsley, "Gretchen Young Signs," *Los Angeles Times*, April 15, 1927, page A8.
28. Grace Kingsley, "Colleen Moore's Plans," *Los Angeles Times*, March 4, 1927, page A8.
29. Gerald Duffy's account of development of "When Irish Eyes are Smiling," Colleen Moore Controversy, Warner Bros. Archives.
30. "It Was Expensive 'Thrill,'" *Los Angeles Times*, March 6, 1927, page C21.
31. "When Irish Eyes Are Smiling," lyrics by Chauncey Olcott & George Graff, Jr., music by Ernest R. Ball, 1912.
32. Gerald Duffy's account of development of "When Irish Eyes Are Smiling," Colleen Moore controversy, Warner Bros. Archives.
33. Colleen Moore Controversy, *Naughty but Nice*, page 22, Warner Bros. Archives.

34. Ibid., *When Irish Eyes Are Smiling*, page 23, Warner Bros. Archives.
35. Ibid.
36. Ibid.
37. Wire quoted in letter to: Edwin Loeb, from: Rowland, May 26, 1927, re Moore/McCormick situation, Colleen Moore controversy, Warner Bros. Archives.
38. The writer of the original song, "When Irish Eyes Are Smiling," with Chauncey Olcott, he had died on March 18, 1932.
39. Wire quoted in letter to: Edwin Loeb, from: Rowland, May 26, 1927, re: Moore/McCormick situation, Colleen Moore Controversy, Warner Bros. Archives.
40. Gerald Duffy's account of development of *When Irish Eyes Are Smiling*, Colleen Moore Controversy. Warner Bros. Archives.
41. "History of First National," page 48, box 15494A, Warner Bros. Archives.
42. "West Coast Stock Sold By Lesser," *Los Angeles Times*, February 25, 1926, page A18.
43. "Giant Theater Merger Forms," *Los Angeles Times*, April 28, 1927, page A1.
44. "History of First National," page 49, box 15494A, Warner Bros. Archives.
45. "Merger of Film Units Completed," *Los Angeles Times*, April 20, 1927, page A13.
46. "History of First National," page 51, box 15494A, Warner Bros. Archives.
47. "First National Convention Is Arranged Here," *Los Angeles Times*, April 21, 1927, page A15.
48. "Film Fans to Be Real Boss," *Los Angeles Times*, May 20, 1927, page A8.
49. There were, in fact, *two* film conventions in town that week. At the Biltmore, 200 Metro-Goldwyn-Mayer delegates made similar reports to their production heads. Both conventions were scheduled to run concurrently until Tuesday night.
50. "Film Fans to Be Real Boss," *Los Angeles Times*, May 20, 1927, page A8.
51. "Rothacker Will Take Film Post," *Los Angeles Times*, May 23, 1927, page A11.
52. "John McCormick to Star Own Wife," *Border Cities Star* (Windsor, Ontario, Canada), June 4, 1927, page 5.

Chapter 31

1. It is unclear if Colleen was writing about an invitation from the January or May event. On page 182 of *Silent Star*, Colleen supposes that "after he [John] was dropped as production head at First National ... he felt he was no longer such a big shot," while his wife and many of his friends were still in important positions. In fact, both events were held before the split from First National. John would have still been head of production. Colleen's writings seem to suggest it occurred in May, owing to her reference to a banquet, which was held that month. However, there appears to be documentation of her attendance at the May event. Evidence suggests that her missed invitation was to the January event. The Academy has no definitive list of those invitees of the January gathering, but at least one book refers to Colleen among those invited: Norbert B. Laufenberg's *Entertainment Celebrities* (Bloomington, IN: Trafford Publishing, 2005), page 868.
2. "History of the Academy," Academy of Motion Picture Arts and Sciences, http://www.oscars.org/academy/history-organization/history.html (March 16, 2011).
3. "Academy Opens; 275 Attending" *Variety*, May 18, 1927, pages 9, 17–18. The article lists "those who attended the affair." Both Colleen and John McCormick are listed. (Thanks to Libby Wertin, Reference Librarian at the Margaret Herrick Library, for finding this information and the information on the January and May events for me.)
4. Ibid.
5. Mervyn LeRoy and Richard Kleiner, *Mervyn LeRoy: Take One* (New York: Hawthorn, 1974), page 74. LeRoy's version of the events substantiates Colleen's in *Silent Star*, at least in terms of order; no mention is made in either Mervyn's or Colleen's accounts of the several days between John quitting, and his and Colleen's departure.
6. She states that he came to her bungalow with news they were leaving a week after drying out from his last bender. However, this timing is uncertain: he would have been host to the First National convention, and had commitments prior to that. There are several days after his May 26 telegram to John C. Bullwinkle and June 3, during which John leaves no paper trail. It is possible that he disappeared for several days, leaving Colleen to fend for herself, and then returned and told her they were leaving.
7. Telegram to: First National, from: Colleen, May 24, 1927, Colleen Moore Controversy, #16079B, Warner Bros. Archives.
8. *Los Angeles Times*, May 24, 1927, page A1.
9. Letter to: First National, from: Colleen, undated but presumably May 25, Colleen Moore Controversy, #16079B, Warner Bros. Archives.
10. There had been two conventions in town recently: 200 delegates from MGM had met at the Biltmore, while 375 delegates for First National had met at the Ambassador. In the *Los Angeles Times*, a photograph in the May 20 issue (page A8), identifies John as one of the "big guns" of the convention.
11. "Parisian Star Counts 350 New Fans in a Week," *Los Angeles Times*, May 29, 1927, page 15.
12. Telegram to: Samuel Spring, from: R.W. Perkins, May 25, 1927, Colleen Moore Controversy, #16079B, Warner Bros. Archives.
13. Letter to: Colleen, from: Richard Rowland, May 25, 1927, Colleen Moore Controversy, Colleen Moore Controversy, #16079B, Warner Bros. Archives.
14. Telegram to: John C. Bullwinkle, from: John McCormick, May 26, 1927, Colleen Moore Controversy, #16079B, Warner Bros. Archives.
15. Telegram to: Charles Einfeld, from: CF Chandler, May 25, 1927, Colleen Moore Controversy, #16079B, Warner Bros. Archives.
16. Telegram to: Charles Einfeld, from: R.A. Rowland, May 25, 1927, Colleen Moore Controversy, #16079B, Warner Bros. Archives.
17. Letter to: Richard Rowland, from: Colleen, May 26, 1927, Colleen Moore Controversy, #16079B, Warner Bros. Archives.
18. Letter to: Richard Rowland, Al Rockett, and Mervyn LeRoy from: Gerald C. Duffy, May 26, 1927, outlining his account of the May 26 meeting, Colleen Moore Controversy #16079B.
19. Letter from: Richard Rowland to: Edwin Loeb, May 26, outlining his account of the May 26 meeting, Colleen Moore Controversy, #16079B, Warner Bros. Archives.
20. Letter to: Richard Rowland, Al Rockett, and Meryn LeRoy from: Gerald C. Duffy, May 26, 1927, outlining his account of the May 26 meeting, Colleen Moore Controversy, #16079B, Warner Bros. Archives.
21. Letter from: Richard Rowland to: Edwin Loeb, May 26, outlining his account of the May 26 meeting, Colleen Moore Controversy, #16079B, Warner Bros. Archives, School of Cinema-Television, University of Southern California.
22. *Los Angeles Times*, May 27, 1927, page A11.
23. "Film Row Unhealed, Resignation of John McCormick From First National Stands," *Los Angeles Times*, May 28, 1927, page A2.
24. *Los Angeles Times*, May 29, 1927, page I2
25. Letter to: Al Rockett, from: Colleen Moore, June 1, 1927, Colleen Moore Controversy, #16079B, Warner Bros. Archives
26. Grace Kingsley, "Will Make Twelve Abroad," *Los Angeles Times*, October 13, 1926, page A8.
27. Letter to: R.W. Perkins, from: Sam Spring, June 2, 1927, Colleen Moore Controversy, #16079B, Warner Bros. Archives.
28. Letter to: Samuel Spring, from: R.W. Perkins, June 2, 1927, Colleen

Moore Controversy, #16079B, Warner Bros. Archives.

29. Moore, *Silent Star*, page 177. Colleen's account of the split from First National begins here, with John breaking the news that they were leaving.

30. Ibid., pages 177–8. Date based upon telegram from Sam Spring, dated that day, and stating that he had met with both John and Colleen and that John had announced they would both soon leave for New York.

31. Monday, June 13.

32. Telegram to: R.A. Rowland, from: Sam Spring, June 3, 1927. (While Sam says he intends to leave that night, he actually left the following day.) Colleen Moore Controversy, #16079B, Warner Bros. Archives.

33. Moore, *Silent Star*, pages 177–8. According to Colleen, immediately after being told by John in her bungalow that they would leave for New York, she called Richard to plead LeRoy's case.

34. Ibid. Colleen's own account in *Silent Star* has her completely in the dark. This seems to run contrary to the report that Sam made of the couple meeting them; it is possible that they met Sam together, and thereafter it was just he and John, but it is hard to imagine Colleen leaving the men to discuss her future, without her presence. Colleen always exercised as much control over her career as possible.

35. Leroy, *Mervyn LeRoy: Take One*, page 74. (It should be noted that Mervyn identifies his first film with himself as director and Colleen as star was to be *Peg o' My Heart*.)

36. *Los Angeles Times*, June 4, 1927, page A8.

37. "John McCormick to Star Own Wife," *Border Cities Star* (Windsor, Ontario, Canada), June 4, 1927, page 5.

Chapter 32

1. Moore, *Silent Star*, page 178.

2. "Departing Liners Take Many Abroad," *New York Times*, June 10, 1927, page 18.

3. "Three Liners to Sail; Only One for Europe," *New York Times*, June 15, 1927, page 46.

4. *Syracuse Herald*, June 10, 1927, page 12.

5. Telegram to: Edwin J. Loeb, from R.W. Perkins, June 11, 1927, Colleen Moore Controversy #16079B, Warner Bros. Archives.

6. *Davenport Democrat and Leader* (IA), June 17, 1927, page 30.

7. Colleen made no reference to this in *Silent Star*, but given the content of his comments as reported in the previous chapter's telegrams and his confidence in his own sales ability, this was undoubtedly his aim. Aside from mentioning his drinking and his purchase of tickets for Europe, Colleen gives no account of John's whereabouts. It appears it was just Colleen and Cleeve in her hotel room, wiling away the time until John made his next move.

8. "Colleen Moore Typifies American Girl Everyone Loves, Says Maker of Picture 'Orchids and Ermine,'" *Kingsport Times* (TN), July 10, 1927, page 8.

9. "Want Colleen Moore to Arbitrate Claim," *New York Times*, June 18, 1927, page 15.

10. "Colleen Moore Must Arbitrate Movie Contract," *Atlanta Constitution*, June 24, 1927, page 1.

11. This is the report of June 13, 1927, compiled by L.R. Martineau at the request of Edwin J. Loeb, of materials from the Colleen Moore unit at First National, creating a detailed chronology of her productions. It is referred to as the "Colleen Moore Controversy" files, #16079B, Warner Bros. Archives.

12. Telegram to: Ned Marin, from: Perkins, June 18, 1927, Colleen Moore Controversy #16079B, Warner Bros. Archives.

13. "Colleen Moore and Company Reconciled," *Los Angeles Times*, July 5, 1927, page 1.

14. Norbert Lusk, "Peace Reigns in Studio Row," *Los Angeles Times*, July 10, 1927, page C13. This same column reported sharp criticism of Colleen's last effort, *Naughty but Nice*: "It is considered a silly, cheap picture, its trite story quite unworthy of Colleen." In spite of this view, it was doing well around the country: "It probably will continue to keep the star at the top of the box office heap."

15. Letter to: Colleen Moore, from: S. Spring, Colleen Moore Legal papers file #16079b, Warner Bros. Archives.

16. Clearance Sheet, Colleen Moore Amendment, file #2727, Warner Bros. Archives.

17. Letter to: Colleen, from: S. Spring, July 6, 1927, Colleen Moore legal file #2727, Warner Bros. Archives.

18. Colleen Moore legal file 6 of 7 #2727, Warner Bros. Archives.

19. Andre Soares's interview with Joseph Yranski in "Colleen Moore and Her Wild Oat," Alt Film Guide, April 27, 2007, http://www.altfg.com/blog/actors/colleen-moore-and-her-wild-oat/ (January 29, 2011).

20. "Another stout sea-going craft is the *Cojo*, which Colleen Moore and her husband, John McCormick, bought on the east coast recently." Oshkosh *Daily Northwestern* (WI), September 12, 1927, page 11. Reported as "chartered" for the return trip in Myra Nye's column, "Society of Cinemaland," *Los Angeles Times*, July 24, 1927, page 24. Reported by Grace Kingsley as being "their new craft," named the *Heigh-Ho*, "M'Cormicks Prolong Absence," *Los Angeles Times*, July 28, 1927, page A8.

21. Marquis Busby, "New Screen Duo in Offing," *Los Angeles Times*, July 8, 1927, page A8.

22. Grace Kingsley, "M'Cormicks Prolong Absence," *Los Angeles Times*, July 28, 1927, page A8.

23. *Port Arthur News* (TX), August 21, 1927, page 12.

24. Letter to: Sam Spring, August 30, 1927, Colleen Moore Legal file 6 of 7 #2727, Warner Bros. Archives.

25. Edward F. Cline started with Mack Sennett; it is claimed in virtually every book that mentions him that he came up with the idea for Sennett's Bathing Beauties.

26. "Theater," *Le Mars Globe-Post* (IA), August 18, 1927, page 8.

27. "Marshall Neilan to Direct Colleen Moore in Next Film," *Mansfield News* (OH), September 11, 1927, page 12.

28. Letter from W.R. Rathacker to Sam Springs, August 30, 1927, Colleen Moore Legal File 2727A-6, Warner Bros. Archives.

29. "Professor LaTour" was the name of King Vidor's character in the mentalist act he and Colleen put together in Truckee during the shooting of *The Sky Pilot*.

30. "Tell the World" (*Her Wild Oat*) file A-145, Warner Bros. Archives.

31. "New York Day-by-Day," by O.O. McIntyre, *Coshocton Tribune* (OH), September 29, 1927, page 12.

32. Letter, September 30, 1927, from: R.W. Allison, to: Cosmopolitan Productions. "Please find check #43731 in the amount of $500.00 covering the services of the Marion Davies' quartet for the week ending 9/24/27." The quartet also worked the week ending September 17, 1927, and was again paid $500. "Tell the World" (*Her Wild Oat*) file A-145, Warner Bros. Archives.

33. This harkens back to the confusion of roles in *Orchids and Ermine*.

34. October 12, 1927, from: Mr. Butler, to: Mr. Obringer. A Boeing Air transport plane was used, its propeller damaged in Griffith Park. Boeing did not charge for the use of the airplane but did ask for reimbursement for gas, oil and pilot's half-day compensation. "Tell the World" (*Her Wild Oat*) file A-145, Warner Bros. Archives.

35. "Colleen's Wild Ride," *Pittsburgh Press* (PA) December 25, 1927 page 38.

36. Letter to: Obringer, from: Marin, October 28, 1927, Warner Bros. Archives.

37. Tino Balio, *The American Film Industry* (Madison: University of Wisconsin Press, 1985), page 237.

38. Douglas Gomery, *The Coming of Sound: A History* (New York: Routledge, 2005), page 38.

39. Tino Balio, *The American Film Industry*, page 239.

Chapter 33

1. Telegram to: Perkins, from: Rothacker, November 29, 1927, Colleen Moore legal file #5 of 7, folder 2727A, Warner Bros. Archives.
2. Colleen Moore Legal Papers, folder 1, #16079b, Warner Bros. Archives.
3. *San Antonio Express* (TX), November 13, 1927, page B17.
4. Myra Nye, "Society of Cinemaland," *Los Angeles Times*, November 13, 1927, page C36.
5. This is an assumption on my part. In *Silent Star* (page 184), Colleen writes that she saw Gary Cooper in a western while visiting Catalina Island for location work on the film *Oh, Kay!* However, *Oh Kay!* would not be in production for some time. If she had spotted Cooper in a western film at Catalina Island, it might have been on an earlier visit, though with her schedule running up to *Lilac Time*, it's difficult to know when that might have been. I assume that Colleen had seen Cooper at a time when she knew the part of the romantic interest needed to be filled, and her only lengthy break between *Her Wild Oat* and *Lilac Time* was her trip to Arrowhead. In *Silent Star*, however, it appears that John was with her in the audience when she noticed the actor, so it is entirely possible that she saw some other showing with John. She writes further that when John persuaded Paramount to loan Cooper out for the film, he had been at work on *Wings*, which was released in late 1927.
6. Joseph Yranski retells Colleen's story that she had been away on a chartered yacht with family while John stayed to work on post-production of *Her Wild Oat*. The newspapers have no mention of Colleen and family chartering a yacht until about the same time one year later: the *Aimee*, on which they sailed the southern waters of California for an extended break between films. Here, as with the timing of Colleen noticing Gary Cooper, I assume that the trip Colleen might have been on was her vacation with her mother and childhood friend.
7. Soares interview with Yranski. Also, *Silent Star*, page 213.
8. Letter to: First National, from: Colleen Moore, December 2, 1927, Colleen Moore legal file 6 of 7 #2727, Warner Bros. Archives.
9. Letter to: First National, from: Loeb, Walker and Loeb, December 2, 1927, Colleen Moore legal file 6 of 7 #2727, Warner Bros. Archives.
10. Letter to: First National, from: Colleen Moore, December 6, 1927, Colleen Moore legal file 6 of 7 #2727, Warner Bros. Archives.
11. Telegram to: Perkins, from: Rothacker, November 29, 1927, Colleen Moore legal file 5 of 7, folder 2727A, Warner Bros. Archives.
12. Letter, October 28, 1927 from: Marin, to: Obringer, Colleen Moore legal file 6 of 7, folder 2727a, Warner Bros. Archives
13. "*Her Wild Oat* for Dec. 25th Release," *Motion Picture World*, December 24, 1927, page unknown. Joseph Yranski Collection, *Her Wild Oat* Clippings Folder.
14. Letters to C.E. Graves, Frank Baker Aircraft and Anderson Boarding and Supply, Colleen Moore Legal Papers, folder 1, #16079b, Warner Bros. Archives.
15. El Toro was the site of the Marine Corps Air Station El Toro from 1942 until it was decommissioned in 1999.
16. "The New Pioneers; Finding the Good Life in Orange County's Suburban Frontier," *Los Angeles Times*, March 27, 1994, http://articles.latimes.com/1994-03-27/news/mn-39202_1_rancho-santa-margarita (January 31, 2011).
17. "Producer Seeks British Soldier," *Oakland Tribune*, December 12, 1927, page O-8.
18. "Male Lead Still Open Is Report," *Mansfield News* (OH), December 21, 1927, page 15.
19. "Film Flickers," *Syracuse Herald*, September 19, 1927, page 9.
20. *Davenport Democrat and Leader* (IA), October 16, 1927, page 20.
21. "Comings and Goings," *Los Angeles Times*, December 11, 1927, page C28.
22. "Colleen Plans New Year," *Los Angeles Times*, December 25, 1927, page C17.
23. Mordaunt Hall, "The Screen; Her Dilemma," *New York Times*, February 6, 1928, page 12.
24. Mae Tinee, "There's Pleasant Aftertaste to Picture from Porter Novel," *Chicago Daily Tribune*, December 20, 1927, page 29.
25. First National's information states the camp was built for 150, with a mess hall capable of feeding 200. Though a remote location, it is possible that not everyone involved in the film was at the tent city all the time (in spite of what the newspaper story will claim in the next paragraph), so the figure of 300 people could be accurate.
26. "Buelah's Hollywood Letter," *Syracuse Herald* (NY), February 5, 1927, page 4.
27. During the Second World War, Cleeve volunteered for the Army Air Forces, but did not qualify. Living in Florida at the time, he volunteered for the Civil Air Patrol. As Lieutenant Cleeve Morrison, he had mechanical troubles and ditched his airplane into the Gulf of Mexico, an event that was photographed. Telephone interview with Alana Morison, 2008, and photographs in family album, Judy Coleman Collection.
28. "Lucky Kinship," *Billings Gazette* (MT), January 15, 1928, page 5.
29. In *Little Orphant Annie* and *A Hoosier Romance*. Colleen was always happy to be reunited with former cast members.
30. *Suburbanite Economist* (Chicago), February 3, 1928, page 3.
31. Another pilot was Charles Stoffer, who had also flown in the war. "Plane Crash for Camera," *New York Times*, April 1, 1928, page 122.
32. Ibid.
33. Letter of February 18 to: R.J Obringer, from: C.M. Movius, M.D. Also, letter of February 20 to: C.E. Anderson, from: R.J. Obringer, New York Indemnity Co., explaining the bill. Interestingly, C.M. Movius, B.S.M.D., is listed in the company stationery as an OB/GYN. Colleen Moore folder #2723A, Warner Bros. Archives.
34. There were 16 aircraft in the air at one time, according to "Plane Crash for Camera," *New York Times*, April 1, 1928, page 122.
35. "Frenchmen Have Innings in Colleen Moore Film," *Suburbanite Economist* (Chicago), March 3, 1928, page 3.
36. Lee Shippey, "Lee Side o' L.A.," *Los Angeles Times*, June 23, 1929, page B4.
37. It would be the last silent scenario of his career. Matthew Kennedy, *Edmund Goulding's Dark Victory: Hollywood's Genius Bad Boy* (Madison: University of Wisconsin Press, 2004), page 70.
38. Letter to: Edmund Goulding, January 18, 1928, explaining conditions of contract relating to production tentatively titled "The Kitten" (Release title: *Tomorrow*). *Happiness Ahead* folder, Warner Bros. Archives, School of Cinema-Television, University of Southern California.
39. "Hollywood Filmography," February 4, 1928, page unknown, the Joseph Yranski Collection.
40. Grace Kingsley, "Colleen Moore Changes Title," *Los Angeles Times*, February 14, 1928, page A10.
41. Table of Gross Income on Colleen Moore Pictures (gross domestic earnings to December 31, 1928):
Flaming Youth—$680,030. 31
Sally—$610,210. 47
Irene—$735,648. 57
Colleen Moore legal file #13100a, Warner Bros. Archives.
42. Grace Kingsley, "Mervyn LeRoy Signs Again," *Los Angeles Times*, February 16, 1928, page A9.
43. Grace Kingsley, "First National Keeps Star," *Los Angeles Times*, March 6, 1928, page A10.
44. While the story reports these events happening at "the studio," the French village sets were built at El Toro,

and the number of extras and amount of material quoted would have been large enough to severely overpopulate the First National studio.
　45. "Many Stars," *Charleston Daily Mail* (WV), February 26, 1928, page 2.
　46. The system was reported as the "Firestone" system in "First National Gets Audible Movie Rights," *New York Times*, April 19, 1928, page 23.
　47. "Talking Films in New Line-up," *Los Angeles Times*, April 20, 1928, page 5.
　48. Donald Crafton, *The Talkies: American Cinema's Transition to Sound, 1926–1931* (New York: Charles Scribner's Sons, 1999), page 193.
　49. "Chester B. Bahm's Stage and Film Chat," *Syracuse Herald*, March 7, 1928, page 9.
　50. Kennedy, *Edmund Goulding's Dark Victory: Hollywood's Genius Bad Boy.*
　51. Goulding had directed less than a half-dozen films by 1928. While he didn't direct this Colleen Moore vehicle, he would go on to direct *Grand Hotel* at the height of the Depression.
　52. "Seiter Will Direct Colleen's Next One," *Charleston Daily Mail* (WV), April 1, 1928, page 2.
　53. *Evening Independent* (St. Petersburg, FL), March 31st, 1928, page 4.
　54. Brownlow, "*The Parade's Gone By...*," page 41.
　55. William K. Everson, *American Silent Film* (New York: Da Capo Press, 1998), page 146.
　56. "Projection Jottings," *New York Times*, April 29, 1928, page X5.
　57. Grace Kingsley, "Neal Dodd Marries Them," *Los Angeles Times*, April 4, 1928, page A10.
　58. Memo to: Obringer, from: John McCormick, April 2, 1928, Colleen Moore legal file 2727A, Warner Bros. Archives.

Chapter 34

　1. Dan Thomas, "Movie Chat," *Olean Times* (NY), April 10, 1928, page 13.
　2. *New York Times*, April 8, 1928, page X7.
　3. Memos to: Obringer, from: McCormick, April 14, 1928, Colleen Moore Legal File 4 of 7, Warner Bros. Archives.
　4. "Colleen Moore is Enjoying Vacation," *Mansfield News* (OH), May 20, 1928, page 17.
　5. "Talking Films in New Line-up," *Los Angeles Times*, April 20, 1928, page 5.
　6. Earle E. Crowe, "Talking Picture New Era," *Los Angeles Times*, April 24, 1928, page 12.
　7. "First National to Rush Synchronization," *Los Angeles Times*, May 16, 1928, page 1.
　8. "Early End of Silent Film Seen," *Los Angeles Times*, June 2, 1928, page 1.
　9. Moore, *Silent Star*, page 231.
　10. Los Angeles Steam Ship Company. Originally named *Grossef Kurfurst*, a former German liner, the ship had been purchased and renamed *City of Los Angeles* in December 1921. René De La Pedraja Tomán, *A Historical Dictionary of the U.S. Merchant Marine and Shipping Industry: Since the Introduction of Steam* (Westport, CT: Greenwood, 1994), page 320.
　11. *Los Angeles Times*, May 12, 1928, page 13.
　12. "It's Her Golden Dream Isle," *Los Angeles Times*, May 12, 1928, page A3.
　13. Grace Kingsley, "Colleen's New Accomplishment," *Los Angeles Times*, May 17, 1928, page A8.
　14. "W.R. Rothacker to Retire from Film Business," *Los Angeles Times*, May 30, 1928, page A9.
　15. Brian Taves, *P.G. Wodehouse and Hollywood: Screenwriting, Satires, and Adaptations* (Jefferson, NC: McFarland, 2006), page 15.
　16. Elsie was a writer, actress and entertainer who had taken to the stage at an early age. During the First World War she was the only woman allowed at the front lines, where she entertained the troops and earned the nickname "Sweetheart of the AEF (Allied Expeditionary Forces). Jacqueline Jones Royster, *Profiles of Ohio Women, 1803–2003* (Athens: Ohio University Press, 2003), page 225. In May 1928, she was back on the stage, doing impersonations of Beatrice Lillie, Ethel and John Barrymore, Fannie Brice and Will Rogers, among others, and "in her various incarnations she takes on the physical, moral and spiritual aspects ... [so that] she is so nearly like them that for all practical purposes—she is them." Philip K. Scheuer, "Elsie Janis Leads New Vaudeville," *Los Angeles Times*, May 22, 1928, page A11.
　17. Grace Kingsley, "Alan Hale with Colleen," *Los Angeles Times*, June 6, 1928, page A8.
　18. "Sparks from Studios," *New York Times*, May 20, 1928, page 105.
　19. 9174 Sunset, Los Angeles, California; the headwaiter was Count Andre Tolstoi and the owner was General T. Lodijensky, formerly of the Russian Imperial Army.
　20. "Blast Wrecks Gay Café After Film Stars Flee," *Chicago Tribune*, June 8, 1928, page unknown.
　21. "Colleen Moore Enjoys Work in Bathing Suits," *Mansfield News* (OH), July 16, 1928, second section, page 2.
　22. Norbert Lusk, "Studio Merger Believed Near," *Los Angeles Times*, June 17, 1928, page C13.
　23. "Rothacker Off on Trip East," *Los Angeles Times*, July 17, 1928, page A13.
　24. "History of First National," page 50box 15494A, Warner Bros. Archives
　25. Ibid., page 48.
　26. Cari Beauchamp, *Joseph P. Kennedy Presents: His Hollywood Years* (New York: Knopf, 2009), pages 179–180.
　27. Ibid., page 180.
　28. "Colleen Moore in 'Happiness Ahead' at the Capitol," *Reading Eagle* (PA), July 8, 1928, page 10.
　29. Norbert Lusk, "Critics Like Talking Film," *Los Angeles Times*, Jun 24, 1928, page C9.
　30. "'John Knows, I Ask him,' Says Colleen Moore," *Davenport Democrat And Leader* (IA), June 10, 1928, page 21.
　31. "Stories on Louise Brooks Not All True, Is Indicated," *Reno Evening Gazette* (NV), June 2, 1928, page 6.
　32. Ibid.
　33. Beauchamp, *Joseph P. Kennedy Presents: His Hollywood Years*, page 198.
　34. Edward Mitchell, "Many Heads Fall Before Kennedy," *Sun* (Baltimore) August 19, 1928, page B8.
　35. Beauchamp, *Joseph P. Kennedy Presents: His Hollywood Years*, page 199.
　36. "Al Rockett Moves Up in Film World," *Los Angeles Times*, July 26, 1928, page A11.
　37. Fred A. Miller, who, with J. Harvey McCarthy, built the Carthay Circle Theater. ("Carthay" was a corruption of the name "McCarthy.")
　38. "Premiere of *Lilac Time* Set," *Los Angeles Times*, July 3, 1928, page 11.
　39. "Business of Sound Movie Not So Easy," *Washington Post*, July 8, 1928, page 48.
　40. Walker was a renowned playboy. "His penchant for frequenting nightclubs and enjoying the company of celebrities, including actress Betty Compton, earned him the nicknames Beau James, and the Night Mayor." Ralph J. Caliendo, *New York City Mayors* (Bloomington, IN: Xlibris Corporation, 2010), page 55.
　41. "'Jimmie' Walker Appears," *Oxnard Daily Courier* (CA), July 10, 1928, page 3.
　42. Suzanne Tarbell Cooper, Amy Ronnebeck Hall, and Marc Wanamaker, *Theatres in Los Angeles* (Charleston, SC: Arcadia, 2008), page 55.
　43. *California, 1826–1926* (Catalog of paintings hung in the Tower room of the Carthay Circle Theatre) (Published by the Carthay Circle Theatre; printed by Guy W. Finney Company, 1926.)
　44. Federal Writers' Project, *Los Angeles: A Guide to the City and Its Environs*, U.S. History Publishers, pages 185–186.
　45. The film was a silent one-reeler, and made on the fly. Described as a glorified home movie, it is presumed lost.
　46. Moore, *Silent Star*, page 186. The Photophone system recorded sound on a separate "sound camera." Later ver-

sions of the system would have the sound printed onto the same film stock as the image, but for *Lilac Time*, the sound was on a separate strip.
 47. "First Look at Protégé," *Washington Post*, September 9, 1928, page A2.
 48. Eddie Brandstatter's famous Montmartre Cafe (originally the Sixty Club) on Hollywood Blvd.
 49. Marquis Busby, "'Lilac Time' Worthy Film," *Los Angeles Times*, July 18, 1928, page A11.
 50. Moore, *Silent Star*, page 184.
 51. Cover, "Hollywood Filmography," August 4, 1928, vol. 8 no, 31., Colleen Moore Legal File #13100a, Warner Bros. Archives.
 52. Clipping by Marion of Hollywood, *Screenland*, October 1928, Joseph Yranski Collection.
 53. *Lilac Time* Program, Joseph Yranski Collection.
 54. Marquis Busby, "*Lilac Time* Worthy Film," *Los Angeles Times*, July 18, 1928, page A11.
 55. *Motion Picture News*, September 8, 1928, page unknown, the Joseph Yranski Collection.
 56. "Tour Takes Her Far from Circle," *Los Angeles Times*, July 24, 1928, Page 11.
 57. Colleen Moore Legal #2727a File 3 of 7, Warner Bros. Archives.
 58. Grace Kingsley, "Seiter's Four," *Los Angeles Times*, April 26, 1928, page A8.
 59. Colleen Moore Legal #2727a File 3 of 7, Warner Bros. Archives.
 60. Tom Geraghty wrote *Synthetic Sin* and would also write *Smiling Irish Eyes* and *Footlights and Fools*. He had written *Harold Teen*, which was directed by Mervyn LeRoy, and *Waterfront*, directed by William Seiter.
 61. Colleen Moore Legal #2727a File 3 of 7, Warner Bros. Archives.
 62. A "Bald-headed schooner" is a gaff-rigged schooner without topsails.
 63. "Oxnard and Vicinity," *Oxnard Daily Courier* (CA), August 25, 1928, page 4.
 64. Marquis Busby, "Oh, for a Sailor's Life," *Los Angeles Times*, August 26, 1928, page D11.
 65. One known Vitaphone short featuring George Jessel is the 1926 Vitaphone short VA-534. The Vitaphone Project, http://www.picking.com/vitaphone52.html (February 20, 2011). Jessel had originated the lead character in the stage version of *The Jazz Singer* and was slated to play the lead in the film, until the ending was changed. Jessel passed on the role and it went to Al Jolson, and the rest is history. George Albert Jessel, *So Help Me: The Autobiography of George Jessel* (Whitefish, MT: Kessinger, 2006), pages 87–88.
 66. Ibid., page 96.
 67. "Making Over the Movies," *Popular Science*, vol. 113, no. 3, September 1928, page 15.

Chapter 35

 1. James O. Spearing, "Now the Movies Go Back to Their School Days," *New York Times*, August 19, 1928, page 71.
 2. Ibid.
 3. Wade Werner (Associated Press Staff Writer), "Screen Life in Hollywood," *Corsicana Daily Sun* (TX), August 18, 1928, page 3.
 4. "Hair Still Her Crowning Glory," *Los Angeles Times*, August 9, 1928, page A10.
 5. Adela Rogers St. Johns, "Mary Got Her Hair Wet," *Photoplay*, vol. 20 no. 2, July 1921, pages 35, 51.
 6. Mordaunt Hall, "Colleen Moore's Latest Film," *New York Times*, September 2, 1928, page 87.
 7. *Oakland Tribune*, August 27, 1928, page 22.
 8. Marquis Busby, "Hilarity Plentiful in *Oh, Kay*," *Los Angeles Times*, August 27, 1928, page A7.
 9. Grace Kingsley, "William Seiter is to Direct Colleen," *Los Angeles Times*, August 16, 1928, page A6.
 10. Colleen Moore Legal File 2 of 7, 9/1/28–12/22/28.
 11. *Pygmalion*: Based on the 1914 play by George Bernard Shaw, which told the story of the transformation of Cockney flower girl Eliza Doolittle, under the tutelage of Prof. Henry Higgins. The story would have been a natural vehicle for Colleen, but she had done several transformation stories before. In addition, the transformation from Cockney accent to apparently an upper-class accent would have been a perfect vehicle for a talking film, not a silent.
 Coquette: Made into a film with Mary Pickford in 1929.
 The Constant Nymph: This drama would be made into a film under the same title in 1934, and 1943, the latter version directed by Edmund Goulding.
 Sunny: Made into a film in 1930, starring Marilyn Miller, and directed by William Seiter.
 Funny Face: Broadway musical comedy, with music by George and Ira Gershwin.
 12. Colleen Moore Legal File 2 of 7, 9/1/28–12/22/28, Warner Bros. Archives.
 13. Ibid.
 14. Ibid.
 15. Ibid.
 16. Edward Mitchell, "Kennedy's Departure Astonishes," *Sun* (Baltimore), September 9, 1928, page MO7.
 17. Earle E. Crowe, "Pathe's Place Uncertain," *Los Angeles Times*, September 2, 1928, page B8.
 18. Douglas Gomery, *Shared Pleasures: A History of Movie Presentation in the United States* (Madison: University of Wisconsin Press, 1992), page 40.
 19. Harry Carr, "The Lancer in Hollywood; A Big Deal," *Los Angeles Times*, September 2, 1928, page C12.
 20. "History of First National," pages 52–53.
 21. "Warners' Increase Holdings," *Los Angeles Times*, September 27, 1928, page 18.
 22. Edwin Schallert, "Deal Spells New Alignment," *Los Angeles Times*, October 7, 1928, page C15.
 23. Moore, *Silent Star*, page 190. "But Can She Talk?" is the title of Chapter 10.
 24. "'Synthetic Sin' Shown," *New York Times*, October 11, 1927, page 26.
 25. Gerald Martin Bordman, *American Theatre: A Chronicle of Comedy and Drama, 1914–1930* (New York: Oxford University Press), 1995, page 329.
 26. "Film Extra Happy over his Contract," *Charleston Daily Mail* (WV), September 2, 1928, page 5.
 27. "Theatrical and Picture Gossip," *Waterloo Evening Courier* (IA), October 6, 1928, page 14.
 28. *Charleston Daily Mail* (WV), November 18, 1928, page 3.
 29. "Nears Goal of Stardom," *Sandusky Star Journal* (OH), November 2, 1928, page 1.
 30. "New Dahlia Named After Colleen Moore," *Montana Standard* (Butte), November 14, 1928, page 10.
 31. Frank Lloyd was the director, as mentioned later in the article, and the film was *Adoration*, with Antonio Moreno. The film was released in December 1928.
 32. "Movie Tears and Laughter Fail to Mix Successfully," *Syracuse Herald* (NY), October 14, 1928. Page X3.
 33. "Colleen Goes Black Face," *Los Angeles Times*, November 18, 1928, page K4.
 34. Movie Man, "Around the Movies," *Gleaner* (Kingston, Jamaica), November 24, 1928, Special Magazine Section, page 3.
 35. "Theatrical and Picture Gossip," *Waterloo Evening Courier* (IA), December 29, 1928, page 12.
 36. Katherine T. Von Blon, "How Lulls Are Spent," *Los Angeles Times*, October 6, 1928, page A9.
 37. Cass Warner Sperling, Cork Milner, and Jack Warner, *Hollywood Be Thy Name: The Warner Brothers Story* (Lexington: University Press of Kentucky, 1998), page 150.
 38. Ibid., 1998, page 118.
 39. Interview, Joesph Yranski, March 3, 2011.
 40. Anthony Slide, *Silent Topics: Essays on Undocumented Areas of Silent Film* (Metuchen, NJ: Scarecrow Press, 2005), pages 77–79.
 41. Roy J. Pomeroy would direct several films, gaining the position of director merely by virtue of his being the sound engineer for Paramount. He started with *Interference*, Paramount's

first talking film, in 1929, and went on to direct *Inside the Lines*, in 1930, and *Shock*, in 1934.
   42. Slide, *Silent Topics: Essays on Undocumented Areas of Silent Film*, page 88.
   43. "Voices Tested," *Los Angeles Times*, October 7, 1928, page C10.
   44. Colleen wrote that she had been tested at the Warner Bros. studio, and that the man testing her had been a "young engineer" who was not concerned with film or the arts, but only what the machine said about Colleen's voice. (*Silent Star*, pages 191–192.) It is possible that Colleen was also tested on the Warner Bros. lot in addition to the test at the Lasky studio, but if so, it was not reported. While Colleen was not with Paramount, several other actors and actresses mentioned in the article cited were with other studios at that time as well. Colleen further describes being baffled when the young engineer tells her to speak into the microphone, to which she replies, "What's a microphone?" In fact, Colleen had been making radio appearances for years and had spoken into any number and type of microphones. It is unlikely that the microphone used for her test was so alien to her in appearance that she did not know what it was.
   45. Colleen describes a conversation between several of the big franchise holders while headed westbound on the Santa Fe Chief. Unless the conversation was recounted to her at some later point, it would have been impossible for Colleen to know what had been said, and by whom. Because of this, it seems more likely that portion of *Silent Star* was an addition of Adela Rogers St. Johns. None of the newspapers of the day make mention of a time during that year where all the individuals described were in Los Angeles simultaneously.
   46. Letter to: First National, from: Colleen Moore, October 2, 1928, Colleen Moore Legal File #2 of 7, 2727A, Warner Bros. Archives.
   47. "Stories on Louise Brooks Not All True, Is Indicated," *Reno Evening Gazette* (NV), June 2, 1928, page 14.
   48. Jerome Beatty was Director of the Publicity and Advertising Department, *Film Daily Yearbook*, page 732.
   49. The description of the letter circulated by Beatty is based upon a telegram from Colleen. Neither the letter Beatty wrote and circulated nor the original letters written by John excerpted therein exists in the current Warner Bros. archives, therefore their contents are a matter of speculation. Their absence, no doubt, reflects a rather unflattering opinion expunged before the rest of the documentation surrounding the incident was archived.
   50. Telegram to: Ned Depinet, from: Colleen Moore, October 4, 1928,
Colleen Moore file #12631B, Warner Bros. Archives.
   51. "War Romance Soon to Vacate," *Los Angeles Times*, September 6, 1928, page A9.
   52. "Criterion Will Show Air Drama," *Los Angeles Times*, November 12, 1928, page A7.
   53. From "Key City Grosses, *Film Daily Yearbook 1929*, pages 865–887. A selection of its grosses are as follows: California Theater, San Francisco: November 10, $19,000; November 17, $14,000.
   St. Francis Theater, San Francisco: December 1, $6,500; (4 days) December 8, $3,000.
   Grand Central Theater, St. Louis: August 18, $22,000; August 25, $15,000; September 1(?); September 8, $15,700. (Compare to *The Jazz Singer*, January 7–March 3, average $14,000, minus January 7, February 11, and March 3 with no totals available).
   Strand Theater, New York: December 15, $36,200; December 22, $28,600.
   Central Theater, New York: August 11–December 1, average $13,870, total $235,800 (17 weeks).
   Carthay Circle Theater, Los Angeles: July 21 ($5 for premiere)–$19,000; average July 28–September 22, $13,533 (nine weeks), total $121,800.
   Roosevelt Theater, Chicago: August 18, $22,000; August 25, $31,500; September 1, $24,000; September 8, $27,500; September 15, $20,000.
   54. Telegram to: Colleen Moore, from: Ned Depinet, October 5, 1928, Colleen Moore file #12631B, Warner Bros. Archives.
   55. Moore, *Silent Star*, page 218.
   56. Grace Kingsley, "Neil Hamilton Wins Big Lead," *Los Angeles Times*, October 20, 1928, page A10.
   57. "Films to Cost Seven Millions," *Los Angeles Times*, November 12, 1928, page A3.
   58. "Colleen Moore Spending Vacation," *Charleston Daily Mail* (WV), November 18, 1928, page 3.

Chapter 36

   1. Memo to: Colleen Moore, from: Al Rockett, December 21, 1928, Colleen Moore legal file #13100A, Warner Bros. Archives.
   2. Rosiland Shepard, "Mother to Colleen," *Los Angeles Times*, December 16, 1928, page C8.
   3. E. J. Fleming, *The Fixers: Eddie Mannix, Howard Strickling, and the MGM Publicity Machine*, page 112.
   4. Memo to: Obringer, from: McCormick, December 4, 1928, Colleen Moore Legal File, 2 of 7, Warner Bros. Archives.
   5. Memo to: Colleen Moore, from: Al Rockett, December 21, 1928, Colleen
Moore Legal File # 13100A, Warner Bros. Archives.
   6. "Feature Film Plans Mapped," *Los Angeles Times*, December 31, 1928, page A3.
   7. Letter to: First National, from: Loeb, Walker and Loeb, February 18, 1929. Colleen Moore Legal File 1 of 7, Warner Bros. Archives.
   8. "Clara Bow Leads Film List," *Los Angeles Times*, January 3, 1929, page A3.
   9. "A Melancholy Dane," *Los Angeles Times*, January 9, 1929, age 11.
   10. Marquis Busby, "'Synthetic Sin' Ranks with Best," *Los Angeles Times*, January 21, 1929, page A7.
   11. "Colleen Scores in New Picture," *Evening Independent* (St. Petersburg, FL), March 22, 1929, page 7.
   12. Mordaunt Hall, "An Absurdity," *New York Times*, January 13, 1929, page 115.
   13. It should be noted that for quite some time into its productions, and occasionally after its release in First National papers, *Why Be Good* was still referred to as "That's a Bad Girl."
   14. Whitney Williams, "*Flaming Youth* Flames Once Again," *Los Angeles Times*, February 3, 1929, page K3.
   15. While the purchase was reported in early January, it is possible that the couple had been negotiating for the house months before. In *Silent Star*, Colleen states that they purchased their Bel Air home in 1927, and that when it was completed after a year and a half, they moved in.
   16. "Colleen Moore and McCormick Buy New Home," *Los Angeles Times*, January 8, 1929, page A9.
   17. Letter to: First National, from: Colleen Moore, January 7, 1929, John McCormick files #2726B, Warner Bros. Archives, School of Cinema-Television, University of Southern California.
   18. Grace Kingsley, "Colleen and John Returning," *Los Angeles Times*, January 24, 1929, page A10.
   19. Cooper, et. al., *Theatres in Los Angeles*, page 109.
   20. Alma Whitaker, "*Lilac Time* Presented," *Los Angeles Times*, January 7, 1929, page A7.
   21. Letter to: Al Rockett, from: John McCormick, February 19, 1928, Colleen Moore Legal File #1 of 7, Warner Bros. Archives.
   22. Letter to: First National, from: Loeb, Walker and Loeb, February 18, 1929, Colleen Moore legal file #1 of 7, Warner Bros. Archives.
   23. Colleen Moore Legal File #2727, Warner Bros. Archives.
   24. Contract of February 27, 1929, Colleen Moore Legal File #13100a, Warner Bros. Archives.
   25. Amendment to John McCormick Contract, February 26, 1929, John McCormick file #2726B, Warner Bros. Archives.

26. Letter to: First National, from: Colleen Moore, March 28, 1929, Colleen Moore Legal File #13100a, Warner Bros. Archives.
27. Marquis Busby, "Seiter Company Wears Shamrock," *Los Angeles Times*, March 20, 1929, page A9.
28. Herbert Beerbohm Tree had been in *Old Folks at Home* for Triangle, just before Colleen's arrival in Hollywood.
29. Moore, *Silent Star*, page 194.
30. Mae Tinee, "Here Are Two Movies Full of Moral Intent," *Chicago Daily Tribune*, March 20, 1929, page 37.
31. Marquis Busby, "Flapper Up Again for Inspection," *Los Angeles Times*, March 16, 1929, page 7.
32. Marquis Busby, "Seiter Company Wears Shamrock," *Los Angeles Times*, March 20, 1929, page A9.
33. James Hall would appear in *Dangerous Nan McGrew*, a story originally proposed for Colleen, in 1930; *The Canary Murder Case*, in 1929, and *Rolled Stockings*, in 1927, both with rival flapper Louise Brooks; and *The Fleet's In*, in 1928, and *The Saturday Night Kid*, in 1929, with Colleen's primary flapper rival, Clara Bow.
34. Claude Gillingwater appeared with Colleen in *Naughty but Nice*, in 1927, and *Oh, Kay!*, in 1928.
35. Mollie Merrick, "Hollywood in Person," *Atlanta Constitution*, April 30, 1929, page A3.
36. Rosiland Shaffer, "Colleen Moore Movie as Irish as Spuds; 'Twin Beds' in Film Rendering Is Futuristic," *Chicago Daily Tribune*, April 14, 1929, page G9.
37. "Chorus Signed for *Smiling Irish Eyes*," *Charleston Daily Mail* (WV), May 12, 1929, page 6.
38. Moore, *Silent Star*, pages 198–199.
39. Reviewers of the time felt that Colleen had a fine singing voice. While she was not satisfied with her performance and with the way the sound equipment at the time recorded it, she was likely not as bad as she thought.
40. Letter to: First National, from: Colleen Moore, March 28, 1929, Colleen Moore Legal File #13100a, Warner Bros. Archives.
41. Letter to: Rockett, from: Obringer, circa April 9, 1929, Colleen Moore Legal File 1 of 7, Warner Bros. Archives.
42. Dorothy Herzog, "Behind the Scenes in Hollywood," *Carbondale Daily Free Press* (IL), April 26, 1929, page 6.
43. Letter to: Rockett, from: Obringer, circa April 9, 1929, Colleen Moore Legal File 1 of 7, Warner Bros. Archives.
44. Letter to: Rockett, from: Obringer, May 2, 1929, Colleen Moore Legal File, folder #1 of 7, Warner Bros. Archives.
45. "Wife Asks Divorce from Film Writer," *Los Angeles Times*, October 7, 1927, page 3.
46. "Bargain Day in Courthouse for Filmland," *Chicago Daily Tribune*, May 21, 1929, page 18.
47. Letter to: Rockett from: Obringer, May 2, 1929, Colleen Moore Legal File, folder #1 of 7. Warner Bros. Archives.
48. "Seiter Directs Colleen Again," *Los Angeles Times*, May 30, 1929, page A7.
49. *Charleston Daily Mail*, June 23, 1929, page 6.
50. *Decatur Review* (IL), June 2, 1929, page 27.
51. "Hollywood Notes," *New York Times*, June 30, 1929, page X4.
52. "New Heat Records Attained in Interior," *Los Angeles Times*, June 22, 1929, page A2.
53. "Hot Wave Due to Continue," *Los Angeles Times*, June 24, 1929, page A1.
54. *Lowell Sun* (MA), July 27, 1929, page 4.
55. Eddie Bush, Paul Gibbons and Bill Seckler, Brunswick Records: Chicago and regional sessions, by Ross Laird, Brunswick-Balke-Collender Company. Brunswick Radio Corporation, edited by Brunswick-Balke-Collender Company, Greenwood Publishing Group, 2001, page 1312. Earl Burtnett's orchestra backed up the trio on their radio broadcasts.
56. "Biltmore Trio Takes Part in Moore Talker," *Los Angeles Times*, June 30, 1929, page 15.
57. The Charles G. Clarke Collection at the Margaret Herrick Library contains lyrics to several for the songs written for *Footlights and Fools*, including corrections and changes made, in folder #17, Margaret Herrick Library, Academy of Motion Picture Arts and Sciences.
58. While there was the clause in her contract for a voice double to be used in her productions, when necessary, Colleen nevertheless insisted that she had done her own singing.
59. Alma Whitaker, "One-reeler First Work of Seiter," *Los Angeles Times*, November 17, 1929, page B14.
60. "In Hollywood," *Lowell Sun* (MA), July 17, 1929, page 4.
61. Grace Kingsley, "Colleen Moore Leaves," *Los Angeles Times*, July 9, 1929, page A8.
62. Letter to: R.W. Perkins, from: unknown, July 12, 1929, Colleen Moore Legal File, #1 of 7.

Chapter 37

1. Harry Evans, "Movies," *Life*, vol. 94, no. 2440, August 9, 1929, page 26 and 33.
2. Norbert Lusk, "Colleen Moore a Personal Hit," *Los Angeles Times*, July 28, 1929, page 15.
3. "The Screen," *New York Times*, July 24, 1929, page 30.
4. In *Silent Star*, Colleen describes moving into house the alone after John disappeared on a bender before a big social event, which was held in September.
5. Lee Shippey, "Lee Side o' L.A.," *Los Angeles Times*, June 23, 1929, page B4.
6. Moore, *Silent Star*, pages 211–214.
7. Most of her jewelry had gone into the making of her dollhouse, the Fairy Castle.
8. Moore, *Silent Star*, page 214.
9. Ibid. Colleen describes this scene as happening during the making of *Footlights and Fools*. However, the social event she mentions happening the next day — a luncheon honoring Winston Churchill — was on September 19, some two months later, and doubtless was a memorable event.
10. Ibid., pages 214–216.
11. Mollie Merrick, "Hollywood in Person," *Atlanta Constitution*, April 11, 1930, page 8.
12. Colleen and John had traveled to New York together. In *Silent Star*, Colleen's mother tells her not to return to the house after the choking incident, a no-nonsense bit of advice. I place the final attack on Colleen after her recovery, in November, based on the fact that she and John had been traveling together the month before, and that she would not have been with him, unsupervised, after the attack.
13. "Colleen Moore, Ill, Returns from East," *Los Angeles Times*, October 30, 1929, page A2.
14. "Undergoes Operation for Appendicitis," *Chicago Tribune*, November 4, 1929, page unknown.
15. "Colleen Moore in 'Footlights and Fools' coming to Rialto," *Hamilton Daily News* (OH), January 2, 1930, page 14.
16. Mae Tinee, "Colleen in New Film Startles Her Friends," *Chicago Daily Tribune*, December 22, 1929, page F1.
17. "Colleen Moore Pleases," *New York Times*, November 9, 1929, page 1.
18. In her testimony, as reported in the *San Mateo Times*, Colleen placed her return from the hospital in February, though there are no reports that her stay in the hospital lasted nearly two months. "Ugly Moods of Hubby Get Colleen Moore Divorce," *San Mateo Times*, May 5, 1930, page 1.
19. "Colleen Moore's Suit for Divorce Disclosed," *Los Angeles Times*, April 15, 1930, page A1.
20. Myra Nye, "Society of Cinemaland; With the 'Ambassadors,'" *Los Angeles Times*, February 16, 1930, page A21.
21. "Ugly Moods of Hubby Get Colleen Moore Divorce," *San Mateo Times*, May 5, 1930, page 1.

22. Moore, *Silent Star*, pages 218–219.
23. "Colleen Moore Reveals Plan to Seek Divorce," *Los Angeles Times*, April 10, 1930, page A1.
24. "Colleen Moore's Suit for Divorce Disclosed," *Los Angeles Times*, April 15, 1930, page A1.
25. "Ugly Moods of Hubby Get Colleen Moore Divorce," *San Mateo Times*, May 5, 1920, page 1.
26. Ibid., page 3.
27. "Colleen Moore Divorced but Shies at Camera Lens," *Los Angeles Times*, May 14, 1930, page A1.
28. "Says She Will Wed Former Husband of Colleen Moore," *Chicago Daily Tribune*, May 3, 1931, page 18.
29. "Cries at Colleen Moore; New Wife Quits Director," *Chicago Daily Tribune*, July 29, 1931, page 4.
30. Muriel Babcock, "Whispers in the Wings," *Los Angeles Times*, April 20, 1932, page 7.
31. Edwin Schallert, "Star's Debut Gala Affair," *Los Angeles Times*, April 19, 1932, page A9.
32. Alma Whitaker, "Stage Work Preferred by Colleen," *Los Angeles Times*, April 17, 1932, page B1.
33. Grace Kingsley, "Colleen Moore Wanted," *Los Angeles Times*, April 22, 1932, page A9.
34. Chapin Hall, "In Hollywood's Bustling Studios," *New York Times*, September 4, 1932, page X3.
35. Edwin Schallert, "News and Reviews of the Stage, Screen and Music; Gossip of Studio and the Theater; Hollywood Casualties," *Los Angeles Times*, June 20, 1933, page A7.
36. Ibid., July 1, 1933, page A7.

Bibliography

Books

Atlanta City Directory, 1908. Atlanta: Foote and Davies, 1908.

Atlanta City Directory, 1910. Atlanta: Foote and Davies, 1910.

Balio, Tino. *The American Film Industry*. Madison: University of Wisconsin Press, 1985.

Beauchamp, Cari, *Joseph P. Kennedy Presents: His Hollywood Years*. New York: Knopf, 2010, 179–180, 198–199.

Bordman, Gerald Martin. *American Theatre: A Chronicle of Comedy and Drama, 1914–1930*. New York: Oxford University Press, 1995.

Brownlow, Kevin. *The Parade's Gone By....* Berkeley: University of California Press, 1968.

Burbank, California: A Home City. Publisher unknown, 1927.

Burke, Thomas. *Twinkletoes: A Tale of Limehouse*. New York: McBride, 1918.

Butler, David, and Irene Kahn Atkins. *David Butler*. Issue 5 of Directors Guild of America Oral History Series. Metuchen, NJ: Scarecrow, 1993.

Cameron, Elspeth. *Canadian Culture: An Introductory Reader*. Toronto: Canadian Scholars', 1997.

The Chicago Blue Book of Selected Names of Chicago and Suburban Towns. Chicago: Chicago Directory, 1914.

Clark, Thomas Dionysius, and John D.W. Guice. *The Old Southwest, 1795–1830: Frontiers in Conflict*. Norman: University of Oklahoma Press, 1996.

Cooper, Walter G. *The Cotton States and International Exposition and South, Illustrated: Including the Official History of the Exposition*. Atlanta: Illustrator, 1896.

Cozad, W. Lee. *Those Magnificent Mountain Movies: The Golden Years 1911–1939*. Lake Arrowhead, CA: Rim of the World Historical Society, 2002.

Crafton, Donald, *The Talkies: American Cinema's Transition to Sound, 1926–1931*. New York: Charles Scribner's Sons, 1999, 193.

Cullen, Frank, *Vaudeville, Old & New: An Encyclopedia of Variety Performers in America, Volume 1*. New York: Routledge, 2007, 652.

Dorothy. "The Play's the Thing," *The Young Woman's Journal* (Church of Jesus Christ of Latter-Day Saints, Young Women's Mutual Improvement Association, Juvenile Instructor Office), April 1907.

Durgnat, Raymond, and Scott Simmon. *King Vidor, American*. Berkeley: University of California Press, 1988.

Dyer, Frank Lewis, and Thomas Commerford Martin. *Edison: His Life and Inventions*. New York: Harper & Brothers, 1910.

Eyman, Scott. *Empire of Dreams: The Epic Life of Cecil B. DeMille*. New York: Simon and Schuster, 2010.

Federal Writers' Project. *Los Angeles: A Guide to the City and Its Environs*. New York: Hastings House, 1941.

Fields, Armond. *Maude Adams: Idol of American Theater, 1872–1953*. Jefferson, NC: McFarland, 2004.

Fleming, E. J. *The Fixers: Eddie Mannix, Howard Strickling, and the MGM Publicity Machine*. Jefferson, NC: McFarland, 2005.

_____. *Paul Bern: The Life and Famous Death of the MGM Director and Husband of Harlow*. Jefferson, NC: McFarland, 2009.

_____. *Wallace Reid: The Life and Death of a Hollywood Idol*. Jefferson, NC: McFarland, 2007.

Forbes, Mrs. A. S. C. *California Missions and Landmarks: El Camino Real*. Los Angeles: self-published, 1915.

Gandy, Joan W., and Thomas H. Gandy. *Natchez: City Streets Revisited*. Charleston, SC: Arcadia, 1999.

Gilman, Daniel Colt, Harry Thurston Peck, and Frank Moore Colby. *The New International Encyclopædia*. New York: Dodd, Mead, 1903.

Golden, Eve. *Golden Images: 41 Essays on Silent Film Stars*. Jefferson, NC: McFarland, 2001.

Gomery, Douglas, *The Coming of Sound: A History*. New York: Routledge, 2005, 38.

_____. *Shared Pleasures: A History of Movie Presentation in the United States*. Madison: University of Wisconsin Press, 1992.

Hall, Clarence A. *Natural History of the White-Inyo Range, Eastern California*. Berkeley: University of California Press, 1991.

Healy, George W., Jr. *A Lifetime on Deadline*. Gretna, LA: Pelican, 1976.

Higginbotham, Sylvia. *Marvelous Old Mansions: And Other Southern Treasures*. Winston-Salem, NC: John F. Blair, 2000.

Hogan, Edmond K. *The Work of the Railway Carman*. Kansas City, MO: Brotherhood Railway Carmen of America, 1921.

Hudson, Robert P. *Michigan: A Summer and Health Resort State*. Michigan: State Board of Health, 1878.

The Indiana Centennial, 1916: A Record of the Celebration of the One Hundredth Anniversary of Indiana's Admission to Statehood, Indiana Historical Collections (Volume 5). Indianapolis: Indiana Historical Bureau and Harlow Lindley, 1919.

Jeansonne, Glen. "Cathrine Curtis and the Women's National Committee to Keep the U. S. out of War," *Women of the Far Right: The Mothers' Movement and World War II*. Chicago Studies in Ethnomusicology Series. University of Chicago Press, 1997.

Jensen, Richard D. *The Amazing Tom Mix: The Most Famous Cowboy of the Movies*. Bloomington, IN: iUniverse, 2005.

Jessel, George Albert. *So Help Me: The Autobiography of George Jessel*. Whitefish, MT: Kessinger, 2006.

Kanin, Garson. *Hollywood: Stars and Starlets, Tycoons and Flesh-Peddlers, Moviemakers and Moneymakers, Frauds and Geniuses, Hopefuls and Has-Beens, Great Lovers and Sex Symbols*. New York: Viking, 1974.

Kennedy, Matthew, *Edmund Goulding's Dark Victory: Hollywood's Genius Bad Boy*. Madison: University of Wisconsin Press, 2004, 70.

Kennedy, Samuel V. *Samuel Hopkins Adams and the Business of Writing*. Syracuse: Syracuse University Press, 1999.

Kirkpatrick, Sidney. *Cast of Killers*. New York: Dutton, 1986.

Klumph, Inez, and Helen Klumph. *Screen Acting, Its Requirements and Rewards*. New York: Falk, 1922.

Kobal, John. *People Will Talk*. New York: Knopf, 1985.

Kofoed, Jack. *Moon over Miami*. New York: Random House, 1955.

Kotsilibas-Davis, James. *The Barrymores, The Royal Family in Hollywood*. New York: Crown, 1981.

Lahue, Kalton C., *Dreams for Sale: The Rise and Fall of the Triangle Film Corporation*. Cranbury, NJ: A. S. Barnes, 1971.

Lang, Gerhard K., and Oskar Gareis. *Ophthalmology: A Pocket Textbook Atlas*. Stuttgart, NY: Thieme, 2007.

Laufenberg, Norbert B. *Entertainment Celebrities*. Bloomington, IN: Trafford, 2005.

LeRoy, Mervyn and Richard Kleiner, *Mervyn LeRoy: Take One*. New York: Hawthorn, 1974, 74.

Lewis, Kevin, and Arnold Lewis. "Include Me Out: Samuel Goldwyn and Joe Godsol." *Film History* (vol. 2, no. 2). Bloomington: Indiana University Press, 1988.

Lowrey, Carolyn. *The First One Hundred Noted Men and Women of the Screen*. New York: Moffat, Yard, 1920.

Lyons, Louis S., and Josephine Wilson. *Who's Who Among the Women of California: An Annual Devoted to the Representative Women of California*. San Francisco, Los Angeles: Security, 1922.

Miyao, Daisuke. *Sessue Hayakawa: Silent Cinema and Transnational Stardom*. Durham: Duke University Press, 2007.

Monaghan, Elizabeth A. *What to Eat and How to Prepare It*. New York: George H. Doran, 1922.

Moore, Colleen. *Silent Star*. Garden City, NY: Doubleday, 1968.

Mordden, Ethan. *Ziegfeld: The Man Who Invented Show Business*. New York: St. Martin's Press, 2008, 194.

Morella, Joe, and Edward Z. Epstein. *The "It" Girl: The Incredible Story of Clara Bow*. New York: Delacorte Press, 1976.

Morrill, Gulian Lansing. *On the Warpath*. Self-published, 1918.

Morrison, Michael A. *John Barrymore, Shakespearean Actor*. Cambridge (England): Cambridge University Press, 1999.

Musser, Charles. *Before the Nickelodeon: Edwin S. Porter and the Edison Manufacturing Company*. Berkeley: University of California Press, 1991.

Norman, Teresa. *A World of Baby Names*. New York: Perigee, 2003.

Oderman, Stuart. *Lillian Gish: A Life on Stage and Screen*. Jefferson, NC: McFarland, 2000.

Oemler, Mrs. Marie Conway. *Slippy McGee: Sometimes Known as the Butterfly Man*. New York: Century, 1920.

Ogle (George A.) and Company. "North Middle part of the City of Port Huron," in *Standard Atlas* of St. Clair County, Michigan: Geo. A. Ogle, 1897.

Our Country: East. Boston: Perry Mason, 1898.

Parker, Gilbert. "She of the Triple Chevron": *The Works of Gilbert Parker* (Volume 1). New York: Scribners, 1912.

Patterson, Frances Taylor. *Cinema Craftsmanship: A Book for Photoplaywrights*. New York: Harcourt, Brace, 1920.

Peterson, Bernard L. "Sally in Our Alley," *A Century of Musicals in Black and White: An Encyclopedia of Musical Stage Works By, About, or Involving African Americans*. Westport, CT: Greenwood, 1993.

Pizzitola, Louis. *Hearst Over Hollywood: Power, Passion, and Propaganda in the Movies*. New York: Columbia University Press, 2002.

Polk's Hillsdale City and County Directory 1905–1906. Detroit: R. L. Polk, 1905.

Port Huron 1902 Directory. Port Huron, MI: Wolverine Directory, 1902.

Port Huron Directory 1899–1900. Port Huron, MI: Riverside Printing, 1899.

Rinehart, Mary Roberts. *Affinities: and Other Stories.* New York: George H. Doran, 1920.

Rochelson, Meri-Jane. *A Jew in the Public Arena: The Career of Israel Zangwill.* Detroit: Wayne State University Press, 2008.

Royster, Jacqueline Jones. *Profiles of Ohio Women, 1803–2003.* Athens: Ohio University Press, 2003.

Sanborn Fire Insurance Maps, Atlanta, Ga. vol. 4, sheet 495; vol. 1, sheet 50; and vol. 2, sheet 185. Pelham, NY: Sanborn Map, 1911.

Scheinin, Richard. *Field of Screams: The Dark Underside of America's National Pastime.* New York: W.W. Norton, 1994.

Slide, Anthony, *The Kindergarten of the Movies: A History of the Fine Arts Company.* Metuchen, N.J.: Scarecrow, 1980, 21, 92, 116.

_____, *Silent Topics: Essays on Undocumented Areas of Silent Film.* Metuchen, NJ: Scarecrow, 2005.

Smith, C. E. "Report on Cause and Correction of Foundation Troubles of Box Factory at Natchez, Mississippi," *Proceedings of the American Society of Civil Engineers* (Volume 46). New York: The Society, 1920.

Smyth, J. E., and Thomas Schatz. *Edna Ferber's Hollywood: American Fictions of Gender, Race, and History.* Texas Film and Media Studies Series. Austin: University of Texas Press, 2009.

Sperling, Cass Warner, Cork Milner, and Jack Warner. *Hollywood Be Thy Name: The Warner Brothers Story.* Lexington: University Press of Kentucky, 1998.

Starr, Jimmy. *Barefoot on Barbed Wire: An Autobiography of a Forty-year Hollywood Balancing Act.* Lanham, MD: Rowman & Littlefield, 2001.

Taves, Brian. *P.G. Wodehouse and Hollywood: Screenwriting, Satires, and Adaptations.* Jefferson, NC: McFarland, 2006.

Thirteenth Census of the United States, 1910: Population by Counties and Minor Civil Divisions, 1910, 1900, 1890. Washington, D.C.: Government Printing Office, 1912.

Tomán, René De La Pedraja. *A Historical Dictionary of the U.S. Merchant Marine and Shipping Industry: Since the Introduction of Steam.* Westport, CT: Greenwood, 1994.

Vidor, King. *A Tree Is a Tree.* New York: Samuel French, 1981.

Wanamaker, Marc, *Hollywood 1940–2008.* Charleston, SC: Arcadia, 2009.

Wing, Ruth, ed., *The Blue Book of the Screen.* Hollywood, CA: Pacific Gravure, 1923.

Wolfe, David A., and Eric J. Mash. *Behavioral and Emotional Disorders in Adolescents: Nature, Assessment, and Treatment.* New York: Guilford, 2008.

Wurtzel, Lillian Semenov, and Carla Winter. *William Fox, Sol M. Wurtzel and the Early Fox Film, Letters 1917–1923.* Jefferson, NC: McFarland, 2001.

Zeitz, Joshua, *Flapper: A Madcap Story of Sex, Style, Celebrity, and the Women who Made America Modern.* New York: Crown Publishers, 2007, 238.

Internet

Andress, Richard. "Film Censorship in New York State," *New York State Archives.* http://www.archives.nysed.gov/a/research/res_topics_film_censor.shtml (March 19, 2010).

"Atlanta, Foote and Davies Company (Atlanta, Ga.)," American *Memory, Library of Congress*, Call Number: G3924.A8A3 1919 .F6. http://hdl.loc.gov/loc.gmd/g3924a.pm001230 (April 19, 2011).

"Baker Grand Theatre; Natchez, MS," Cinema Treasures. http://cinematreasures.org/theater/31644/ (March 6, 2010).

"Birds EyeView of the City of Hillsdale, Hillsdale Co., Mich. 1866; drawn & published by A. Ruger," *American Memory, Library of Congress*, Call Number: G4114.H65A3 1866 .R8. http://hdl.loc.gov/loc.gmd/g4114h.pm003510 (April 19, 2011).

Connell, Mike. "Part 5: Bright ideas gave city status; Inventors and attitude made Port Huron an early industrial leader," *Port Huron Times Herald*, 2007. http://www.thetimesherald.com (October 4, 2007).

"Disc-Overies." The Vitaphone Project. http://www.picking.com/vitaphone52.html (February 20, 2011).

"History of Edison Motion Pictures: Origins of Motion Pictures — the Kinetoscope." Library of Congress, http://international.loc.gov/ammem/edhtml/edmvhist.html (October 12, 2010).

"History of the Academy." Academy of Motion Picture Arts and Sciences. http://www.oscars.org/academy/history-organization/history.html (March 16, 2011).

"History of the Actors Fund." The Actor's Fund. http://www.actorsfund.org (April 5, 2010).

"History of the Hollywood Bowl Shell." Hollywood Bowl. http://www.hollywoodbowl.com/about/bowl-shell.cfm (January 7, 2011).

"Irene." Internet Broadway Data Base. http://www.ibdb.com/production.php?id=6724 (December 2, 2010).

"Johnny Wilson, alias: Giovanni Francisco Panica; Norman Selby, alias: Kid McCoy; Louis C. Wallach, alias: The Fighting Dentist. "http://boxrec.com/ (October 20, 2010).

"Money-Mad Indians Give Peaceful Town a Thrill." *Camera*, vol. 6 no. 1, page 11, compiled by Joe Moore, with assistance from the special collections staff of Arizona State University, Tempe AZ. http://www.slapsticon.org/mugshots/Camera-Jun3023.htm (February 22, 2010).

"The New Pioneers: Finding the good life in Orange County's suburban frontier." *Los Angeles Times*, March 27, 1994. http://articles.latimes.com/1994-03-27/news/mn-39202_1_rancho-santa-margarita (January 31, 2011).

Rayport, Jeffrey. "The Virus of Marketing," *Fast Company Magazine*, December 31, 1996. http://www.fastcompany.com/magazine/06/virus.html (September 3, 2010).

"Route of the California Limited—'Santa Fe All the Way.'" Rumsey Map Collection. http://www.davidrumsey.com/maps900046-24543.html (March 3, 2010).

"Sally Joy Brown: The Housewives' Friend." *The Chicago History Journal*. http://www.chicagohistoryjournal.com/2008/10/sally-joy-brown-housewives-friend.html (January 3, 2011).

Soares, Andre. "Colleen Moore and *Her Wild Oat*," *Alt Film Guide*, April 27, 2007. http://www.altfg.com/blog/actors/colleen-moore-and-her-wild-oat/ (January 29, 2011).

"Strand Theatre; Tampa, FL." Cinema Treasure website. http://cinematreasures.org/theater/8513 (July 25, 2010).

"World's Most Advanced Post Production Sound Facility to Open at Warner Bros. Studios in Winter 2005." Warner Bros. http://wbpostproduction.warnerbros.com/news/pps_fac_pr.pdf (July 10, 2010).

Young, Ann. "Early Film Studios in Santa Cruz County." *Santa Cruz Public Libraries*. http://www.santacruzpl.org/history/articles/295/ (October 13, 2010).

Index

Numbers in **_bold italics_** indicate pages with photographs.

Abel, David 32
Academy of Motion Picture Arts and Sciences 188
Actor's Fund Festival 79
Adams, Samuel Hopkins (writer) 59, 113
Adoree, Renee 215
Affinities **_102_**–103
Aimee (chartered yacht) **_220_**–221, 224
Ain't She Sweet 200; see also *Her Wild Oat*; *Tell the World*
American Mutoscope and Biograph Company 7
American Vitagraph Company 107, 109–110
Anderson, Gilbert M. "Brohcho Billy" 22
Antony and Cleopatra 237
April Showers 114–115
Arbuckle, Roscoe "Fatty" 53, 91
Armat, Thomas 5, 6
Arrowhead Hot Springs 184–185, 204
Arthur, George K. 160
Arthur J. Klein (trophy) 145
Associated First National 3, 59, 72–73, 102, 112–113, 124, 127, 130–131
Associated Producers 64, 67
Astor, Gertrude 92, 109–110
Atkins, Irene Kahn 70
Aylett, Jack 214

The Bad Boy 30–33
Badger, Clarence 127–129
Bailey, Frankie 172
Balaban, A.J. 162
Balaban, Barney 162
Balaban and Katz, Inc. 162–163, 225
Balkan Love 229
Ball, Ernest 186
Banzhaf, Albert H.T. 38, 39
Barnes, T. Roy 64
Barrows, James O. 78
Barry, John A. 38–39
Barry, Wesley 63, 65, 72
Barrymore, John 73–**_74_**; *Clair de Lune* (play) 76
Barrymore, Lionel 247
Baxter, Warner 107, 109–110
Beahan, Charles 224
Beal, Dolly **_159_**
Beatty, Jerome 229–230

Beau Geste 230
Beaudet, Louise 141
beauties of *Flaming Youth* 122, 123; see also *Flaming Youth*
Beauty Parlor 248
Belcher, Ernest 172
S.S. *Berengaria* 154
Besserer, Eugenie 42–**_43_**, 207–208
The Better 'Ole 203
Bidwell, Eli Clark 37, 38–39
"Biograph Girl" 20
Bishop Paiutes (Native Americans) 121; see also *The Huntress*
The Bitterness of Sweets 96, 98–99, 102, 111; see also *Look Your Best*
Black Oxen 128
Black Oxen (book) 117, 126; see also Bow, Clara
Blackie, Boston 117; see also *Through the Dark*
Blank, A.H. 225
Blue, Monte 36
Board, J.L. "Lew" 7; see also Kelly, Elizabeth
Bobbed Hair 140
Bonner, Joe 103
Bonner, Priscilla 115
Boothby, W.C. 199
Borden, Olive 218
Borzage, Frank 110–111, 115
Bow, Clara 126, 128–129, 162, 233
Bowers, John 69–70, 103, 138
Brabin, Charles 20, 138, 169, 174
Bracken, Monica 99
Brockwell, Gladys 169, 171
Broken Blossoms 158, 169
Broken Chains 102, 104, 105, 110
Broken Hearts of Broadway 115–116
Brook Evans 223
Brooks, Louise 150, 206, 217, 229
Brownlee, Frank 144
Brush, Katherine 235; see also *Footlights and Fools*
Bryan, Al 241; see also *Smiling Irish Eyes*
Bryan, William Jennings 76, 79
Bull, C.S. **_101_**
Bullwinkle, John C. 190
Burkan, Nathan 197–198
Burning Daylight 218
The Busher 46
Bushman, Francis X. 18
Butler, David 69–70

Campbell, Colin 41, 61

Carthay Circle Theater 218–219, 230
Cassell, Duncan 156, 161, 202
Cathrine Curtis Corporation 67
Ceballos, Larry 239
censorship 85, 88, 89, 91
Chambers, Robert W. 229
Chandler, C.F. Chandler 190
Chaplin, Charles 26, 59, 93, 97, 160, 215, 219
Chaplin, Sydney 133
Chautard, Emile 106
Chester "Chet" Withey 28, 32
Chicago Daily News scenario contest 93; see also *Broken Chains*; Westover, Winifred
The Children 223–224
The Chink and the Child 158; see also *Twinkletoes*
Christie, Al 53–54, 56, 59–60, 62, 64–66
Christie, Charles 54, 60
Christie Comedies 56
Christie Comedy Company 54, 61, 64, 72
Christie Studio 56, 57–58, 62–63, 66
A Church Mouse 247
S.S. *City of Los Angeles* 214
Clarissa and the Post Road 147
Clark, Marguerite 18
Clawson, Elliott J. 49, 51
Clifford, Ruth 115
Clipped Wings (proposed film) 231
"Clipped Wings" (short story) 224; see also *Clipped Wings*
Cohan, George M. 188
Cojo (yacht) 199
Collier, Constance 237
Collins, Monte 95
"Come Back to Erin" ("Return to Erin") 239, 243; see also *Smiling Irish Eyes*
Come on Over 94, 238
Common Property 51–52
Compson, Betty 53
Connolly, Jack 51
Conselman, William 161
The Constant Nymph 223
Cooley, Hallam 183, 201
Cooper, Gary 206, 209
Cooper, Miriam 72
Coquette 223
Cosmopolitan Productions 61, 110–111, 118

291

Cotton States and International Exposition (1895) 5, 6
Counterfeit 135; see also *Flirting with Love*
Cowl, Jane 199; see also *Lilac Time*
Cox, Clarence 234
Crandall, Mr. and Mrs. Harry M. 149
Crawford, Joan 223
Cross, "Doc" Leach (Louis C. Wallach; "The Fighting Dentist") 115
Cummings, Irving 116, 143, 247
Currier, Frank 73
Curtis, Cathrine 67–69
The Cyclone 55

Dangerous Nan McGrew 224, 228
Daniels, Bebe 161
Daphne Goes Down 161
Darlin' 96; see also *Come on Over*
Darmond, Grace 64, 66
The Daughter of Mother McGinn (book) 117; see also *Through the Dark*
Davenport, Milla 139
Davis, Mildred 149
Daw, Marjorie 66
Day, Shannon 88
De Grasse, Sam 34
Delicatessen 161, 164–166; see also *Look Your Best*
DeMille, Cecil B. 135, 188
DeMille, Mrs. William 79
Dempsey, Jack 175, 215, 218
Depinet, Ned 229–230
The Desert Flower **144**, 147, 158, 249
The Desert Flower (play) 143; see also *The Desert Flower*
The Devil's Claim 58
Dexter, Elliott 122
Dierker, Hugh 78
Dillon, John F. 117
Dinty 63–66, 68, 72, 75, 87
The Divine Lady 226
Dix, Richard 88, 89, 92, 215
Don Juan 203
Donlin, Mike "Turkey Mike" 164
Dove, Billie 226
Dresser, Louise 141
Drew, Florence 93
Duffy, Gerald C. 184–185, 189–193, 201, 240
Duffy, Marjorie 240; see also Duffy, Gerald C.
Dunn, Winifred 163–164

Earl Burtnett's Biltmore Trio 241; see also *Smiling Irish Eyes*
Early to Bed 232, 234–325
East of the Setting Sun see *Balkan Love*
Edison, Thomas 7–8, 23, 109
Edison Trust 23, 41; see also Motion Pictures Patents Company
Edwards, R.G. 204
Edwards, Snitz 121
The Egg Crate Wallop 50–53
1895 Cotton States and International Exposition 5, 6
Einfeld, Charles 190

Electrical Research Products 213
Ella Cinders 163–166, 227
Ella Cinders (comic strip) 161; see also *Ella Cinders*
Elvidge, June 106
Errol, Leon 141–142
Essanay Company 22, 24–25, 149
Exceptional Pictures Corporation 61

Fabian, Warner 113–114, 130–132; see also Adams, Samuel Hopkins
Fairbanks, Douglas 188
Fairbanks, Douglas, Jr. 249
Famous Players Film Corporation 23; see also Zukor, Adolph
Famous Players–Lasky Corporation 33, 59, 135, 157, 162, 186
FBO (Film Booking Offices of America) 216–217, 224
Ferber, Edna 137–138; see also *So Big*
Ferguson, Helen 25–26
Fine Arts Film Company 34, 36–37, 39, 165
Finkelstein and Ruben 131, 225
Firnatone (sound process) 209, 213–214, 217
First National Burbank Studio 165–167, 181, 187, 227
First National Exhibitor's Circuit, Inc. 33; see also Associated First National
First National Motion Pictures Corporation 187
First National Pictures, Inc.: developments 59, 67, 72, 86, 114, 127, 147, 155, 157, 163, 165, 186, 214–216, 224–225; sound 213, 221
First National Productions (developments) 127, 135, 140
First National–Vitaphone 239–240
Fitzgerald, F. Scott 101; *This Side of Paradise* 113; *Tales of the Jazz Age* 113
Fitzmaurice, George 199, 205–207, 218–219, 247
Flaming Youth 121, **125**, 127, 129–133, 142, 147, 157–158, 208, 234
Flaming Youth (novel) 113; see also *Flaming Youth*
flappers, first appearances 66, 100, 113
The Fleet's In 233
Flesh 248
Fletcher, Billy 99
Flirting with Love 135–136
Foolish Wives 89
Footlights and Fools 235–236, 239–242, 244–246
For Sale 135
Ford, James 226
Forman, Tom 114–115
Forsaking All Others 106, 107, 110
"Forsaking All Others" (short story) see *Forsaking All Others*
Fort, Garrett 224
Fox, William 23, 41, 49, 155, 185, 216
Fox bear (Theda Bear-a) 49
Fox Films 46, 54, 154, 186, 216, 225

Francisco, Betty 238
Freulich, Henry 174, 181
Funny Face 223–224

Garden of Eden 182
Garner, Jack 141
A Garret in Paris 231
Geraghty, Carmelita **123**, 125
Geraghty, Tom 219, 223, 238
Gibbons, Cedric 104, 188
Gilbert, Jack (John) 46
Gillingwater, Claude 157, 238
Glazer, Benjamin 208
Glyn, Elinor 79
Goldbeck, Willis 202
Goldfish, Samuel 23; see also Goldwyn, Samuel
Goldwyn, Samuel 87, 88
Goldwyn Pictures 93, 96, **98–99**, **100**, 102, 105, 107, 110
Goldwyn Studio 92–95
Gore, A.L. 186; see also Gore Bros.
Gore, Mike 186; see also Gore Bros.
Gore Bros. 154–155
Goulding, Edmund 208–210
Grace, Dick 207
Grauman, Sid 79, 188
Graves, Ralph 93, **94**
Gray, Lawrence 215
Green, Al 93, 141, 158–157, 161, 164, 247; *In Hollywood with Potash and Perlmutter* 142
Grieve, Harold 234, 245
Griffith, Corinne 225–226
Griffith, D.W. 14, 23–25, 28–29, 34–39, 41–42, 53, 59, 93, 158, 218

Hackett, Raymond 241
Haines, William 247
Hale, Alan 215
Hall, Al 204, 226
Hall, James 206, 243
Hamilton, Neil 234
Hands Up! 36
Happiness Ahead 210–**212**, 213, 216, 219
Hardy, Sam 175
Harlan, Kenneth 35, 114–115, 169
Harris, Mildred 28–29, 31, 34
Harron, Robert 28–29, 31–32, 34–35, 38, 248
Haskin, Byron 104
Hatton, Frederick and Fanny 199; see also *Synthetic Sin*
Haver, Phyllis 134, 138
Hawkley, Clifford B. 186
Hawley, Clifford 209
Hayakawa, Sessue 58
Hayes, George "Gabby" 238
Hays, Will H. 179
"He Fooled 'Em All" (short Story) see *His Nibs*
Hearst, William Randolph 11
Heart of Maryland 83
Heart to Heart 212
Hearts of the World 36, 39, 40
Held, John 113
Her Bridal Night-mare 58–59
Her Wild Oat 200–201, 204–206, 251

Index

Here Is My Heart 208; see also *Happiness Ahead*
Herring, Aggie 109
Hersholt, Jean 166
Hickox, Sid *159*, 219, 234–236
Hiers, Walter 64, **65**
His Nibs 61–62, 93
Holt, Jack 149
Holubar, Allen 102, 104, 105
Holy Names Academy 20
A Hoosier Romance 41–42, 44
Howey, Walter 14–15, 21–22, 24–25, 27, 41, 91, 111, 218
Hoyt, Nancy 224
Hudson, Earl 116–117, 125, 131, 133, 138
Hugh Dierker Photodrama Producing Company 61
Hughes, Lloyd 126, 141, 144, 163
Hughes, Rupert 79, 87, 88, 92, 93, 97, **106**, 238
Hughes, Rush 92
The Huntress 117–119, **120**, 121, 126

Ince Studio 102, 103, 110
influenza 109
International Academy of Motion Picture Arts and Sciences 188; *see also* Academy of Motion Picture Arts and Sciences
Intolerance 27–29, 34–36
Irene 147–148, 156, 158–161, 208
Irene (musical) 147; see also *Irene*
Irish themes or image 25, 34, 63, 77, 90, 95–97, 101, 114–115, 160, 184, 238
Irving Cummings Productions 115
It Must Be Love 166, 171–172, 232

Jack Dempsey–Gene Tunney fight 175
Jasmine, Arthur 49
The Jazz Singer 203, 227
"Jeannine, I Dream of Lilac Time" (song) 227; see also *Lilac Time*
Jenkins, Charles Francis 5–6
Jennings, Al 36, 79
Jessel, George 221
Johnston, Julanne 170, 219, 226, 238, 246
Jolson, Al Jolson 203, 219, 227
Jones, Aaron "King Jones" 15; *see also* "nickelodeon" phase of motion pictures
Josephson, Julien 161
Julian, Rupert 38

Kane, Diana 219
Katz, Samuel 162
Keith, Donald 162
Keith-Albee-Orpheum (theater chain) 216–217
Kelly, Agnes 7–**8**; *see also* Morrison, Agnes
Kelly, Elizabeth "Liberty" 7, **14**, 21, 24
Kelly, John Patrick 7, 9; *see also* Kelly, Mary
Kelly, Mary 9, 11–13, 17, 19, 25, 27, 32–34, 37, 42, 45, 72, 86, 90, 95, 125, 139, 248

Kennedy, Joseph 216–217, 219, 224
Kent, Larry 201
"Killarney Rose" 186
Kingsley, Grace (columns) 37, 78, 81, 87–89, 103, 108, 138, 145–146, 184, 200, 242–243
Kossloff, Theodore 67, 98

Ladies of the Mob 233
Laemmle, Carl 22–23, 27, 89
Lake Alice 116
Lambert, Reita 224
Landis, Cullen 106–107
Landry, George 119
Langdon, Harry 160, 163, 164
Lasky, Jesse 188, 213
Lasky-DeMille Barn 162
Lawrence, D.H.: *Women in Love* 113
Lawrence, Florence 172; *see also* "Biograph Girl"
Lee, Gwen 175, 201
Lerner, Mary see *Forsaking All Others*
LeRoy, Mervyn 141–*142*, 145, 159, 163, 173, 176–177, 181–182, 184–186, 188–193, 195, 200, 208, 218, 223, 227, 240, 247
Lescalle, Ward 102
Lesser, Sol 73, 79, 108, 155
Levee, M.C. 140, 165, 179, 187, 192, 194
Lewis, Sinclair 113; *Main Street* 113
Lieber, Robert 186, 213, 225
Lighton, Louis D. 116
Lilac Time 43, 182, 199–200, 202, 204–***207***, 208–209, 213, 217–219, 221, 226–227, 230, 234–235, 237, 239–240
Lilac Time (play) 199; see also *Lilac Time*
Lilies of the Field 135
Little Orphant Annie 42–**43**, 44–45, 61, 75, 87
"Little Orphant Annie" (poem) 42
Lloyd, Frank 226
Lloyd, Harold 160, 228
Loeb, Edwin 189, 194, 196
Loeb, Walker and Loeb 205, 235; see also Loeb, Edwin
Long Pants 184
Look Your Best **98–99**, *106*, 111, 226
Loos, Anita 248
Loring, Hope 116
The Lotus Eater 73–**74**, 75–76
Louis Robinson Ranch 205; see also *Lilac Time*
Love, Bessie 28, 160
Lowe, Edmund 210
Loy, Myrna 193
Lubin, Sigmund "Pop" 224
Lubitsch, Ernst 247
Lucille Love 18
Lucky Boy 221
Lyon, Ben 128, 138

MacCurdy, James Kyle 116
Mackaill, Dorothy 219
S.S. *Majestic* 150
S.S. *Malolo* 213
The Man in the Moonlight 49–52
March, Fredric 241

March, Iris 160
Marin, Ned 182, 191–192, 202
Marion, George, Jr. 223
Marshall, Tully 116, 169
Marshall Neilan Productions 86
Martineau report 198
Mason, Dan 141
Mason, Grace Sartwell 147
Mastbaum, Jules 224
Mathis, June 140–142, 147, 161
S.S. *Mauretania* 197
Mayer, Louis B. 114, 188
Mayer-Schulberg Studio 114
McCord, T.D. 153–158
McCormick, John 23, 72, 79, 95, 115–116, 206; Athletic Club (Los Angeles) 119; break with First National 189, 191, 197; drinking 119, 125, 132, 176, 179–181, 213, 227–228, 244–246; engagement to Colleen Moore 96, *122*; engagement to Dorothy Mackaill 247; engagement to Mae Clark 247; First National Western General Manager of west coast productions 156; First National Western Representative 79, 146; First National's western press representative 79; marriage to Janet Gattis 247; meeting Colleen 88, 90; parents 125, violence 176–177, 245–246; Waters, Bessie 72
McCoy, "Kid" (Norman Selby) 115
McCutcheon, George Barr 229
McDonald, Farrell 93
McGee, James L. 42
McGregor, Malcolm 104, 166
McGuire, Kathryn 183, 209, 226
McGuire, Tom 114
McGuirk, John 186, 213
McKean, Marie 204
Merriam, Charlotte 112, 128
Metro-Goldwyn 138
Metro-Goldwyn-Mayer (MGM) 247, **248**
Military Mary 223
Miller, Carl 157
Miller, Marilyn 141
Mills, Alyce 162
Minter, Mary Miles 31
Miss George Washington 181
Miss Nobody 163
Mitchell, Mr. and Mrs. Walter 125
Mix, Tom 46–**48**, 49, 51, 54–**55**, 56–57
Mixville 55
Montross, Lynn and Lois Seyster 233
Moore, Cleve 207; *see also* Morrison, Cleeve
Moore, Colleen: baseball 52; bungalow 159–160; devotees 172–173; divorce 246–247; dollhouse 213–214, 249; engagement 96; European tour 149–*151*, **152–154**; John's drinking 119; Mrs. John McCormick 181; neck injury 145–***146***, 147; publicity 79–**80**, *180*; rumors of romance 73, 86, 89, 96; sound 202, 228; wedding ***122–124***, 125–***126***

Moore, Colleen, contracts: Christie 60; Cosmopolitan 108, 111; First National (1923) 108, 116–117, 122, 135; First National first option (of 1923 contract) 135; First National amendment and second option (of 1923 contract) 140; First National (1925) 155, 157; First National amendment (of 1925 contract) 136; First National (1926) 164, 171, 179, 182, 185, 189–191, 193–194, 196–198; First National (1927) 199, 204–205, 208, 211; First National (1928) 212, 225, 229, 235–236; First National (1929) 235–236, 239, 242; Goldwyn *101*, 105; Griffith 24, 26–27, 37–39; MGM 247–248; Neilan 65–66; Selig 40, 42, 44; Warner Bros. (rejected by John) 230

Moore, Colleen, films of: *Affinities 102*–103; *April Showers* 114–115; *The Bad Boy* 30–33; *Broken Chains* 102, 104, 105, 110; *Broken Hearts of Broadway* 115–116; *The Busher* 46; *Common Property* 51–52; *The Cyclone* 55; *The Desert Flower 144*, 147, 158, 249; *The Devil's Claim* 58; *Dinty* 63–66, 68, 72, 75, 87; *The Egg Crate Wallop* 50–53; *Ella Cinders* 163–166, 227; *Flaming Youth* 121, *125*, 127, 129–133, 142, 147, 157–158, 208, 234; *Flirting with Love* 135–136; *Footlights and Fools* 235–236, 239–242, 244–246; *Forsaking All Others* 106, 107, 110; *Hands Up!* 36; *Happiness Ahead* 210–*212*, 213, 216, 219; *Her Bridal Nightmare* 58–59; *Her Wild Oat* 200–201, 204–206, 251; *His Nibs* 61–62, 93; *A Hoosier Romance* 41–42, 44; *The Huntress* 117–119, *120*, 121, 126; *Irene* 147–148, 156, 158–161, 208; *It Must Be Love* 166, 171–172, 232; *Lilac Time* 43, 182, 199–200, 202, 204–*207*, 208–209, 213, 217–219, 221, 226–227, 230, 234–235, 237, 239–240; *Little Orphant Annie* 42–*43*, 44–45, 61, 75, 87; *Look Your Best 98*–*99*, *106*, 111, 226; *The Lotus Eater* 73–*74*, 75–76; *The Man in the Moonlight* 49–52; *Naughty but Nice* 182–184, 199, 226; *The Ninety and Nine* 107, 109–110; *The Nth Commandment* 110–*111*, 112, 114; *Oh, Kay* 204, 208, *212*–216, 218, 221, 223; *An Old Fashioned Young Man* 34–36; *Painted People* 133, 135; *The Perfect Flapper* 133–135, 147; *The Power and the Glory* 248; *A Roman Scandal* 57, 58; *Sally* 94, *141*, 147–148, 152–153, 158, 208; *The Savage* 38, 49; *The Sky Pilot* 67–*68*, *69*–73, 75, 87, 103; *Slippy McGee* 78–*80*, 81–*82* , *83*–84, 111, 142; *Smiling Irish Eyes* 240–241, 243; *So Big 137*–*138*, 139–141, 143, 148, 150, *152*–153, 158, 168, 170, 184, 248; *So Long Letty* 63, 64–*65*, 66, 72, 84, 103; *Social Register* 248–249; *Success at Any Price* 249; *Synthetic Sin* 199–200, 204, 208, 211–212, 219, 223–228, 231, 233, 237; *Through the Dark* 117–*118*, *119*, 133, 143; *Twinkletoes* 158, 161, 163–165, 168–175, 181–182, 199, 237; *The Wall Flower* 87–88, 92–93, *97*, *100*; *We Moderns* 147, 153, *155*–158, 169; *When Dawn Came 61*–62, 78, 87; *Why Be Good?* 230–235, 23; *The Wilderness Trail* 47–*48*, 49, 52, 54

Moore, Colleen, flapper 101–102, 107–108, 113, 127, 131, 133–139, 149, 217, 223, 233, 237

Moore, Colleen, suggested or unproduced films: *Ain't She Sweet* 200; *Balkan Love* 229; *Beauty Parlor* 248; *Brook Evans* 223; *The Children* 223–224; *Clarissa and the Post Road* 147; *Clipped Wings* 231; *The Constant Nymph* 223; *Coquette* 223; *Dangerous Nan McGrew* 224, 228; *Early to Bed* 232, 234–325; *Flesh* 248; *Funny Face* 223–224; *Garden of Eden* 182; *A Garret in Paris* 231; *Military Mary* 223; *Miss George Washington* 181; *Miss Nobody* 163; *Pygmalion* 223; *Red-Headed Woman 248*; *The Richest Girl in the World* 212; *The Richest Girl on Earth* 219, 224; "Rogue's Moon" 229; *Roundabout* 224; *Shebo* 158, 161, 163; *Something with a Kick* 184; *Sunny* 223; *Susi* 223; *Turn Back the Clock* 248

Moran, Polly 172
Moreno, Antonio 98, *99*, 226
Morgan, Ira H. 67
Morley, Karen 248
Morosco, Oliver 78, 111
Morrill, G.L. "Golightly" 89; *see also* Sunset Inn
Morrison, Agnes 9, 13–15, 17, 21, 24–27, 32–34, 42, 45, 47–48, 54, 68, 72–75, 89–90, 116, 119, *123*, 125
Morrison, Charles Runnles *85*, 146
Morrison, Cleeve 11, 14, 17–*19*, 20–21, 24, 64, *68*, *95*, 115, 124–125, 134–135, 157, 196–197, 221, 240, 245; *see also* Moore, Cleve
Morrison, James 111
Morrison, Kathleen: American Stock Company 17, 19; Atlanta, GA 17–19; baseball 22; birth 9; Chicago, IL 11, 14, 17, 21–22, 24–27; Chicago studios 22; dolls 10, 12–*13*, 15; Essanay film test 25–26; eyes 12, 25–26; Hillsdale, MI 12–14; "Kathleen's Collection" 12; McCormick, Kathleen Morrison 147; Motion Picture Patents Company (MPPC) 22, 23, 41, 109; Port Huron, MI 9–11; Tampa, FL 19–22, 24, 25; Warren, PA 19; *see also* Moore, Colleen, entries

Motion Picture Benefit 80; *see also* Actor's Fund Festival
Mulhall, Jack 157, 175
Mullan, George V. 197, 199
Murfin, Jane 199; see also *Lilac Time*
Murphy, Edna Murphy 193, 218
Murray, Charles 79, 160
Murray, Mae 193
Meyer, George W. 241; see also *Smiling Irish Eyes*
Myers, Carmel 32–33

Naughty but Nice 182–184, 199, 226
Nazimova, Alla 149, 151
Neilan, Marshall 63, 65, 73, *75*, 97, 119, 200–201, 206, 247–248; *Go and Get It* 63; *The Harbor City Mystery* 63
"nickelodeon" phase of motion pictures 15–16
Nilsson, Anna Q. 73
The Ninety and Nine 107, 109–110
The Ninety and Nine (1916 Vitagraph Blue Ribbon Feature) 109; see also *The Ninety and Nine*
The Nth Commandment 110–*111*, 112, 114
"The Nth Commandment" (short story) see *The Nth Commandment*

Oakman, Wheeler 83, 87
Obringer, Roy 211–212, 223, 239
O'Connor, Kathleen 93, *94*
O'Connor, Loyola O'Connor 34
O'Connor, Mary 37
Oh, Kay! 204, 208, *212*–216, 218, 221, 223
Oh What a Life 200
An Old Fashioned Young Man 34–36
"Old Killarney Fair" (song) 239; see also *Smiling Irish Eyes*
O'Malley, Pat 66
O'Mally, Pat 164
"Ophelia Will Fool You" (song) 241; see also *Footlights and Fools*
Orchids and Ermine 171, 173–*176*, 177–178, 181–182, 189–190, 199
Ostriche, Muriel 141
Otterson, John 202
Our Dancing Daughters 223
The Outcast 226

Painted People 133, 135
Paramount 23, 50, 111, 129, 161–162, 186, 206, 216, 225, 230
Pathé 53, 215–216, 224
Payson, Blanche 99
The Perfect Flapper 133–135, 147
Perkins, R.W. 190, 194, 196, 205, 242
Peter Pan (play) 14–15, 184
Phantoscope 5, 6
Phillips, Eddie 112
Photophone (sound process) 217, 219
Pickford, Mary 20, 23, 28, 32, 59, 63, 85, 97, 172, 188, 228
Pickford-Fairbanks lot 92

"Pilly Pom Pom Plee" (song) 241; see also *Footlights and Fools*
Plumb, Charles 161
Pomeroy, Roy J. 228
Poucher, Ralph 213–214
Powell, Paul 50
The Power and the Glory 248
The Power of a Lie 107
Preferred Pictures 114
Price, Kate 93, 95, 144, 160
The Prince of Graustark 24
Printzlau, Olga 114
Producers Security Corporation 62
Prohibition 59–60, **80**, 214
Publix Theaters 162
Pygmalion 223

Ramish, Adolph 155
Ray, Charles 46, 50, 65, 79, 139
RCA (Radio Corporation of America) 217, 228
Red Hair 233
Red-Headed Woman **248**
Reed, Donald 183
Reynolds, Lynn F. 120
Rich, Walter J. 202
The Richest Girl in the World 212
The Richest Girl on Earth 219, 224
Riley, James Whitcomb 42, 44
Rinehart, Mary Roberts 92
RKO (Radio-Keith-Orpheum) 249
Roach, Hal 53
The Road to Dublin 184; see also *When Irish Eyes Are Smiling*
Robertson-Cole Company 61–62, 64
Rockett, Al 155–156, 191, 193, 214, 219, 223, 230–231, 235, 240
Rogue's Moon 229
Roland, Ruth 160
Rolled Stockings 206; see also Brooks, Louise; Hall, James
Rolph, James "Sunny Jim" 127
A Roman Scandal 57, 58
Roscoe, Alan 136
Rosing, Bodil 232, 237
Rossheim, Irving D. 186, 215–216
Rothacker, W.R. 187, 190, 192, 199, 205, 213–214, 216
Roundabout 224; see also *Clipped Wings*
Rowland, Gilbert 162
Rowland, Richard A.: First National 108, 112–113, 117, 135, 147, 150, 155–156, 181, 185, 199, 216; John's break with First National 189–191, 195, 198; Metro Pictures Corporation 59
Ruggles, Wesley 78, 81, 83

St. Denis, Ruth 183
St. Johns, Adela Rogers 88, 97, 125, 202, 222
Sale, Charles "Chic" 60–62, 65, 93
Salisbury, Monroe 38, 49, 50
Sally 94, **141**, 147–148, 152–153, 158, 208
Sally (Ziegfeld show) 140; see also *Sally*
"Sally in Our Alley" (song) 140; see also *Sally*

Salmon, Nat 104
Santell, Alfred 173, 175–176
Santschi, Thomas 45
Sarnoff, David 217
The Savage 38, 49
Schip, Carlo 141
Schulberg, B.P. 114
Schulte, P.J. 159; see also Moore, Colleen: bungalow
Scott, Albert 247
Scott, LeRoy 135; see also *Flirting with Love*
Scott, Theodore J. 234
Seddon, Margaret 117
Seiter, William A. 210, 223, 227, 231, 234–236, 240; *Little Church Around the Corner* 210
Selig, Col. William 41, 44, 45
Selig Polyscope 41; Allesandro studio 41; Chicago studio 22, 41; Edendale studio 41
Sellon, Charles 210
Selwyn, Clarissa 157
Semon, Larry 109
Sennett, Mack 53
Sent for Out see *Come on Over*
Seymour, Clarine 53
Seymour, Harry 141
Shearer, Norma 228, 247
Shebo 158, 161, 163
Shilkret, Nathaniel 217, 227
Shumway, L. C. **61**, 78
Sills, Milton 158, 225
The Singing Fool 225
Single Wives 136
Skouras Brothers 225
The Sky Pilot **67**–**68**, **69**–73, 75, 87, 103
Slippy McGee 78–**80**, 81–**82**, **83**–84, 111, 142
Slippy McGee, Sometimes Known as the Butterfly Man (novel) see *Slippy McGee*
The Smart Aleck (film) 62, 65–66; see also *His Nibs*
"The Smart Aleck" (story) 61
Smiling Irish Eyes 240–241, 243
"Smiling Irish Eyes" (song) 239; see also *Smiling Irish Eyes*
Smith, Cliff 55
Smith, David 109
Smith, Frederick James 74
So Big **137**–**138**, 139–141, 143, 148, 150, **152**–153, 158, 168, 170, 184, 248
So Big (book) 137; see also *So Big*
So Long Letty 63, 64–**65**, 66, 72, 84, 103
So Long Letty (musical) 61; see also *So Long Letty*
Social Register 248–249
Something with a Kick 184
songs: "Come Back to Erin" ("Return to Erin") 239, 243; "If I Can't Have You" 241; "Jeannine, I Dream of Lilac Time" 227; "Killarney Rose" 186; "Old Killarney Fair" 239; "Ophelia Will Fool You" 241; "Pilly Pom Pom Plee" 241; "Return to Erin" 243; "Smiling Irish Eyes" 239; "Then I'll

Ride Home with You" 239; "A Wee Bit o' Love" 239; "You Can't Believe My Eyes" 241
Spearing, James O. 222
Spring, Samuel 189, 194–195, 199
Stanley, Forrest 117
Stanley Corporation 186, 215–216, 224–225
Stark, Pauline 28
Stedman, Myrtle 141
Sternberg, Josef von 247
Stone, Arthur 166
Stone, Beatrice 17, 19; see also Stone, Jack
Stone, Jack 18, 207, 221, 240
Stone, Roy 171, 174
Striker, Joseph 128
Stroheim, Erich von 229
Success at Any Price 249
Sunny 223
Sunset Inn 89
Sunshine Alley see *April Showers*
Susi 223
Swamp Angel 125–129; see also *Painted People*
Swanson, Gloria 53, 181, 215
Sweet, Blanche 89, 160
Synthetic Sin 199–200, 204, 208, 211–212, 219, 223–228, 231, 233, 237
Synthetic Sin (play) 199

Tally, Thomas L. 33, 108
Talmadge, Constance 160
Talmadge, Norma 93, 143, 155, 160, 181
Tampa neighbors 20
Tashman, Lilyan 210
Taylor, Estelle 215, 218, 247
Taylor, Rex 158
Tearle, Conway 128, 135–136
Technicolor 158, 161
Tell the World 200; see also *Her Wild Oat*
Temperament 135–136; see also *Flirting with Love*
Thalberg, Irving 188
That's a Bad Girl 230; see also *Why Be Good?*
"Then I'll Ride Home with You" (song) 239; see also *Smiling Irish Eyes*
Through the Dark 117–**118**, **119**, 133, 143
Titania's Palace 213, 249
Todd, Harry 69
Tomorrow 208; see also *Happiness Ahead*
Torrence, David 107
Torrence, Ernest 104
Tree, Herbert Beerbohm 237
Triangle Film Corporation 27, 33, 36
Triangle Fine Arts Studio 28, 34–**35**, 38, 40
Tully, Richard Walton 117
Turn Back the Clock 248
Turner, Florence (Vitagraph Girl) 20
Turner and Dahnken 33; see also Associated First National

Twinkletoes 158, 161, 163–165, 168–175, 181–182, 199, 237
Twinkletoes (book) 158; see also *Twinkletoes*

United Artists 245
United Studio lot *120*, 140, 162, 164–165
Universal Blue Bird 38–39
Universal City 27, 49, 52, 88–89
Universal Jewel 106
Universal Pictures 23, 38, 49, 56, 89, 110
Unsell, Eve 114

Valentino, Rudolph 172
Valli, Virginia 160, *185*
Vane, Myrtle 114
Velez, Lupe 219, 228
Victor Talking Machine Company 213
Vidor, Florence 160
Vidor, King 65, *67*, 68, *69*–71
Vidor Village (studio) 67
Vitagraph Prospect Boulevard lot 241
Vitaphone Corporation 202–203
Vitaphone (sound process) 209
Volstead Act 59, 85

Walker, Mayor James "Jimmy" 218–219
The Wall Flower 87–88, 92–93, *97*, *100*

Wallace, May 107
Walsh, Raoul 72, 247
Wampas Frolic (1920) 96; (1924) 144–*146*
Warner, Harry 227
Warner, Jack 227
Warner Bros. 202, 213, 224–224, 229–230
Warner Bros.–First National 224, 227, 231
Warren, Mary 93
We Moderns 147, 153, *155*–158, 169
"We Moderns" (play) 147; see also *We Moderns*
Webb, Millard 183, 247
"A Wee Bit o' Love" (song) 239; see also *Smiling Irish Eyes*
Wellman, William 162
West Coast Theatres 154
Western Electric 202, 228
Westover, Winifred 103, 182
Wharton, Edith 113, 224: *The Age of Innocence* 113
When Dawn Came *61*–62, 78, 87
When Irish Eyes Are Smiling 184, 188–192, 195, 198–199, 224, 231–232, 235–236, 238–240
Where There's a Will 224, 228
Whitlock, Lloyd 110
Why Be Good? 230–235, 237
The Wilderness Trail 47–*48*, 49, 52, 54
Wilkinson, Sir Nevile and Lady Beatrix 213

Williams, J.D. 108
Wilson, Carmelita 234
Wilson, Johnny ("Giovanni Francisco Panica") 115
Wilson, Carey 96, 102, 104, 141, 182, 184–*185*, 206, 214, 230, 235, 240
Windsor, Claire 104, 160
Wings 207
Woods, Frank 28, 37, 39
World Series (1926) 176
Wright, Alfred 194

Yearsley, C.L. 108
Yorke, Edith 83
"You Can't Believe My Eyes" (song) 241; see also *Footlights and Fools*
Young, Gretchen 183; *see also* Young, Loretta
Young, Loretta 226
Young, Polly Ann 183
A Young Gentleman of the Old School 35; see also *An Old Fashioned Young Man*

Zanuck, Darryl F. 218
Ziegfeld, Florenz 141–142
Zukor, Adolph 23, 33, 59, 111, 157, 162, 167, 216

www.ingramcontent.com/pod-product-compliance
Lightning Source LLC
Chambersburg PA
CBHW080800300426
44114CB00020B/2782